Claiming Space

Cosmopolitan–Vernacular Dynamics in World Literatures

The four books in this limited series are an outcome of a major Swedish research project called 'Cosmopolitan–Vernacular Dynamics in World Literatures', the aim of which has been to intervene – not least methodologically – in the current disciplinary development of world literature studies. The series is united by a common introductory chapter and approaches the vernacular in world literature across a range of fields, such as comparative literature, postcolonial literature and literary anthropology.

More information on the research project can be found at Worldlit.se.

The books in this series are available as open access through the Bloomsbury Open Access programme and are available on www.bloomsburycollections.com. They are funded by the Riksbankens Jubileumsfond.

Series Editor
Stefan Helgesson

Volumes in the Series
Claiming Space: Locations and Orientations in World Literatures
Edited by Bo G. Ekelund, Adnan Mahmutović and Helena Wulff

Literature and the Making of the World: Cosmopolitan Texts, Vernacular Practices
Edited by Stefan Helgesson, Helena Bodin and Annika Mörte Alling

Northern Crossings: Translation, Circulation and the Literary Semi-periphery
By Chatarina Edfeldt, Erik Falk, Andreas Hedberg, Yvonne Lindqvist, Cecilia Schwartz and Paul Tenngart

Vernaculars in an Age of World Literatures
Edited by Christina Kullberg and David Watson

Claiming Space

Locations and Orientations in World Literatures

Edited by
Bo G. Ekelund, Adnan Mahmutović and Helena Wulff

BLOOMSBURY ACADEMIC
NEW YORK • LONDON • OXFORD • NEW DELHI • SYDNEY

BLOOMSBURY ACADEMIC
Bloomsbury Publishing Inc
1385 Broadway, New York, NY 10018, USA
50 Bedford Square, London, WC1B 3DP, UK
29 Earlsfort Terrace, Dublin 2, Ireland

BLOOMSBURY, BLOOMSBURY ACADEMIC and the Diana logo are
trademarks of Bloomsbury Publishing Plc

First published in the United States of America 2022
This paperback edition published 2023

Volume Editors' Part of the Work © Bo G. Ekelund, Adnan Mahmutović
and Helena Wulff, 2022
Each chapter © Contributors

Cover design by Namkwan Cho
Cover image © Shutterstock.com

Library of Congress Cataloging-in-Publication Data
Names: Ekelund, Bo G., editor. | Mahmutovic, Adnan, editor. | Wulff, Helena, editor.
Title: Claiming space : locations and orientations in world literatures /
edted by Bo G. Ekelund, Adnan Mahmutovic and Helen Wulff.
Description: New York : Bloomsbury Academic, 2021. | Series: Cosmopolitan-vernacular
dynamics in world literatures | Includes bibliographical references and index. | Summary: "Explores
forms of aesthetic worlding and processes of translation and distribution in relation
to the spatial and territorial politics of literary practices"– Provided by publisher.
Identifiers: LCCN 2021007991 (print) | LCCN 2021007992 (ebook) | ISBN 9781501374104 (hardback) |
ISBN 9781501374111 (ebook) | ISBN 9781501374128 (pdf)
Subjects: LCSH: Place (Philosophy) in literature. | Liminality in literature. |
Space and time in literature.
Classification: LCC PN56.P49 C43 2021 (print) |
LCC PN56.P49 (ebook) | DDC 809/.93358–dc23
LC record available at https://lccn.loc.gov/2021007991
LC ebook record available at https://lccn.loc.gov/2021007992

ISBN: HB: 978-1-5013-7410-4
          PB: 978-1-5013-7414-2
          ePDF: 978-1-5013-7412-8
          eBook: 978-1-5013-7411-1

Series: Cosmopolitan–Vernacular Dynamics in World Literatures

Typeset by Integra Software Services Pvt. Ltd.

To find out more about our authors and books visit www.bloomsbury.com
and sign up for our newsletters.

Contents

Notes on contributors   vi

Acknowledgements   viii

Series introduction – The cosmopolitan–vernacular dynamic:
Conjunctions of world literature *Stefan Helgesson, Christina Kullberg,*
Paul Tenngart and Helena Wulff   ix

Introduction – Land, language, literature: Cosmopolitan and
     vernacular claims to place *Bo G. Ekelund*   1

1   One world literature *with* Chinua Achebe and Flora Nwapa
     Paula Uimonen   29

2   The locations and orientations of South African literature:
     From Sol Plaatje to Peter Abrahams *Ashleigh Harris*   59

3   Dislocation in Ahmad Saadawi's *Frankenstein in Baghdad* and
     Hassan Blasim's *The Madman of Freedom Square* *Tasnim Qutait*   85

4   Locating the literature of Hawai'i *Sally Anderson Boström*   111

5   Sites of solidarity and circuits of Second World reading:
     Ralph de Boissière's *Crown Jewel* and the locations of the
     proletarian novel *Bo G. Ekelund*   137

6   Core: Ecologies of Muslim-American writing *Adnan Mahmutović*   169

7   Locations, orientations and multiple temporalities in the
     contemporary, 'global' Latin American novel *Jobst Welge*   193

8   Ambiguous arrival: Emotions and dislocations in the
     migrant encounter with Sweden *Helena Wulff*   217

Afterword – At home in the world *Deborah Reed-Danahay*   236

Index   250

Contributors

Sally Anderson Boström is a researcher at Uppsala University. Her areas of interest include island literature and creole languages. In 2019, she was a guest researcher at the University of Hawai'i at Hilo.

Bo G. Ekelund is Associate Professor of English Literature at Stockholm University. His articles within the field of the sociology of literature have been published in *Poetics*, *Novel* and *Ariel*, among other journals. He is currently working on a geometric study of the construction of fictional space in thirty-two Caribbean novels.

Ashleigh Harris is Professor of English Literature at Uppsala University. She is the author of *Afropolitanism and the Novel: De-Realizing Africa* (2019) and is currently working on a monograph entitled 'Literary Form Beyond the Book in Southern Africa'. Her recent research has been focused on literary forms circulating outside of the formal book and publishing industry in Sub-Saharan Africa.

Adnan Mahmutović is Writer-in-Residence and Associate Professor of English Literature at Stockholm University. His academic work includes *Ways of Being Free: Authenticity and Community in Works by Rushdie, Ondaatje and Okri* (2012), *Visions of the Future in Comics* (2018) and *The Craft of Editing* (2019). His creative work includes *Thinner than a Hair* (2010), *How to Fare Well and Stay Fair* (2012) and *At the Feet of Mothers* (2020).

Tasnim Qutait is a postdoctoral researcher at Uppsala University. Her research interests are in translation studies and world literature with a focus on the Middle East and North Africa. Her book *Nostalgia in Anglophone Arab Literature: Nationalism, Identity and Diaspora* is forthcoming from Bloomsbury in May 2021.

Deborah Reed-Danahay is Professor of Anthropology at the University at Buffalo. Her publications include six books and numerous journal articles and book chapters. Her most recent book is *Bourdieu and Social Space: Mobilities, Trajectories, Emplacements* (2020). Her current interests include the history and methodologies of cultural anthropology, personal narrative, migration and the nation state. She has conducted fieldwork in France, England and the United States.

Paula Uimonen is Professor of Social Anthropology at Stockholm University. She specializes in digital anthropology as well as the anthropology of art, media, globalization, visual culture and world literature. Her recent publications include the monograph *Invoking Flora Nwapa: Nigerian Women Writers, Femininity and Spirituality in World Literature* (2020) and the co-edited volume *Connect to Collect: Approaches to Collecting Social Digital Photography in Museums and Archives* (2020). Paula's current research deals with Swahili Ocean Worlds.

Jobst Welge is Professor of Romance Literature and Cultural Studies at Leipzig University, with a special focus on the Hispanophone and Lusophone areas. His research concerns the theory and history of the novel as well as questions of cultural authority in the early modern period. His recent publications include the study *Genealogical Fictions: Cultural Periphery and Historical Change* (2015) and the co-edited volume *Unendlichkeiten: Lesarten einer (post-)modernen Denk- und Textfigur* (2020).

Helena Wulff is Professor of Social Anthropology at Stockholm University. Her publications include eleven books and (co-)edited volumes, as well as numerous journal articles and book chapters. Among her recent publications are the edited volume *The Anthropologist as Writer: Genres and Contexts in the Twenty-First Century* (2016) and the book *Rhythms of Writing: An Anthropology of Irish Literature* (2017). Her research is in literary anthropology, currently focused on migrant writing in Sweden.

Acknowledgements

This book is available as open access through the Bloomsbury Open Access programme and is available on www.bloomsburycollections.com. The open-access edition of this text was made possible by *Riksbankens Jubileumsfond*.

Generous funding from this foundation also made possible the scholarly work undertaken within the research programme 'Cosmopolitan and Vernacular Dynamics in World Literatures'. This volume is one of the many results of that programme. The editors and authors also wish to acknowledge the pivotal role played by Stefan Helgesson in launching, energizing, and guiding the programme.

Series introduction

The cosmopolitan–vernacular dynamic: Conjunctions of world literature

Stefan Helgesson, Christina Kullberg, Paul Tenngart and Helena Wulff

'World literature is not an object, it's a *problem*'. This was Franco Moretti, famously, in 2000.[1] But what is the problem of world literature today, two decades later? In broad strokes, the disciplinary challenge would seem to be the same: to devise methods and reading practices that offer alternatives to entrenched national and civilizational frameworks. Scholarship within world literature shares a fundamentally *comparative* urge, whereby discrete languages, times and locations of literature are considered in conjunction. But 'conjunction' is in fact the nub of the problem, as this is supposedly not just an older version of comparative literature under a new name. Instead, conjunction can be conceptualized through a wide number of temporalities, scales, geographies, generic constellations, languages and ideological perspectives – all of them susceptible to historical change.

Moretti proposed a world-systemic model, inspired by Immanuel Wallerstein, which has since developed into a strong but by no means exclusive or uncontested methodological premise of world literature. Deep-time approaches focusing on imperial formations, translation-based approaches, Alexander Beecroft's ecologies of literature – all offer distinct ways of investigating conjunction and connection.[2] What they do not always offer is mutual compatibility. Instead, the most productive way to delineate world literature today might be to consider it as a set of procedures and methods rather than a coherent body of theory. As a scholarly field, it provides in the first instance a space of conversation and intellectual exchange *across* specializations that may also enable reconfigured empirical and critical investigations within those specializations.

This give-and-take among different disciplinary locations has shaped the work leading up to the four volumes presented here. Emerging from a long-running

---

[1] Franco Moretti, 'Conjectures on World Literature', *New Left Review* 1 (2000): 55.
[2] Alexander Beecroft, *An Ecology of World Literature* (London: Verso, 2015).

project based in Sweden, and involving researchers from comparative literature, anthropology, intellectual history and a range of language departments, the basic methodological wager of our work differs from much else that has been published in the field of world literature. Avoiding hard-wired systemic, deterministic or 'global' claims, what we call the *cosmopolitan–vernacular dynamic* (which can also be read as *vernacular–cosmopolitan*) offers itself not as a distinct theory, but as a methodological starting point – akin to an *Ansatzpunkt* in Erich Auerbach's sense[3] – from which to explore the resonances and connections between widely diverse literary texts and cultures.

To explain the motivations behind such a methodology, we need to make a detour into the current state of world literature studies. Undergirding this sprawling field is the political and ethical intuition that literary knowledge in our crisis-ridden, globalized and racialized world – even in its (anticipated) post-Covid-19 shape – requires new modes of scholarly attention. To speak from our own contemporary vantage point in Scandinavia, it is clear that the joint impact of the cultural Anglosphere, migration from Europe, the Middle East, Africa and Asia, the cultural policies of the EU and the ubiquitous presence of digital media not only weaken the explanatory value of the nation state and the national language as the privileged loci of the production and reading of literature in Sweden today, but also invite reconsiderations of an earlier literary history in the region. Similar shifts in the production of literature and in the literary imagination can be registered elsewhere across the world, shifts that prompt us to rethink how we read and contextualize literature. The road to such a revised conception of literary studies leads, however, to a garden of forking paths. This is one important lesson to be learned from the twenty-odd years since Moretti's lively provocation in the year 2000.

Common to the turn-of-the-millennium interventions by Moretti and David Damrosch (less so Pascale Casanova, whose concern was consecration) was an emphasis on circulation – quite literally on how texts move and are received in diverse contexts. This deceptively simple perspective counters what Jerome McGann once called 'textual idealism', which treats texts as if they were just magically 'there'.[4] Instead, the circulational perspective allows us to engage the material, spatial and historical unconscious of literature as texts in movement. This approach has been developed by Beecroft, Venkat Mani, Sandra Richter

---

[3] Erich Auerbach, 'Philologie der Weltliteratur', in *Weltliteratur: Festgabe für Fritz Strich zum 70. Geburtstag*, ed. Walter Muschg and Emil Staiger (Bern: Francke, 1952), 39–50.
[4] Jerome McGann, *The Textual Condition* (Princeton: Princeton University Press, 1991), 7.

and Yvonne Leffler, among others.[5] Increasingly, as in contributions to Stefan Helgesson and Pieter Vermeulen's *Institutions of World Literature* or in Ignacio Sánchez-Prado's study of Mexican literature, this tends towards studies of market dynamics and, not least, the sociology of translation.[6] However, the most rigorous large-scale studies of circulation are to be found within computational literary studies (CLS) which involves an even more fundamental shift towards quantitative methods than the sociology of translation. Not surprisingly, given his coinage of 'distant reading', CLS has become Moretti's main field of activity at the Stanford Literary Lab.[7] Even as the merits and drawbacks of CLS are being debated, the achievements in all these interlinked areas of investigation attest firmly to the *complexity* of studying world-literary circulation.[8] This knowledge is not just readily available, nor does it amount merely to an external study of literature, but it is rather of crucial relevance both to the empirical and theoretical understanding of how literary cultures evolve.

Having said that, a striking alternative development over the last ten years has been the proliferation of interpretive, qualitative methods in world literature studies. Often on the basis of strong theorizations of the world-concept, and sometimes pitched polemically against the circulation approach, researchers have attempted to read 'the world' through specific literary works, rather than through Morettian 'distant reading' (which is ideally suited for digital methods). The epistemic assumption in these interpretive models follows the synechdochal logic of *pars pro toto*, or the part standing in for the whole. Eric Hayot was early to embark on this path in *On Literary Worlds* (2012), an ambitious but all too brief attempt to bring world literature studies – understood as a global

5 B.Venkat Mani, *Recoding World Literature: Libraries, Print Culture, and Germany's Pact with Books* (New York: Fordham University Press, 2017); Sandra Richter, *Eine Weltgeschichte der deutschsprachigen Literatur* (Munich: Bertelsmann, 2017); Yvonne Leffler, *Swedish Nineteenth-Century Literature and World Literature: Transnational Success and Literary History* (Gothenburg: Göteborg University, 2020).

6 Stefan Helgesson and Pieter Vermeulen, eds., *Institutions of World Literature: Writing, Translation, Markets* (New York: Routledge, 2016); Ignacio Sánchez Prado, *Strategic Occidentalism: On Mexican Fiction, the Neoliberal Book Market, and the Question of World Literature* (Evanston: Northwestern University Press, 2018). On the sociology of translation, see Johan Heilbron, 'Book Translation as a Cultural World-System', *European Journal of Social Theory* 2, no. 4 (1999): 429–44; Johan Heilbron, 'Obtaining World Fame from the Periphery', *Dutch Crossing: Journal of Low Countries Studies* 44, no. 2 (2020): 136–44; Abram de Swaan, *Words of the World: The Global Language System* (Cambridge: Polity Press, 2001); Gisèle Sapiro, ed., *Translatio: le marché de traduction en France à l'heure de la mondialisation* (Paris: CNRS éditions, 2008); Hélène Buzelin and Claudio Baraldi, 'Sociology and Translation Studies: Two Disciplines Meeting', in *Border Crossings: Translation Studies and Other Disciplines*, ed. Yves Gambier and Luc van Doorslaer (Amsterdam: John Benjamins, 2016), 117–39.

7 Moretti, 'Conjectures', 56–8. See also litlab.stanford.edu.

8 Nan Z. Da, 'The Computational Case against Computational Literary Studies', *Critical Inquiry* 45 (2019): 601–39.

extension of literary studies – to bear on, in principle, *any* given work of literature, regardless of origin or period. Emily Apter's much publicized *Against World Literature* (2013) instead championed linguistic specificity – coded as the 'Untranslatable' – as the normative locus of a worldly reading. A related tendency has been the regionally or linguistically restricted conception of literature X *as* world literature, with the francophone *littérature-monde* as a high-profile example, but also evident in many (not all) titles in Bloomsbury's 'Literatures as World Literature' series. Building on Moretti's world-systemic inclination, the Warwick Research Collective (WReC) has elaborated a significantly different conception of world-literature (with a hyphen) as the aesthetic registration of combined and uneven development in the capitalist world-system – but this, too, has issued in a mode of close interpretive attention to literary texts, rather than distant reading. Other, more or less distinct examples of this interpretive turn in world literature studies can be cited, such as Francesca Orsini's concept of the multilingual local, pitched in opposition to systemic approaches, Debjani Ganguly's work on the global novel, Ottmar Ette's 'transarea' approach, Pheng Cheah's phenomenology of 'worlding literature' and Birgit Neumann and Gabriele Rippl's notes on world-making.[9] A point of relevance to our work is that while the most rigorous systemic approaches, represented here by WReC, speak of world-literature in the singular, the implication of, for example, Hayot's, Apter's or Orsini's perspectives is to consider *literatures* as an inevitably plural phenomenon – even in contexts of exchange and translation. At stake here, ultimately, is the relative theoretical weighting of determinacy and contingency in interpretive practices. Our work does not collectively pursue one or the other of these angles, but most contributions tend to side with contingency and hence the plural conception of literature.

Having said so, it must be stressed that each volume in this series has a distinct methodological profile of its own. As its title indicates, *Northern Crossings* deals with aspects of circulation to and from Sweden – understood in structural terms as a semi-periphery rather than a reified national space. It is in that sense the most systemically oriented volume in this series. *Claiming Space*, by contrast, approaches the narrative inscription of places around the world mainly through interpretive

---

[9]   Francesca Orsini, 'The Multilingual Local in World Literature', *Comparative Literature* 67, no. 4 (2015): 345–74; Debjani Ganguly, *This Thing Called the World: The Contemporary Novel as Global Form* (Durham, NC: Duke University Press, 2016); Ottmar Ette, *TransArea: A Literary History of Globalization*, trans. Mark W. Person (Berlin: De Gruyter, 2016); Pheng Cheah, 'Worlding Literature: Living with Tiger Spirits', *Diacritics* 45, no. 2 (2017): 86–114; Birgit Neumann and Gabriele Rippl, 'Anglophone World Literatures: Introduction', *Anglia* 135, no. 1 (2017): 1–20.

methods. *Literature and the Making of the World* configures its object of inquiry as 'literary practice' (both intra- and extratextual) and combines for that reason text-focused readings with book-historical and anthropological methods of inquiry. *Vernaculars in an Age of World Literatures*, finally, with its focus on the concept of the vernacular, combines interpretive readings with large-scale historical analyses.

As mentioned, it is the working hypothesis of the cosmopolitan–vernacular dynamic that brings these studies together. In the simplest and most general terms, this assumes that literature in different times is shaped through a combination of cosmopolitan and vernacular orientations. Indeed, the cosmopolitan–vernacular dynamic, we claim, *is precisely what is at stake in the world literature field*: not just the outward success or failure of certain texts, genres or literary languages, nor just the 'refraction' of *national* literatures,[10] but rather the always situated negotiation of cosmopolitan and vernacular orientations in the temporal unfolding of literary practice. The further implication – which extends beyond our contributions – is that such a methodology might allow for the articulation of 'universality' after the collapse of 'universalism'.[11]

Just as importantly, however, the cosmopolitan–vernacular dynamic should be understood as a falsifiable postulation: in the hypothetical case of Beecroft's 'epichoric', or strictly local, literary ecology it would hardly be meaningful to talk of a cosmopolitan orientation.[12] The opposite point, that there might be texts, genres and modes of writing without any vernacular connection at all, is harder to make – but it is the case, for example, that standard Arabic or *fusha* can function as a cosmopolitan written standard that runs parallel to local (spoken) Arabic dialects.[13] We are not claiming, in other words, that the cosmopolitan–vernacular dynamic *must* apply in all literary contexts. Even more importantly, it does not operate in just one mode, nor is it necessarily always successful. To speak of the cosmopolitan–vernacular dynamic is an open proposition, in the sense that it does not prescribe in advance any particular weighting of cosmopolitan or vernacular tendencies. Although the cosmopolitan–vernacular dynamic is fundamentally a question of how literary values are shaped, just *how* these values should be understood and assessed can only be discovered by examining the particular case.

[10] David Damrosch, *What is World Literature?* (Princeton: Princeton University Press, 2003), 281.
[11] Markus Messling, *Universalität nach dem Universalismus: über frankophonen Literaturen der Gegenwart* (Berlin: Matthes & Seitz, 2019).
[12] Beecroft, *Ecology*, 33.
[13] Shaden M. Tageldin, 'Beyond Latinity, Can the Vernacular Speak?', *Comparative Literature* 70, no. 2 (2018): 114–31.

In adopting the cosmopolitan–vernacular perspective, we acknowledge our debt to Sheldon Pollock, whose magisterial macro-historical analysis of pre-modern literary cultures in South Asia and Europe in *The Language of the Gods in the World of Men* offered a path-breaking comparison not just of the cosmopolitan literatures of Sanskrit and Latin, but more importantly of the historical constructedness of vernacular literatures. *Contra* the Romanticist assumption of vernacular authenticity and immediacy, Pollock (and Beecroft after him) argued that a historical approach to vernacular literatures will show how they tend to be elite projects shaped in reaction against a dominant cosmopolitan Other (such as the literate cultures of Latin and Sanskrit). To *literize* (standardize through writing) and *literarize* languages coded as vernaculars are to be understood as deliberate, politically motivated actions.[14]

Illuminating though such an explanatory model is, it should not be taken at face value as a transhistorical constant, nor need it be restricted to macro-historical analyses but can be applied equally to closer textual study. Contrary to Pollock's pre-modern focus, our four volumes engage with literature from the last 200 years (about half of the primary sources are contemporary), an epoch which marks a radical new departure in literary history. This is when *Weltliteratur* was conceptualized in the wake of the accelerating commodification of print literature, the emergence of comparative philology and the entrenchment of (and resistance to) European nationalism and imperialism. It is, hence, an era when cosmopolitan and vernacular orientations in literature have been reconfigured drastically in relation not least, if not only, to the cultural authority of 'the West'. An important aspect of this process has been the accelerating *vernacularization* of languages and literatures in all parts of the world. This needs to be understood in two ways. First, vernacularization entails the positioning of named languages, registers of language or local knowledges as inferior in the field of power, as for instance Aamir Mufti discusses in the context of India and Pakistan.[15] But, secondly, vernacularization also involves the deliberate elevation of vernaculars, including what we more broadly call the 'domain of vernacularity', as a resource for the construction of national or socially distinct literatures. Given the constitutively relational nature of vernacularization, this process needs to be thought of as unstable: it can change over time (an obvious example being how European vernaculars such as English

---

[14] Sheldon Pollock, *The Language of the Gods in the World of Men* (Berkeley: University of California Press, 2006), 4–5.

[15] Aamir Mufti, *Forget English! Orientalisms and World Literatures* (Cambridge, MA: Harvard University Press, 2016).

and French became cosmopolitan, imperial languages), as well as shift momentarily across space (Spanish being transformed into an immigrant vernacular in the United States). Or, as has often been the case in Africa, a *literary* vernacularity has had to be crafted through adopted, formerly imperial languages.

With its connections to comparative philology and the German romantic aesthetics of Herder, Goethe, Schlegel and Schleiermacher, among others, post-eighteenth-century vernacularization is a deeply ambivalent affair: its value-coding can be programmatically positive yet grounded in untenable essentializations of race and ethnicity.[16] A particularly effective challenge to this legacy has been the interrogation of language boundaries and 'artefactualized' languages, along with the critique of the 'monolingual paradigm'.[17] These debates are relevant to our work, not least since discourses of the vernacular have often been a tool for establishing a monolingual paradigm that effaces translingual conceptions of language.[18] Our heuristic employment of the term allows, however, for an alternative take on mono- and multilingualism. If the vernacular indicates a *relation*, it may entail a heteroglossic or translingual register 'within' a named language (vernacular varieties of English, say), as much as an identity as a separate language vis-à-vis a dominant other (which, for example, was the position of Wolof in relation to imperial French). The social dimension of the vernacular also draws our attention to the relativity of communities of comprehension – the intimacy of a vernacular to one group will be perceived as opacity by others. Such fluidity in the definition and nature of the vernacular chimes well with the critique of linguistic 'bordering', but – and this is important

---

[16] For more on this, see John K. Noyes, *Herder: Aesthetics against Imperialism* (Toronto: University of Toronto Press, 2015); Baidik Bhattacharya, 'On Comparatism in the Colony: Archives, Methods, and the Project of *Weltliteratur*', *Critical Inquiry* 42 (2016): 677–711; Mufti, *Orientalisms*; Siraj Ahmed, *Archaeology of Babel: The Colonial Foundation of the Humanities* (Stanford: Stanford University Press, 2018).

[17] Jan Blommaert, *The Sociolinguistics of Globalization* (Cambridge: Cambridge University Press, 2010), 4; Yasemin Yildiz, *Beyond the Mother Tongue: The Postmonolingual Condition* (New York: Fordham University Press, 2012). See also Richard Bauman and Charles Briggs, *Voices of Modernity: Language Ideologies and the Politics of Inequality* (Cambridge: Cambridge University Press, 2003); Daniel Heller-Roazen, *Echolalias: On the Forgetting of Language* (New York: Zone Books, 2005); Naoki Sakai, 'How Do We Count a Language? Translation and Discontinuity', *Translation Studies* 2, no. 1 (2009): 71–88; Lisbeth Minaard and Till Dembeck, 'Introduction: How to Challenge the Myth of Monolingualism?', *Thamyris/Intersecting* 28 (2014): 9–14; Robert Stockhammer, 'Wie deutsch ist es? Glottamimetische, -diegetische, -pithanone, und -aporetische Verfahren in der Literatur', *Arcadia* 50 (2015): 146–72; David Gramling, *The Invention of Monolingualism* (New York: Bloomsbury, 2016); Julia Tidigs and Markus Huss, 'The Noise of Multilingualism: Reader Diversity, Linguistic Borders and Literary Multimodality', *Critical Multilingualism Studies* 5, no. 1 (2017): 208–35; Stefan Helgesson and Christina Kullberg, 'Translingual Events: World Literature and the Making of Language', *Journal of World Literature* 3, no. 2 (2018): 136–52.

[18] As discussed in an African context by Moradewun Adejunmobi in *Vernacular Palaver: Imaginations of the Local and Non-native Languages in West Africa* (Clevedon: Multilingual Matters, 2004).

– it also factors the wholly contextual dimension of social hierarchies into the analysis.[19] This has two consequences. One is that it acknowledges the de facto importance of artefactualized language, particularly within literature, despite its *theoretical* untenability. In the world of publishing, the authority of standard varieties of English, French or Arabic – including their publishing infrastructures – cannot be wished away. Hence, when terms such as 'centre' and 'periphery' are used in *Northern Crossings* in the context of translational exchanges, this is not a normative judgement, but rather an attempt at descriptively conceptualizing a given state of affairs.

The other consequence is that a social conception of language opens up towards a wider frame of analysis. As argued in *Vernaculars in an Age of World Literatures* and elsewhere in our volumes, the vernacular is not 'just' a linguistic matter, but implies rather an entire domain of vernacularity. This can be understood in metonymic terms as that which relates to proximate, intimate, domestic or local experiences and sensibilities, particularly in their linguistic registration. It has tremendous aesthetic as well as persuasive potential, but is also ideologically ambiguous. As Moradewun Adejunmobi's important work on West Africa shows, it is naive to assume that promotions of the vernacular are always 'intrinsic and unproblematic exemplars of minority politics'.[20] On the contrary, what she calls 'discourses of the vernacular' have, intermittently, justified asymmetries of power under colonialism, as well as supported the political aspirations of subordinated groups, notably by those 'at the forefront of interaction with the dominant foreign culture'.[21] The dynamics of the vernacular will, in brief, always be strictly context-sensitive. From this it follows that an assessment of its political tenor can only be issued a posteriori.

If, when we embarked on this project, we found that the vernacular was an ignored or undertheorized term in world literature studies, this has changed to some extent in recent years. An important line of questioning in this regard concerns the extent to which the very term 'vernacular' is possible to use outside of its particular European-latinate genealogy. Tageldin, for one, has observantly noted the instability of the term's field of reference – it is 'terminological quicksand'[22] – but her account of Arabic supports rather than refutes the

---

[19] Sakai, 'How Do we Count', 71.
[20] Moradewun Adejunmobi, 'Major and Minor Discourses of the Vernacular: Discrepant African Histories', in *Minor Transnationalism*, ed. Françoise Lionnet and Shu-mei Shih (Durham, NC: Duke University Press, 2005), 179.
[21] Adejunmobi, 'Major and Minor', 191.
[22] Tageldin, 'Beyond Latinity', 115.

heuristic value of using the term 'vernacular' comparatively: it is often the case, we find, that when the vernacular transforms into a deliberate literary project, 'middle registers' of writing which fixate the flux of spoken language abound. In literary practice, that is to say, the vernacular oscillates between being a medium and being a citation within the medium. Interestingly, this need not work very differently in oral or performative modes of verbal art, which also exhibit the qualities of craftedness and quotability.[23] Against this backdrop, the value of a 'comparativist assessment of vernacular styles and political practices across the globe', as Sieglinde Lemke puts it, should be evident.[24]

We should note here that much of the critique *against* world literature as a field of study has argued that the vernacular is what world literature leaves behind. If the basic motivation for world literature as a disciplinary commitment could be described in terms of a cosmopolitan ethics, this has, in turn, often been accused of being an elitist, Eurocentric or politically aloof concern. There is by now an entire subfield of debates in this vein whose most common articulation has been that of postcolonialism 'versus' world literature.[25] The more recent contributions to this discussion tend, however, also to identify points of convergence between these positions. Our take on this is that if postcolonialism is ideologically primed to speak on behalf of the vernacular (whose proximity to concepts such as the subaltern or indigeneity should not pass unnoticed), an actual attention to vernacular orientations also shows their relevance far beyond strictly postcolonial concerns. We are, in other words, claiming that the cosmopolitan–vernacular optic engages the postcolonial perspective, without effacing or supplanting it.

---

[23] Karin Barber, *The Anthropology of Texts, Persons and Publics* (Cambridge: Cambridge University Press, 2007).

[24] Sieglinde Lemke, *The Vernacular Matters of American Literature* (Basingstoke: Palgrave Macmillan, 2009), 9.

[25] Mads Rosendahl Thomsen, *Mapping World Literature: International Canonization and Translational Literatures* (London: Continuum, 2008); Peter Hitchcock, *The Long Space: Transnationalism and Postcolonial Form* (Stanford: Stanford University Press, 2010); Graham Huggan, 'The Trouble with World Literature', in *A Companion to Comparative Literature*, ed. Ali Behdad and Dominic Thomas (Oxford: Blackwell, 2011), 490–506; Subramanian Shankar, *Flesh and Fish Blood: Postcolonialism, Translation, and the Vernacular* (Berkeley: University of California Press, 2012); Gayatri Spivak, 'The Stakes of a World Literature', in *An Aesthetic Education in the Era of Globalization*, Gayatri Spivak (Cambridge, MA: Harvard University Press, 2012), 455–66; Robert J. C. Young, 'World Literature and Postcolonialism', in *The Routledge Companion to World Literature*, ed. Theo D'haen, David Damrosch and Djelal Kadir (Oxon: Routledge, 2011), 213–22; Elleke Boehmer, 'The World and the Postcolonial', *European Review* 22, no. 2 (2014): 299–308; Stefan Helgesson, 'Postcolonialism and World Literature: Rethinking the Boundaries', *Interventions* 16, no. 4 (2014): 483–500; Joseph Slaughter, 'World Literature as Property', *Alif* 34 (2014): 39–73; Bhavya Tiwari and David Damrosch, eds., Special issues on world literature and postcolonial studies, *Journal of World Literature* 4, no. 3 (2019) and 5, no. 3 (2020); Elke Sturm-Trigonakis, ed., *World Literature and the Postcolonial* (Berlin: Springer, 2020).

At this point, however, it is of some urgency also to address the
cosmopolitan dimension of our methodology. As mentioned, world literature
and cosmopolitanism were revived as concerns in academia more or less
in tandem in the post-1989 phase: if world literature is underwritten by a
fundamentally cosmopolitan ethos of openness towards the other, it also
offers the more philosophical concerns of cosmopolitanism an empirical field
of study. Even more importantly, the gradual turn from such philosophically
normative approaches to a descriptive conception of cosmopolitanism as 'a
characteristic and possession of substantial social collectivities, often nonelite
collectivities that had cosmopolitanism thrust upon them', offers yet further
scope for its coupling with world literature.[26] Not unlike Pollock, who considers
cosmopolitanism as something people 'do rather than something they declare,
as practice rather than proposition', our own work in these volumes is informed
not by any a priori definition of what a cosmopolitan space or stance is, but,
again, by a relational premise: terms such as 'cosmopolitan', 'cosmopolitanism'
and 'cosmopolitanization' have meaning only insofar as they set themselves
off against other modes of belonging, or, better, other orientations.[27] But to
complicate things further, cosmopolitan orientations, insofar as they are
verbalized, must have a *specific* linguistic signature; this signature, in turn,
might more often than not be positioned as vernacular. Conversely, vernacular
orientations may, under the right conditions (such as an attachment to a global
language) have a cosmopolitan appeal. An example of the latter could be the
Antillean French of Patrick Chamoiseau's Goncourt-winning novel *Texaco*
(1992). An example of the former is Rabindranath Tagore's famous lecture in
1907 on world literature, held in the late colonial period when Tagore's Bengali –
a formidable language of literature and erudition – was still regarded by the
British as a vernacular.[28] It is in other words crucial to think of the cosmopolitan
and the vernacular orientations as *different* but not as mutually exclusive
opposites, in a schematic sense. Homi Bhabha, not least, has inspired such a view
by speaking of vernacular cosmopolitanism.[29] To grasp how these orientations

[26] Bruce Robbins and Paulo Horta, eds., *Cosmopolitanisms* (New York: New York University Press, 2017), 3.
[27] Sheldon Pollock, 'Cosmopolitan and Vernacular in History', *Public Culture* 12, no. 3 (2000): 593.
[28] Rabindranath Tagore, 'Vishva Sahitya', 1907, trans. Rijula Das and Makarand R. Paranjape, in *Rabindranath Tagore in the 21st Century*, ed. D. Benerjii (New Delhi: Springer, 2015), 277–88.
[29] Homi K. Bhabha, 'Unsatisfied: Notes on Vernacular Cosmopolitanism', in *Text and Nation: Cross-Disciplinary Essays on Cultural and National Identities*, ed. Laura Garcia-Morena and Peter C. Pfeiffer (London: Camden House, 1996), 191–207; Pnina Werbner, 'Vernacular Cosmopolitanism', *Theory, Culture & Society* 23, no. 2–3 (2006): 496–8.

might interact, it is therefore imperative to emphasize that the cosmopolitan–vernacular dynamic is also, and fundamentally, a matter of translation – which could be illustrated by how Tagore's lecture is only accessible to us who are writing this introduction in its English version. As with the vernacular, however, the cosmopolitan tendencies are also ambiguous when translation enters the picture. If cosmopolitan orientations are at work whenever transnational structures or agents – be it anglophone, French, Chinese or any other cross-cultural exportation of literature – exercise their power over less well-endowed literary spaces, it may equally be the case that the cosmopolitan orientation of translational practice creates intercultural channels and mindsets that challenge isolationist tendencies. As Robbins and Horta explain, cosmopolitanism has always both a positive and a negative definition. In positive terms, it embraces a wider humanity; in negative terms, it fosters detachment. This duality also applies to literary modes of cosmopolitanism, which indicates how *location* must always be factored into the cosmopolitan–vernacular analysis, even if it is a negatively conceived locality (as a consequence of detachment). There is, strictly speaking, no 'world space', no vaguely conceived orbit 'out there' where world literature exists in its separate realm. Instead, any postulation or imaginary of a wider world necessarily implies a particular 'here'. This premise is made explicit in *Claiming Space*, whose readings are organized by way of the two terms 'location' and 'orientation', and in *Literature and the Making of the World*, where the focus on literary practice links the textual and fictive aspects of literature to the emplaced and linguistically inflected work of writers, editors or, in one case, a maker of scrapbooks. The word 'world' emerges here as double-coded, as both the lifeworld once theorized by Hannah Arendt and others, and as an imagined world with a wider scope – and this imagined world, it turns out, is typically nurtured by modes of writing, much as Don Quixote once mistook his romances for the world.

The world, then, can be made and sustained through literary practice, a perspective which also offers a particularly strong motivation for our incorporation of anthropological approaches to literature in our volumes. Not only is the immediate relevance of anthropology evident when engaging terms such as 'vernacular', 'cosmopolitan' and 'world', but we also claim that the defamiliarizing gaze of anthropology on the literary domain helps literary scholarship to move beyond excessive textualism. The work of Karin Barber serves as a rich source of inspiration, but there is also a long-running debate on the relation of literature to ethnography as well as a subfield of literary anthropology which has grown rapidly in recent years.[30] In the latter instance in particular, there has been a consistent development of methods for cultural, temporal and biographical contextualization of literary texts relating to vernacular–cosmopolitan dynamics. A central idea here is that the anthropologist and the author are fellow intellectuals and thus the author's commentary is key to understanding issues such as choice of topic, the writing process, the literary career, the publishing industry and the literary market, as well as the circulation of books. This, juxtaposed with the anthropologist's ethnographic observations, can reveal analytical aspects of world literature that are not obvious from the texts alone. It is for this reason that our volumes integrate contributions that build on anthropological methods such as ethnographic observations during literary festivals, readings and book launches, combined with extensive in-depth interviews of authors.

Our four volumes will appear in staggered fashion in 2021 and 2022, so depending on when exactly you as reader are encountering this general introduction, not all of them may yet be available. Regardless, we will end by briefly describing their profile.

As already indicated, *Claiming Space*'s contribution to our larger project is its specification of the cosmopolitan and vernacular vectors in terms of 'location' and 'orientation'. This enables a refined analysis of spatial imaginaries in literature. This volume pays attention to language, forms of aesthetic worlding and processes of translation and distribution, while its edge is turned towards the spatial and territorial politics involved in literary practices and works in the late twentieth and early twenty-first centuries. Locations, we argue, are inhabited or claimed by means of vernacular or cosmopolitan strategies, choices that are also visible in the orientations bound up with these sites. In dialogue with the critical geopolitics of culture, with sociology and anthropology, our attention to

---

[30] On literature and ethnography, see Eleni Coundouriotis, *Claiming History: Colonialism, Ethnography, and the Novel* (New York: Columbia University Press, 1999); Gaurav Desai, *Subject to Colonialism: African Self-Fashioning and the Colonial Library* (Durham, NC: Duke University Press, 2001); Vincent Debaene, *L'Adieu au voyage. L'ethnologie française entre science et littérature* (Paris: Gallimard, 2010); Christina Kullberg, *Poetics of Ethnography in Martinican Narratives: Exploring the Self and the Environment* (Charlottesville: University of Virginia Press, 2013); Justin Izzo, *Experiments with Empire: Anthropology and Fiction in the French Atlantic* (Durham, NC: Duke University Press, 2019). For examples of literary anthropology, see: Nigel Rapport, *The Prose and the Passion: Anthropology, Literature and the Writing of E. M. Forster* (Manchester: Manchester University Press, 1994); Marilyn Cohen, ed., *Novel Approaches to Anthropology: Contributions to Literary Anthropology* (New York: Lexington Books, 2013); Helena Wulff, *Rhythms of Writing: An Anthropology of Irish Literature* (London: Bloomsbury, 2017); Oscar Hemer, *Contaminations and Ethnographic Fictions: Southern Crossings* (Cham: Palgrave, 2020); Paula Uimonen, *Invoking Flora Nwapa: Nigerian Women Writers, Femininity and Spirituality in World Literature* (Stockholm: Stockholm University Press, 2020).

literary locations and orientations brings spatial particularity into the reckoning of vernacular and cosmopolitan relationality. Explicitly expressed or implied, manifesting itself sometimes as *dis*-location and *dis*-orientation, the claiming of space by any symbolic means necessarily is revealed as a constant effect of literary practice.

Vernaculars in an Age of World Literatures attempts to theorize the vernacular. As indicated in the discussion above, our point of departure is that the vernacular is always plural: not limited to language alone but comprising various types of expressions, material objects, people and environments. Moreover, its significance and value change with time and context. From a European point of view, it has been identified with the consolidation of national literatures, but in other contexts it has been associated with diaspora and movements of the marginalized or else, like in early twentieth-century China, it needs to be adapted to a specific literary and linguistic tradition to be useful as a concept. Sometimes, but not always, it works as an expression of resistance to the hegemony of cultural centres. Yet this seemingly inherent heterogeneity and variability is precisely what makes the vernacular a productive concept for rethinking world literature today. In nine case studies approaching a select number of narratives from the long twentieth century, from more or less marginal contexts, the volume explores how the concept may be put into practice and demonstrates how vernaculars operate within different literary, critical, cultural and political circumstances.

In the collectively authored *Northern Crossings* we analyse cosmopolitanizing and vernacularizing translational processes from the point of view of the literary semi-periphery. Literary traffic to and from Swedish displays a nuanced palette of diverse intercultural relations. The world literary system has hitherto been predominantly described from a binary centre–periphery perspective. A focus on the semi-periphery makes visible other important phenomena in the formation of interlingual literary flows. Our studies show that the logic of integration into new literary cultures does not follow one set of principles or a single pattern. The strategies employed by publishers, translators and other intermediaries in adapting the foreign text to a new literary culture always put the cosmopolitan–vernacular dynamic into play, but exactly what processes are implemented depends on a wide range of variables, such as genre, narrative technique, literary style, textual and authorial position in source and target cultures, publishing agendas, translator profiles and overall relations between specific literary cultures.

Literature and the Making of the World, finally, engages the cosmopolitan-vernacular dynamic by focusing on a range of literary practices and materialities. In its first section, 'Worlds in texts', the world-making potential of place, genre and language is explored in readings of, among other things, French nineteenth-century novels, Lu Xun's 'A Madman's Diary' and Siberian exile writing. The second section, 'Texts in worlds', looks at literary journals, the profession of travel writers, the social world of a scrapbook keeper in Harlem and the trajectory of a contemporary novel in the Indian language Kannada with a view to fleshing out, in an anthropological spirit, the 'world' of world literature as an experiential and embodied category. In contrast to macro-scale varieties of world literature studies, the empirically fine-grained contributions to this volume bring close reading, book history, ethnography and historical contextualization to bear on its selected instances of literary practice.

Bibliography

Adejunmobi, Moradewun. *Vernacular Palaver: Imaginations of the Local and Non-native Languages in West Africa*. Clevedon: Multilingual Matters, 2004.

Adejunmobi, Moradewun. 'Major and Minor Discourses of the Vernacular: Discrepant African Histories'. In *Minor Transnationalism*, edited by Françoise Lionnet and Shu-mei Shih, 179–97. Durham, NC: Duke University Press, 2005.

Ahmed, Siraj. *Archaeology of Babel: The Colonial Foundation of the Humanities*. Stanford: Stanford University Press, 2018.

Apter, Emily. *Against World Literature: On the Politics of Untranslatability*. London: Verso, 2013.

Arendt, Hannah. 1958. *The Human Condition*. Chicago: Chicago University Press, 1998.

Auerbach, Erich. 'Philologie der Weltliteratur'. In *Weltliteratur: Festgabe für Fritz Strich zum 70. Geburtstag*, edited by Walter Muschg and Emil Staiger, 39–50. Bern: Francke, 1952.

Barber, Karin. *The Anthropology of Texts, Persons and Publics*. Cambridge: Cambridge University Press, 2007.

Bauman, Richard and Charles Briggs. *Voices of Modernity: Language Ideologies and the Politics of Inequality*. Cambridge: Cambridge University Press, 2003.

Beecroft, Alexander. *An Ecology of World Literature*. London: Verso, 2015.

Bhabha, Homi K. 'Unsatisfied: Notes on Vernacular Cosmopolitanism'. In *Text and Nation: Cross-Disciplinary Essays on Cultural and National Identities*, edited by Laura Garcia-Morena and Peter C. Pfeiffer, 191–207. London: Camden House, 1996.

Bhattacharya, Baidik. 'On Comparatism in the Colony: Archives, Methods, and the Project of *Weltliteratur*'. *Critical Inquiry* 42 (2016): 677–711.

Blommaert, Jan. *The Sociolinguistics of Globalization*. Cambridge: Cambridge University Press, 2010.

Boehmer, Elleke. 'The World and the Postcolonial'. *European Review* 22, no. 2 (2014): 299–308.

Boehmer, Elleke. *Postcolonial Poetics: 21st-Century Critical Readings*. Cham: Palgrave Macmillan, 2018.

Buzelin, Hélène and Claudio Baraldi. 'Sociology and Translation Studies: Two Disciplines Meeting'. In *Border Crossings: Translation Studies and Other Disciplines*, edited by Yves Gambier and Luc van Doorslaer, 117–39. Amsterdam: John Benjamins, 2016.

Casanova, Pascale. *La République mondiale des lettres*. Paris: Seuil, 1999.

Cheah, Pheng. 'What Is a World? On World Literature as World-Making Activity'. *Daedalus* 13 (2008): 26–38.

Cheah, Pheng. *What Is a World? On Postcolonial Literature as World Literature*. Durham, NC: Duke University Press, 2016.

Cheah, Pheng. 'Worlding Literature: Living with Tiger Spirits'. *Diacritics* 45, no. 2 (2017): 86–114.

Cohen, Marilyn, ed. *Novel Approaches to Anthropology: Contributions to Literary Anthropology*. New York: Lexington Books, 2013.

Coundouriotis, Eleni. *Claiming History: Colonialism, Ethnography, and the Novel*. New York: Columbia University Press, 1999.

Da, Nan Z. 'The Computational Case against Computational Literary Studies'. *Critical Inquiry* 45 (2019): 601–39.

Damrosch, David. *What Is World Literature?* Princeton: Princeton University Press, 2003.

Debaene, Vincent. *L'Adieu au voyage. L'ethnologie française entre science et littérature*. Paris: Gallimard, 2010.

Desai, Gaurav. *Subject to Colonialism: African Self-Fashioning and the Colonial Library*. Durham, NC: Duke University Press, 2001.

de Swaan, Abram. *Words of the World: The Global Language System*. Cambridge: Polity Press, 2001.

Ette, Ottmar. *TransArea: A Literary History of Globalization*, trans. Mark W. Person. Berlin: De Gruyter, 2016.

Ganguly, Debjani. *This Thing Called the World: The Contemporary Novel as Global Form*. Durham, NC: Duke University Press, 2016.

Gramling, David. *The Invention of Monolingualism*. New York: Bloomsbury, 2016.

Hayot, Eric. *On Literary Worlds*. Oxford: Oxford University Press, 2012.

Heilbron, Johan. 'Book Translation as a Cultural World-System'. *European Journal of Social Theory* 2, no. 4 (1999): 429–44.

Heilbron, Johan. 'Obtaining World Fame from the Periphery'. *Dutch Crossing: Journal of Low Countries Studies* 44, no. 2 (2020): 136–44.

Helgesson, Stefan. 'Postcolonialism and World Literature: Rethinking the Boundaries'. *Interventions* 16, no. 4 (2014): 483–500.

Helgesson, Stefan and Christina Kullberg. 'Translingual Events: World Literature and the Making of Language'. *Journal of World Literature* 3, no. 2 (2018): 136–52.

Helgesson, Stefan and Pieter Vermeulen, eds. *Institutions of World Literature: Writing, Translation, Markets*. New York: Routledge, 2016.

Heller-Roazen, Daniel. *Echolalias: On the Forgetting of Language*. New York: Zone Books, 2005.

Hemer, Oscar. *Contaminations and Ethnographic Fictions: Southern Crossings*. Cham: Palgrave, 2020.

Hitchcock, Peter. *The Long Space: Transnationalism and Postcolonial Form*. Stanford: Stanford University Press, 2010.

Huggan, Graham. 'The Trouble with World Literature'. In *A Companion to Comparative Literature*, edited by Ali Behdad and Dominic Thomas, 490–506. Oxford: Blackwell, 2011.

Izzo, Justin. *Experiments with Empire: Anthropology and Fiction in the French Atlantic*. Durham, NC: Duke University Press, 2019.

Kullberg, Christina. *Poetics of Ethnography in Martinican Narratives: Exploring the Self and the Environment*. Charlottesville: University of Virginia Press, 2013.

Laachir, Karima, Sara Marzagora and Francesca Orsini. 'Significant Geographies: In Lieu of World Literature'. *Journal of World Literature* 3, no. 3 (2018): 290–310.

Leffler, Yvonne. *Swedish Nineteenth-Century Literature and World Literature: Transnational Success and Literary History*. Gothenburg: Göteborg University, 2020.

Lemke, Sieglinde. *The Vernacular Matters of American Literature*. Basingstoke: Palgrave Macmillan, 2009.

Mani, B.Venkat. *Recoding World Literature: Libraries, Print Culture, and Germany's Pact with Books*. New York: Fordham University Press, 2017.

McGann, Jerome. *The Textual Condition*. Princeton: Princeton University Press, 1991.

Messling, Markus. *Universalität nach dem Universalismus: über frankophonen Literaturen der Gegenwart*. Berlin: Matthes & Seitz, 2019.

Minaard, Lisbeth and Till Dembeck. 'Introduction: How to Challenge the Myth of Monolingualism?' *Thamyris/Intersecting* 28 (2014): 9–14.

Moretti, Franco. 'Conjectures on World Literature'. *New Left Review* 1 (2000): 54–68.

Mufti, Aamir. *Forget English! Orientalisms and World Literatures*. Cambridge, MA: Harvard University Press, 2016.

Neumann, Birgit and Gabriele Rippl. 'Anglophone World Literatures: Introduction'. *Anglia* 135, no. 1 (2017): 1–20.

Noyes, John K. *Herder: Aesthetics against Imperialism*. Toronto: University of Toronto Press, 2015.

Orsini, Francesca. 'India in the Mirror of World Fiction'. In *Debating World Literature*, edited by Christopher Prendergast, 319–33. London: Verso, 2004.

Orsini, Francesca. 'The Multilingual Local in World Literature'. *Comparative Literature* 67, no. 4 (2015): 345–74.

Pollock, Sheldon. 'Cosmopolitan and Vernacular in History'. *Public Culture* 12, no. 3 (2000): 591–625.

Pollock, Sheldon. *The Language of the Gods in the World of Men*. Berkeley: University of California Press, 2006.

Rapport, Nigel. *The Prose and the Passion: Anthropology, Literature and the Writing of E. M. Forster*. Manchester: Manchester University Press, 1994.

Richter, Sandra. *Eine Weltgeschichte der deutschsprachigen Literatur*. Munich: Bertelsmann, 2017.

Robbins, Bruce and Paulo Horta, eds. *Cosmopolitanisms*. New York: New York University Press, 2017.

Rosendahl Thomsen, Mads. *Mapping World Literature: International Canonization and Translational Literatures*. London: Continuum, 2008.

Sakai, Naoki. 'How Do We Count a Language? Translation and Discontinuity'. *Translation Studies* 2, no. 1 (2009): 71–88.

Sánchez Prado, Ignacio. *Strategic Occidentalism: On Mexican Fiction, the Neoliberal Book Market, and the Question of World Literature*. Evanston: Northwestern University Press, 2018.

Sapiro, Gisèle, ed. *Translatio: le marché de traduction en France à l'heure de la mondialisation*. Paris: CNRS éditions, 2008.

Shankar, Subramanian. *Flesh and Fish Blood: Postcolonialism, Translation, and the Vernacular*. Berkeley: University of California Press, 2012.

Slaughter, Joseph. 'World Literature as Property'. *Alif* 34 (2014): 39–73.

Spivak, Gayatri. 'The Stakes of a World Literature'. In *An Aesthetic Education in the Era of Globalization*, Gayatri Spivak, 455–66. Cambridge, MA: Harvard University Press, 2012.

Stockhammer, Robert. 'Wie deutsch ist es? Glottamimetische, -diegetische, -pithanone, und -aporetische Verfahren in der Literatur'. *Arcadia* 50 (2015): 146–72.

Sturm-Trigonakis, Elke, ed. *World Literature and the Postcolonial*. Berlin: Springer, 2020.

Tageldin, Shaden M. 'Beyond Latinity, Can the Vernacular Speak?'. *Comparative Literature* 70, no. 2 (2018): 114–31.

Tagore, Rabindranath. 'Vishva Sahitya'. 1907. Translated by Rijula Das and Makarand R. Paranjape. In *Rabindranath Tagore in the 21st Century*, edited by D. Benerjii, 277–88. New Delhi: Springer, 2015.

Tidigs, Julia and Markus Huss. 'The Noise of Multilingualism: Reader Diversity, Linguistic Borders and Literary Multimodality'. *Critical Multilingualism Studies* 5, no. 1 (2017): 208–35.

Tiwari, Bhavya and David Damrosch, eds. Special issues on world literature and postcolonial studies. *Journal of World Literature* 4, no. 3 (2019) and 5, no. 3 (2020).

Uimonen, Paula. *Invoking Flora Nwapa: Nigerian Women Writers, Femininity and Spirituality in World Literature*. Stockholm: Stockholm University Press, 2020.

Warner, Michael. 'Publics and Counterpublics'. *Public Culture* 14, no. 1 (2002): 49–90.

Warwick Research Collective (WReC). *Combined and Uneven Development: Towards a New Theory of World-Literature*. Liverpool: Liverpool University Press, 2015.

Werbner, Pnina. 'Vernacular Cosmopolitanism'. *Theory, Culture & Society* 23, no. 2–3 (2006): 496–8.

Wulff, Helena. *Rhythms of Writing: An Anthropology of Irish Literature*. London: Bloomsbury, 2017.

Yildiz, Yasemin. *Beyond the Mother Tongue: The Postmonolingual Condition*. New York: Fordham University Press, 2012.

Young, Robert J. C. 'World Literature and Postcolonialism'. In *The Routledge Companion to World Literature*, edited by Theo D'haen, David Damrosch and Djelal Kadir, 213–22. Oxon: Routledge, 2011.

Introduction

Land, language, literature: Cosmopolitan and vernacular claims to place

Bo G. Ekelund

Land and language

Land and language combine to make up much of the world. Land without language is a sort of bare earth, the 'uninscribed earth' that Gayatri Spivak took to be the state of any part of the globe that awaits worlding.[1] Language without land holds the precarious existence of Volapük or Esperanto, whose universalism makes claims for the whole world, but no claims for any particular part of it.[2] Within the cosmopolitan–vernacular dynamic, the literary claims to land, to places, to territories, are made with the different linguistic and literary means made possible by a given state of that combination, and by the aspirations that preceding worldings have given rise to.[3]

The opportunities to inhabit and claim locations physically are more constrained than the opportunities to do so symbolically, while it is important to

---

[1] Gayatri Spivak, 'Three Women's Texts and a Critique of Imperialism', *Critical Inquiry* 12, no. 1 (1985): 243. The idea of 'worlding' has since seen many developments and refinements in different directions. I take my lead from the 'worlding project', see Rob Wilson and Christopher Leigh Connery, eds., *The Worlding Project: Doing Cultural Studies in the Era of Globalization* (Berkeley: North Atlantic Books, 2007).

[2] See Roberto Garvía, *Esperanto and Its Rivals: The Struggle for an International Language* (Philadelphia: University of Pennsylvania Press, 2015). Also note Lu Jiande's interesting claim that 'world literature came to China hand in hand with the spread of that [internationalist] idea of Esperanto', made in 'Dialogue Section B. The Interactions Between the Local and the Universal: A Few Thoughts After Listening to the Talk of Professor Damrosch', *Tensions in World Literature: Between the Local and the Universal*, ed. Weigui Fang (Singapore: Palgrave, 2018), 329.

[3] For the literal-minded, I will quote from Karl Marx's *Capital*, Volume 3, with a slight addition of my own: 'For the sake of completeness, it should be noted that what we understand here by land also includes water, etc. in so far as this [is inhabited or claimed] and appears as an accessory to the land' (London: Penguin, 1991), 752.

realize that symbolic resources are also scarce. In globalization, the former sort of opportunity is shrinking, with the unprecedented scale of migrations and the extreme rise in real estate prices in 'desirable' locations being two different indices of that contraction. The European feudal warlords' motto 'nulle terre sans seigneur' resonates, with later conceptions of res nullius or terra nullius still being invoked in arguments over territorial claims.[4] The mastery of space, of all space, underlies all forms of domination. Despite the absence of large-scale territorial wars in the past half-century, military violence still guarantees and disputes the drawing of borders. The claim made with the sword, however, is not sufficient. Political sovereignty, legal claims and economic possession of land all demand language in a constantly ongoing struggle over the right to inhabit and control territory. More than just a matter of states and their sovereign territories, these conflicts extend to the relentless dispossession of the great majority of their access to land *within* states as well. A good example is the recent proposal to criminalize trespass in England and Wales, curtailing the already limited right to roam in these lands even further: except for landowners, who are a tiny proportion of the population, people in England have no right of access to 92 per cent of the land of their country. As George Monbiot observes, 'no form of wealth is more fiercely contested than land'.[5] To contest that wealth, and to enjoy it, requires more than open coercion and legal documents: the more complete claim to spaces requires the kind of language we call literary. Bringing together anthropologists and literary scholars, this book will focus on such literary claims to land.

Literary claims are one of many symbolic forms for inhabiting or claiming land, forming part of the cultural work that helps confirm or contest the distribution of land and our access to it.[6] Such symbolic claims are not hard to find. On the day that this paragraph was first drafted, the news reported on New Zealand filmmaker Taika Waititi's *land acknowledgement* at the Academy

[4] To take just one example, there is a large literature on the dispute over the Senkaku/Diaoyu islands, in which the Japanese government cites the terra nullius principle, while the Chinese government claims historic title.

[5] George Monbiot, 'Lockdown is nothing new. We've been kept off the land for centuries', *The Guardian*, 22 April 2020. www.theguardian.com/commentisfree/2020/apr/22/lockdown-coronavirus-crisis-right-to-roam?CMP=Share_iOSApp_Other

[6] There is no coherent or restricted field of study that specializes in the symbolic and physical struggle over territorial claims. Generally speaking, that would be the field of politics in its broadest sense. However, we find related inquiries in recent anthropological works such as Gabriella Gahlia Modan's *Turf Wars: Discourse, Diversity, and the Politics of Place* (Malden: Blackwell, 2007) and a helpful discussion in Setha Low's *Spatializing Culture: The Ethnography of Space and Place* (London: Routledge, 2016). For a broad overview of political geography and conflicts over territory, see David Storey's *Territory: The Claiming of Space* (Harlow: Pearson, 2001).

Awards ceremony in Hollywood, which extended explicit recognition to the 'Tongva, Tataviam, and the Chumash' as 'the first people of this land on which our motion picture community lives and works'.[7] The practice of expressing a 'land acknowledgement' is gaining ground, and for those new to the game there is 'A guide to indigenous land acknowledgment' on the website of the Native Governance Center.[8] The guide helpfully and pedagogically leads the reader through issues of motivation and decorum, concluding with the observation that land acknowledgement is 'merely a starting point' for a process that includes a commitment to returning land. The symbolic acknowledgement of previous inhabitation and possession should, therefore, be a prequel to renewed inhabitation by those who have been dispossessed. The debate triggered by Waititi's statements revolved around the status of his speech act, critics seeing in it not so much a starting point than an ineffectual symbolic gesture, the logic of the spectacle at work at the very apex of the society of the spectacle, the Hollywood Academy Awards ceremony.

It is prudent to observe that nothing is merely symbolic and to reiterate that land and language make up the world, even as we recognize that land acknowledgements are not the same thing as handing territory over from control by, say, the US state to control by indigenous people. The use of the Chumash name Malibu does not hand the real estate of that beach city over to the Chumash, but it registers their historical presence, as the street name Cahuenga Boulevard in Los Angeles supplies a linguistic trace back to the Tongva and Tataviam peoples' inhabitation of the area. The ability of American English to absorb the indigenous names for its own onomastic purposes gives notice that the dynamic between the vernacular and the cosmopolitan also plays out between the indigenous and the colonizer's language. In literature too: Cahuenga becomes available for the hard-boiled vernacular of Raymond Chandler, who placed his private eye Philip Marlowe in the 'Cahuenga Building' on Hollywood Boulevard. That literary claim received its belated confirmation when the square at the intersection of that street and Cahuenga Boulevard was named 'Raymond Chandler Square'.[9]

[7] Quoted in Nick Martin, 'The Dissonance of a Land Acknowledgment at the Oscars', *The New Republic*, 10 February 2020. https://newrepublic.com/article/156520/dissonance-land-acknowledgment-oscars

[8] Native Governance Center, 'A Guide to Indigenous Land Acknowledgement'. https://nativegov.org/a-guide-to-indigenous-land-acknowledgment/

[9] Paul Zollo, 'Chandler Square', *Los Angeles Times*, 7 October 1988. www.latimes.com/archives/la-xpm-1998-oct-07-me-29977-story.html

As this winding example shows, symbolic claims and symbolic forms of inhabitation of place combine land and language in intricate ways that produce sedimentations of linguistic and other traces. In his influential article on literary worlds, Eric Hayot seizes on Chandler's work as one of those cases in which the ensemble of novels produces a recognizable 'world', more precisely a 'noir world' which operates 'as an *approach* to the actual world, heightening one's awareness of certain real-world features'.[10] Among those features, it is safe to say, the indigenous inhabitation of what is now the Cahuenga building's whereabouts, is absent. Chandler's noir world claims Los Angeles in complex ways, yes, but his characters inhabit this world on terms that favour white men, with a highly ambivalent place for Mexicans or Hispanic Americans. As an aesthetic world partly constituted by 'relations to and theories of the lived world', as Hayot claims when he moves towards generalization from his examples, Chandler's world combines his distinctive 'American vernacular' with the land of southern California in ways that to some extent make up that part of the world. Raymond Chandler Square is just the most public sign that this literary claim to place supports social principles of vision and division.[11]

This kind of tangible recognition that literary works have successfully attached themselves to space is found across the world, so that, given the requisite capital of mobility, we can walk in the Lu Xun Park in Shanghai, saunter down Rue Maryse Condé in Guadeloupe or walk along Jorge Luis Borges street in Buenos Aires, while writers' house museums are sprinkled all over the globe, from Oamaru, New Zealand (Janet Frame) to Östra Ämtervik, Sweden (Selma Lagerlöf), from Isla Negra, Chile (Pablo Neruda) to Cradock, South Africa (Olive Schreiner), from Kolkata (Rabindranath Tagore) to Reykjavík (or, rather, a few miles outside the city: Halldór Laxness), not to mention the abundance of such museums in cities such as Moscow, London, Paris, Dublin or New York.[12] Literary tourism affects the social production of space in other ways, too, with guided tours that take visitors to the mean streets of Chandler in LA or the Nordic noir streets of Lisbeth Salander's Stockholm.[13] This world of literary museums and monuments

[10] Eric Hayot, 'On Literary Worlds', *Modern Language Quarterly* 72, no. 2 (June 2011): 136.
[11] Hayot, 'On Literary Worlds', 137. For an insightful discussion of Chandler as an 'experimenter in the American vernacular', in his own words, see Daniel Peter Linder Molin, *The American Detective in Translation* (Salamanca: Ediciones Universidad de Salamanca, 2011), 94–5.
[12] See Anne Trubek, *A Skeptic's Guide to Writers' Houses* (Philadelphia: University of Pennsylvania Press, 2010) and Nicola J. Watson, *The Author's Effects: On Writer's House Museums* (Oxford: Oxford University Press, 2020).
[13] 'In A Lonely Place: Raymond Chandler's Los Angeles', Esotouric Tours into the Heart of Los Angeles. https://esotouric.com/chandler/; Annika S. Hipple, 'In the Footsteps of Lisbeth Salander: A Walking Tour of Stieg Larsson's Stockholm', *Real Scandinavia*. http://realscandinavia.com/in-the-footsteps-of-lisbeth-salander-a-walking-tour-of-stieg-larssons-stockholm/

is unequal, too. The UNESCO designation 'city of literature' gives evidence of the geographically skewed literary valorization of different parts of the world, with twenty-four of the thirty-nine cities in Europe, one in Africa.[14]

These reified proofs of successful literary inhabitations and claims of space are conspicuous but at the same time superficial in comparison to the constant process by which literary works trade in the value of places or engage in the valorization of sites that as yet have no literary pedigree. One fundamental principle behind this process is expressed by the main character of Alasdair Gray's novel *Lanark*, as he seeks to explain the lack of appreciation for Glasgow, 'a magnificent city', by contrasting it with 'Florence, Paris, London, New York. Nobody visiting them for the first time is a stranger because he's already visited them in paintings, novels, history books and films. But if a city hasn't been used by an artist not even the inhabitants live there imaginatively'.[15] The implication is that the literary 'use' of cities – and other locations – makes those places accessible for an appropriation that is otherwise less substantial. Not all novels take up the burden of preparing a visitor for the imaginative experience of a city, but literary works and practices cannot but contribute to an imaginative priming directed at locations in the world.[16]

That dimension of literature's cultural work is most often present at a deep level, while other features are highlighted. To return to the border between Mexico and the USA that plays an important part in Chandler's novels, it remains a highly disputed geography. On and around this border between two states, land and language combine in struggles over the worlding of these areas. Jobst Welge's chapter in the present volume contributes to the analysis of the kinds of claims that are made concerning this borderland. In this introductory

---

[14] UNESCO, 'Creative Cities Network'. https://en.unesco.org/creative-cities/. A list of the literary cities can be generated by a search in the 'Creative Cities' map.

[15] Alasdair Gray, *Lanark* (New York: Braziller, 1985), 243.

[16] It would be our argument that this is so even with fictional worlds or storyworlds that seem to sever or displace their relation to the actual world quite radically. Clearly such cases would involve a more complex approach to the ways that literature builds the shared world by building its own worlds. The refusal of reference, tout court, was and remains a particularly literary privilege, intensely cultivated by some modernist and postmodernist writers, often taking their cue from Mallarmé's poetics of antirepresentation, a literature that, in Jacques Rancière's formulation, 'exiled itself from any country of its own', in *Mute Speech: Literature, Critical Theory, and Politics* (New York: Columbia University Press, 2011), 130. Forgoing any direct symbolic claim on land, such literary strategies strengthen the indirect valorization of the place that makes possible the refusal of place, the social space of a highly autonomous literary practice. Here, Pascale Casanova's analysis of a literary world space and Bourdieu's insistence on the reciprocal force of social and physical space seem apt instruments for understanding the location and orientation involved (Casanova, *The World Republic of Letters* (Cambridge, MA: Harvard University Press, 2004); Bourdieu 'Site Effects', in *The Weight of the World* (Stanford: Stanford University Press, 1999)).

discussion, however, where it is useful to raise topical rather than analytical–historical illustrations, we should note the debate over Jeanine Cummins's *American Dirt*, a novel about a Mexican woman and her son fleeing drug cartel violence in Acapulco, attempting to find a safe harbour in the USA, migrating across the border.[17] The intense and often acrimonious debate over *American Dirt* focused on who is authorized to tell stories about particular experiences, but also included questions about the composition of the publishing industry that performs much of that authorization. In a struggle over the right to decide who gets to 'own' the literary treatment of the migration experience of Latinx migrants to the USA, lines were drawn around issues of literary quality or the lack of it, and around cultural appropriation or the freedom to write creatively about others. The position-takings depended on the use of what is now increasingly defined as 'platforms' with access to different media: Oprah Winfrey's influential book club, the publishing company, the key reviews (the *New York Times Book Review*, *The Guardian*) and diverse groups of writers taking up collective stances using hashtags such as #ownvoices and #DignidadLiteraria.

The stakes involved in this debate are clearly of some moment, and they include the literary claim to a territory that is geoculturally and geopolitically contested. The spatial claims associated with *American Dirt* found an inflated expression in one of the heavyweight blurbs for the novel, by Sandra Cisneros: 'This book is not simply the great American novel; it's the great novel of *las Americas*. It's the great world novel! This is the international story of our times. Masterful.'[18] While it would have been controversial to go straight from 'great American novel' to 'great world novel', the mediating enlargement via the entire hemisphere (and note the shift then to Spanish) points to the importance of those borderlands. The dustjacket flap of the novel reproduced a bilingual motto that Cummins had taken as a compass direction for her work, 'También de este lado hay sueños. On this side, too, there are dreams.' Reproduced from graffiti on the border wall at Tijuana, the motto articulates the border with the language that can cross such borders, even as the full stop in the middle of the quote indicates how they may also perform boundary-work that enforces the division. Thirty years after the publication of Gloria Anzaldúa's seminal work *Borderlands/La Frontera*, Cummins's novel made claims on this unsettling territory that conjure up all the previous ones, be they military, political or symbolic.[19] For the literary claims, a

---

[17] Jeanine Cummins, *American Dirt* (New York: Flatiron, 2020).
[18] Cummins, *American Dirt*, back cover.
[19] Gloria Anzaldúa, *Borderlands/La Frontera: The New Mestiza* (San Francisco: Aunt Lute, 1987).

geocritical study would yield a large volume of instances, including prominently Cormac McCarthy's *Blood Meridian*, his *Border Trilogy* and Valeria Luiselli's *Lost Children Archive*, to mention just a few titles.[20]

These examples lead up to a fundamental idea guiding this book: their dimension of claiming space needs to be seen as having a conceptual or analytical autonomy that calls for a particular readiness on the part of scholarship. It is a readiness that is not only to be triggered by these specific borderlands, or territories that are otherwise manifestly contested, but a more general preparedness. It is, to some extent, a conceptual configuration that will bring the study of literary claims to space into what is now best called a geocultural framework.

The geocultural perspective

The geocultural perspective entered different disciplines in significant ways in the early 1990s, at roughly the same time as the formation of 'critical geopolitics'.[21] From its influential introduction by Immanuel Wallerstein, who conceived of geoculture as the hidden doxa of the capitalist world-economy, it was inflected as a more flexible notion by Ulf Hannerz, who saw the geocultural imagination as a way of thinking about the 'distribution of things cultural, somehow cultural, over territories and their human populations'.[22] For our purposes, the stress on distribution is salutary, since the geocultural dimension of human expressive practices must needs be apportioned in time and space. An important modulation was added by Walter Mignolo, who saw at that point in time a 'new geocultural politics of location' that was marked by being 'territorially detached' in various ways.[23] This detachment served Mignolo as a way of shifting the focus away from the

---

[20] For a discussion that summarizes some main themes connected to the borderlands, see Ramón Saldívar, 'The American Borderlands Novel', in *The Cambridge History of the American Novel*, ed. Leonard Cassuto, Clare Virginia Eby and Benjamin Reiss (Cambridge: Cambridge University Press, 2011).

[21] See Simon Dalby, 'Critical Geopolitics: Discourse, Difference, and Dissent', *Environment and Planning D: Society and Space* 9 (1991): 261–83; K. J. Dodds and J. D. Sidaway, 'Locating Critical Geopolitics', *Environment and Planning D: Society and Space* 12 (1994): 515–24; and Gearoid Ó Tuathail, *Critical Geopolitics: The Politics of Writing Global Space* (Minneapolis: University of Minnesota Press, 1996).

[22] Immanuel Wallerstein, *Geopolitics and Geoculture: Essays on the Changing World-System* (Cambridge: Cambridge University Press, 1991); Ulf Hannerz, 'Geocultural Scenarios', in *Frontiers of Sociology: The Annals of the International Institute of Sociology*, Vol. 11, ed. Peter Hedström and Björn Wittrock (Leiden: Brill, 2009), 268.

[23] Walter D. Mignolo, 'Afterword: Human Understanding and (Latin) American Interests: The Politics and Sensibilities of Geocultural Locations', *Poetics Today* 16, no. 1 (1995): 174.

reference to any given territory, instead seeking out the 'locus of enunciation', that is, the site from which such references are made. We wish to keep both dimensions: the politics of location always involve claiming space. That claim will indeed be made from a locus of enunciation, but will be directed *at* a location which may but need not correspond to that site of speech. Inhabiting one location, we may claim another one, while being oriented towards yet another. To give an account of the geocultural work that literary practices, texts and institutions carry out, the distinct problematic of particular locations and orientations must be in the picture.

Literary texts and practices, we argue in this volume, are ways of inhabiting or claiming space that constantly shift, assemble and reassemble, expand and contract the 'world' that undergirds world literature. They do so by mobilizing language and form along the spectrum of the cosmopolitan–vernacular dynamic. It is a geocultural or even geopolitical practice, if we understand these terms to include symbolic acts that affect the construction of geographical boundaries while also, always, affecting the value of given locations.[24] In this perspective, 'world literature' is itself a stage in the geocultural politics of location. We agree with Aamir Mufti that far from promoting a borderless world, world literature takes part in the border-construction or boundary-work that all symbolic claims on space are bound up with.[25] However, the politics of location and orientation that literary works and practices inevitably participate in cannot be limited to national borders, nor can the nature of their claims be predicted on the basis of the emergence of world literature in any specific discipline or place. World literature is constantly in the process of being made, but not on conditions of our own choosing, nor even on conditions imposed by the discipline; writers and critics are engaged in preparing us for living imaginatively in different parts of a world whose borders are in dispute. As Tasnim Qutait shows in Chapter 3, literary works may also allow us to imaginatively live through processes of apparent unworlding and dissolution of state structures. The use of horror and magic realism in the works of Ahmed Saadawi and Hassan Blasim vernacularizes these cosmopolitan modes to represent post-invasion Iraq. In the case of Saadawi, the relocation of Mary Shelley's *Frankenstein* to Baghdad invokes globalized horror to represent violence rendered routine. Blasim, meanwhile, turns to dream logic, magical realism and metafictional elements to reflect on writing about Iraq from the diaspora. These strategies have allowed their texts to

---

[24] See Caren Irr, *Toward the Geopolitical Novel: U.S. Fiction in the Twenty-First Century* (New York: Columbia University Press, 2014), for a survey of recent US novels that extend the geographical scope of the political novel.

[25] Aamir Mufti, *Forget English!* (Cambridge, MA: Harvard University Press, 2016).

travel as examples of Iraqi fiction that fit into current paradigms of world literature, introducing the unfamiliar within recognizable frames. Working in the registers of horror, dream and split ontologies, Saadawi and Blasim perform the geocultural work of placing Iraq as a central location in a world of shock and awe.

Invoking a geocultural order and geopolitics is not to be taken as a sign of disciplinary hubris, but as a modest way of registering the fact that literary works and practices cannot avoid having an impact on the symbolic and physical making of the world. Combining land and language, literature valorizes place. Literature prepares individuals and groups for living imaginatively in cities and in countrysides, in sweatshops, in oil fields, on the floor of stock exchanges, in shanty towns and in penthouses, on the moon, on Mars, beyond the visible stars. Such imaginative inhabitation need not be something to be applauded: it is to be found in populations being primed to occupy territories where others have lived for a long time, a mobilization based on stories of ancient rights to place. Whether it prompts aggressive territoriality or the convivial sharing of land, it is a dimension of literary texts that needs further, systematic exploration.

The conceptual couple: Location and orientation

This book seeks to add to a geocultural and geopolitical understanding of world literature by insisting on the centrality of a conceptual pair, locations and orientations. In the chapters that follow, they serve some quite general and some quite concrete functions. First, they allow for continuity and dialogue with existing paradigms of world literature studies. Second, they operate across geographical scales: the Americas can be a location; so can the Savannah in Port-of-Spain or a house in Buffalo, NY. Third, they may be attached to systemic and structural forms of analysis as well as to phenomenological ones, to Newtonian space as well as to relative space-time or relational spacetime.[26] These first three propositions set out the openness of the concepts.[27] We add three analytical obligations that limit that openness, pushing the pair more resolutely towards empirical work. Fourth, then, locations and orientations in literary works stand in some knowable relation to locations and orientations outside of those texts. Fifth, locations and orientations stand in an irrevocable relationship to one

---

[26] See David Harvey's distinctions in *Cosmopolitanism and the Geographies of Freedom* (New York: Columbia University Press, 2009), 134–41.

[27] See Pierre Bourdieu's discussion of open concepts in *An Invitation to Reflexive Sociology* (Chicago: University of Chicago Press, 1992), 95–6.

another: there can be no location without an orientation, and every orientation presupposes a location. Sixth, locations and orientations are always the properties of social agents or of cultural objects made by social agents; as such, they appear either as forms of inhabitation or as claims on space.

Locations and orientations are properties of social agents or of cultural objects

To continue with the last proposition, a location, in our use of the term, is not a point in space that somehow exists in itself. Rather, the term designates the way that an individual, a group or a cultural object, such as a text, inhabits or claims a place or position at a given time. That means that location (and orientation) is a social relation between an agent and a space. We are not talking here of positions in social space, in the sense Pierre Bourdieu has developed, although any understanding of location certainly draws in the intricate relations between positions in social space and the physical spaces we can inhabit or claim.[28] The ability to inhabit or claim, or to appropriate physical space more generally, directly depends on the possession of various forms of capital so that 'social space translates into physical space', albeit in mediated, '*blurred*' forms.[29] The use of the word 'space' here is not meant to indicate some significant preference with regard to space and place: as inhabited and claimed, location is closer to place, but the distribution of inhabitations, claims and orientations only becomes fully open to explanation within a spatial structure which relates not only places, but more abstract spatial entities as well. For the study of literary objects, practices and persons and their distribution in the world, a location is that meaningful connection between object or person and place that can help us understand the larger distribution. Conversely, from some larger mapping, it is always meaningful to move to individual locations within it.[30] A person or object existing for a brief

---

[28] See Bourdieu, 'Site Effects'; also see Deborah Reed-Danahy for a helpful overview of Bourdieu's thinking about space, with a particular focus on mobility, in *Bourdieu and Social Space* (New York: Berghahn, 2019).

[29] Bourdieu, 'Site Effects', 124.

[30] In the emphasis on particular ways of claiming and inhabiting locations, our approach shares the 'bottom-up' methodology of the project on Multilingual Locals and Significant Geographies, while in our insistence on matters of the larger distribution of such claims, it differs significantly from that project. Studies of particular locations and orientations are a first step in the attempt to understand the mechanisms that allow certain geographies to become significant, while others remain insignificant. The critique voiced by the Significant Geographies group against what they variously call reductive, flattening and positivist Marxist approaches seems from this perspective symptomatic of a desire to forgo any systematic reckoning of the symbolic and material resources that do indeed condition such attributions of significance. See Karima Laachir, Sara Marzagora and Francesca Orsini, 'Significant Geographies *in lieu* of World Literature', *Journal of World Literature* 3 (2018): 290–310.

moment in one spot does not make that spot a location in our sense. A location is a property of someone or something, a feature that belongs to a person or object in some significant manner, with at least some duration. Residence is a term that might indicate such a relation, and even temporary residence will serve as location as long as it is meaningful within the larger context we are considering. Take Jamaica Kincaid's description of a brief stopover in Kathmandu in her travel book *Among Flowers: A Walk in the Himalayas*:

> We spent three days on the roof of our hotel in Kathmandu, cleaning and drying seeds, labeling them, numbering the packets, getting them ready to be inspected and shipped out, after proper inspection by the proper authorities, to our gardens in Wales (for Bleddyn and Sue), Kingston, Washington (for Dan), and North Bennington, Vermont (for me).[31]

Grammar is obliging here, with the possessive pronouns indicating a claim to the hotel as well as the gardens: our hotel, our gardens. Such an explicit assertion, however, is not a requirement for location to be a property of an individual. In the sense given here, a site need only be meaningfully associated with that person, not owned by her. Kincaid goes on to give her readers the local colour that gives substance to the non-place of the hotel, before reflecting, in the concluding passage of the book, on the 'strangeness of [her] situation', gathering seeds for a Vermont garden in Nepal.[32] The added details make the hotel readable as more than just a convenience, a temporary necessity of no real import. The sensuous particulars say that the writer's location here consists not only in the strangeness of treating place instrumentally, but also in the need to convey its substance as a lived place. Since it is a shared location, the hotel generates different orientations: Wales, Washington state, Vermont. In this case, the location is subservient to those orientations, which is part of how it is inhabited or claimed. On the hotel roof, the vernacular seeds are prepared to become cosmopolitan, to undergo 'proper inspection' before their further movement into a larger world. Whether we are analysing the distribution of seeds and plants, or the distribution of 'prominent literary figures'[33] or of hotels, the location enters the geocultural reckoning along with some entity that inhabits it or claims it in some fashion.

---

[31] Jamaica Kincaid, *Among Flowers: A Walk in the Himalayas* (Washington, DC: National Geographic Society, 2005), 187.

[32] Kincaid, *Among Flowers*, 189.

[33] *Among Flowers* is a book in the National Geographic Directions series, in which famous authors – 'some of the world's most prominent and highly regarded literary figures' – write about various destinations, offering some fascinating conjunctions of literary gazes and well-known or even iconic places.

No location without an orientation

In the conceptual scheme adopted here, locations presuppose orientations and vice versa: they are 'co-constitutive'.[34] Our study of world literature or the literatures of the world would ask, wherever it found a location, what orientation or orientations that location is bound up with. Such a question can be asked in many registers, and within different horizons and at varying scales, but we take it that it is always worth asking; we assume, too, that the answers are never given beforehand. The particular case must be fully investigated. The explicit orientation asserted by Jamaica Kincaid for herself and her seeds may appear quite straightforwardly to be Vermont in the example we have looked at. Extending our analysis of the way her text produces locations and orientations, we find that it shares with Washington and Wales a more general character within a particular distribution of goods (and evils): they are places of comfort: 'We wanted to leave and our destination was beyond Kathmandu, our destination was home and the comfort and beauty of our gardens.'[35] In this way, the analysis of location and orientation will move from the singular to the composite, to entanglements, to distant horizons, from concrete to more abstract determinations, pushing the analysis of the case to find its exemplarity.

The necessity of investigating the particular case derives from the fact that there is no single law describing the logic of location and orientation. It is, for example, not a given that a peripheral location implies an orientation towards a central one; one cannot deduce that an Irish modernist is oriented towards Paris.[36] However, that is not to say there may not be forces in play that make one orientation more likely than others, as is surely often the case. These forces are sometimes more overtly 'political', sometimes less so.

In Chapter 4, Sally Anderson Boström brings up a case in which questions of location and orientation animate a politics of place. Questions of who gets to write the literature of Hawai'i, where it is written, and what language it is written in, dominate debates that began in the mid-twentieth century and continue today. Central to the question of who can lay claim to the islands' literature, Anderson Boström observes, is the contentious issue of what it means to be

---

[34] Helena Wulff, 'Introduction to Part 2', *World Literatures: Exploring the Cosmopolitan-Vernacular Exchange*, ed. Stefan Helgesson et al. (Stockholm: Stockholm University Press, 2018), 103.

[35] Kincaid, *Among Flowers*, 181.

[36] I am alluding to Casanova's discussion of Samuel Beckett in *The World Republic of Letters*, 319–20, which does not, it should be pointed out, commit the mistake of such a deduction. See also the extended analysis in Casanova's earlier work, *Samuel Beckett: Anatomy of a Literary Revolution* (London: Verso, 2006), 75–84.

'local' and the place of Hawai'i Creole English – or 'pidgin' – in that debate. Focusing on a comparison between Maxine Hong Kingston's *Hawai'i One Summer* (1978) and Lois-Ann Yamanaka's *Blu's Hanging* (1997), Anderson Boström shows how these two authors' differing orientations – writing about Hawai'i from within as a 'local' or from within as an 'outsider' – reveal different perspectives on the vernacular and different orientations towards the mainland United States. By paying attention to the local dynamics involved in writing about Hawai'i, this analysis provides another particular case with broad implications for the geocultural study of literature. Both authors are emotionally invested in the location of Hawai'i, but their appropriations of space accentuate different geocultural relations. In this case and the others presented here, the locations-and-orientations perspective is a tool for relational thinking. Its relationality is first inscribed in the location–orientation couple, but then extends to ever-widening questions regarding the geocultural distributions and claims of spatial, symbolic and material goods. Within this expanding horizon we engage with the dynamic between cosmopolitan and vernacular tendencies as fundamentally informing the way that locations and orientations are shaped within the realm of expressive practices, including, more narrowly, the production, reproduction and circulation of literature.

Knowable relations to the lived world

Our objects of study include, centrally, literary works. Using diverse methods – close reading, distant reading, historicizing and contextualizing, interviews and fieldwork – we assume that locations and orientations can be analysed in literary works. Here, too, the particular case must be given its due. While we take it that the relations between the location–orientation complex in the text is related in some understandable way to locations and orientations outside of it, seconding Eric Hayot's dictum that aesthetic worlds are 'always relations to and theories of the lived world',[37] we do not posit that the mechanisms of mediation are always the same. Writers who operate according to mimetic protocols produce literary works that will repay a different sort of scrutiny than writers who work within the expectations of an expressive literary ideology.[38] Writers may

[37] Hayot, 'On Literary Worlds', 137.
[38] This contrast, one of many possible, picks up M. H. Abrams's argument in *The Mirror and the Lamp* (Oxford: Oxford University Press, 1953).

explicitly refuse to pin down the parallel between fictional location and actual place, like Peter Abrahams in *This Island Now*, explored by Ashleigh Harris in Chapter 2 of the present volume. However, as Harris demonstrates, that refusal may form an implicit invitation to the reader to construct this parallel as something much more complex than simply a choice of 'the particular island on which he or she wants this story played out'.[39] Abrahams's novel, seen in this light, stages its locations to allow for an orientation back towards South Africa, or perhaps even an expanded pan-African purview, looking towards other horizons of confinement and emancipation. Harris sets Abrahams's novel in a productive juxtaposition with Sol Plaatje's *Mhudi*, located in the country of the Barolong in the mid-nineteenth century but oriented, as a novel written in English, towards a cosmopolitan reader. Harris argues that the orientation towards the world from Plaatje's location at the beginning of the twentieth century gets radically disoriented by the creation of the apartheid state, and as such, the vector of worldliness promised by literature in Plaatje's early writings gets inverted by apartheid isolationism. As such, Abrahams's novel presents us with the inverse view to Plaatje's: if Plaatje was concerned first and foremost with taking Setswana culture, language and history to the world, Abrahams turns the global world view back on apartheid isolationism. The construction of the relation between literary location/orientation and its counterparts in a social and historical world – in this case and others – passes through a whole network of individuals, groups and institutions, differently configured in any given case.

Fidelity to that complexity in the cases we study implies a certain plurality of approaches, with anthropological perspectives alongside close readings and studies of the circulation of books. Different modes of reading or disciplinary projects may adopt the location/orientation pair for various purposes, but they will be under particular analytical obligations because of this adoption. In its simplest form, those obligations boil down to asking the two questions, what is the particular location we are asked to reckon with (in this text, in this situation, in this practice)? And, what are the orientations bound up with that location? Or, if an orientation rather than a location is what claims our analytical attention: what locations does it presuppose or conjure up? The answers to these questions then have a bearing on the geocultural work being carried out.

---

[39] See Chapter 2, this volume.

The levels of analysis, structures, individuals, phenomenology and physics

While those questions insist on particularity, they do not limit our conceptual pair to investigations at a micro-level. The particular locations of a hotel roof in Kathmandu or a fictional Caribbean island exist within a larger distribution of places. The experiences of the dislocated writers studied by Helena Wulff in Chapter 8 are singular, but point to the near-systemic distribution of writers who have been driven from one point on the globe to another.[40] Focusing on three autobiographical accounts of arrival by writers who have migrated to Sweden during different periods of time and circumstances, Wulff argues that these writings can be understood as literary cosmopolitanism from within, and thus vernacular forms. The stories register the writers' changing orientations to their locations, not only to Sweden, but also to their countries of origin, over time. This is an orientation that also includes a sense of dislocation. Journeying towards their moment of arrival, these migrants and refugees obviously share an orientation to Sweden. Writing of the arrival itself plumbs deeply personal experiences, while revealing larger structures involved in the migrant encounter with Sweden. Each phenomenological orientation evokes the structural distribution of socio-geographically constituted perspectives. In this regard, as in all others, the world of world literature is one but unequal, to echo again Moretti's phrase that stands at the beginning of the current formation of 'world literature'.[41] The number of Swedish writers in exile in Greece, Iran or Afghanistan does not match the number of Greek, Iranian or Afghani writers in exile in Sweden. That is to say that the location–orientation perspective does not simply lend itself to analyses of both structural and individualizing kinds, but insistently refers the structure back to the individual and vice versa. As Pascale Casanova says, authors are all 'prisoner[s] of particular points of view'.[42] The challenge remains to explore not only such individual points of view but the architecture of the prison as well.

That architectural dimension can be pursued at the level of an apartment floor plan or a Discrete Global Grid, as long as we see a location at either level as the property of someone or something. That opposition seems to suggest that location as understood within a phenomenological mode of knowledge is tied

---

[40] I prefer not to speak of systems or systemic effects, taking that to imply a downgrading of agency which seems to me unwarranted.
[41] Franco Moretti, 'Conjectures on World Literature', *New Left Review* 1 (2000): 55–6.
[42] Casanova, *The World Republic*, 10.

to circumscribed places, while the objectivist mode would then be the default setting for larger spatial entities. However, the acceptance of different scales is a point distinct from the accommodation of different methodologies. Take the Rio Declaration's language about '[r]ecognizing the integral and interdependent nature of the Earth, our home'.[43] The earth as 'our home' spells out a kind of ideal belonging in a metaphor that telescopes two distant levels. A study aimed at finding ways of communicating the need for changes in environmental policy found that the metaphor of a planetary 'home' 'resonated with climate experts as well as diverse subpopulations of the general public, including conservatives and climate-change deniers'.[44] This construction of the planet as a location that is the property of every human being is ideological in both the bad and the good sense: it mystifies the unequal access to the goods of the planet, while it shapes an orientation towards a future state of this distribution; in other words, it creates a horizon that enables orientations.[45] This example shows not just one exceptionally resonant point on the scale of possible locations, but it also shows how orientation activates temporality. The idea that earth is our home is in one sense true while at the same time it is obviously false, because we are far from achieving that state of social relationships. 'The earth, our home' is a horizon towards which the Rio Declaration signatories formally oriented themselves from their locations, or perhaps from the location of the hangar-like 'Riocentro', outside the city. As a conceptual metaphor, the target domain of the earth is mapped onto the source domain of the home, but of course both words are in themselves non-literal. As a literary artefact, 'the earth is our home' reminds us that at the largest geographical scale, locations are entirely imaginary, or even fictional. At the same time, 'home' is phenomenologically anchored: it is where the heart is, where a feeling results from the act of hanging up one's hat or wiping one's shoes on the welcome mat. Structural distribution and embodied experience may both enter analytically where location makes its home.[46]

---

[43] 'Rio Declaration on Environment and Development', *Report of the United Nations Conference on Environment and Development*, 12 August 1992. www.un.org/en/development/desa/population/migration/generalassembly/docs/globalcompact/A_CONF.151_26_Vol.I_Declaration.pdf.

[44] Paul H. Thibodeau, Cynthia M. Frantz and Matias Berretta, 'The Earth is Our Home: Systemic Metaphors to Redefine Our Relationship with Nature', *Climatic Change* 142, no. 1–2 (May 2017): 287–300. https://doi.org/10.1007/s10584-017-1926-z

[45] See Darko Suvin, 'Locus, Horizon, and Orientation: The Concept of Possible Worlds as a Key to Utopian Studies', *Utopian Studies* 1, no. 2 (1990): 69–83.

[46] When David Damrosch and David L. Pike talk about works of 'world literature' engaging in a conversation with contexts 'into which they travel away from home' it is clear that 'home' is not thought of as 'the earth, our home' ('Preface', *The Longman Anthology of World Literature*, 2nd edition, vol. D: The Seventeenth and Eighteenth Centuries (New York: Longman, 2009), xvi.

The analytical obligations of the location/orientation approach do not prescribe that the analysis *has* to move from the phenomenological or everyday inhabitation of place, with its embodied orientation to other place, to the structural (and, inevitably, political) distribution of the access to places, either by way of inhabitation or orientation. It does say that such a move is always possible, and it says the move can originate at either point. It is worth noting at this point that the word 'orientation' appeared in English first as a way of speaking generally about the way churches or graves, as instances in an ensemble of many cases, are aligned in relation to the points of the compass. However, that abstract noun came into use long after the verb 'to orient', which signifies the alignment of a church or grave towards the east, and the verb in turn was preceded by the noun orient, which, of course, means East. Orientation is anthropological, religious and political here, at the level of classifiable phenomena, and belongs to a geography that is symbolic and physical at the same time. Locations and orientations constantly bundle together the symbolic, the social and the physical, the body and the object world. As Sara Ahmed has shown in her decisive intervention into the question of phenomenological orientation, the alignments presupposed by phenomenology are themselves aligned or misaligned with racial, sexual and political classifications.[47]

Geographical scales

In short, geographical scales are not exact equivalents of the opposition between structural and phenomenological approaches to location and orientation. Our conceptual pair lends itself to different approaches, but also to sites of varying size and scope, to places with distant or proximate horizons. In that sense, it is 'scale-sensitive' in the sense proposed by Nirvana Tanoukhi: it *follows* not just the material processes that shape a landscape but also the symbolic processes through which locations are claimed, the way 'zone[s] of autonomy' are created.[48] In Paula Uimonen's study of the gendered literary worlds of West African fiction in Chapter 1, the focus shifts from the community town of Oguta, to the larger territory denoted by 'Igbo society', to Nigeria, to West Africa, to Africa and then to various points on the map that index the reception of texts written by Flora Nwapa and Chinua Achebe, with 'today's globalized world' as a final horizon. These are all different

---

[47] Sara Ahmed, *Queer Phenomenology: Orientations, Objects, Others* (Durham, NC: Duke University Press, 2006).

[48] Nirvana Tanoukhi, 'The Scale of World Literature', *New Literary History* 39, no. 3 (2008): 610. doi:10.1353/nlh.0.0051.

locations, inhabited or claimed in different ways, generating different orientations. Seen as properties of Nwapa or Achebe, however, they respond to that analytical obligation mentioned above. What Uimonen shows is that such locations, whether inhabited, claimed or ascribed, are subject to a logic of gendering which is not universal, but the local or translocal effect of a politics of location. To advance a more gender-balanced and decentred appraisal of world literature, she concludes with a conceptualization of one world literature as a pluriverse of aesthetic worlds, providing another horizon towards which scholarship may orient itself.[49]

Our understanding of location and orientation at different scales factors in not just politics or the pervasive effect of gendered principles of vision and division, but also the effects of literary conventions. In literary texts, shifts of geographical scale are often built into the construction of locations in that peculiar double reference we know as allegory. As Adnan Mahmutović observes in his analysis of Michael Muhammad Knight's novel *Taqwacores*, the novel uses a house in Buffalo as a 'microcosm containing the macrocosm', thereby shifting the reader's focus between the particularity of the single locality and the larger orbit of 'the cosmopolitan house of Islam'.[50] In this way, Knight uses location to answer the demands of the global novel while keeping faith with the sensuous particulars of the genre's traditional mission. Moreover, in Chapter 6, Mahmutović shows how this formal juggling involves the creation of a new vernacular that can mediate between scales. A house, a village, a metropolis, a nation, the planet – the size or scope depends on the politics of location, the configuration of literary expectations and the larger principles of vision and division that writers abide by or betray. By deploying the open conceptual pair of locations and orientations, we can register those forms of fidelity and infidelity at different – combined and uneven – geographical scales.

Continuity and dialogue with existing paradigms of world literature studies

In these preliminary remarks, we have stressed conceptual openness and an analytical obligation that puts a limit on that openness. It is time to consider the distinctiveness and usefulness of this approach within the expanding

---

[49] Our approach is in that sense compatible with Shu-mei Shih's insistence on the capacity for scaling, while it insists on the particular location or orientation as the key unit. Shih speaks of 'the capacity to scale up to the world and down to the text' but our approach scales up to the world as location and down to the individual location(s) claimed in the text or by the text. 'World Studies and Relational Comparison', *PMLA* 130, no. 2 (March 2015): 434. https://doi.org/10.1632/pmla.2015.130.2.430.

[50] Adnan Mahmutović, 'Literary Ecologies and Post-9/11 Muslim Writing', *World Literatures: Exploring the Cosmopolitan-Vernacular Exchange*, ed. Stefan Helgesson et al. (Stockholm: Stockholm University Press, 2018), 146. https://doi.org/10.16993/bat

universe of the world literature debate. As our first point stipulated, we do not see this conceptual base as the means to break with existing paradigms, or as a broom with which to clear some entirely new space for our own studies. The location/orientation pair is open enough to function within the different but overlapping environments activated by Franco Moretti, Pascale Casanova and David Damrosch – if we take these three as the founders of the current discourse on world literature – as well as most conceptual environments formed and expanded by the reactions against them.[51] We agree with Mads Rosendahl Thomsen that the different approaches to world literature are, in practice, 'domains that cannot be fully integrated', but at the same time we endorse work on locations and orientations that provisionally suspend judgement on the final validity of one or the other.[52] For us, that validity, however, will be affected by the analytical obligation of the location/orientation perspective, which insists on the geocultural work done when literary works and practices claim space.

A brief example will serve to illustrate what that obligation would entail. Take Moretti's well-debated formula of the compromise between foreign (read core-derived) form and local (read peripheral) materials: for us, the question of what is inhabited as a local site or a central one is itself always part of the analysis, as is the question of what is claimed as a foreign, distant source. Broadly, we agree with Moretti that the world is indeed unequal and its inequalities are structural and knowable, but the distribution of the means of inhabiting and claiming particular locations allows for counter-structural effects within the structure. Such effects are acknowledged by Moretti, as in the example of the formal innovations of the Latin American Boom, and we take it that both his general formula and this particular formation of innovation and dissemination would profit from and be modified by a systematic study of the locations and orientations involved. Such a study would, for instance, have to think about the institutional location of Columbia University, the growing puissance of New York in transnational cold war culture, and the migratory patterns that gave the

---

[51] This foundational trio appears differently from different locations. A search in Google's Ngram function for the years 1990 to 2008 registers no statistically significant mentions of David Damrosch if one limits the search to either German, French or Spanish. Moretti is the most common reference in German and English. On the other hand, Damrosch is a cornerstone in US-dominated discussions of world literature, and typical of the American connection between teaching and world literature.

[52] Mads Rosendahl Thomsen, *Mapping World Literature: International Canonization and Transnational Literatures* (London: Bloomsbury, 2008), 20. Thomsen is comparing Damrosch, Moretti and Casanova when making this observation.

'visible translator' Gregory Rabassa what he calls his 'piebald [circumstances]'.[53] These latter included grandparents born in four different countries, a childhood in Yonkers and a farm in New Hampshire and a spell as cryptographer in the US Army. But it is the location of Columbia College that makes possible Rabassa's editorial post in the cosmopolitan little magazine the *Odyssey Review* for which Rabassa scouted for Latin American titles.[54] From there, the translations of Julio Cortázar's *Rayuela*, as *Hopscotch* (1966), and Gabriel García Márquez's *Cien años de soledad*, as *One Hundred Years of Solitude* (1970), followed, and the North American relay of the Latin American Boom had been initiated. In Pascale Casanova's account of the Boom, it is the Nobel Prize awarded to Miguel Asturias (in 1967) that stands as a sort of starting gun for the boom, but Stockholm is far from the most urgent location to be factored into that history.[55]

As this example shows, the location/orientation approach tends to reintroduce individual actors, but it does so in the spirit of an impossibly large 'collective biography', in the sense established by the work of mainly French sociologists of culture.[56] Particular authors, translators, critics, publishers and so on are part of the real, collective history that produces the phantom of world literature, and our approach takes each individual case to involve claims for parts of that world. To insist on the concrete concept of a location that is bound up with an agent inhabiting or claiming it is a way of resisting the 'derealization' of literary works and authors.[57] For example, Damrosch's definition of world literature as a 'mode of reading' that manifests itself as 'a form of detached engagement with worlds beyond our own place and time' is destabilized by the analytical obligation to take into account a particular reader's '*own* place and time' and how that possession of space

---

[53] Gregory Rabassa, *If This Be Treason: Translation and Its Dyscontents* (New York: New Directions, 2006), 29.

[54] The *Odyssey Review* published two European and two Latin American stories in each issue (Rabassa, *If This Be Treason*, 24). See also María Constanza Guzmán, *Gregory Rabassa's Latin American Literature: A Translator's Visible Legacy* (Lewisburg: Bucknell University Press, 2011), 58–9; and Deborah N. Cohn, *The Latin American Literary Boom and U.S. Nationalism During the Cold War* (Nashville: Vanderbilt University Press, 2012), 101–4.

[55] Casanova, *The World Republic*, 325. It should be added that French translations of Cortázar had preceded Rabassa's: Laure Guille-Bataillon translated *Los Premios* as *Les gagnants* in 1961 and *Rayuela* as *Marelles* in the same year as Rabassa's English translation. The former title had been translated into English by Elaine Kerrigan in 1965 as *The Winners*, too. But it is the success of Rabassa's translations that stand out in this conversion of vernacular or at least national literary forms into recognizable goods on a cosmopolitan literary market.

[56] See Donald Broady, 'French Prosopography: Definition and Suggested Readings', *Poetics* 30 (2002): 381–5.

[57] Pierre Bourdieu, *The Field of Cultural Production: Essays on Art and Literature*, edited by Randal Johnson (Cambridge: Polity, 1993), 32. See also 'How to Read an Author', *Pascalian Meditations* (Stanford: Stanford University Press, 2000), 85–92.

makes possible a particular mode of reading.[58] In this regard, the anthropological concern with the ineluctable locatedness of authors, readers and other actors – see Paula Uominen's discussion of the celebrations of Flora Nwapa's novel *Efuru*'s fiftieth anniversary in this volume – is a major resource for our approach.

While Damrosch and others object to Moretti's systemic approach to literature, and Moretti finds yet another close reading a redundancy, we find that locations and the orientations bound up with them can be explored both by the close reading of texts – whether they have travelled from home or not – and by structural studies that consider distribution and diffusion. What our perspective adds is the obligation to consider the way the closely read text or disseminated formal feature is bound up with locations (and the orientations generated within them). That obligation means more than shifting the focus to processes of localization and domestication, or to interdependencies and hybridities, since the particular form of the location/ orientation nexus is precisely the object of our inquiry. In Chapter 7, a series of recent novels by Latin American writers, primarily those by Valeria Luiselli and Álvaro Enrigue, are shown to variously negotiate local, vernacular registers with a cosmopolitan, transnational orientation. Reading closely and comparatively, Jobst Welge finds in these texts palimpsest-like landscapes that appear to harbour different temporalities, such as the haunting presence of historical traces. These novels produce orientations and analogies between past and present, between places and dislocations. The often auto-fictional component of these works points to the dislocated, multiple-oriented figure of the contemporary 'Latin American' writer. These novels sustain hemispheric literary claims while insisting on the linguistic and historic heterogeneity of locations that resist being translated into present territorial bounds.

The cosmopolitan–vernacular dynamic as *Ansatzpunkt*

Highlighting the *form* given to the location/orientation dyad, the dynamic of the cosmopolitan and the vernacular enters as a decisive dimension or *Ansatzpunkt* which denotes both formal features and substantial components of the practices of inhabiting and claiming place.[59] The cosmopolitan and the vernacular invite

---

[58] David Damrosch, *What Is World Literature?* (Princeton: Princeton University Press, 2003), 281.

[59] See Stefan Helgesson, 'General Introduction: The Cosmopolitan and the Vernacular in Interaction', *World Literatures: Exploring the Cosmopolitan-Vernacular Exchange*, ed. Stefan Helgesson et al. for a discussion of this dynamic as a sort of Auerbachian *Ansatzpunkt* (Stockholm: Stockholm University Press, 2018), 8.

linguistic considerations, above all, but it should be clear that language is just one dimension of this dynamic. If we think of the linguistic choices open to a writer as part of what they can do with their overall resources, there is good reason to see in cosmopolitan and vernacular modes a reflection or an expression of the spatial dimension of social resources: mobility and autochthony.[60] This opposition is no simple binary, since the capital of autochthony may be precisely what makes mobility possible; also, a firmly local set of resources may manifest themselves as an orientation towards transnational horizons.[61] With that caveat concerning the terminology, a matrix suggests itself, showing a logical set of alternatives. Tables and boxes have a propensity to reify whatever is put within them, so the borders between the cells in Table 1 must be considered permeable, even as they perform an analytical function we take to be useful:

Table 1 The Matrix of Cosmopolitan/Vernacular Location/Orientation

	Cosmopolitan orientation	Vernacular orientation	Mixed orientation
Cosmopolitan location			
Vernacular location			
Mixed location			

In Chapter 5, Bo G. Ekelund's discussion of Ralph de Boissière's *Crown Jewel*, the island's capital, Port-of-Spain, is inhabited and claimed by a range of characters, placed along the creole continuum as holding distinct positions in a social space that is partly cosmopolitan, partly vernacular. Underlying the local struggles of workers in the novel, focused as they are on the vernacular bread and butter, or roti and pilaf, is an orientation towards a workers' international. No doubt all cases of locations and orientations are to some extent mixed, but the literary critic's task is to ask about the dominant dimension, as here, in a vernacular location that is claimed in the spirit of solidarity that leads outward to a shared cosmopolitanism. It can never be a matter of mechanically inserting a given location into the table, of course. The types are not to be found as substances existing in reality; instead,

---

[60] See Jean-Noel Retière, 'Capital d'autochtonie', in *Dictionnaire critique et interdisciplinaire de la participation*, ed. Ilaria Casillo et al. (Paris: GIS Démocratie et Participation, 2013).

[61] David Goodhart's distinction between members of an 'anywhere' class and a 'somewhere' class captures a good deal of this distribution of spatial resources, but does so by reifying certain aspects of this distribution into some existing, fully formed groups of a kind he has himself constructed. *The Road to Somewhere: The Populist Revolt and the Future of Politics* (Oxford: Oxford University Press, 2017).

each alternative is a helpmeet for the analysis of 'particular cases of the possible'. This phrase is intended to highlight the power of a particular case that is dealt with in its particularity without being separated from the larger forces that make that particularity possible. Unlike models that take singularity as their cornerstone, the analysis of locations and orientations grant the irreducible features of the individual case while insisting on those features that point to affinities, homologies and common conditions of emergence. Not quite a typology, then, the location/orientation analysis lends itself to typological questions, and several contributions in this book ask those questions in the terms supplied by Alexander Beecroft in his influential proposal to think about world literatures as appearing in the form of different ecologies. As Harris and Mahmutović show, configurations of location and orientation may fit into Beecroft's types or they may show how the ecologies cannot quite contain the tensions produced by the particular case. Within a given ecology, the orientations represented by the literary work may presume horizons that lie outside that configuration.

What do our particular cases of the possible say about the relations between the vernacular and the cosmopolitan in literary claims to space? The overwhelming impression is that the authors studied here claim places by skating and sliding on the cosmopolitan–vernacular continuum: vernacularizing cosmopolitan forms (Ahmed Saadawi and Hassan Blasim), using vernacular registers to calibrate orientations towards a cosmopolitan horizon (Valeria Luiselli and Álvaro Enrigue), taking the language and culture of the 'small world' to the 'large world' in a cosmopolitan language (Sol Plaatje), forging new translingual and vernacular forms in order to establish new cosmopolitan horizons (Michael Muhammad Knight), manoeuvring the creole continuum to claim places for an international expansion of social space (Ralph de Boissière), disrupting the very sense of cosmopolitan mobility by narrating moments of arrival as multiple and unfinished (Theodor Kallifatides, Duraid Al-Khamisi, Ali Zardadi), probing the inseparability of vernacular language and 'home' (Lois-Ann Yamanaka) or wedding vernacular forms to the exploration of a local female experience that transcends the masculine forms of literary recognition (Flora Nwapa). The claim to a place is a claim for its legitimacy, and for literary works and practices, that means its literary value, its right to be approved for literarization and librarization. While many literary claims to place no doubt do little more than add confirmation to what is already recognized, the chapters in this book focus on works that try to legitimate the illegitimate, to prime readers for imaginatively living in a larger world.

In the end, the analytical obligations outlined here, like any obligation, will have to prove their force by the degree to which they authorize the claims made in the following chapters about literary texts, practices and authors. It seems to us incontestable that literature constitutes a geocultural practice, mobilizing vernacular or cosmopolitan resources as it makes up the world by combining land and language, underwriting the allocation of access to locations while fuelling the orientations that may serve to upset that distribution.

Bibliography

Abrams, M. H. *The Mirror and the Lamp*. Oxford: Oxford University Press, 1953.

Ahmed, Sara. *Queer Phenomenology: Orientations, Objects, Others*. Durham, NC: Duke University Press, 2006.

Anzaldúa, Gloria. *Borderlands/La Frontera: The New Mestiza*. San Francisco: Aunt Lute, 1987.

Bourdieu, Pierre. 'Site Effects'. In *The Weight of the World*, trans. Priscilla Parkhurst Ferguson et al. Stanford: Stanford University Press, 1999, 123–9.

Bourdieu, Pierre. *An Invitation to Reflexive Sociology*. Chicago: University of Chicago Press, 1992.

Bourdieu, Pierre. *The Field of Cultural Production: Essays on Art and Literature*, edited and with an introduction by Randal Johnson. Cambridge: Polity Press, 1993.

Bourdieu, Pierre. *Pascalian Meditations*. Stanford: Stanford University Press, 2000.

Broady, Donald. 'French Prosopography: Definition and Suggested Readings'. *Poetics* 30 (2002): 381–5.

Casanova, Pascale. *The World Republic of Letters*. Cambridge, MA: Harvard University Press, 2004.

Casanova, Pascale. *Samuel Beckett: Anatomy of a Literary Revolution*. London: Verso, 2006.

Cohn, Deborah N. *The Latin American Literary Boom and U.S. Nationalism During the Cold War*. Nashville: Vanderbilt University Press, 2012.

Cummins, Jeanine. *American Dirt*. New York: Flatiron, 2020.

Dalby, Simon. 'Critical Geopolitics: Discourse, Difference, and Dissent'. *Environment and Planning D: Society and Space* 9 (1991): 261–83.

Damrosch, David. *What Is World Literature?* Princeton: Princeton University Press, 2003.

Damrosch, David and David L. Pike. 'Preface'. *The Longman Anthology of World Literature*, 2nd edition. Vol. D. New York: Longman, 2009, xv–xix.

Dodds, K. J. and J. D. Sidaway, 'Locating Critical Geopolitics'. *Environment and Planning D: Society and Space* 12 (1994): 515–24.

Garvía, Roberto. *Esperanto and Its Rivals: The Struggle for an International Language.* Philadelphia: University of Pennsylvania Press, 2015.

Goodhart, David. *The Road to Somewhere: The Populist Revolt and the Future of Politics.* Oxford: Oxford University Press, 2017.

Gray, Alasdair. *Lanark.* New York: Braziller, 1985.

Guzmán, María Constanza. *Gregory Rabassa's Latin American Literature: A Translator's Visible Legacy.* Lewisburg: Bucknell University Press, 2011, 58–9.

Hannerz, Ulf. 'Geocultural Scenarios'. *Frontiers of Sociology: The Annals of the International Institute of Sociology.* Vol. 11, edited by Peter Hedström and Björn Wittrock, 267–88. Leiden: Brill, 2009.

Harvey, David. *Cosmopolitanism and the Geographies of Freedom.* New York: Columbia University Press, 2009.

Hayot, Eric. 'On Literary Worlds'. *Modern Language Quarterly* 72, no. 2 (June 2011): 129–61.

Helgesson, Stefan. 'General Introduction: The Cosmopolitan and the Vernacular in Interaction'. *World Literatures: Exploring the Cosmopolitan–Vernacular Exchange,* edited by Stefan Helgesson, Annika Mörte Alling, Yvonne Lindqvist and Helena Wulff, 1–11. Stockholm: Stockholm University Press, 2018. https://doi.org/10.16993/bat

Hipple, Annika S. 'In the Footsteps of Lisbeth Salander: A Walking Tour of Stieg Larsson's Stockholm'. *Real Scandinavia.* http://realscandinavia.com/in-the-footsteps-of-lisbeth-salander-a-walking-tour-of-stieg-larssons-stockholm/.

'In A Lonely Place: Raymond Chandler's Los Angeles'. https://esotouric.com/chandler/.

Irr, Caren. *Toward the Geopolitical Novel: U.S. Fiction in the Twenty-First Century.* New York: Columbia University Press, 2014.

Kincaid, Jamaica. *Among Flowers: A Walk in the Himalayas.* Washington, DC: National Geographic Society, 2005.

Laachir, Karima, Sara Marzagora and Francesca Orsini. 'Significant Geographies *in lieu* of World Literature'. *Journal of World Literature* 3 (2018): 290–310.

Low, Setha. *Spatializing Culture: The Ethnography of Space and Place.* London: Routledge, 2016.

Lu Jiande, 'Dialogue Section B. The Interactions Between the Local and the Universal: A Few Thoughts After Listening to the Talk of Professor Damrosch'. In *Tensions in World Literature: Between the Local and the Universal,* edited by Weigui Fang, 325–30. Singapore: Palgrave, 2018.

Mahmutović, Adnan. 'Literary Ecologies and Post-9/11 Muslim Writing'. *World Literatures: Exploring the Cosmopolitan–Vernacular Exchange,* edited by Stefan Helgesson, Annika Mörte Alling, Yvonne Lindqvist and Helena Wulff, 140–49. Stockholm: Stockholm University Press, 2018. https://doi.org/10.16993/bat

Martin, Nick. 'The Dissonance of a Land Acknowledgment at the Oscars'. *The New Republic,* 10 February 2020. https://newrepublic.com/article/156520/dissonance-land-acknowledgment-oscars.

Marx, Karl. *Capital*. Vol. 3. 1894, edited by Friedrich Engels, trans. David Fernbach. London: Penguin, 1991.

Mignolo, Walter D. 'Afterword: Human Understanding and (Latin) American Interests: The Politics and Sensibilities of Geocultural Locations'. *Poetics Today* 16, no. 1 (1995): 171–214.

Modan, Gabriella Gahlia. *Turf Wars: Discourse, Diversity, and the Politics of Place*. Malden: Blackwell, 2007.

Molin, Daniel Peter Linder. *The American Detective in Translation: The Translation of Raymond Chandler's Novels into Spanish*. Salamanca: Ediciones Universidad de Salamanca, 2011.

Monbiot, George. 'Lockdown is nothing new. We've been kept off the land for centuries'. *The Guardian* 22 April 2020. www.theguardian.com/commentisfree/2020/apr/22/lockdown-coronavirus-crisis-right-to-roam?CMP=Share_iOSApp_Other

Moretti, Franco. 'Conjectures on World Literature'. *New Left Review* 1 (2000): 54–68.

Mufti, Aamir. *Forget English!* Cambridge, MA: Harvard University Press, 2016.

Native Governance Center, 'A Guide to Indigenous Land Acknowledgement'. https://nativegov.org/a-guide-to-indigenous-land-acknowledgment/.

Ó Tuathail, Gearoid. *Critical Geopolitics: The Politics of Writing Global Space*. Minneapolis: University of Minnesota Press, 1996.

Rabassa, Gregory. *If This Be Treason: Translation and Its Dyscontents*. New York: New Directions, 2006.

Rancière, Jacques. *Mute Speech: Literature, Critical Theory, and Politics*. New York: Columbia University Press, 2011.

Reed-Danahy, Deborah. *Bourdieu and Social Space*. New York: Berghahn, 2019.

Retière, Jean-Noel. 'Capital d'autochtonie'. *Dictionnaire critique et interdisciplinaire de la participation*, edited by Ilaria Casillo et al. Paris: GIS Démocratie et Participation, 2013.

'Rio Declaration on Environment and Development'. *Report of the United Nations Conference on Environment and Development*. 12 August 1992. www.un.org/en/development/desa/population/migration/generalassembly/docs/globalcompact/A_CONF.151_26_Vol.I_Declaration.pdf.

Saldívar, Ramón. 'The American Borderlands Novel'. In *The Cambridge History of the American Novel*, edited by Leonard Cassuto, Clare Virginia Eby and Benjamin Reiss, 1031–45. Cambridge: Cambridge University Press, 2011.

Shih, Shu-mei. 'World Studies and Relational Comparison'. *PMLA* 130, no. 2 (March 2015): 430–38. https://doi.org/10.1632/pmla.2015.130.2.430

Spivak, Gayatri Chakravorti. 'Three Women's Texts and a Critique of Imperialism'. *Critical Inquiry* 12 no. 1 (1985): 243–61.

Storey, David. *Territory: The Claiming of Space*. Harlow: Pearson, 2001.

Suvin, Darko. 'Locus, Horizon, and Orientation: The Concept of Possible Worlds as a Key to Utopian Studies'. *Utopian Studies* 1, no. 2 (1990): 69–83.

Tanoukhi. Nirvana. 'The Scale of World Literature'. *New Literary History* 39, no. 3 (2008): 599–617. doi:10.1353/nlh.0.0051.

Thibodeau, Paul H., Cynthia M. Frantz and Matias Berretta. 'The Earth is Our Home: Systemic Metaphors to Redefine Our Relationship with Nature'. *Climatic Change* 142, no. 1–2 (May 2017): 287–300. https://doi.org/10.1007/s10584-017-1926-z

Thomsen, Mads Rosendahl. *Mapping World Literature: International Canonization and Transnational Literatures*. London: Bloomsbury, 2008.

Trubek, Anne. *A Skeptic's Guide to Writers' Houses*. Philadelphia: University of Pennsylvania Press, 2010.

UNESCO. 'Creative Cities Network'. https://en.unesco.org/creative-cities/

Wallerstein, Immanuel. *Geopolitics and Geoculture: Essays on the Changing World-System*. Cambridge: Cambridge University Press, 1991.

Watson, Nicola J. *The Author's Effects: On Writer's House Museums*. Oxford: Oxford University Press, 2020.

Wilson, Rob and Christopher Leigh Connery, eds. *The Worlding Project: Doing Cultural Studies in the Era of Globalization*. Berkeley: North Atlantic Books, 2007.

Wulff, Helena. 'Introduction to Part 2'. *World Literatures: Exploring the Cosmopolitan–Vernacular Exchange*, edited by Stefan Helgesson, Annika Mörte Alling, Yvonne Lindqvist and Helena Wulff, 103–106. Stockholm: Stockholm University Press, 2018. https://doi.org/10.16993/bat.i. License: CC-BY.

Zollo, Paul. 'Chandler Square'. *Los Angeles Times*, 7 October 1988. www.latimes.com/archives/la-xpm-1998-oct-07-me-29977-story.html.

One world literature *with* Chinua Achebe and Flora Nwapa

Paula Uimonen

Introduction: African locations and gendered orientations in world literature

When approached from a geocultural perspective, the location of African writers points to interesting transnational dynamics in world literature, even more so when appraised in relation to gendered orientations.[1] Scholars have underscored how a writer's *location* is 'not simply a geographical, historical, or cultural context but a standpoint, a position, an *orientation*'.[2] They have also highlighted that the 'constraint of location in the form of geographical tag or label' has been particularly pertinent for 'Asian and African writers', regardless of 'wherever they may actually live'.[3] Indeed, in a recent discussion on 'the relationship between *location* and creative practice' Eileen Julien notes that 'creative texts by Africans have generally been defined *spatially*: They come from "Africa"'.[4] While the geocultural labelling of 'African writers' is well known, much less attention has been paid to how gendered orientations intersect with African locations, the

---

[1] An earlier version of this chapter, 'After Achebe: Flora Nwapa and African Women in World Literature' was submitted to TFA@60, the 60th anniversary celebration of *Things Fall Apart*. The paper was to be presented in Abuja on 24 July 2018, but the event was cancelled. Another version was presented at a conference organized by the European Association of Social Anthropologists (EASA): Paula Uimonen, 'Who was Flora Nwapa? Gender and Power in World Literature', paper presented at EASA 2018, Stockholm, 15 August 2018.

[2] Francesca Orsini and Laetitia Zecchini, 'The Locations of (World) Literature: Perspectives from Africa and South Asia', *Journal of World Literature* 4 (2019): 2, emphasis added.

[3] Orsini and Zecchini, 'The Locations of (World) Literature', 2.

[4] Eileen Julien, 'The Critical Present: Where is "African Literature"?', in *Rethinking African Cultural Production*, ed. Frieda Ekotto and Kenneth Harrow (Bloomington and Indianapolis: Indiana University Press, 2015), 20, emphasis in original.

Claiming Space

relationality of which can offer interesting insights into the cultural dynamics of cosmopolitan and vernacular (dis)locations and (dis)orientations.[5]

In this chapter, I will explore African locations and gendered orientations with the help of two pioneering writers, Chinua Achebe and Flora Nwapa. Through *Things Fall Apart*, Chinua Achebe claimed a space for African literature in the world literary canon, the global success of which speaks to cosmopolitan aspirations and imaginaries.[6] By comparison, Flora Nwapa's *Efuru*,[7] the first internationally published novel in English by an African woman writer, has not received anywhere near as much attention, indicating how the politics of location intersect with gender hierarchies in literary canon formation. In both cases, the writers claimed a place for their local Igbo communities in geocultural imaginaries of Africa, thus diversifying vernacular locations in literary mappings of the world, while their cosmopolitan style of writing, mixing English with vernacular words and idioms, benefited from their postcolonial location, addressing readers at home as well as in the world at large.[8] From a gender perspective, a closer look at the writers' aesthetic world-making reveals interesting cultural dynamics, which I will discuss in terms of literary gendering, while teasing out some problematic aspects of hyper-canonical dislocation and scholarly disorientation. Drawing on ethnographic fieldwork in Nigeria during the Efuru@50 literary festival, the analysis then shifts focus to the cultural context of Flora Nwapa's literary production, to elaborate on the social distribution of gendered orientations in vernacular cultural locations.

In an effort to advance world literary theory by way of anthropology, I will draw on globalectics,[9] which I will ultimately fuse with one world anthropology,[10] while paying attention to gender complementarity.[11] Focusing on gender, I hope

[5] See also Paula Uimonen, 'Zuhura the African Lioness: Performance Poetry, Digital media and the Transnational Tangle in World Literature', in *World Literatures: Exploring the Cosmopolitan-Vernacular Exchange*, eds. Stefan Helgesson, Annika Mörte Alling, Yvonne Lindqvist and Helena Wulff (Stockholm: Stockholm University Press, 2018), 129–39; Paula Uimonen, 'Muse and Power: African Women Writers and Digital Infrastructure in World Literature', *Anthropology and Humanism* 44, no. 1 (2019): 20–37.

[6] Chinua Achebe, *Things Fall Apart* (London: Heinemann, 1962).

[7] Flora Nwapa, *Efuru* (London: Heinemann, 1966).

[8] For theoretical elaborations on geocultural ideas of mapmaking in the global oecumene, see Ulf Hannerz, *Writing Future Worlds: An Anthropologist Explores Global Scenarios* (London: Palgrave Macmillan, 2016).

[9] Ngũgĩ wa Thiong'o, *Globalectics: Theory and the Politics of Knowing* (New York: Columbia University Press, 2014).

[10] Tim Ingold, 'One World Anthropology', *HAU: Journal of Ethnographic Theory* 8, no. 1/2 (2018): 158–71.

[11] Chikwenye Okonjo Ogunyemi, *Africa Wo/Man Palava, The Nigerian Novel by Women* (Chicago: The University of Chicago Press, 1996).

to address some existing knowledge gaps, noting that scholars have suggested that 'Gender might possibly be the elephant in the room in world literature.'[12] But the multifaceted complexities of gender are not easily dealt with, especially within the parameters of prevailing theory. By insisting on plurality and multi-logue, a globalectical perspective can help us move beyond established theoretical binaries, especially the tendency to place the local/particular/vernacular in opposition to the global/universal/cosmopolitan. Such analytical binaries are also evident in critical feminist theory, which tends to assume a conflictual opposition between male and female genders. While a feminist sensibility can highlight the masculinist orientation of dominant theory, it is worth paying closer attention to different gender theories. Through my discussion of literary gendering in the works of Nigerian/Igbo writers, I hope to bring forth the value of vernacular gender theory, acknowledging that gender difference does not have to imply inequality or opposition, but can be appreciated in terms of gender complementarity.

Chinua Achebe and cosmopolitan orientations in world literature

Through the publication of *Things Fall Apart* in 1958 Chinua Achebe secured a place for African literature in the world literary canon, breaking through its European dominance. The novel was republished in 1962 as the first volume in the canonical Heinemann African Writers Series and its global success has been remarkable. It is considered to be 'the most widely read African novel; it has been translated into more than 60 languages and has sold over 10 million copies.'[13] In anthologies of world literature, *Things Fall Apart* has typically been located 'with Africa' and 'against Europe', emphasizing 'the need Achebe felt to present Africa "from the inside"', not least as a counter narrative to European novels on Africa.[14] In his famous lecture on the racist depiction of Africa in Joseph Conrad's *Heart of Darkness*, Achebe defiantly declared: 'And the question is whether a novel which celebrates this dehumanization, which depersonalizes

---

[12] Stefan Helgesson and Mads Rosendahl Thomsen, *Literature and the World* (London and New York: Routledge, 2020), 162.

[13] Terri Ochiagha, *Achebe and Friends at Umuahia: The Making of a Literary Elite* (Woodbridge: James Currey, 2015), 1.

[14] Brian Doherty, 'The Center Cannot Hold: The Development of World Literature Anthologies', *Alif: Journal of Comparative Poetics* 34 (2014): 106.

a portion of the human race, can be called a great work of art. My answer is: No, it cannot.'[15] Achebe's claim for a place for African writers was thus oriented towards literary decolonization, which African writers championed.[16] Reflecting its centrality in world literature canons, *Things Fall Apart* has been described as 'hyper-canonical within the counter-canon'.[17] In addition to being 'Africa's most famous novel',[18] even 'the *exemplary* novel of Africa' and an 'instance of world literature',[19] the novel is referred to as an example of *literary cosmopolitanism*.[20]

The cosmopolitan orientation ascribed to *Things Fall Apart* has largely rested on the assumption that African writers are oriented towards non-African readers. In her seminal text on the extroverted African novel, in which she used *Things Fall Apart* as a telling example, Eileen Julien suggested that '"the African novel" is recognized as such precisely because it is characterized by extroversion and engagement with what is assumed to be European or global discourses'.[21] In a later article, she clarified that she was only referring to a genre, not African novels at large, and that extroverted novels 'do not intentionally address international readers', rather they are 'extroverted because of the selective way in which they are read and then anointed'.[22] Other scholars have noted that it might be 'more accurate to conceive of "extroversion" as dependent on particular readers than fixed in a text's form'.[23] Indeed, Achebe himself countered the supposedly extroverted orientation of African literature: 'I don't know if African writers always have a foreign audience in mind. What I know is that they don't have to. At least I know I don't have to.'[24] He cited the previous year's sales figures of *Things Fall Apart* to prove his point: 'about 800 copies in Britain; 20,000 in Nigeria; about 2,500 in all other places'. Olabode Ibironke has suggested that

---

[15] Chinua Achebe, 'An Image of Africa: Racism in Conrad's *Heart of Darkness*', *Massachusetts Review* 18 (1977): 6.

[16] Ngũgĩ wa Thiong'o, *Decolonising the Mind: The Politics of Language in African Literature* (London: James Currey, 1986).

[17] Doherty, 'The Center Cannot Hold', 100.

[18] Mũkoma wa Ngũgĩ, *The Rise of the African Novel: Politics of Language, Identity and Ownership* (Ann Arbor: University of Michigan Press, 2018), 2.

[19] Helgesson and Rosendahl Thomsen, *Literature and the World*, 3–4.

[20] Graham Huggan, *The Postcolonial Exotic: Marketing the Margins* (New York: Routledge, 2001), 27.

[21] Eileen Julien, 'The Extroverted African Novel', in *The Novel: History, Geography and Culture*, ed. Franco Moretti (Princeton: Princeton University Press, 2006), 685.

[22] Eileen Julien, 'The Extroverted African Novel, Revisited: African Novels at Home, in the World', *Journal of African Cultural Studies* 30, no. 3 (2018): 377.

[23] Nathan Suhr-Sytsma, 'The Extroverted African Novel and Literary Publishing in the Twenty-First Century', *Journal of African Cultural Studies* 30, no. 3 (2018): 342.

[24] Chinua Achebe cited in Olabode Ibironke, 'African Writers Challenge Conventions of Postcolonial Literary History', in *Rethinking African Cultural Production*, ed. Frieda Ekotto and Kenneth Harrow (Bloomington and Indianapolis: Indiana University Press, 2015), 43.

the conflation of 'place of publication' with the 'location of the primary reading public' has perpetuated misconceptions of the extroverted orientation of African literature.[25] Even so, 'the view of African literature as primarily an export product, aimed at a largely foreign audience' is still common.[26] Even scholars who recognize the 'multifocality' of African literature make a distinction between global African literature, published in Europe and America, and locally published African literature, concluding that it is the former that comprises the 'market category, African literature, a form of world literature', while the latter 'remain outside of the postcolonial, as a literary category'.[27]

If we appraise world literature through the prism of global capitalism, as in a world-literature system structured on inequality, then the global market category of African literature is quite telling of the 'hierarchy of constitutive elements governed by specific "logics" of determination and relationality'.[28] African literature can then be equated with a market category of world literature according to the racist and sexist logic of global capitalism.[29]

But from a globalectical perspective, we can appreciate the cosmopolitan orientation of *Things Fall Apart* in terms of a multi-logue with a culturally diverse readership. One distinguishing characteristic of postcolonial locations is that they are always linked to other places elsewhere, but not exclusively to metropolitan centres. Schooled in English literature by their colonial masters, writers like Achebe paid tribute to their European counterparts: 'Achebe's titles, like *Things Fall Apart* and *No Longer at Ease*, are homages to the writer's intellectual formation'.[30] But while intertextuality with European literature was 'remarkable', Ngũgĩ wa Thiong'o has underlined that these novels were 'not derivatives', but 'a synthesis forged in resistance', which 'speaks to Africa, the formerly colonized, and the world'.[31]

The point of speaking to *both* Africa *and* the world should not be taken lightly, a cosmopolitan orientation reflected in Achebe's choice of language. His cosmopolitan use of English mixed with vernacular words and idioms in

---

[25] Ibironke, 'African Writers Challenge Conventions of Postcolonial Literary History', 43.

[26] Huggan, *The Postcolonial Exotic*, 34.

[27] Madhu Krishnan, *Contemporary African Literature in English: Global Locations, Postcolonial Identifications* (Basingstoke: Palgrave Macmillan Limited, 2014), 161–3.

[28] WReC, *Combined and Uneven Development: Towards a New Theory of World-Literature* (Liverpool: Liverpool University Press, 2015), 8.

[29] Immanuel Wallerstein, 'Culture as the Ideological Battleground of the Modern World-System', *Theory, Culture & Society* 7, no. 2–3 (1990): 31–55.

[30] Thiong'o, *Globalectics*, 42–3.

[31] Thiong'o, *Globalectics*, 43.

Igbo, or what Mũkoma wa Ngũgĩ refers to as Africanized English, was aimed
at 'fashioning out an English which is at once universal and able to carry his
peculiar experience'.[32] Achebe's insistence on 'speaking of African experiences
in a world-wide language'[33] affirmed the decolonizing ambitions of African
writers at the time, since 'English was useful in the national, Pan-African, and
international fronts' of liberation struggle.[34] Interestingly enough, the choice
of a cosmopolitan language meant that novels could be dislocated from their
national/vernacular origins and relocated in other nations.[35] This transnational
and transcultural mobility was by no means limited to the African continent, but
captures the cosmopolitan orientation of postcolonial locations, since 'writers
from the colonial world always assumed an extranational dimension'.[36]

Rather than attributing Achebe's cosmopolitan orientation to his presumed
gravitation towards metropolitan centres, we can look at it the other way around,
acknowledging that 'the colony was the real depository of the cosmopolitan'.[37]
In anthropology, cosmopolitanism has been described as an 'orientation',
characterized by 'intellectual and [a]esthetic openness toward divergent cultural
experiences' and a 'willingness to engage with the Other'.[38] More recently,
anthropologists have paid attention to variations in cosmopolitanisms,[39] while
recognizing the need to decolonize Kantian cosmopolitanism.[40] In world literature
studies, cosmopolitanism is often located in the global circulation of literature,
capturing the orientation of literary works, as in literary cosmopolitanism,[41]
or a mode of reading, as in cosmopolitan criticism.[42] While scholars have
acknowledged a 'cosmopolitan desire' in readerships of world literature for quite
some time, even though it may have entailed 'an acceptance of a Eurocentric,
racist outlook', attitudes have changed, and 'today "cosmopolitanism" necessarily
entails anti-racism and a non-Eurocentric outlook'.[43]

[32] Chinua Achebe cited in Ngũgĩ, *The Rise of the African Novel*, 47.
[33] Achebe cited in Ngũgĩ, *The Rise of the African Novel*, 51.
[34] Ngũgĩ, *The Rise of the African Novel*, 51.
[35] Ngũgĩ, *The Rise of the African Novel*, 45.
[36] Thiong'o, *Globalectics*, 54.
[37] Thiong'o, *Globalectics*, 52.
[38] Ulf Hannerz, *Transnational Connections: Culture, People, Places* (London and New York: Routledge, 1996), 103.
[39] Hannerz, *Writing Future Worlds*.
[40] Paula Uimonen, 'Decolonising Cosmopolitanism: An Anthropological Reading of Immanuel Kant and Kwame Nkrumah on the World as One', *Critique of Anthropology* 40, no. 1 (2019): 81–101.
[41] Huggan, *The Postcolonial Exotic*.
[42] Robert Spencer, *Cosmopolitan Criticism and Potcolonial Literature* (Basingstoke: Palgrave Macmillan, 2011).
[43] Helgesson and Rosendahl Thomsen, *Literature and the World*, 137.

Perhaps the *kaleidoscopic* view of globalectics can offer a cosmopolitan reorientation, to complement advances towards a more *stereoscopic* appraisal of world literature.[44] Scholars appraising *Things Fall Apart* as an *example* of world literature note that the novel's multifaceted intertextuality and multilayered location may come across as 'an important anomaly'.[45] Acknowledging the novel's intricate complexity, they suggest it can be appraised from both *affirmative* (intrinsic qualities, canonization, cosmopolitanism, intercultural dialogue) and *critical* (gaps, omissions, inequalities, colonialism, unequal power relations) perspectives, thus adopting a more 'stereoscopic view of world literature'.[46] To move beyond the binary lens of a stereoscopic view, we can also approach world literature from a globalectical perspective, thus getting a more kaleidoscopic view of world literature. For instance, by probing the complexities of gender, we can aspire to more holistic appraisals of both literary aesthetics and the power relations of an uneven world-literature system.

Flora Nwapa and claiming women's space in the African literary canon

It was only in 1966 that a woman writer entered the African literary canon, Flora Nwapa, whose debut novel *Efuru* was published as number 26 in the canonical Heinemann African Writers Series. Her second novel *Idu* was published as number 56 in the series in 1970, but she remained the only Nigerian woman writer in the series for almost a decade, until the publication of Buchi Echemeta's *The Joys of Motherhood* in 1979. Out of 270 numbered titles published in the series from 1962 to 1987, only fourteen titles were written by women, by ten different women writers from eight different countries.[47] More female writers have been added over time, but in my research in Tanzania and Nigeria, female writers have often discussed the male dominance of the African literary canon, typically referring to the elevated status of Chinua Achebe, Ngũgĩ wa Thiong'o and Wole Soyinka.

---

[44] Helgesson and Rosendahl Thomsen, *Literature and the World*, 6.
[45] Helgesson and Rosendahl Thomsen, *Literature and the World*, 3.
[46] Helgesson and Rosendahl Thomsen, *Literature and the World*, 3–6.
[47] The writers were: Mariama Bâ (Senegal), Charlotte Bruner (USA), Buchi Emecheta (Nigeria), Nadine Gordimer (South Africa), Bessie Head (Botswana), Doris Lessing (UK/Zimbabwe), Martha Mvungi (Tanzania), Rebeka Njau (Kenya), Flora Nwapa (Nigeria), Alifa Rifaat (Egypt). James Currey, *Africa Writes Back: The African Writers Series & The Launch of African Literature* (Oxford: James Currey, 2008), 301–308.

While Chinua Achebe is celebrated for placing African literature on the world literature map, Flora Nwapa is recognized for claiming a literary space for African women. Honoured as the 'Mother of African Women's Writing', Flora Nwapa has been described as a 'trailblazer' in the 'world literary canon' in recognition of her pioneering role.[48] In addition to being the first internationally published female African writer in English, Flora Nwapa was also the first female publisher in Africa. She set up her own publishing company Tana Press in 1977, not least to facilitate the local production of women's and children's literature. From the outset, Flora Nwapa addressed the absence, marginality and one-sided portrayals of women in male-authored African literature. In her own words:

> I try to project the image of women positively. I attempt to correct our menfolks when they started writing, when they wrote little or less about women, where their female characters are prostitutes and ne'er-do-wells. I started writing to tell them this is not so.[49]

Unlike her male fellow writers, Flora Nwapa portrayed women in a variety of roles, from rural traders to cosmopolitan urbanites, in a diversity of settings, from Igbo towns to cities like Lagos, London and Hamburg. Women were also depicted in relation to men: fathers, husbands, brothers, sons, colleagues and friends. In addition to capturing traditional everyday life, Nwapa wrote about social transformations in Nigeria, usually from women's perspective. She addressed race relations during colonialism as well as corruption and elitism in post-independence political leadership, not to mention the horrors of the civil war in Biafra. One of the leitmotifs in Nwapa's writings was women's economic independence.

Flora Nwapa's women-centred storytelling has been positively recognized by scholars of African women's literature.[50] Her path-breaking counter narratives to the male dominated canon are well known, and her books are still taught

---

[48] Marie Umeh, ed., *Emerging Perspectives on Flora Nwapa: Critical and Theoretical Essays* (Trenton and Asmara: Africa World Press, 1998), 9.

[49] Flora Nwapa cited in Marie Umeh, 'The Poetics of Economic Independence for Female Empowerment: An Interview with Flora Nwapa', *Research in African Literatures* 26, no. 2 (1995): 27.

[50] Adeola James, *In Their Own Voices: African Women Writers Talk* (London: James Currey, 1990); Henrietta Otokunefor and Obiageli Nwodo, eds., *Nigerian Female Writers: A Critical Perspective* (Lagos: Malthouse Press Ltd, 1989); Stephanie Newell, ed., *Writing African Women: Gender, Popular Culture and Literature in West Africa* (London: Zed Books, 2017); Umeh, *Emerging Perspectives on Flora Nwapa*; see also Paula Uimonen, 'Cosmopolitan Feminism: From Flora Nwapa's *Efuru* to Chimamanda Ngozi Adichie's *We Should all be Feminists*', paper presented at Efuru@50, Maiduguri, 1 December 2016.

in courses on African literature, especially in Nigeria and the United States. Flora Nwapa has also inspired succeeding generations of Nigerian women writers, from Buchi Emecheta to Chimamanda Ngozi Adichie. The title of Emecheta's classic *The Joys of Motherhood* was inspired by the concluding lines of *Efuru*. More recently, while underlining the 'magic' influence of Achebe's books, Adichie recognized how 'important' Flora Nwapa was to her: 'there was something about her that was very familiar, the sorts of stories that I heard in my hometown'.[51]

Similarly to Chinua Achebe, Flora Nwapa led a transnational life, albeit more firmly anchored in Nigeria. Although it was unusual for women to receive higher education at the time, she graduated from Queen's College in Lagos and the University College, Ibadan, following which she also got a diploma in education from the University of Edinburgh. In addition to writing books, she had a professional career in teaching and university administration and after the civil war as the first female Commissioner in then East Central State. Unlike Achebe, who lived a large part of his life in the USA, Nwapa never moved away from Nigeria, but her biography details her many travels overseas.[52] She was often invited to conferences and participated in book fairs in Africa, Europe and the USA.[53] Like Achebe, Nwapa wrote in English, addressing both national and international audiences, while her stories captured the transnational entanglements of everyday life in late colonial and post-independence Nigeria. Similarly to Achebe, Nwapa articulated her stories with translingual fluency. Not only did she intersperse her English texts with Igbo, Oguta and Yoruba words and proverbs, she also managed to portray a diversity of vernacular styles, thus capturing ethnic, gendered and classed variations in language. The Igbo scholar Ezeigbo has underlined the aesthetic value of 'Nwapa's perfect control of local color, tonal inflections in dialogue, and rhythms of rural lifestyle in all their complexities', especially the 'speech rhythms and mannerisms of Igbo rural women', concluding that this is what 'largely defines her significant linguistic and stylistic contribution to African fiction'.[54]

[51] Chimamanda Ngozi Adichie interviewed by Aaron Brady 2013. https://www.salon.com/2013/07/14/chimamanda_ngozi_adichie_race_doesnt_occur_to_me_partner/
[52] Umeh, *Emerging Perspectives on Flora Nwapa*, 673–9.
[53] Marie Umeh, *Flora Nwapa, a Pen and a Press* (New York: Triatlantic Books of NY, 2010), 113.
[54] Theodora Akachi Ezeigbo, 'Myth, History, Culture, and Igbo Womanhood in Flora Nwapa's Novels', in Marie Umeh, ed., *Emerging Perspectives on Flora Nwapa: Critical and Theoretical Essays* (Trenton and Asmara: Africa World Press, 1998), 68.

The unequal legacies of the Father and Mother of modern African literature

Chinua Achebe and Flora Nwapa are recognized as the Father and Mother of modern African literature respectively, a complementary status that encapsulates many layers of relationality. Both studied at the University College, Ibadan, which is considered the birthplace of modern Nigerian literature. As editor of the African Writers Series, Achebe facilitated the publication of *Efuru*, while his writings inspired Flora Nwapa to write about her local community, albeit from a woman's perspective. Similarly to Achebe, Flora Nwapa got involved in publishing, to develop literary production in Nigeria. Flora Nwapa and Chinua Achebe were friends and their families were interrelated, with Chinua Achebe being the godfather of Nwapa's only son Uzoma Nwakuche. Nwapa (1931–1993) and Achebe (1930–2013) were contemporaries, born during late colonialism, their professional careers intertwined with post-independence nation-building, both in positions corresponding to their elite backgrounds and high levels of education. Ethnically Igbo, both wrote about Igbo culture and society, while their pioneering roles in Nigerian, African and world literature have influenced succeeding generations.

But the Father and Mother of modern African literature have enjoyed very different legacies in literary history. Although both contributed to the formation of the African literary canon, Nwapa has not received anywhere near as much attention or praise as Achebe. Nwapa's absence in world literature anthologies can be contrasted with Achebe's hyper-canonical position.[55] While a handful of biographies on Chinua Achebe have been published, only one has been written on Flora Nwapa, and it is out of print.[56] In a recent book on African publishing, there are eight entries on Chinua Achebe, but none on Flora Nwapa, despite her being the first female publisher on the continent.[57]

Even Heinemann treated the two authors quite differently, promoting Chinua Achebe, while undervaluing Flora Nwapa. In the famous *Africa Writes Back*, published in conjunction with the fiftieth anniversary celebration of *Things Fall Apart*, Achebe's key role as writer and editor is highlighted repeatedly.[58] Meanwhile,

---

[55] Doherty, 'The Center Cannot Hold'.

[56] Umeh, *Flora Nwapa, a Pen and a Press*.

[57] Kiarie Kamau and Kirirmi Mitambo, eds., *Coming of Age: Strides in African Publishing. Essays in Honour of Dr. Henry Chakava@70* (Nairobi: East African Publishers Ltd., 2016).

[58] Currey, *Africa Writes Back*.

in the chapter on Nigerian literature, Flora Nwapa is recognized as a 'skilled story-teller' and 'the first writer to put women at the centre', yet her work is belittled by the comment 'although her early heroines tend to emerge as "worshipful servant-wives to erring husbands", as *The Companion [to African Literature]* put it'.[59] In a recent interview, James Currey could not even remember where he had met Nwapa, guessing it must have been in Ibadan.[60] In scholarly analyses of her writing career, it has been ascertained that Flora Nwapa experienced 'multiple marginality' as an African and female writer, since Heinemann 'regarded her as a "minor writer" and therefore did not bother to print and distribute her books locally and internationally when they were in demand, as they would have if she came from a so called first-world country'.[61] This discrimination had dire consequences: 'According to Flora Nwapa, Heinemann's placing her in the literary backwaters resulted in the piracy of her books locally and the death of her voice globally'.[62]

The marginalization of Flora Nwapa points to gender hierarchies in the appraisal of African writers' location. While Chinua Achebe has been celebrated as a cosmopolitan writer, his first novel acclaimed as *the African novel*, Flora Nwapa has been dislocated from cosmopolitan circuits, relegated to a domestic sphere associated with vernacularity. One could hardly claim that aesthetic differences account for this glaring gap, nor is it enough to point to postcolonial power relations, but from a gender perspective there is something to be said concerning the omission of women writers in the annals of literary history around the world. The gender imbalance in literary canon formation is receiving more attention, as noted in a recent study which acknowledged that 'The male dominance in just about any version of a world literary canon is plain to see'.[63] Reviews of anthologies of literary history have demonstrated that 'the gender of literary history is indisputably masculine'.[64] This is not due to a lack of women writers, but rather that their literary works have been ignored, neglected or forgotten in literary history.[65] Instead, the world literature canon privileges male-

---

[59] Currey, *Africa Writes Back*, 43.

[60] James Currey interviewed by Onyeka Nwelue in his documentary film *The House of Nwapa* (2016).

[61] Umeh, 'The Poetics of Economic Independence for Female Empowerment', 22.

[62] Umeh, 'The Poetics of Economic Independence for Female Empowerment', 22.

[63] Helgesson and Rosendahl Thomsen, *Literature and the World*, 162.

[64] Debra Castillo, 'Gender and Sexuality in World Literature', in *The Routledge Companion to World Literature*, ed. Theo D'haen, David Damrosch and Djelala Kadir (London and New York: Routledge, 2012), 394.

[65] Jenny Bergenmar and Katarina Leppänen, 'Gender and Vernaculars in Digital Humanities and World Literature', *NORA-Nordic Journal of Feminist and Gender Research* 25, no. 4 (2017): 232–46; Helena Wulff, *Rhythms of Writing: An Anthropology of Irish Literature* (London: Bloomsbury, 2017).

authored novels, while undervaluing other forms like folklore and children's literature as well as stories depicting everyday life, which are common features in women's writings.[66] This hierarchical ordering is also evident in how gender tends to be categorized alongside indigenous and non-Western, thus asserting the Western-centric masculinity of literary history.[67] The gender imbalance in literary canons can be related to how a 'masculine bias of the canon exemplifies a wider process by which hegemonic discourses – especially on gender and race – are established', a 'process of devaluation' that is clearly at work in 'domains of high culture'.[68] A male bias is also noticeable in world literature studies, attesting to masculinist centralism in literary scholarship.[69] Feminist scholars have even highlighted literary scholarship to exemplify how theory is gendered, raced and classed.[70] Rather tellingly, it is primarily female and feminist scholars who have addressed the gender gap in world literature, an imbalance that can hopefully be addressed by future scholarship.

A more gender sensitive appraisal of world literature is clearly needed, but it needs to be culturally astute. Scholars have argued that gender sensitive and feminist analyses offer effective tools for revealing the gendered power structures and ideological parameters operating in literary history and canon formation processes.[71] Such work can for instance show 'the importance of gender as a mediating category in the circulation of literature',[72] while rectifying the 'absence of gender both theoretically and numerically'.[73] But gender sensitive analyses should also recognize that feminism may have its limitations, indicating the need to pay greater attention to more culturally sensitive gender theory, as discussed below.

---

[66] Margaret R. Higonnet, 'Editor's Introduction', *Comparative Critical Studies* 6, no. 2 (2009): 138–40.

[67] Castillo, 'Gender and Sexuality in World Literature', 394.

[68] Katherine Lutz, 'The Gender of Theory', in *Women Writing Culture*, ed. Ruth Behar and Deborah A. Gordon (Berkeley: University of California Press, 1995), 250.

[69] Gayatri Chakravorty Spivak, *In Other Worlds* (London and New York: Routledge, 1998).

[70] Lutz, 'The Gender of Theory', 251.

[71] Katarina Helena Leppänen, 'Reflections on Gender and Small Languages in World Literature Scholarship: Methods of Inclusions and Exclusions', in *World Literatures: Exploring the Cosmopolitan-Vernacular Exchange*, ed. Stefan Helgesson, Annika Mörte Alling, Yvonne Lindqvist and Helena Wulff (Stockholm: Stockholm University Press, 2018), 89–99; Bergenmar and Leppänen, 'Gender and Vernaculars in Digital Humanities and World Literature'.

[72] Chatarina Edfeldt, 'Gender and the Circulation of African Lusophone Literature into the Portuguese Literary System', in *World Literatures: Exploring the Cosmopolitan-Vernacular Exchange*, ed. Stefan Helgesson, Annika Mörte Alling, Yvonne Lindqvist and Helena Wulff (Stockholm: Stockholm University Press, 2018), 369.

[73] Bergenmar and Leppänen, 'Gender and Vernaculars in Digital Humanities and World Literature', 237.

Literary gendering and aesthetic worldmaking

Literature creates imaginary worlds, often serving as a reflection or commentary on social worlds. Indeed, world literature can fruitfully be thought of in terms of *literary worldmaking*, a creative process through which worlds are not only imagined but also narrated into existence.[74] Reflecting the cultural location and orientation of the writer, a *literary world* can be conceptualized as a diegetic unity created through the text, culturally constructed *aesthetic worlds* that constitute 'relations to and theories of the lived world'.[75]

Literary worldmaking is also a gendering process. Since *aesthetic worldedness* is about 'the relation that a work establishes between the world inside and the world outside itself',[76] literature interplays with the cultural construction of gender. As a fluid form of situated knowledge, we can appreciate that gender is 'not about fixed *location* in a reified body, female or otherwise, but about nodes in fields, inflections in *orientations*'.[77] Gender should thus be appreciated as a *historical* social construct, productively approached as a process of *gendering* rather than a static given in social relations.[78] As an aesthetic form of worldmaking, literature offers interesting insights into this gendering process.

A comparison of *Things Fall Apart* and *Efuru* brings forth how literary gendering can create rather different aesthetics worlds. In these novels, the gendering process is already visible in the opening lines, with the introduction of gendered characters. *Things Fall Apart* starts with 'Okonkwo was well known throughout the nine villages and even beyond. His fame rested on personal achievements.'[79] By comparison, *Efuru* starts with 'They saw each other fairly often and after a fortnight's courting she agreed to marry him.'[80] It is only in the second paragraph that *she* is introduced: 'Efuru was her name. She was a remarkable woman.' In contrast to *Things Fall Apart*, which has a male protagonist with women appearing mostly in the margins, in *Efuru* the story is narrated from

---

[74] Pheng Cheah, 'What Is a World? On World Literature as World-Making Activity', *Daedalus* 137, no. 3 (2008): 26–38.

[75] Eric Hayot, 'On Literary Worlds', *Modern Language Quarterly* 72, no. 2 (2011): 137.

[76] Hayot, 'On Literary Worlds', 137.

[77] Donna Haraway, 'Situated Knowledges: The Science Question in Feminism and the Privilege of Partial Perspective', *Feminist Studies* 14, no. 3 (1988): 588, emphasis added.

[78] Oyèrónké Oyěwùmí, 2011. 'Introduction: Gendering', in *Gender Epistemologies in Africa: Gendering Traditions, Spaces, Social Institutions, and Identities*, ed. Oyèrónké Oyěwùmí (New York: Palgrave Macmillan, 2011).

[79] Chinua Achebe, *Things Fall Apart* (Greenwich, CT: Fawcett Publications, Inc., 1959), 7.

[80] Flora Nwapa, *Efuru*, 50th Anniversary Edition (Oguta: Tana Press Ltd., 2016), 7.

a woman's perspective, with a diversity of female characters, from the virtuous Efuru to the malignant gossiper Omirima, not to mention the female deity Uhamiri. Even so, the female characters are always related to men and one of the most important relations in the book is the one between Efuru and her father.

Things Fall Apart offers interesting insights into postcolonial politics of literary gendering. Although Achebe's novel may come across as a patriarchal rendering of traditional Igbo society, Nkiru Nzegwu has insisted that contrary to the modern myth of a traditional patriarchy, precolonial Igbo society was nonpatriarchal.[81] She traces the epistemological problem of misrepresentation to the imperialist ideological beliefs of early European ethnographers, Christian missionaries and educationists, whose patriarchal nuclear family model was embraced by Western-educated Igbo elites after independence. She argues that Achebe's *Things Fall Apart* popularized this patriarchal model of traditional society, even though the 'Okonkwo model' was neither universal, nor traditional.[82] When read in the context of Igbo society, it becomes clear that far from endorsing the patriarchal system introduced during colonialism, Achebe's portrayal of the misogynist Okonkwo offered a stinging critique of patriarchal family relations. During the fiftieth anniversary celebration of *Things Fall Apart* in New York in 2008, Chinua Achebe himself was quoted as saying: 'All the problems Okonkwo has from beginning to end are related to ignoring the female! And that is where he is *a flawed hero*.'[83]

By comparison, Nwapa's feminine aesthetic worlds offer a different politics of literary gendering, centred on women's empowerment from a womanist perspective. As much as she focused on women, Nwapa's gendering was not gynocentric; it did not exclude men, nor did it romanticize women, but it addressed gender relations from a critical angle. In the context of the Nigerian literary complex, Nwapa's *Efuru* has been described as representative of a new genre, described as the 'women-and-men novel', which typically had a woman protagonist and dealt with different aspects of gender, a genre mostly although not exclusively written by women.[84] But Flora Nwapa was not just a pioneering

---

[81] Nkiru Nzegwu, *Family Matters: Feminist Concepts in African Philosophy of Culture* (SUNY series, feminist philosophy) (Albany: State University of New York Press, 2006).

[82] Nzegwu, *Family Matters*, 17.

[83] Chinua Achebe cited in Sabine Jell-Bahlsen, 'Nneka: Is Mother Still Supreme in Igboland? Reflections on the Biography of *Eze Mmiri*, Madame Martha Mberekpe of Orsu-Obodo, 1934–2007', in *Against All Odds: The Igbo Experience in Postcolonial Nigeria*, ed. Apollos Nwauwa and Chima Korieh (Abia State, Nigeria: Goldline & Jacobs Pub, 2011), 196, emphasis in original.

[84] Wendy Griswold, *Bearing Witness: Readers, Writers, and the Novel in Nigeria* (Princeton: Princeton University Press, 2000), 168.

female writer, she was also a womanist. As a womanist, she used fiction to promote women's rights, her characters serving as role models for women, while challenging patriarchal practices and structures.[85] Nwapa's literary worldmaking could thus correct literary misrepresentations of African women, while offering strategies for women in times of social transformation.[86] Similarly to other women writers, Nwapa's works helped raise women's 'consciousness for self-discovery, self-definition, and self-appreciation as a full human being, *not inferior or superior to man, but just different*'.[87]

Although both authors' understanding of gender was more multifaceted than their writings conveyed, aesthetic worlds tend to take on lives of their own, as novels are read in different locations with different orientations. The politics of gendered orientation become particularly poignant when aesthetic worlds are dislocated from the complexities of their cultural origins and circulated in spheres of other cultural orientations. Let us now turn to an analysis of how literary gendering interplays not only with aesthetic worldmaking but also with the situated knowledge and cultural (dis)orientation of scholarly readings, not least when it comes to knowledge hierarchies in gender theory.

Cultural dislocation and vernacular gender theory

By virtue of being the most widely read African novel, Achebe's *Things Fall Apart* has had an enormous impact on geocultural imaginaries of Africa. In May 2018, the BBC even declared *Things Fall Apart* to be number five among 'The top 10 stories that shaped the world.'[88] Achebe's aesthetic worldmaking and literary gendering has thus been influential well beyond literature. The global circulation of this hyper-canonical classic brings forth some problematic aspects of the relation between literary gendering and gender theories of the world.

---

[85] Sabine Jell-Bahlsen, 'Flora Nwapa and Oguta's Lake Goddess: Artistic Liberty and Ethnography', *Dialectical Anthropology* 31 (2007): 253–62; Chikwenye Okonjo Ogunyemi, *Africa Wo/Man Palava: The Nigerian Novel by Women* (Chicago: The University of Chicago Press, 1996).

[86] Theodora Akachi Ezeigbo, 'Gender Conflict in Flora Nwapa's Novels', in *Writing African Women: Gender, Popular Culture and Literature in West Africa*, ed. Stephanie Newell (London: Zed Books, 2017).

[87] Safoura Salami-Boukari, *African Literature: Gender Discourse, Religious Values, and the African Worldview* (New York: African Heritage Press, 2012), xxv, emphasis added.

[88] www.bbc.com/culture/story/20180521-the-top-10-stories-that-shaped-the-world.

Nzegwu has highlighted how the famous philosopher Martha Nussbaum used *Things Fall Apart* to validate her thesis of universal sexism.[89] Discussing the main character Okonkwo's fear of weakness in terms of fear of 'female' emotion, Nussbaum concluded that the notion that 'women are emotional, emotions female' had been a familiar view in Western and non-Western traditions for thousands of years, a perspective used to exclude women.[90] As Nzegwu has pointed out, Nussbaum's decontextualized reading of the novel rendered a distorted interpretation of Igbo society and a false homogenization of non-Western tradition, which was then used as a basis for feminist analysis with universal claims.[91] If Nussbaum had read *Efuru* instead, her hypothesis might have taken a different turn.

Feminist literary scholars have also used *Things Fall Apart* to discuss sexist politics in African literature, again without fully appreciating the cultural complexities of gender. In her critique of Eurocentric and androcentric literary standards in canonical African literature, Florence Stratton has argued that *Things Fall Apart* favoured patriarchy: 'when the novel is read with a view to examining its relation to patriarchal ideology, the portrayal appears as a means of legitimizing male domination'.[92] Stratton's allegations of sexism have been challenged by Nigerian feminist scholar Obioma Nnaemeka, who has discussed her analysis as an example of 'the pitfalls of a radical feminist criticism in its full regalia of arrogance, prejudice, and separatism'.[93] For instance, while Stratton reads Okonkwo as representative of male violence against women, Nnaemeka argues that such one-sided readings miss the novel's paradoxes and contradictions, as it captures cultural ideals as well as deviations: 'Okonkwo is simultaneously normative and marginal'.[94] In other words a flawed hero, as Achebe himself expressed it.

These disorientations in Western feminist theorizing of African literature can be related to cultural dislocations and so-called anthropological readings. As

---

[89] Nkiru Nzegwu, 'Feminism and Africa: Impact and Limits of the Metaphysics of Gender', in *A Companion to African Philosophy*, ed. Kwasi Wiredu (Blackwell Publishing Ltd, 2005).

[90] Martha Nussbaum, 'Emotions and Women's Capabilities', in *Women, Culture and Development: A Study of Human Capabilities*, ed. Martha Nussbaum and Jonathan Glover (Oxford: Oxford University Press, 1995), 360.

[91] Nzegwu, 'Feminism and Africa'.

[92] Florence Stratton, *Contemporary African Literature and the Politics of Gender* (New York: Routledge, 1994), 37.

[93] Obioma Nnaemeka, 'Feminism, Rebellious Women, and Cultural Boundaries: Rereading Flora Nwapa and her Compatriots', *Research in African Literatures* 26, no. 2 (1995): 96.

[94] Nnaemeka, 'Feminism, Rebellious Women, and Cultural Boundaries', 99.

canonical novels circulate well beyond the writer's cultural context, they are also subject to a process of cultural dislocation, a cultural rupture through which the novel is relocated into other cultural imaginaries. Sometimes these geocultural imaginaries are disoriented by what has been described as the *anthropological exotic*, a mode of perception and consumption that 'allows for a reading of African literature as the more or less transparent window onto a richly detailed and culturally specific ... African world'.[95] Graham Huggan notes that the anthropological exotic has been influential in the marketing and reception of *Things Fall Apart* and the African Writers Series at large, 'the anthropological dimensions of literary texts often touted as virtually unmediated representations of African society, culture and history'.[96] More recently, Ngũgĩ has noted that 'African literature across multiple generations has suffered a kind of Africa-Is-a-Country literary criticism that, in place of diverse aesthetics, reads it as anthropology'.[97]

African scholars have challenged the ethnocentric orientation of Western feminist scholarship on epistemological grounds, insisting on closer attention to cultural context, as opposed to anthropological readings. For instance, Nnaemeka has encouraged a situated position of what she calls *inoutsiders* in analyses of African literature, to avoid 'the trap of creating African history and anthropology out of African novels'.[98] Far from being critical of anthropology or foreign scholarship in Africa per se, she has emphasized the importance of *cultural literacy*, underlining that 'African texts, as cultural productions, must not be decontextualized from the cultural contexts that gave them life and to which they refer'.[99] Similarly, scholars who are familiar with the cultural locations of African literature emphasize the need for more contextual analyses. For instance, Julien calls attention to how 'deep engagement with contextual factors' is becoming increasingly pertinent to appreciate literary production in today's globalized world.[100] Such deep engagement can be difficult to achieve without scholarly relocation, given the structural constraints of literary circulation. As Newell has pointed out: 'West African societies overflow with local, culturally

[95] Huggan, *The Postcolonial Exotic*, 37.
[96] Huggan, *The Postcolonial Exotic*, 53.
[97] Ngũgĩ, *The Rise of the African Novel*, 13.
[98] Nnaemeka, 'Feminism, Rebellious Women, and Cultural Boundaries', 87.
[99] Obioma Nnaemeka, 'Introduction: Imag(in)ing Knowledge, Power, and Subversion in the Margins', in *The Politics of (M)Othering: Womanhood, Identity and Resistance in African Literature*, ed. Obioma Nnaemeka (London: Routledge, 1997), 22.
[100] Julien, 'The Critical Present', 25.

specific constructions of gender which circulate in literature' but much of this material is 'unknown to researchers outside the country of production'.[101] Since only a fragment of African literature circulates in the global market, scholars who are located at a distance need to devise other strategies to capture context.

One way of contextualizing literary gendering is to pay more attention to vernacular gender theory. Literature can be read as 'fictionalized theory', as aesthetic worlds that 'reinscribe and foreground teleological, ontological, and epistemological insights and praxes relevant to the specific histories and politics that preceded the fictional texts'.[102] By emphasizing vernacular theory, Juliana Makuchi diversifies prevailing theory, demonstrating that 'there can be no one, "unified" post-colonial literature or theory, just as there is no one, "unified" feminist theory, but rather feminist theories that offer diverse and differing voices within feminism(s)'.[103] In her own analysis of gender in African women's writing, Makuchi highlights the *shifting locations* of gender inequalities, along with multiple identities and multidirectional *social locations*, a fluidity that subverts and nuances conceptions of gender in dominant feminist theory.[104] Similarly, using vernacular gender theory, Chikwenye Okonjo Ogunyemi interrogates the literary work of Nigerian women writers by way of African womanism, arguing that it is 'communal in its orientation', thus more applicable than the 'rhetorical, polemical, and individualistic' thrust of Western feminism.[105]

Another example can be drawn from my anthropological work on the *Lake Goddess* in Flora Nwapa's works. This female water deity (also known as Uhamiri, Ogbuide or Mammywater) is a recurring feature in Flora Nwapa's aesthetic worlds, from her first novel *Efuru* to her last, posthumously published novel *The Lake Goddess*.[106] Since the Lake Goddess is a prominent water deity in Igbo/Oguta cosmology, Flora Nwapa's literary depictions can be related to vernacular theories of the lived world. In addition to capturing myths she had learned through the storytelling of her foremothers,[107] Flora Nwapa carried out research in her community, interviewing priestesses and other devotees.[108] Scholars have noted how Nwapa's works portray local practices and beliefs with

---

[101] Newell, *Writing African Women*, 1.

[102] Juliana Makuchi, *Gender in African Women's Writing. Identity, Sexuality, and Difference* (Bloomington: Indiana University Press, 1997), 20.

[103] Makuchi, *Gender in African Women's Writing*, 19.

[104] Makuchi, *Gender in African Women's Writing*, 32–3.

[105] Ogunyemi, *Africa Wo/Man Palava*, 119.

[106] Flora Nwapa, *The Lake Goddess* (Oguta: Tana press Ltd., 2017).

[107] Ogunyemi, *Africa Wo/Man Palava*.

[108] Jell-Bahlsen, 'Nneka: Is Mother Still Supreme in Igboland?'

considerable accuracy: 'I find *The Lake Goddess* almost anthropological in its narrative.'[109] But since Nwapa's literary narratives constitute aesthetic worlds, we can appreciate the critical distinction signalled by the word 'almost'. As noted by Sabine Jell-Bahlsen, an anthropologist specialized in Igbo/Oguta cosmology who knew the writer personally, Flora Nwapa used her artistic liberty to recreate and reconfigure indigenous cosmology, according to her womanist agenda.[110] It was only by learning more about vernacular gender theory, in this case African womanism,[111] that I could better appreciate the cultural nuances in Nwapa's aesthetic worlds, which I have discussed elsewhere in terms of womanist worldmaking.[112]

Gendered orientations in vernacular locations at the Efuru@50 celebration

In 2016, Efuru@50 was celebrated in five cities across Nigeria, an event that carried the slogan *Flora Nwapa: Pioneer of African women literature.*[113] In 2018, *Things Fall Apart* was to be celebrated as TFA@60, with the theme *Things Fall Apart: 60 Years On.* The diamond jubilee of TFA@60 was planned to be celebrated in seven cities in Nigeria, as well as ten African countries, Europe and the USA. The difference in scope and scale is worth noting as it speaks to gendered power structures in world literature. However, since the grandiose plans for TFA@60 never materialized, there is also something to be said for ambiguities and paradoxes in world literature, even in celebrations of hyper-canonical literature.

At Efuru@50, Flora Nwapa was given due recognition for her pioneering accomplishments in claiming a space for African women writers. Keynote speakers at the event were high-profile women writers and intellectuals like

[109] Ifi Amadiume, 'Religion, Sexuality, and Women's Empowerment in Nwapa's *The Lake Goddess*', in *Emerging Perspectives on Flora Nwapa: Critical and Theoretical Essays*, ed. Marie Umeh (Asmara and Trenton: Africa World Press Inc, 1998), 519.

[110] Jell-Bahlsen, 'Flora Nwapa and Oguta's Lake Goddess'.

[111] Ogunyemi, *Africa Wo/Man Palava*.

[112] Paula Uimonen, *Invoking Flora Nwapa: Nigerian Women Writers, Femininity and Spirituality in World Literature* (Stockholm: Stockholm University Press, 2020).

[113] In addition to the Efuru@50 event in Nigeria, several commemorative events and activities took place in 2016. A round table on Flora Nwapa was organized at the African Literature Association (ALA) annual meeting in Atlanta. Anthropologist Sabine Jell-Bahlsen presented a paper on Efuru@50 at the annual Igbo conference at SOAS in London. Onyeka Nwelue produced a documentary film *The House of Nwapa*, combining archival film materials with interviews and other forms of footage.

Bolanle Awe, Zaynab Alkali and Theodora Akachi Ezeigbo. Most of the scholars who presented papers were female, many of them analysing Nwapa's literary legacy from a feminist or womanist angle. In Abuja, several male scholars presented papers using feminist theories, while considerable debate erupted on feminism and gender equality in Owerri. In Lagos, the event attracted some 150 people, in Maiduguri over 500 and in Enugu some 700 people came to the celebration, including the deputy governor Honourable Mrs Cecilia Ezeilo, who gave her posthumous accolade to Flora Nwapa, while the First Daughters of Enugu State gave her the award *Nwada Igbo Gara Uzo Oma* (A First Daughter of Igbo Land Who Travelled on a Good Journey).

Efuru@50 was a highly ritualized event through which Flora Nwapa's literary legacy was revived and immortalized.[114] Since she joined her ancestors in 1993, Flora Nwapa had gradually fallen into oblivion on the literary scene. As noted by Denja Abdullahi, President, Association of Nigerian Authors (ANA) in the documentary film *The House of Nwapa*: 'Flora Nwapa, sometimes her memory is like fading away in Nigerian literary landscape. So people have not really done enough to celebrate her as one of the earliest Nigerian female novelists.'[115] By 2016, many of Flora Nwapa's books were out of print, or circulated as pirated copies in Nigeria. Through Efuru@50, Nwapa's colleagues and friends could revive her legacy, their eloquent tributes testifying that Efuru was indeed a remarkable woman, and so was Flora Nwapa. The presence of Flora Nwapa's three children underscored the social significance of the event, while the presence of students pointed to a literary future.

'Okomma!' (mighty sword) titled men of Igbu society exclaimed as they walked into the lecture room in Owerri, ritually greeting each other by clashing their ceremonial swords. They had travelled all the way from Oguta to honour Flora Nwapa, who they referred to by her prestigious title, *Ogbuefi* (killer of cow). Among them were Flora Nwapa's brother, Chief Christopher Nwapa, and they were welcomed by her son, Uzoma Nwakuche, both titled men. These traditional cultural leaders took turns making brief comments about *Efuru* in relation to Oguta culture. In writing the novel, Flora Nwapa was 'showing how Oguta was and how it was growing', an elderly titled man remarked, not least 'the palm produce market', which was centred in Oguta. 'Our women, Oguta women, played very, very important roles in the market', he underlined. The women used

---

[114] Uimonen, *Invoking Flora Nwapa*.
[115] Onyeka Nwelue, *The House of Nwapa* (2016).

the money to help their families and their husbands, so Efuru was an average Oguta woman, who helped her husband and family by trading, he explained. 'Efuru decided on her own, to follow her *chi*', even though her husband did not lend her a hand as he was supposed to. In traditional Oguta society, husbands and wives worked together for the family, he concluded. As often happened during the Efuru@50 celebration, the fictional character Efuru was discussed as if she had been a living person, while Flora Nwapa's literary text was treated as some kind of historical documentation of traditional Oguta culture. When discussing the novel, community leaders from Flora Nwapa's hometown pointed out where fictional characters in the novel had departed from cultural ideals. While the main character Efuru had been a model Oguta woman, her two consecutive husbands had clearly not lived up to their family duties. The characters in the novel were thus appraised according to cultural norms.

While the titled men from Oguta addressed differences between aesthetic worlds and social worlds, it was disjunctions between cultural norms and feminist theory that created quite a stir in the scholarly debate that followed. Several female scholars used feminist or womanist theory to discuss *Efuru* and other literary works by Nigerian women writers. One scholar discussed the character Efuru as a proto-feminist, another one interrogated patriarchal assumptions in *Efuru*, while two others emphasized how Flora Nwapa portrayed women's independence. While some participants appreciated their critical insights, others challenged feminist analyses on cultural grounds. Meanwhile, the Igbo chairman kept repeating the cultural significance of *complementary binaries* and the cultural logic of *duality*. He recounted that in precolonial culture women had a strong position in society, but they were degraded by the influence of Arabic and European cultures. Throughout the heated discussions, the chairman kept insisting on gender complementarity as a core value.

Discussions among cultural insiders exemplify how literary texts can move between fact and fiction, reflecting the dynamic interplay of location and orientation in readership. Unlike anthropological readings from a culturally distant location, whereby fiction is treated as fact, cultural insiders can appreciate aesthetic worlds as fictitious representations of social words. Differences in cultural proximity play a key role in this process, since the geocultural imaginaries of cultural insiders and outsiders are mediated by their cultural location. But cultural location is not merely related to a place but also to social position. In this particular instance, we can note how cultural authorities like the titled members of Igbu society related to Efuru as an Oguta woman, while celebrating the author of *Efuru* as a chronicler of Oguta culture. Scholars of literature related to Flora Nwapa as a pioneering female writer, whose literary works depicted gender relations and social transformations, while the chairman acted as a cultural gatekeeper, confident in his cultural expertise. Although readings by cultural insiders can differ markedly from those of cultural outsiders, it should become clear that gendered orientations are also socially distributed within a given cultural location.

As much as the Efuru@50 celebration in Owerri may come across as a very local event in a vernacular location, it also exemplifies the transnational relationality and cosmopolitan orientation of postcolonial African locations. The languages spoken at the event (Oguta, Igbo and English), vocalized the participants' translocal and transnational outlook, while their statements evoked a historical trajectory of transcultural encounters, from colonial times to contemporary globality. Coming together to celebrate the novel *Efuru* and the writer Flora Nwapa, they were also connected to the global market of the world-literary system, while my presence as the only international participant assured that the event would be duly documented in scholarly accounts with global circulation, like the documentary film Efuru@50, distributed on YouTube.[116] Indeed, as I have discussed elsewhere, Efuru@50 extended Flora Nwapa's fame well beyond the event, an expansion of intersubjective space-time that speaks to the complex entanglements of African literature, well beyond the materiality of literary objects.[117]

One world literature and gender complementarity

As discussed in the introductory chapter of this volume, location and orientation can be cross-fertilized with cosmopolitan and vernacular, thus producing various conceptual pairs to interrogate the complexity of world literature. In this chapter, I have used the kaleidoscopic lens of globalectics to tease out some of these interlinkages in relation to African locations and gendered orientations. Focusing on two pioneering writers, Chinua Achebe and Flora Nwapa, I have discussed their works in relation to gendered claims of place in canon formation as well as the intricacies of literary gendering in aesthetic worldmaking. But given world literature's preoccupation with the *world*, I would like to conclude this text with

---

[116] https://www.youtube.com/watch?v=EndOXak9ESQ
[117] Uimonen, *Invoking Flora Nwapa.*

some abstractions, drawn from a fusion of literary and anthropological theory. So let me take note of the caveat that the cosmopolitan and vernacular 'should not be thought of as opposites but as two modes – or vectors – of literary worldliness that may interact, merge or contest each other', thus constituting 'thoroughly relational terms'.[118] It is especially the *relationality* of the cosmopolitan/universal and the vernacular/particular that I wish to probe further, by way of globalectics, one world anthropology and gender complementarity.

'Globalectics is derived from the shape of the globe', Thiong'o explains, emphasizing that 'On its surface there is no one center; any point is equally a center'.[119] He elaborates that 'Globalectics embraces wholeness, interconnectedness, equality of potentiality of parts, tension, and motion. It is a way of thinking and relating to the world, particularly in the era of globalism and globalization'.[120] Comparatively, Pheng Cheah has argued for a more normative understanding of the world, emphasizing 'openness' and 'being-with of all peoples, groups and individuals', as opposed to a world defined in terms of global capitalism.[121] To explore the world in world literature, I would like to adopt Thiong'o's globalectic vision of *wholeness* and move along with Cheah's *being-with*, even extending it into *becoming-with*, by way of anthropological theory. The world as a totality can be rethought through *one world anthropology*.[122] As a philosophical inquiry, one world anthropology explores the relation between universality and particularity, singularity and plurality, based on the core principle that 'the inhabited world is indeed *one*'.[123] The oneness of the world ties in well with world literature, capturing its totality. But what makes one world anthropology even more compelling is the notion that the world is *conversation* and to inhabit the world is to join the conversation. This is comparable with Cheah's suggestion that the world has 'a narrative structure', it is 'formed by the telling of stories',[124] and Eric Hayot's postulation that 'A world is conversant with itself'.[125]

[118] Stefan Helgesson, 'General Introduction: The Cosmopolitan and the Vernacular in Interaction', in *World Literatures: Exploring the Cosmopolitan-Vernacular Exchange*, ed. Stefan Helgesson, Annika Mörte Alling, Yvonne Lindqvist and Helena Wulff (Stockholm: Stockholm University Press, 2018), 2.

[119] Thiong'o, *Globalectics*, 8.

[120] Thiong'o, *Globalectics*, 8.

[121] Pheng Cheah, 'World against Globe: Toward a Normative Conception of World Literature', *New Literary History* 45, no. 3 (2014): 326.

[122] Ingold, 'One World Anthropology'.

[123] Ingold, 'One World Anthropology', 158, emphasis in original.

[124] Cheah, 'World against Globe', 325.

[125] Eric Hayot, *On Literary Worlds* (Oxford: Oxford University Press, 2012), 54.

Tim Ingold identifies *correspondence* as an organizational principle of the world. Moving beyond notions of assembly or rhizome, he suggest that 'parts are not components that are added *to* one another but movements that carry on *alongside* one another', and in relating to one another they 'co-respond'.[126] He underlines that 'the relations that make up the whole are not *between* but *along*', thus contrasting the along-ness of correspondence with the between-ness of interaction, like the distinction between the words '*and*' and '*with*'.[127] Thinking through world literature with one world anthropology has certain epistemological advantages. Instead of thinking of the cosmopolitan–vernacular in terms of interactions and exchanges, we can see these modes as movements of differential correspondence. This postulation has several bearings on world literature. First of all, it insists on world literature as a whole, empirically denoting all the literatures of the world, instead of a structurally constrained aesthetic hierarchy of literary objects in global circulation. Secondly, the parts that make up world literature are always in movement, their location spatiotemporally dispersed alongside one another, their orientation in multidirectional correspondence with one another. World literature is thus not an assembly of all literatures in the world, but a constantly shifting literary constellation, an emergent world literature.

The worldmaking capacity of literature makes world literature a particularly interesting case for one world theorizing. As Hayot convincingly argues: 'aesthetic worlds tell us something about the history of the idea of the world', therefore 'they not only reflect it but help conceive it'.[128] This is comparable with Thiong'o's postulation that 'literature mimics the creation of the universe'.[129] World literature is a particularly good example of the worlding of the world, its ontogenesis, since 'the world is a conversation; it is not the object of our conversation. In this conversation lies *ontogénèse*, the becoming of being'.[130] While the notion of one world literature accommodates the cultural diversity of aesthetic worlds, the ontogenesis of worldmaking begs for a more processual approach, to 'think of difference in terms of *differentiation* rather than *diversity*'.[131] This is a critical distinction, since differentiation captures the way in which parts are related to the whole, not as separate entities, but as something that emerges from within,

[126] Ingold, 'One World Anthropology', 160.
[127] Ingold, 'One World Anthropology', 159.
[128] Hayot, 'On Literary Worlds', 159, n 38.
[129] Thiong'o, *Globalectics*, 17.
[130] Ingold, 'One World Anthropology', 169, emphasis in original.
[131] Ingold, 'One World Anthropology', 161, emphasis in original.

according to the 'principle of interstitial differentiation'.[132] It also captures the perpetual movement of the world, its ontogenesis, since diversity refers to *being different*, while differentiation refers to *becoming different*.[133]

The principle of interstitial differentiation has a direct bearing on the relationality of the cosmopolitan and the vernacular in world literature. It reaffirms the relationality of the global/universal and the local/particular in location and orientation, insisting that the parts of the whole emerge from within, alongside one another, rather than through binary opposition or interaction. And it decentres and decolonizes world literature along the lines of a globalectical imagination, insisting that 'any center is the center of the world', while any 'specific text can be read as a mirror of the world'.[134] Through interstitial differentiation we can also appreciate the significance of gender complementarity in one world literature. In Igbo culture, gender complementarity is valued as an important aspect of social balance, in recognition of men and women being different, yet equal. If we acknowledge gender as an important aspect of differentiation emerging from within and alongside one world literature, the notion of gender complementarity offers a way to develop more equitable gendered orientations in the scholarly appraisal of the many cultural locations of aesthetic worldmaking. While keeping in mind the intrinsic value of gender complementarity, let us envisage what one world literature might look like:

> World literature would be like the sea or the ocean into which all streams from all corners of the globe would flow. The sea is constituted of many rivers, some of which cross many fields, but the rivers and their constituent streams do not lose their individuality as streams and rivers.[135]

Concluding musings *with* Chinua Achebe and Flora Nwapa

As suggested in the title, my aim in this chapter has been to explore one world literature *with* Chinua Achebe and Flora Nwapa. Inspired by Igbo cultural ideals of gender complementarity, I am using *with* on purpose, thus paying tribute to *both* the Father *and* the Mother of modern African literature. I would now like to invoke their cultural location for some concluding thoughts on one world literature.

---

[132] Ingold, 'One World Anthropology', 166.
[133] Ingold, 'One World Anthropology', 162.
[134] Ngũgĩ wa Thiong'o, 'A Globalectical Imagination', *World Literature Today* 87, no. 3 (2013): 42.
[135] Thiong'o, *Globalectics*, 55.

Chinua Achebe's and Flora Nwapa's literary works constitute aesthetic worlds that correspond with other literary worlds in the making of world literature, thus participating in the multi-logue correspondence that is the world. Their complementary location and orientation in African literature articulate the relationality of aesthetic and social worlds. In the global marketplace, their literary texts are hierarchically ordered according to the racist and sexist logic of global capitalism, but fortunately their narratives offer cultural imaginaries of other worlds. In their Igbo social worlds, men and women have complementary roles and identities, which in turn intersect with other cultural identities, in continually shifting locations and orientations. Through their literary texts, these writers can recreate and reconfigure their social worlds in conversation with readers around the world. Since their books exist in material form, these conversations continue long after the writers' departure from the physical world, when their individual *chi* have been reunited with *Chi-Ukwu*, the great life force that is the creator and leader of their universe, in the eternal cycle of life. Similarly to other aesthetic worlds, their literary narratives articulate different forms of worldmaking, creative expressions of interstitial differentiation in the never-ending conversation that is the ontogenesis of the world. Stories like how the lake goddess Ogbuide and the river god Urashi flow alongside one another at that spectacular confluence in Oguta lake, where the blue and brown waters meet and correspond, in a continuous movement of natural and spiritual complementarity.

Bibliography

Achebe, Chinua. *Things Fall Apart*. 1958. London: Heinemann, 1962.

Achebe, Chinua. *Things Fall Apart*. Greenwich, CT: Fawcett Publications, Inc., 1959.

Achebe, Chinua. 'An Image of Africa: Racism in Conrad's *Heart of Darkness*', *Massachusetts Review* 18, 1977.

Amadiume, Ifi. 'Religion, Sexuality, and Women's Empowerment in Nwapa's *The Lake Goddess*'. In *Emerging Perspectives on Flora Nwapa: Critical and Theoretical Essays*, edited by Marie Umeh, 515–29. Asmara and Trenton: Africa World Press Inc., 1998.

Bergenmar, Jenny and Katarina Leppänen. 'Gender and Vernaculars in Digital Humanities and World Literature'. *NORA – Nordic Journal of Feminist and Gender Research* 25, no. 4 (2017): 232–46.

Castillo, Debra. 'Gender and Sexuality in World Literature'. In *The Routledge Companion to World Literature*, edited by Theo D'haen, David Damrosch and Djelal Kadir, 393–403. London and New York: Routledge, 2012.

Cheah, Pheng. 'What Is a World? On World Literature as World-Making Activity'. *Daedalus* 137, no. 3 (2008): 26–38.

Cheah, Pheng. 'World against Globe: Toward a Normative Conception of World Literature'. *New Literary History* 45, no. 3 (2014): 303–29.

Currey, James. *Africa Writes Back: The African Writers Series & the Launch of African Literature*. Oxford: James Currey, 2008.

Doherty, Brian. 'The Center Cannot Hold: The Development of World Literature Anthologies'. *Alif: Journal of Comparative Poetics* 34 (2014): 100–124.

Edfeldt, Chatarina. 'Gender and the Circulation of African Lusophone Literature into the Portuguese Literary System'. In *World Literatures: Exploring the Cosmopolitan–Vernacular Exchange*, edited by Stefan Helgesson, Annika Mörte Alling, Yvonne Lindqvist and Helena Wulff, 369–82. Stockholm: Stockholm University Press, 2018.

Ezeigbo, Theodora Akachi. 'Gender Conflict in Flora Nwapa's Novels'. 1997. In *Writing African Women: Gender, Popular Culture and Literature in West Africa*, edited by Stephanie Newell, 95–104. London: Zed Books, 2017.

Ezeigbo, Theodora Akachi. 'Myth, History, Culture, and Igbo Womanhood in Flora Nwapa's Novels'. In *Emerging Perspectives on Flora Nwapa: Critical and Theoretical Essays*, edited by Marie Umeh, 51–76. Trenton and Asmara: Africa World Press Inc., 1998.

Griswold, Wendy. *Bearing Witness: Readers, Writers, and the Novel in Nigeria*. Princeton: Princeton University Press, 2000.

Hannerz, Ulf. *Transnational Connections: Culture, People, Places*. London and New York: Routledge, 1996.

Hannerz, Ulf. *Writing Future Worlds: An Anthropologist Explores Global Scenarios*. London: Palgrave Macmillan, 2016.

Haraway, Donna. 'Situated Knowledges: The Science Question in Feminism and the Privilege of Partial Perspective'. *Feminist Studies* 14, no. 3 (1988): 575–99.

Hayot, Eric. 'On Literary Worlds'. *Modern Language Quarterly* 72, no. 2 (2011): 129–61.

Hayot, Eric. *On Literary Worlds*. Oxford: Oxford University Press, 2012.

Helgesson, Stefan. 'General Introduction: The Cosmopolitan and the Vernacular in Interaction'. In *World Literatures: Exploring the Cosmopolitan–Vernacular Exchange*, edited by Stefan Helgesson, Annika Mörte Alling, Yvonne Lindqvist and Helena Wulff, 1–11. Stockholm: Stockholm University Press, 2018.

Helgesson, Stefan and Mads Rosendahl Thomsen. *Literature and the World*. London and New York: Routledge, 2020.

Higonnet, Margaret R. 'Editor's Introduction'. *Comparative Critical Studies* 6, no. 2 (2009): 135–48.

Huggan, Graham. *The Postcolonial Exotic: Marketing the Margins*. New York: Routledge, 2001.

Ibironke, Olabode. 'African Writers Challenge Conventions of Postcolonial Literary History'. In *Rethinking African Cultural Production*, edited by Frieda Ekotto and Kenneth Harrow, 29–51. Bloomington and Indianapolis: Indiana University Press, 2015.

Ingold, Tim. 'One World Anthropology'. *HAU: Journal of Ethnographic Theory* 8, no. 1/2 (2018): 158–71.

James, Adeola. *In Their Own Voices: African Women Writers Talk.* London: James Currey, 1990.

Jell-Bahlsen, Sabine. 'Flora Nwapa and Oguta's Lake Goddess: Artistic Liberty and Ethnography'. *Dialectical Anthropology* 31 (2007): 253–62.

Jell-Bahlsen, Sabine. '*Nneka*: Is Mother Still Supreme in Igboland? Reflections on the Biography of *Eze Mmiri*, Madame Martha Mberekpe of Orsu-Obodo, 1934–2007'. In *Against All Odds: The Igbo Experience in Postcolonial Nigeria*, edited by Apollos Nwauwa and Chima Korieh, 195–218. Abia State, Nigeria: Goldline & Jacobs Pub, 2011.

Julien, Eileen. 'The Extroverted African Novel'. In *The Novel: History, Geography and Culture*, edited by Franco Moretti, 667–700. Princeton: Princeton University Press, 2006.

Julien, Eileen. 'The Critical Present. Where is "African Literature"?' In *Rethinking African Cultural Production*, edited by Frieda Ekotto and Kenneth Harrow, 17–28. Bloomington and Indianapolis: Indiana University Press, 2015.

Julien, Eileen. 'The Extroverted African Novel, Revisited: African Novels at Home, in the World'. *Journal of African Cultural Studies* 30, no. 3 (2018): 371–81.

Kamau, Kiarie and Kirimi Mitambo, eds. *Coming of Age: Strides in African Publishing. Essays in Honour of Dr. Henry Chakava@70.* Nairobi: East African Publishers Ltd, 2016.

Krishnan, Madhu. *Contemporary African Literature in English: Global Locations, Postcolonial Identifications.* Basingstoke: Palgrave Macmillan Limited, 2014.

Leppänen, Katarina Helena. 'Reflections on Gender and Small Languages in World Literature Scholarship: Methods of Inclusions and Exclusions'. In *World Literatures: Exploring the Cosmopolitan–Vernacular Exchange*, edited by Stefan Helgesson, Annika Mörte Alling, Yvonne Lindqvist and Helena Wulff, 89–99. Stockholm: Stockholm University Press, 2018.

Lutz, Catherine. 'The Gender of Theory'. In *Women Writing Culture*, edited by Ruth Behar and Deborah A. Gordon, 249–66. Berkeley: University of California Press, 1995.

Makuchi, Juliana. *Gender in African Women's Writing: Identity, Sexuality, and Difference.* Bloomington: Indiana University Press, 1997.

Newell, Stephanie, ed. *Writing African Women: Gender, Popular Culture and Literature in West Africa.* 1997. London: Zed Books, 2017.

Ngũgĩ, Mũkoma Wa. *The Rise of the African Novel: Politics of Language, Identity and Ownership.* Ann Arbor: University of Michigan Press, 2018.

Nnaemeka, Obioma. 'Feminism, Rebellious Women, and Cultural Boundaries: Rereading Flora Nwapa and her Compatriots'. *Research in African Literatures* 26, no. 2 (1995): 80–113.

Nnaemeka, Obioma. 'Introduction: Imag(in)ing Knowledge, Power and Subversion in the Margins'. In *The Politics of (M)Othering: Womanhood, Identity and Resistance in African Literature*, edited by Obioma Nnaemeka, 1–25. London: Routledge, 1997.

Nussbaum, Martha. 'Emotions and Women's Capabilities'. In *Women, Culture and Development: A Study of Human Capabilities*, edited by Martha Nussbaum and Jonathan Glover, 360–95. Oxford: Oxford University Press, 1995.

Nwapa, Flora. *Efuru*. London: Heinemann, 1966.

Nwapa, Flora. *Idu*. Oguta: Tana Press Ltd, 1970.

Nwapa, Flora. *Efuru*. 50th Anniversary Edition. Oguta: Tana Press Ltd, 2016.

Nwapa, Flora. *The Lake Goddess*. Oguta: Tana Press Ltd, 2017.

Nzegwu, Nkiru. 'Feminism and Africa: Impact and Limits of the Metaphysics of Gender'. In *A Companion to African Philosophy*, edited by Kwasi Wiredu, 560–69. Oxford: Blackwell Publishing Ltd, 2005.

Nzegwu, Nkiru. *Family Matters: Feminist Concepts in African Philosophy of Culture*. Albany: State University of New York Press, 2006.

Ochiagha, Terri. *Achebe and Friends at Umuahia: The Making of a Literary Elite*. Woodbridge: James Currey, 2015.

Ogunyemi, Chikwenye Okonjo. *Africa Wo/Man Palava: The Nigerian Novel by Women*. Chicago: The University of Chicago Press, 1996.

Orsini, Francesca and Laetitia Zecchini. 'The Locations of (World) Literature: Perspectives from Africa and South Asia'. *Journal of World Literature* 4 (2019): 1–12.

Otokunefor, Henrietta and Obiageli Nwodo, eds. *Nigerian Female Writers. A Critical Perspective*. Lagos: Malthouse Press Ltd., 1989.

Oyěwùmí, Oyèrónké. 'Introduction: Gendering'. In *Gender Epistemologies in Africa: Gendering Traditions, Spaces, Social Institutions, and Identities*, edited by Oyèrónké Oyěwùmí, 1–7. New York: Palgrave Macmillan, 2011.

Salami-Boukari, Safoura. *African Literature. Gender Discourse, Religious Values, and the African Worldview*. New York: African Heritage Press, 2012.

Spencer, Robert. *Cosmopolitan Criticism and Postcolonial Literature*. Basingstoke: Palgrave Macmillan, 2011.

Spivak, Gayatri Chakravorty. *In Other Worlds*. London and New York: Routledge, 1998.

Stratton, Florence. *Contemporary African Literature and the Politics of Gender*. New York: Routledge, 1994.

Suhr-Sytsma, Nathan. 'The Extroverted African Novel and Literary Publishing in the Twenty-First Century'. *Journal of African Cultural Studies* 30, no. 3 (2018): 339–55.

Thiong'o, Ngũgĩ wa. *Decolonising the Mind: The Politics of Language in African Literature*. London: James Currey, 1986.

Thiong'o, Ngũgĩ wa. 'A Globalectical Imagination'. *World Literature Today* 87, no. 3 (2013):40–42.

Thiong'o, Ngũgĩ wa. *Globalectics: Theory and the Politics of Knowing*. New York: Columbia University Press, 2014.

Uimonen, Paula. 'Cosmopolitan Feminism: From Flora Nwapa's *Efuru* to Chimamanda Ngozi Adichie's *We Should all be Feminists*'. Paper presented at *Efuru@50*, Maiduguri, 1 December 2016.

Uimonen, Paula. 'Who was Flora Nwapa? Gender and Power in World Literature'. Paper presented at *EASA 2018*, the biennial conference of the European Association of Social Anthropologists (EASA), Stockholm 14–17 August 2018.

Uimonen, Paula. 'Zuhura the African Lioness. Performance Poetry, Digital Media and the Transnational Tangle in World Literature'. In *World Literatures: Exploring the Cosmopolitan–Vernacular Exchange*, edited by Stefan Helgesson, Annika Mörte Alling, Yvonne Lindqvist and Helena Wulff, 129–39. Stockholm: Stockholm University Press, 2018.

Uimonen, Paula. 'Muse and Power. African Women Writers and Digital Infrastructure in World Literature'. *Anthropology and Humanism* 44, no. 1 (2019): 20–37.

Uimonen, Paula. 'Decolonising Cosmopolitanism: An Anthropological Reading of Immanuel Kant and Kwame Nkrumah on the World as One'. *Critique of Anthropology* 40, no. 1 (2019): 81–101.

Uimonen, Paula. *Invoking Flora Nwapa: Nigerian Women Writers, Femininity and Spirituality in World Literature*. Stockholm: Stockholm University Press, 2020.

Umeh, Marie. 'The Poetics of Economic Independence for Female Empowerment: An Interview with Flora Nwapa'. *Research in African Literatures* 26, no. 2 (1995): 22–9.

Umeh, Marie, ed. *Emerging Perspectives on Flora Nwapa: Critical and Theoretical Essays*. Trenton and Asmara: Africa World Press Inc., 1998.

Umeh, Marie. *Flora Nwapa, a Pen and a Press*. New York: Triatlantic Books of NY, 2010.

Wallerstein, Immanuel. 'Culture as the Ideological Battleground of the Modern World-System'. *Theory, Culture & Society* 7, no. 2–3 (1990): 31–55.

WReC. *Combined and Uneven Development: Towards a New Theory of World-Literature*. Liverpool: Liverpool University Press, 2015.

Wulff, Helena. *Rhythms of Writing: An Anthropology of Irish Literature*. London: Bloomsbury, 2017.

Documentary films

Nwelue, Onyeka. *The House of Nwapa*, 2016. www.youtube.com/watch?v=3ZT5_YeTPos&feature=youtu.be

Uimonen, Paula. *Efuru@50*, 2017. Produced by Paula Uimonen & Yaki Bozi. www.youtube.com/watch?v=EndOXak9ESQ

2

The locations and orientations of South African literature: From Sol Plaatje to Peter Abrahams

Ashleigh Harris

In this chapter, I read two novels which I hesitate to call simply 'South African', yet which I will nevertheless consider central to the national literature of that country. The first novel, *Mhudi* (1930) by Sol T. Plaatje, already enjoys a central space in the South African canon, often lauded as the first English novel written by a black South African.[1] For this reason, the novel has enjoyed such legitimizing factors as being included on the national high school curriculum. The novel tells the tale of its eponymous protagonist Mhudi and her husband Ra-Thaga as they escape a vicious attack on their village by Mzilikazi, king of the Matabele, in and around the year 1832. The second novel, *This Island Now*, by Peter Abrahams is not quite as highly recognized within the South African canon. Abrahams's *Mine Boy* (1946) enjoys that place, rather, being written on the cusp of apartheid and drawing overt attention to the conditions of black workers under white rule. *This Island Now* has a more oblique relationship to South Africa: it was written after Abrahams went into exile and is set on a fictional island somewhere in the Caribbean, not in South Africa at all.

I use these two very different texts – one intensely located in the country of the Barolong, a Batswana tribe in the early to mid-nineteenth century, and the other set on a fictional island in the Caribbean – to explore South African literature's ambivalent relationship to the world. The novels are separated by thirty-six years, but their different relationships to the world of letters displays the dizzying pace of the loss of local literary traditions as a result of apartheid. Indeed, separating these texts exactly is the historical fulcrum of the inauguration of South African

[1] Stephen Gray, 'Sources of the First Black South African Novel in English: Solomon Plaatje's use of Shakespeare and Bunyan in *Mhudi*', *Munger Africana Library Notes*, no. 37 (December 1976): 6–28.

apartheid in 1948.[2] The argument that follows posits that apartheid disorientated a national literature of South Africa and that we can use these two case studies to demonstrate that disorientation.

In *An Ecology of World Literature: From Antiquity to the Present Day*, Alexander Beecroft opens up new understandings of how literatures emerge, circulate and adapt to their given location and orient themselves in terms of their local, regional, national or even global contexts. Beecroft's six ecologies expand outward from the smallest level of circulation (the epichoric) to the largest (the global). The epichoric is 'the limit-case of literary circulation, where verbal art (frequently though not necessarily, oral) may be transmitted over long periods of time but does not leave the small-scale local community'.[3] Panchoric ecologies 'are those that form in regions with small-scale polities but where literary and other cultural artifacts circulate more broadly through a space that is self-aware of itself as some kind of cultural unity and that define themselves by the exclusion of other polities that do not share that culture'.[4] Cosmopolitan ecologies, writes Beecroft, 'are found whenever a single literary language is used over a large territorial range and through a long period of time'.[5] Vernacular ecologies, in turn, emerge 'out of cosmopolitan ones when sufficient cultural resources accumulate behind some version of a locally spoken language to allow for its use for literary purposes'.[6] The vernacular also consolidates into the next ecology, that of national literature, which Beecroft notes occurs 'together with the emergence of nationalism per se'.[7] Finally, we reach the global ecology, which 'represents another limit-case – the literary circulation that truly knows no borders. As major languages (most obviously, of course, English) escape the bonds of the nation-state, and texts begin to circulate more rapidly around the planet, we may', speculates Beecroft, 'be moving in the direction of just such a borderless world'.[8] Even though Beecroft wishes to resist an 'evolutionary'[9] logic to these ecologies, the centrifugal motion, from the most restricted forms of circulation to the largest possible ones, places them in a temporal line of historical

---

[2]   *Mhudi* was actually completed in 1920, but I nevertheless see its publication date as crucial, since it is in publication that its movement into the world of course begins. I will discuss this matter in relation to Sol Plaatje's translation and orthographic work in more detail below.
[3]   Alexander Beecroft, *An Ecology of World Literature: From Antiquity to the Present Day* (London: Verso, 2015), Kindle, loc. 667 of 7487.
[4]   Beecroft, *An Ecology of World Literature*, loc. 675 of 7487.
[5]   Beecroft, *An Ecology of World Literature*, loc. 684 of 7487.
[6]   Beecroft, *An Ecology of World Literature*, loc. 692 of 7487.
[7]   Beecroft, *An Ecology of World Literature*, loc. 699 of 7487.
[8]   Beecroft, *An Ecology of World Literature*, loc. 715 of 7487.
[9]   Beecroft, *An Ecology of World Literature*, loc. 666 of 7487.

emergence. While these temporalities may then overlap, there is a strong sense that they mark a line of succession, if not progression, 'from antiquity to the present day', as the book's subtitle reveals.

South African literature, however, sits uncomfortably within this schema. This is because colonialism imposed a cosmopolitan language and literature upon literary cultures and then refused any possibilities of the vernacularization of colonial forms excepting in Afrikaans. Apartheid compounded the problem, first by making impossible the achievement of a truly national literature, given that the nation itself did not acknowledge the civil and human rights of the majority of its people, and second by disorienting South Africa's relationship to the globe because of isolationism. This resulted in both a compacted and disoriented set of literary ecologies, which coexisted, competed and confounded one another in ways that complicated South African literature's coming into being as national literature, and its relationship to the world.

As such, in the early to mid-nineteenth century, one can see concurrent examples of at least four of Beecroft's stages: an epichoric oral literature in ǀXam, a language that is now extinct, the panchoric traditions of isiXhosa and isiZulu praise poetry,[10] cosmopolitan forms in English, such as accounts of the African interior that were enjoying global circulation in the metropolitan newspapers of Europe and America,[11] and vernacular processes, such as the translation of John Bunyan's *Pilgrim's Progress* into isiXhosa in 1866,[12] as well as the consolidation of the Afrikaans Language Movement in 1875, which aimed to have Afrikaans legitimated as a language. By the twentieth century, with the increasing support for Afrikaans literature towards the creation of a national (white) literature, and the lack of resources given to the development of indigenous language literatures, the matter had become all-the-more knotted, and by the inauguration of apartheid in 1948, this tangle included both national and global ecologies, in equally disorienting ways.

Through a discussion of *Mhudi* and *This Island Now*, I hope to investigate how the entanglement of Beecroft's ecologies in the South African context might be understood if we take seriously recent calls to decolonize the national canon of South African literature, a canon that remains dominated by English and Afrikaans. I am drawing here on pedagogical and linguistic work of scholars such as Leketi Makalela, who argues that South Africa needs to engage an 'ubuntu

---

[10] Known as *ukubonga* and *izimbongo* respectively.

[11] Such as Nathaniel Isaacs's *Travels and Adventures in Eastern Africa: Descriptive of the Zoolus, their manners, customs etc etc. With a Sketch of Natal* (London: Edward Churton, 1836).

[12] See Isabel Hofmeyr, *The Portable Bunyan: A Transnational History of The Pilgrim's Progress* (Princeton: Princeton University Press, 2004).

trans-languaging' approach to the classroom, in which we appreciate that 'no one language is complete without the other'.[13] Elsewhere, I have applied Makalela's idea to a literary historiography of South Africa, asking the following question: 'Just as an Ubuntu trans-languaging is a necessity for the decolonised curriculum, I wonder what an ubuntu approach to literary form might look like. This would involve necessarily thinking through the complex ways in which written and oral forms, to mould Makalela's linguistic concept to the literary, are "not complete without the other".[14] This idea allows me to read the various ecologies of South African literature as co-constructive of what we can now retroactively posit as a national literature. This not only recuperates indigenous-language literatures for the literary canon – an obvious move in this case – but also puts into perspective the strategic use of English as a global language in the absence of an authentic national literature. Finally, the approach reads all the literatures of South Africa as co-constructive of one another, though obviously with varying power differentials, in such a way that allows us to think more precisely about how the compression of concurrent ecologies influenced the making of the South African canon.

Both of my selected novels illustrate a keen self-awareness of their complicated relationship to colonial history and its linguistic and literary residues. As such, we can read both novels as themselves telling a tale of their location and orientations in the world of letters: *Mhudi* negotiates the problem of the loss of local languages and literatures under the dominant cosmopolitan language and literature of English even as it reached outward to a world of letters. For this discussion, I will be taking up Beecroft's four ecologies of epichoric, panchoric, cosmopolitan and vernacular. In contrast, *This Island Now* engages the ecologies of cosmopolitanism and the nation, by highlighting the twisted temporality of writing a national literature from elsewhere. As such, the chapter picks up on the ways in which colonial and apartheid ideologies dislocated and disoriented South African writing in ways that still require us to rethink the geospatial logic of the very concept of South African literature.

---

[13] Leketi Makalela, '"Our Academics Are Intellectually Colonised": Multi-Languaging and Fees Must Fall', *Southern African Linguistics and Applied Language Studies* 36, no. 1 (2018): 2. 'In order to move away from "linguistic tribes" of the past, teaching African languages can be aligned with the African cultural and epistemological conception of being, ubuntu, which propagates a communal orientation and continuum of social, linguistic and cultural resources and denotes the interconnectedness of all human existence … "I am because you are; you are because we are"' (Leketi Makalela 'Moving Out of Linguistic Boxes: The Effects of Translanguaging for Multilingual Classrooms' *Language and Education* 29, no. 3 (2015): 214).

[14] Ashleigh Harris, 'African Literature as Indigenous History in South Africa's "Decolonize-the-Curriculum" Movement', in *The Routledge Companion to Indigenous Global History*, edited by Lynette Russell and Ann McGrath. Routledge (Forthcoming); Makalela, 'Our Academics', 2.

Writing South Africa into the world: Sol Plaatje's *Mhudi* (1930)

Sol Plaatje was not only the first black writer of an English novel in present-day South Africa, but also a key contributor to debates about the problem of English overwhelming and devastating local languages (in his case, Setswana), and of print culture accelerating this devastation. Plaatje was mission-schooled and worked in a number of different jobs engaged with language in some form or another (he was a teacher, translator, journalist and editor). Although he was a founding member of the political body that would later become the African National Congress (ANC), it is Plaatje's politics of language that is of greatest significance for this chapter. In the early 1900s, Plaatje embarked on an oral preservation project to collect, transcribe and translate Setswana proverbs, which he recognized as a dying cultural form in the face of print culture and English political and educational dominance.

Plaatje's anxiety about the diminishing of Setswana was justified, as can be illustrated in the reception history of his own writings. While his novel *Mhudi* and his account of the lived consequences of the 1913 Native Lands Act, *Native Life in South Africa* (1916), both written in English, have been firmly canonized, his concurrent oral collection project on Setswana proverbs and folk tales received little funding. Although the project resulted in two publications, *Sechuana Proverbs with Literal Translations and their European Equivalents* (1916) and *A Sechuana Reader in International Phonetic Orthography with English Translations* (with Daniel Jones, 1916), they have become relatively obscured historically. Jane Starfield bemoans the fact that the first of these publications, *Sechuana Proverbs*, remains 'under lock and key'[15] at the Africana library of the University of the Witwatersrand, where I myself examined the text thirty years after Starfield made her observation. Neither of these texts have been republished or enjoy wide circulation today.[16] As such, it is clear that the cosmopolitan language of English in the literary expression of the novel was bound to enjoy greater longevity than the oral tradition of proverbs and folk tales in Setswana. Even worse, as Deborah Seddon informs us, Plaatje's failure to

---

[15] Jane Starfield, 'The Lore and the Proverbs: Sol Plaatje as Historian', paper presented to the African Studies Seminar, University of the Witwatersrand, 26 August 1991, 1.

[16] A modernized version of Sechuana Proverbs is available as a pamphlet entitled *Other Proverbs of Sol Plaatje: The First Setswana Author*, ed. B. Malefo and D. S. Matjila (Kimberly: Sol Plaatje Educational Trust, 2010).

raise further funding for his project to archive Setswana oral literatures through the sales of *Mhudi*[17] and through requests to international and local funders (he repeatedly approached his own Chief for support),[18] means that '[we now] only have his letters as evidence for the significant body of Setswana orature he had collected to disseminate in print'.[19] The texts themselves are lost to history.

Also lost to history are four of the six translations of Shakespearean plays that Plaatje completed in Setswana. Plaatje mentions on his title page to *Diphosho-phosho*, a translation of *The Comedy of Errors*, that he had also completed other translations of Shakespeare's *Merchant of Venice* (*Mashoabi-shoabi*), *Much Ado About Nothing* (*Matsapa-tsapa a lefela*), *Julius Caesar* (*Dincho-ncho tsa bo Julius Kesara*) and others ('*Le buka tse dingoe gape*'). Of these, only *The Comedy of Errors* and *Julius Caesar* remain, and they, like *Sechuana Proverbs*, are available only as single copies in a few university archives. Yet the translations that remain and Plaatje's various accounts of his work of translation reveal something crucial about his efforts to use cosmopolitan form and the cultural capital of the English canon strategically for the purposes of both retaining a record of Setswana spoken arts and ensuring the future of the Setswana language in the face of colonial monolingualism.

Deborah Seddon emphasizes how and why Plaatje used proverbs in his translations of Shakespeare:

> Throughout the text of *Diphosho-phosho*, Plaatje employs Setswana proverbs; where appropriate, he translates Shakespeare's language into such indigenous idiomatic forms. Replete with his creative deployment of Setswana idiom, his translation thus both preserves and 'performs' the orature of his own language.[20]

Ndana Ndana, in his substantial analysis of how these proverbs are engaged in the translation, reminds us of the urgency of this work. Plaatje indicates in

---

[17] Plaatje notes in his preface to *Mhudi* that '[t]he book has been written with two objects in view, viz., (a) interpret to the reading public, one phase of the "back of the Native mind"; and (b) with the readers' money, to collect and print (for Bantu schools) Sechuana folktales, which, with the spread of European ideas, are fast being forgotten. It is thus hoped to arrest this process by cultivating a love for art and literature in the vernacular'. Plaatje, *Mhudi*, xi; cited in Ndana Ndana 'Sol Plaatje's Shakespeare: Translation and Transition to Modernity' (PhD diss., University of Cape Town, 2005), 158.

[18] Ndana, 'Sol Plaatje's Shakespeare', 187.

[19] Deborah Seddon, 'Written out, Writing in: Orature in the South African Literary Canon Author(s)', *English in Africa* 35, no. 1 (May, 2008): 138.

[20] Deborah Seddon, 'Shakespeare's Orality: Solomon Plaatje's Setswana Translations', *English Studies in Africa* 47, no. 2 (2004): 90.

his introduction to *Diphoshophosho*, that his key concern was the adulteration of the Setswana language by missionary schools and their orthographies[21] imposed by non-native speakers of the language.[22] These colonial interventions, argued Plaatje, were

> responsible for the deplorable fact that Sechuana is systematically 'murdered' in those schools where the vernacular is taught. The head teacher is usually the white missionary, who, even if a good linguist must, except in rare cases, have the accent and use the idiom of a foreigner, and the pupils invariably drop their mother's accent and speak the language 'as teacher speaks it.' In the course of time, when it is decided to impart the language through native tutors, the latter will be speaking a kind of 'School Sechuana' with accents varying according to their tuition, but all equally alien to native speech.[23]

As Ndana reminds us '[c]oncerns for the extinction of languages are real. It should be remembered that within Plaatje's lifetime, the Koranna language disappeared.'[24] The strategic translation of canonical English texts for the preservation of a vernacular (and its largely oral traditions) becomes a condensed site for understanding the ecologies of the epichoric, the cosmopolitan and the vernacular.[25] If we understand the Setswana oral proverb as an epichoric literary form and then see it reproduced in a printed vernacularization of a cosmopolitan text – in this case a Setswana translation of Shakespeare's *The Comedy of Errors* – the superimposition of these three ecologies in a single text becomes apparent.

---

[21] As Plaatje writes: 'One difficult point in regard to this language is presented by its different systems of orthography. These are five. We have firstly an Anglican spelling of Sechuana; secondly, a Congregational; thirdly, a Lutheran, and fourthly, a Wesleyan, besides the fifth spelling of Sechuana used by the Natives in their own newspapers.' *Sechuana Proverbs with Literal Translations and their European Equivalents* (London: Kegan Paul, Trench, Trubner and Co., 1916) 13; cited in Ndana, 'Sol Plaatje's Shakespeare', 174.

[22] In his introduction to *Diposhoposho*, Plaatje writes: 'It has not been an easy task to write a book such as this in Setswana: it has been both difficult and intricate. But we are driven forward by the demands of the Batswana – the incessant and shrill cries of people exclaiming, "Tau's Setswana will be of no use to us! It is becoming extinct because children are not taught Setswana! They are taught the missionary language! They will lose all trace of our language!" That is why we undertook to tackle this task.' *Diphosho-phosho* (Morija: Morija Press, 1930), ii, translation in Ndana 'Sol Plaatje's Shakespeare', 157.

[23] Plaatje, *Sechuana Proverbs*, 15–16; cited in Ndana, 'Sol Plaatje's Shakespeare', 175.

[24] Ndana, 'Sol Plaatje's Shakespeare', 158.

[25] The panchoric is relevant here, too, and equally entangled in the other three ecologies, insofar as the debate around the orthography of Setswana at the time was dominated by English and Afrikaans speakers who, among other things, considered a single orthography for isiZulu, isiXhosa and Setswana. Such standardizing impulses impose a panchoric stretch to the South African bantu languages.

To mention just one example discussed by Ndana: the final lines of Adriana's plea to her sister Luciana to marry appear in Shakespeare's text thus:

> But if thou live to see like right bereft,
> This fool-begged patience in thee will be left (II.1.40–41).

Plaatje's translation is: '*A ko nyaloe re ke re bone gore a u tla rua pelo telele ea gago e gompieno ekete telele-telele fela jaka telele ea kgomo*',[26] which Ndana translates as 'Marry so that we can see whether you will keep your long heart which presently is as long-long as the large intestine of a cow.'[27] Ndana goes on to explain Plaatje's play on the word *telele*: 'The word is used first as an adjective in the idiom "*rua pelo telele*/keep a long heart/be patient", and then repeated shortly for emphasis in "*telele-telele*/long-long". Lastly, the word is used as a noun in "*telele ya kgomo*/the large intestine/colon of a cow".'[28] Ndana offers an enlightening reading of the significance of the word *telele* in terms of how the themes of marriage and patience, here adapted to a Batswana cultural context, are evoked in the dialogue between Adriana and Luciana. What is of significance for my argument is that this vernacularization of Shakepeare's play entirely reworks it and is in no sense a direct translation (something that Plaatje warns us about in the preface to the play). As such, the cosmopolitan text becomes, I would argue, not only vernacularized, but returned to a smaller circle of distribution – one closer to the epichoric ecology than the vernacular one. The fate of Plaatje's *Sechuana Proverbs*, *Diphosho-posho* and his *Sechuana Reader*, all published in 1916 and all part of his strategy to preserve and extend the significance of Setswana, was indeed a return to almost zero circulation because they are now only available in a handful of copies in a few libraries. And Plaatje's attempts to use a vernacular strategy to bypass the ecology of the growth of a cosmopolitan literature ultimately failed, resulting in the stasis and eventual disappearance of these texts.[29]

What then of his English novel *Mhudi*? Must we read this novel as a surrender to the inevitable dominance of the cosmopolitan language of English? If we apply Beecroft's ecological thinking, *Mhudi* certainly appears to be just that given its very different reception-history to the fate of the texts published in Setswana. Yet,

---

[26] Plaatje, *Diphosho-phosho*, 10.
[27] Ndana, 'Sol Plaatje's Shakespeare', 162.
[28] Ndana, 'Sol Plaatje's Shakespeare', 162.
[29] It is interesting that Plaatje tried to mobilize interest in this project globally, too, as we see in a letter that he wrote to W. E. B. Du Bois on 19 December 1920, where he states: 'I have with me translations of Shakespeare's "Merchant of Venice" and "Julius Caesar" and "Comedy of Errors" which will be very readable to the South African Natives' (Brian Willan, *Sol Plaatje: A Biography* (Johannesburg: Wits University Press, 1984), 262; cited in Ndana, 'Sol Plaatje's Shakespeare', 186).

Mhudi, despite taking the ultimately cosmopolitan form of the novel, is a formally complex text: one which suggests that in the hands of a writer deeply committed to the preservation of his language and its cultural forms, the novel did not simply replace the epichoric oral forms of proverbs and folk tales that coexisted with the development of print culture and book distribution in Southern Africa. Isabel Hofmeyr has argued of the South African context that literary and oral traditions 'can never be neatly separated' and that 'the interaction of orality and literacy cannot be imagined as a straight, evolutionary line in which the written eventually triumphs over the spoken.' Indeed, she proves in her analysis of English written histories and Sesotho oral narratives of The Siege of Makapansgat that the two forms 'can never be neatly separated.'[30] The impossibility of separating, or providing a teleology for, the move from oral to print culture is a matter that troubles the ecologies of the epichoric, the cosmopolitan and the vernacular in the South African context since we see here epichoric indigenous forms altering the deep literary structure of the cosmopolitan form of the novel. As such, vernacularization is not simply about the strategy of engaging the cosmopolitan form to legitimate a vernacular but is also an adaptation of the cosmopolitan form to the local context in which the form circulates. To put this in the terms of this book, this is a reorientation back to the local.

Indeed, as a novel, *Mhudi* cuts a somewhat unexpected form. It is a novel ostensibly about its eponymous character Mhudi, but she disappears for much of the narrative as the narration of historical events overwhelms the development of her personal story. Structurally, the historical event of the Kunana Massacre, in which the Matabele attacked and decimated the Barolong, begins the novel and sets the stage for both Mhudi's and her husband-to-be's exile into the wilderness where they happen upon each other. The next section of the novel describes the happiness of the newly-weds and their eventual reintegration into Batswana society. Mhudi's husband, Ra-Thaga, befriends a Boer named De Villiers, whose people Mhudi openly despises because of their cruelty to their servants. De Villiers is ultimately involved in a successful plot to remove the Matabele king, Mzilikazi, and to force him northwards and out of the land of Ra-Thaga's ancestors, the Barolong. Ra-Thaga becomes a broker between the Batswana tribes and the Boers, and with the Boers' superior firearms, which the Matabele have never seen before, the mission is successful and the Matabele suffer enormous losses, including the son of Mzilikazi. Consequently, the Matabele withdraw to the north. Suddenly the novel returns us to Mhudi who, after a serious illness,

---

[30] Isabel Hofmeyr, 'We Spend Our Years as a Tale That is Told': Oral Historical Narrative in a South African Chiefdom (Johannesburg: Wits University Press, 1993), 12.

ventures out to find Ra-Thaga, fearing for his safety. This begins what reads as a new section of the novel, which returns us to the protagonists and their relationships with one another and takes its view away from the historical aspects of the conflicts between the Matabele and the Barolong. On the way to Thaba Nchu, where she will be reunited with her husband, Mhudi meets Queen Nandi, Mzilikazi's favourite wife, who has been exiled as a result of the jealous actions of his senior wife. Mhudi and Nandi also meet Hannetjie Van Zyl on their travels, a woman who proves to be the only trekker Mhudi trusts because she is kind. In an ending reminiscent of the impossible coincidences of a Shakespearean comedy, the three women all end up happily with their male equivalents in the text (Nandi returns to Mzilikazi in koBulawayo, where the Matabele have now settled), Ra-Thaga and Mhudi are reunited, and Hannetjie marries Ra-Thaga's good friend De Villiers. The novel ends with the image of Ra-Thaga and Mhudi returning to their homeland on a wagon given to Mhudi by De Villiers.

Part historical fiction, part character fiction, then, the novel also engages with Setswana oral traditions in interesting ways. Most obviously, the narration of the historical conflicts between the Matabele and the Barolong is a written and English transcription of, as Plaatje writes in his foreword to the novel, 'stray scraps of tribal history' that he had 'incidentally heard' of this history. Plaatje claims that he 'elicited from old people that the slaying of Bhoya and his companions, about the year 1830, constituted the casus belli which unleashed the war dogs and precipitated the Barolong nation headlong into the horrors described in these pages'.[31] Tim Couzens has published extensively on the historical aspects of the narrative,[32] but these specifics are less important to this argument than the fact that Plaatje used the novel form to transcribe these 'stray scraps of tribal' and oral history.

Furthermore, just as we saw in the case of Plaatje's translation of *The Comedy of Errors*, Setswana proverbs recur throughout the pages of *Mhudi*. These are usually introduced by clear marking phrases such as 'the proverb says'[33] or by placing the proverb itself in inverted commas (for example, 'Korannas argue that the life of the husband of a beautiful woman would "not be worth the value of a mouse skin"'), so as to clearly mark the shift from the free indirect discourse of the narrator to the proverb. For example, '[Ra-Thaga] recalled a Sechuana

[31] Sol Plaatje, *Mhudi* (1930; London: Penguin Modern Classics, 2006), xi.
[32] Tim Couzens, 'The Dark Side of the World: Sol Plaatje's *Mhudi*', *English Studies in Africa* 14, no. 2 (1971): 187–203; Tim Couzens, 'Sol Plaatje's *Mhudi*', *Journal of Commonwealth Literature* 8, no. 1, (1973): 1–19; Tim Couzens, Introduction to *Mhudi*, by Sol T. Plaatje, (London: Heinemann, 1978), 1–20.
[33] For example, see Plaatje, *Mhudi*, 191 and 192.

proverb which his comrade used to quote, viz., "Never be led by a female lest thou fall over a precipice". This proverb appears in *Sechuana Proverbs*, translated there as, 'Big game should never be led by the females, lest they fall over a precipice.'[34] What is particularly interesting about this novelistic inclusion of this particular proverb is the critical distance the novel allows for the use of the proverb. As Phaswane Mpe has argued, Ra-Thaga makes use of the proverb to ignore his wife's advice, which is a mistake.

> The proverb is set against hard facts so that the reader can perceive the naivety of vision of those who accept it. Men are, in a sense, the precipices over which they themselves fall, and it is Mhudi who is proved right. This proverb, whose purpose seems to be to reinforce and perpetuate the subordination of women, actually serves as a criticism in the hard fact that Mhudi is in many ways better than most male characters.[35]

Indeed, the entire narrative of *Mhudi*, as indicated by its title being the name of its female protagonist, counters this proverb. Yet, the narrative strategy Plaatje uses nevertheless enables its inclusion so that the novel archives it and part of the historical cultural values that went into its making.

There are numerous other proverbs in *Mhudi* that appear, too, in Plaatje's 1916 *Sechuana Proverbs*. This possibly explains why almost all of the proverbs in *Mhudi* are attributed to the Barolong characters and, as Mpe notes, 'Ndebele speakers in the novel seldom appear to use proverbs – or to use them properly.'[36] Given Plaatje's commitment to the preservation of Setswana, this is unsurprising, but the novelistic effect of this is that the Matabele are presented as people without history and without a strong sense of connection to their cultural past. Interestingly, a Zulu *induna* (or 'medicine man', as Plaatje puts it) makes use of a Setswana proverb when he says to the Matabele Queen Nomenti, '[y]our orders are confusing … They are uttered in two voices as from the cleft tongue of an alligator.'[37] The proverb corresponds to proverb 721 in *Sechuana Proverbs*: 'You have two tongues like a monitor', which Plaatje glosses with '*Varanus* of Cape Monitor, a terrestrial alligator with a bifid tongue.'[38] We could read this moment as an indication from Plaatje that proverbs circulated panchorically across different languages in the

---

[34] Plaatje, *Sechuana Proverbs*, 34 (Proverb 138).
[35] Phaswane Mpe, 'Sol Plaatje, Orality and the Politics of Cultural Representation', *Current Writing: Text and Reception in Southern Africa* 11, no. 2 (1999): 82.
[36] Mpe, 'Sol Plaatje', 84.
[37] Plaatje, *Mhudi*, 82.
[38] Plaatje, *Sechuana Proverbs*, 97.

region. Or, we could argue that the conversation between the *induna* and Queen
Nomenti, as narrated by Plaatje, is pre-structured by the proverb: that is to say,
the conversation leads towards its culmination in this proverb. If we develop this
second idea, one might suggest that the novel's form is deeply guided by Setswana
oral literature, not only because it includes historical narratives and proverbs, but
because it is structured towards elaborating the underlying cultural, psychological
and historical meanings behind these oral texts.

This idea can be substantiated by considering more carefully the role of
storytelling in the novel. Given Plaatje's statement in his foreword to the novel
that one of his ambitions with this novel was, 'with the readers' money, to collect
and print (for Bantu Schools) Sechuana folk-tales which, with the spread of
European ideas, are fast being forgotten',[39] it is perhaps no surprise that those
very folk tales emerge in and intersect the narrative structure of *Mhudi*. It is
worth keeping in mind that Plaatje published *Sechuana Proverbs* the same year
as he published *A Sechuana Reader in International Phonetic Orthography (with
English Translations)* with Daniel Jones, Reader in Phonetics at the University
of London. *A Sechuana Reader* includes fifteen short texts in Setswana, most
of which are folk tales, but which also include a song, a Socratic dialogue and a
translation of the Lord's Prayer. As he elaborates in his preface to this work, Plaatje
sees phonetics as the most reliable ways of preserving the Setswana language. He
expresses his hope here that a young generation of Batswana can learn through
phonetics the 'correct pronunciation of their mother tongue'.[40] What is also
striking about the folk tales Plaatje includes in *A Sechuana Reader* is that they
often elaborate or explain a proverb. For example, Folktale Six, 'Bulging Cheeks
are a Characteristic of the Cat Family', begins: 'This is a Sechuana proverb. It
originated in the following old story', after which follows a tale explaining the
proverb.[41] Just as these narratives then elaborate proverbs, I would suggest that
Plaatje's novel has just such a didactic structure. Once again, storytelling is not
only then included mimetically in the text, as we see when Mhudi is 'reminded
... of a tale that [she] had heard long ago'[42] and then narrates the story of a man
who saw the sun moving eastwards and died as a result. Rather, the novel itself
might be considered an exegesis on the oral texts that Plaatje wishes to preserve.

---

[39] Plaatje, *Mhudi*, xi.
[40] Sol Plaatje and Daniel Jones, *A Sechuana Reader in International Phonetic Orthography with English Translations* (London: University of London press, 1916), x.
[41] Plaatje and Jones, *A Sechuana Reader*, 10.
[42] Plaatje, *Mhudi*, 23.

This idea is axiomatic for Eileen Pooe who is the first person to be awarded a doctoral degree for a thesis written in Setswana. Her thesis, *Taoto ya Phetsolelo ya* Mhudi *ka Sol T. Plaatje mo Setswaneng jaaka mmusetsagae wa dikwalo tsa Maaforika tsa Seesimane* (October 2019) argues that *Mhudi* is a Setswana novel that must be repatriated, rather than translated, to Setswana for Batswana readers. Pooe's argument draws on the language politics of Plaatje and the fact, as I have discussed above, that his historical position required him to write this novel in English, even as he was desperately attempting to develop written Sestwana as a literary language. Hence, repatriation rather than translation. Indeed, given that so many of the proverbs cited in *Mhudi* appear in Plaatje's 1916 *Sechuana Proverbs*, it seems fair to suggest that the other proverbs he used were probably included in the second volume of *Sechuana Proverbs* that he was working on when he wrote *Mhudi*: 'the significant body of Setswana orature he had collected to disseminate in print' that Deborah Seddon notes has not survived.[43] While the translated and transliterated echoes of these proverbs in *Mhudi* are no replacement for the lost works, they may, at least, help us retrieve some proverbs from that incomplete work. And Pooe's argument about the novel's repatriation would allow the book to become a revived archive of those proverbs.

While Pooe's strategy of repatriation is a reorienting of Plaatje towards the located context of Batswana history and culture, we should not mistake this for a provincializing strategy. Plaatje's language politics was, almost to the book, one that can be understood as belonging to Beecroft's vernacular ecologies, which emerge

> out of cosmopolitan ones when sufficient cultural resources accumulate behind some version of a locally spoken language to allow for its uses for literary purposes. Vernaculars are often developed in the context of new political formations ... their emergence is frequently accompanied either by translations of canonical works from cosmopolitan languages or by texts I call "vernacular manifestoes".[44]

All the works I have cited of Plaatje's involve prefaces or forewords that can be considered as vernacular manifestos. A crucial point to note here, though, is that these manifestos are not only directed towards the speakers of the vernacular but are globally oriented insofar as they advocate the literary legitimacy of the vernacular to a cosmopolitan audience. Plaatje's extensive travels, his communications with key global thinkers and scholars, such as W. E. B. Du Bois,

---

[43] Seddon, 'Written out', 138.
[44] Beecroft, *An Ecology of World Literature*, loc. 697 of 7487.

and his emphasis on not only translating Setswana into English and English into Setswana, but on finding 'European equivalents' to Setswana proverbs, as well as finding African equivalents to European classics,[45] all suggest that his ambitions were cosmopolitan. As Beecroft states of the near impossibility of the limit-case of epichoric fiction, '[i]f one man is an island, it is all the more true ... that no culture is an island',[46] and this is certainly the case for Plaatje's Setswana literature.

Writing South Africa from the world: Peter Abrahams's *This Island Now* (1966)

By 1966, the apartheid state in South Africa was operating as an island, outside of the moral and political pressures mounting against it in the world. In this context, Peter Abrahams, often cited as the second black South African to write a novel in English (*Song of the City* from 1943), published *This Island Now*. While Abrahams's historical novel *Wild Conquest* (1950) made extensive use of *Mhudi* as a source text,[47] the connections between the two writers do not go much further than this. Abrahams's father was Ethiopian and his mother was 'coloured', which is to say of mixed ethnicity. Abrahams left South Africa in 1939 at the age of twenty and, while he returned for work, most specifically to research what would become his 1953 *Return to Goli*, he never returned to live in the country. Instead, Abrahams lived in London and Paris, and eventually settled in Jamaica where he lived until his death in 2018. As Kolawole Ogungbesan states,

> Because, unlike black African writers who followed him, he was not concerned about building up an indigenous reading audience on the African continent (a slow process, considering the problems of literacy, economics, and mass communication) he sought only to meet western literary demands and was hardly interested in traditional African aesthetics.[48]

Yet, one wonders what other options Abrahams had available to him as a writer in exile. I argue that his dislocation from South Africa did not mean that his

[45] For example, he writes, also in 1916, that 'Some of the stories on which ... [Shakespeare's] dramas are based find equivalents in African folk-lore.' Sol Plaatje, 'A South African's Homage', in *A Book of Homage to Shakespeare*, ed. Israel Gollancz (Oxford: Oxford University Press, 1916), 339.
[46] Beecroft, *An Ecology of World Literature*, loc. 1068 of 7487.
[47] See Michael Green, 'History, Nation, and Form in Peter Abrahams's "Wild Conquest"', *Research in African Literatures* 27, no. 2 (1996)and Michael Wade, *Peter Abrahams* (London: Evans, 1972).
[48] Kolawole Ogungbesan, 'A Long Way from Vrededorp: The Reception of Peter Abrahams's Ideas', *Research in African Literatures* 11, no. 2 (Summer, 1980): 188.

writings were not still oriented towards the country, but Abrahams's engagements with South Africa were, first and foremost, mediated by his close connections to the pan-African movement. During his time in London, Abrahams became friends with George Padmore, Kwame Nkrumah and Jomo Kenyatta. Andrea Thorpe examines the impact of Abrahams's involvement with these figures in the development of his pan-Africanist ideas.[49] Thorpe's argument looks at South African writing in London after 1948. She explains:

> By focusing on writing published after 1948, I am of course using as a temporal milestone the beginning of formal apartheid. Therefore, what these texts have in common is that they are a response to the apartheid context, displaced to a non-South African location that is a significant site of South African exile and emigration. London is read through apartheid, and vice versa. Apartheid obviously affected writers differently, depending most importantly on their racial classification under South African law, but also on the moment in which they wrote.[50]

As stated above, I too wish to consider 1948 as a historical fulcrum to set Plaatje's *Mhudi* (published eighteen years before apartheid) and Abrahams's *This Island Now* (published eighteen years after 1948) in productive dialogue with one another, even though Abrahams's text which is distinctly cosmopolitan in language, location, concerns and form, is a far cry from Plaatje's heavily located, though globally oriented, vernacular politics discussed above.

This historical balancing enables me to extend my argument of the collapsing of temporalities between Beecroft's ecologies of literature, this time extending the argument to include the national and global ecologies. Since apartheid legislation denied black South Africans the basic rights of citizenship, the very idea of nationhood was, of course, a deeply troubled one in that context. The consequent exile of many South African black writers meant that as apartheid South Africa was consciously nurturing its Afrikaans and English national literary canon, a dislocated national canon was being written elsewhere. Yet because of the dislocation of exile, the alternative national literature being produced elsewhere during apartheid by writers such as Lewis Nkosi and Es'kia Mphahlele, Alex la Guma, Can Temba, was also being produced, largely, in English and often addressed itself to a global (and also a distinctly pan-African) audience by virtue

---

[49] Andrea Susan Thorpe, 'Cosmos in London: South Africans Writing London after 1948' (PhD diss., University of London, 2016), 36.

[50] Thorpe, 'Cosmos in London', 19.

of taking the South African story out of isolation into the globe. This was all the more important because of the apartheid state's censorship laws, which actively suppressed these versions of life in South Africa in the country itself. As such, the non-authorized version of life under apartheid for black South Africans had to be, of necessity, written elsewhere.

Apartheid thus disrupted any simple or organic evolution from a vernacular literature to a national one (excepting non-political works in Afrikaans and English which clearly followed this pattern). Yet, if we take a closer look at Peter Abrahams's *This Island Now*, ostensibly about African decolonization and the burgeoning African nationalism of the 1960s, we can see how this pan-African reflection on nationalism can be seen as a literary comment on the national circumstances of South African apartheid. In the argument that follows, I illustrate how Abrahams uses his cosmopolitan and pan-African location to write a text that is deeply entangled in the national ecology of South African literature even as it is written from a different location. I would even argue that a truly national South African literature was of necessity dislocated to the global sites of exile until the end of apartheid in 1994.

This Island Now is set on a fictional island and begins with the death of President Moses Joshua, the 'Old Man', as he is known, who has headed the island's one-party state since the end of colonial rule. His death makes way for the presidency of the revolutionary, Albert Josiah, a man who seeks to end the debilitating poverty that most islanders live in. The title of *This Island Now* clearly plays with Caliban's famous statement, 'This island's mine', and its setting has been linked (if tangentially) to Shakespeare's *The Tempest*. Ogungbesan writes that 'Abrahams' nameless island is, like Prospero's, a microcosm of the world.'[51] The island as microcosm of the world here is distinctively the world of the 1960s. Ogungbesan goes on to explain that '[t]he problems which confront President Albert Josiah are more than those of a tiny island in the Caribbean; they are problems which face the whole of the developing countries in general and which have threatened to embroil the big powers in a global war.'[52] Indeed, the novel certainly posits the island as representative of the economic and political troubles faced by postcolonial nation states in the 1960s.

Furthermore, the Caribbean island in this novel is described as being a space in which 'a tiny white minority is in control of all the key areas of real power in

---

[51] Kolawole Ogungbesan, 'The Political Novels of Peter Abrahams', *Phylon* 34, no. 4 (1973): 426.
[52] Ogungbesan, 'The Political Novels', 426.

the land',[53] and, as a land of 'vast inequalities, such great gaps between those who have and those who do not' and in which 'whites who represent less than five per cent of the nation still control something like ninety per cent of its wealth'.[54] Thus, although formally postcolonial, the island is nevertheless still reminiscent of South Africa at that time. This neocolonial racial politics and economics is precisely what the revolutionary character, Albert Josiah, is at pains to resist in the novel. Since he is not the first democratically elected leader of the country, the nation's immediate past is less relevant to him than the living consequences of the colonial past, as we read in his thoughts on the matter:

> The lion does not lie down peacefully with the lamb. The exploiters do not suffer a change of heart and cease to exploit. The great powers do not suddenly discover a morality that tells them it is wrong to manipulate small countries and use their lands as bases and battlefields and their people as living targets in the power game of showing muscle. If this way is wrong then there is no way out for the peoples of the so-called underdeveloped world. The people of that other world were lucky; they had centuries in which to work out their institutions and to grow rich and strong and stable: and of course they had the resources of the underdeveloped world, human and material, at their ready disposal. And in spite of their lip service today they are still bent on exploitation: subtler and more sophisticated it is true, but no less real for that.[55]

Yet, Josiah, like Old Man Joshua before him, ultimately falls into the self-same logic of colonial governance, denying his people the most basic of all human rights: the right to vote. We read, 'at the beginning of the fourth and final year of Josiah's first term of office there had been a referendum and the people had voted – under pressure of a massive and vigorous party campaign – to suspend all further elections until the economic revolution was completed'.[56] The irony here, of course, is that Josiah becomes trapped in the very modes of power that he is attempting to challenge at a global scale. As such, the novel can be read as a rumination on what Achille Mbembe sees as the entangled time of the postcolony, which 'is not a series but an *interlocking* of presents, pasts, and futures that retain their depths of other presents, pasts, and futures, each age bearing, altering, and maintaining the previous ones'.[57] Mbembe's warning that

---

[53] Peter Abrahams, *This Island Now* (London: Faber & Faber, 1966), 135.
[54] Abrahams, *This Island Now*, 136.
[55] Abrahams, *This Island Now*, 268.
[56] Abrahams, *This Island Now*, 266.
[57] Achille Mbembe, *On the Postcolony* (Berkeley: University of California Press, 2001), 16.

the postcolony simply reiterates the colonial *episteme* of its forebears is very much Abrahams's warning to African statesmen of the time, too.

Furthermore, within the literary logic of the novel, the location of the island in *This Island Now* also operates as a heterotopic space, which is to say, as an entanglement of space and not only of time. 'The heterotopia', according to Michel Foucault, 'is capable of juxtaposing in a single real place, several spaces, several sites that are in themselves incompatible'.[58] Abrahams borrows a convention from the theatre in providing a description of the novel's setting. Though he is more specific than the description of scene offered by Shakespeare in *The Tempest* ('A ship at sea: an island'), Abrahams also maintains some vagueness about the setting.[59] He writes:

> *Time:* The present.
>
> *Place:* An Island in the Caribbean
>
> *Nature:* A novel, a work of fiction, in which all persons and places are figments of the imagination; but since the imagination is nurtured by reality the point of departure of this story is the reality of the Caribbean. Each reader is therefore at liberty to decide the particular island on which he or she wants this story played out.[60]

This description of place is specific enough, but the vagueness that creeps in with the direct challenge to the reader to 'decide the particular island on which he or she wants this story played out' stretches the context beyond the Caribbean, too. This stretch is even apparent in the title of the book, which is a quote, not from Shakespeare, but from W. H. Auden's 'Look Stranger'. Written in 1936, the poem is addressed to a stranger ('Look, stranger, on this island now') looking towards the shores of England ('Here at a small field's ending pause/Where the chalk wall falls to the foam'). Abrahams's pan-African background supports the claim that the unspecified island in *This Island Now* might be read across the Atlantic. With Ghana's independence in 1957 and Kenya's in 1963, Abrahams's novel clearly

[58] Michel Foucault, 'Of Other Spaces', *Diacritics* 16 (Spring 1986): 22–7.

[59] I have written elsewhere that 'the literature of decolonization had also found the trope of the island a particularly productive one, especially via the intertextual rejection and rewriting of Shakespeare's ur-text of the colonial encounter, *The Tempest*. In "Caribbean and African appropriations of *The Tempest*," Rob Nixon traces what is now a well-known trajectory of postcolonial appropriations of Shakespeare's play, from C.L.R. James's *The Black Jacobins* (1938), to George Lamming's *The Pleasures of Exile* (1960), to Aimé Césaire's *Une Tempête* (1969) and Edward Kamau Braithwaite's "Caliban" (as part of a cycle entitled "Islands", 1969)'. (Ashleigh Harris, '"The Island is not a Story in Itself": Apartheid's World Literature', *Safundi* 19, no. 3 (2018): 324; citing Rob Nixon, 'Caribbean and African appropriations of *The Tempest*', *Critical Inquiry* 13 (Spring 1987): 557–78.

[60] Abrahams, *This Island Now*, 7.

operates as a warning to his powerful political friends, Nkrumah and Kenyatta, to avoid the fate of the character Albert Josiah. Yet, if the book had been set in Africa, this critique of postcolonial power might have become interpreted as nothing more than a direct commentary on Nkrumah and/or Kenyatta. Instead, by locating his novel in the Caribbean, Abrahams drew out its black Atlantic and pan-African relevance in ways that de-territorialize his warning about postcolonial entanglements in the colonial episteme. We might also argue that this strategy draws attention to the impossibility of writing about national struggles against colonization and of the postcolonial future *in* (even set in) South Africa: by setting the novel in a heterotopic space, Abrahams dramatizes the absence of the nation his novel is oriented towards.

It is not difficult to stretch the significance of the novel to newly formed, postcolonial African nation states, but we have to attend to the text more closely if we are to extend this significance to Robben Island, where in 1966 three of the key leaders of the ANC, Nelson Mandela, Walter Sisulu and Govan Mbeki, sat incarcerated.[61] The context seems, at first glance, incompatible, given the strong hold the apartheid state had over South Africa in 1966, while the island in Abrahams's text is a postcolonial and independent nation. Yet, I wish nevertheless to consider Abrahams's decolonized island in relation to Robben Island, not to suggest a relationship of equivalence, but rather to show how the momentum of decolonization across the African subcontinent exacerbated the symbolic meanings of Robben Island in apartheid South Africa at the time. I have discussed elsewhere how islands were often configured during apartheid to operate as metonyms for Robben Island, which was in turn a strategy to highlight the absence of Robben Island in national discourse at the time:

> the apartheid state went beyond the standard security protocols regarding blackouts on images and information on their prison operations by also imposing a ban on images of its most famous inmate, Nelson Mandela. The island's distance from the mainland helped this process of effacing the abject and outcast space of the prison and its inmates from public and governmentally sanctioned discourse. ... A prison, especially one off the mainland, [provided an easy] site to achieve the sleight-of-hand that made its prisoners and everything that happened there disappear from public view and this invisibility enabled the rule of brutality with impunity there.[62]

---

[61] Indeed, the island's most famous inmate, Nelson Mandela, was moved there just two years prior to the book's publication, in 1964.

[62] Harris, 'The Island is not a Story in Itself', 323.

As such, Robben Island can be seen as the disavowed site of the South African national imaginary that held the entire scaffold of the apartheid myth in place. This disavowal, as with all the other suppressed and censored stories of the brutality of life for black South Africans under apartheid, required anti-apartheid writers to write Robben Island into the national discourse. Thus, to stretch Abrahams's text to cover the political and historical topography of Robben Island is to understand how the island in the novel operates as a heterotopia within a much larger set of pan-African, black Atlantic, global relations.

We get some evidence of Abrahams's intentions in this regard in *A Night of their Own*, published only a year before *This Island Now*. *A Night of their Own* was set in South Africa and more directly took up white anxiety about African decolonization. There, Abrahams addressed a white South African reader thus:

> Black rule may indeed be the terrible thing you fear. From the little we hear and read, it has not been all that terrible in other parts of Africa. But even if it were, because it would be majority rule, there would be hope for good.[63]

It is precisely such white fear that required proponents of apartheid to disavow the spectre of decolonization through myths of containment of this perceived threat. As such, the prison island at the furthermost point of the African continent, becomes a symbolic last frontier of colonial history. In Abrahams's novel, Josiah attempts to isolate his island from those economic and political factors that still exploit the human and material resources of the island. Yet, he finds himself recuperated into colonial flows, caught in a cycle of inevitable return, or of entanglement with the colonial past and the neocolonial present. Josiah is trapped not by the island, but by what surrounds it. This dynamic becomes apparent in *This Island Now* when the character Martha, wishing to claim the island's separateness from the world, says:

> You know, for us who are coloured and who are of the western world, who live in the western world, only this chain of islands is home. Once we leave these islands, we're outsiders. We're outsiders in continental America, in Europe, in Africa, in Asia. Our ancestors came from these great land masses but they are no longer home to us. And so we're outsiders even among those who are like us but who are not of these islands ... We are a new breed, a kind of outpost of the future.[64]

---

[63] Peter Abrahams, *A Night of their Own* (London: Faber and Faber, 1965), 237; cited in Kolawole Ogungbesan, 'The Political Novels of Peter Abrahams', *Phylon* 34, no. 4 (1973): 430.

[64] Abrahams, *This Island Now*, 181.

President Albert Josiah attempts, not unlike the apartheid government in South Africa, to enact Martha's sense of containing the islands, though in his case for political reasons. Seeing the press as 'the most potent weapon in the society, more powerful in its impact on the minds of men than anything else in the country,'[65] Josiah denies the islanders a free press and controls the flow of news media into the country from the rest of the world (a strategy distinctly reminiscent of South African censorship at the time). Yet, despite Martha's wish to create an 'outpost of the future' on the island, and Josiah's related wish to stand alone, outside the flows of colonial and apartheid history, the island is perpetually impacted by precisely these histories. As the historical Mandela sat incarcerated on a prison island, the fictional Josiah, free leader of a decolonized land, finds himself nevertheless incarcerated by his island's entanglements in global, colonial history and its aftermaths. What this means is that the novel not only is oriented towards postcolonial, pan-African nationalism, but also writes the apartheid condition into global history. Josiah remains, in some senses, as unfree as Mandela.

Josiah's urge to, like Martha, make the island an 'outpost of the future' is what keeps him incarcerated. Instead, *This Island Now* offers a cosmopolitan answer to national isolationism by highlighting the ways in which the pan-African world is caught up in global forces that continue colonial *epistemes* and economics. This seems to be the only option available to Abrahams in the absence of a valid national literature. While it was not possible in 1966 for Abrahams to address South African audiences, and because of the decimation of the literary vernacular imagined by Sol Plaatje, this cosmopolitan – even tentatively global – form was one of the only viable options for a black South African writer at that time in history. I suggest that the kind of repatriation required for a novel like *This Island Now* is to give it its place in the national canon of South African literatures, and to see it as indicative of the deferment and dislocation of the ecology of a national literature in that country during apartheid.

Conclusion

Sol Plaatje's *Mhudi* can be placed at the intersection between a cosmopolitan language and form (the English novel) and the process of strategic vernacularization of Setswana oral literatures. Indeed, Tim Couzens went so far

---

[65] Abrahams, *This Island Now*, 189.

as to argue that '*Mhudi*, completed ten years after [the founding of the] Union and eight years after the founding of the ANC, is an attempt to create in mythical and historical terms the first South African national epic.'[66] Peter Abrahams's novel, on the other side of the historical fulcrum of the start of apartheid, mobilizes the same cosmopolitan form (i.e. the English novel), based in a speculative space that might thus be considered to be a cosmopolitan location, to articulate the impossibility of a truly national literature of South Africa under apartheid. What we see in both novels is that colonial and apartheid history complicate the process of vernacularization that would, in Beecroft's account, constitute the basis of a national literature. While Afrikaans literature as a vernacular form was thriving in 1960s South Africa, the failures of the apartheid state to invest in the literary cultures of the rest of the country have had dire consequences, as discussed above in terms of lost translations and other publications by writers of Plaatje's calibre and importance. In a way these two novels dramatize the problem of this missing middle of vernacularization from two different historical perspectives.

This missing middle is, I argue, one of the consequences of colonialism and apartheid that continues to impress itself upon South Africa's national literature to this day. South African literary scholarship and publishing remains dominated by English and Afrikaans. Few comparativist approaches or university courses exist that bring a greater variety of South Africa's eleven national languages to bear on a shared historiography of South African Literature.[67] As such, with different literary traditions experiencing uneven and sometime asynchronous processes of social change, economic support and global spread, the ecologies of South African literatures have been entangled and overlapping. For example, Sol Plaatje's *Sechuana Proverbs* of 1916 is published at the same time as the Afrikaans Language Movement was consolidating its efforts to have Afrikaans recognized as a language and not simply a dialect of Dutch (this was only finally ratified in 1925). This concurrence of language politics had, however, by the 1960s become utterly bifurcated as Afrikaans was by then a national educational and cultural priority while indigenous languages received little to no structural support.[68] While the move from epichoric to national literatures can be seen to be compressed, and even overlapping, in the examples I have discussed, South Africa has not yet

---

[66] Tim Couzens, 'Sol T. Plaatje and the First South African Epic', *English Studies in Africa* 14, no. 1 (1987): 53.

[67] For a longer account of this problem see Harris, 'African Literature as Indigenous History'.

[68] Later still, in 1974, under the Afrikaans Medium Decree of 1974 that was instrumental to the events of the Soweto Uprising, indigenous languages were denied as media of instruction at schools.

articulated a national literature fully accountable to its multilingual literary past. My argument has been that this is because multilingual South African literature has not yet consolidated its various vernaculars on a national level. That is, of course, the work ahead for literary producers in the country. For literary scholars, if we are to seriously consider recent calls to decolonize the curriculum, perhaps the work to hand is to introduce methods that repatriate non-English and non-Afrikaans literatures more committedly to the national canon, dominated as it still is by these two languages. This cannot be seen as a nationalist exercise though: indeed, as this chapter has argued, a re-engagement of the South African literary canon will need to include the multiple locations and orientations of a body of writing that had a distinctly ambivalent relationship to the state.

Bibliography

Abrahams, Peter. *This Island Now*. London: Faber & Faber, 1966.

Abrahams, Peter. *A Night of their Own*. London: Faber and Faber, 1965.

Beecroft, Alexander. *An Ecology of World Literature: From Antiquity to the Present Day*. London: Verso, 2015. Kindle.

Couzens, Tim. 'The Dark Side of the World: Sol Plaatje's *Mhudi*'. *English Studies in Africa* 14, no. 2 (1971): 187–203.

Couzens, Tim. 'Sol Plaatje's *Mhudi*'. *Journal of Commonwealth Literature* 8, no. 1 (1973): 1–19.

Couzens, Tim. Introduction to *Mhudi*, by Sol T Plaatje. London: Heinemann, 1978.

Couzens, Tim. 'Sol T. Plaatje and the First South African Epic'. *English in Africa* 14, no. 1 (1987): 41–65.

Couzens, Tim. 'Moment in the Past: William Tsikinya-Chaka'. *Shakespeare 111 Southern Africa* 2 (1988): 60–66.

Foucault, Michel. 'Of Other Spaces'. *Diacritics* 16 (Spring 1986): 22–7.

Gray, Stephen. 'Sources of the First Black South African Novel in English: Solomon Plaatje's use of Shakespeare and Bunyan in *Mhudi*'. *Munger Africana Library Notes*, no. 37 (December 1976): 6–28.

Green, Michael. 'History, Nation, and Form in Peter Abrahams's "Wild Conquest"'. *Research in African Literatures* 27, no. 2 (1996): 1–16.

Harris, Ashleigh. '"The Island is not a Story in Itself": Apartheid's World Literature'. *Safundi* 19, no. 3 (2018): 321–37.

Harris, Ashleigh. 'African Literature as Indigenous History in South Africa's "Decolonize-the-Curriculum" Movement'. In *The Routledge Companion to Indigenous Global History*, edited by Lynette Russell and Ann McGrath. Routledge. (Forthcoming).

Hofmeyr, Isabel. '*We Spend Our Years as a Tale That is Told*': Oral Historical Narrative in a South African Chiefdom. Johannesburg: Wits University Press, 1993.

Hofmeyr, Isabel. *The Portable Bunyan: A Transnational History of* The Pilgrim's Progress. Princeton: Princeton University Press, 2004.

Isaacs, Nathaniel. *Travels and Adventures in Eastern Africa: Descriptive of the Zoolus, their Manners, Customs etc etc. With a Sketch of Natal*. London: Edward Churton, 1836.

Makalela, Leketi. 'Moving Out of Linguistic Boxes: The Effects of Translanguaging for Multilingual Classrooms'. *Language and Education* 29, no. 3 (2015): 200–217.

Makalela, Leketi. '"Our Academics Are Intellectually Colonised": Multi-Languaging and Fees Must Fall'. *Southern African Linguistics and Applied Language Studies* 36, no. 1 (2018): 1–11.

Mbembe, Achille. *On the Postcolony*. Berkeley: University of California Press, 2001.

Mpe, Phaswane. 'Sol Plaatje, Orality and the Politics of Cultural Representation'. *Current Writing: Text and Reception in Southern Africa* 11, no. 2 (1999), 75–91.

Ndana, Ndana. 'Sol Plaatje's Shakespeare: Translation and Transition to Modernity'. PhD diss., University of Cape Town, 2005.

Nixon, Rob. 'Caribbean and African Appropriations of *The Tempest*'. *Critical Inquiry* 13 (Spring 1987): 557–78.

Ogungbesan, Kolawole. 'The Political Novels of Peter Abrahams'. *Phylon* 34 no. 4 (1973): 419–32.

Ogungbesan, Kolawole. 'A Long Way from Vrededorp: The Reception of Peter Abrahams's Ideas'. *Research in African Literatures* 11, no. 2 (Summer, 1980): 187–205.

Pooe, Eileen Elizabeth. 'Taoto ya Phetsolelo ya Mhudi ka Sol T. Plaatje mo Setswaneng jaaka mmusetsagae wa dikwalo tsa Maaforika tsa Seesimane'. PhD diss., North-West University, South Africa, 2019.

Plaatje, Sol. *Native Life in South Africa Before and Since the European War and the Boer Rebellion*. London: P.S. King, 1916.

Plaatje, Sol. *Sechuana Proverbs with Literal Translations and their European Equivalents*. London: Kegan Paul, Trench, Trubner and Co., 1916.

Plaatje, Sol. 'A South African's Homage'. In *A Book of Homage to Shakespeare*, edited by Israel Gollancz. Oxford: Oxford University Press, 1916.

Plaatje, Sol. *Mhudi*. 1930. London: Penguin Modern Classics, 2006.

Plaatje, Sol. *Other Proverbs of Sol Plaatje: The First Setswana Author*, edited by B. Malefo and D. S. Matjila. Kimberly: Sol Plaatje Educational Trust, 2010.

Plaatje, Sol and Daniel Jones. *A Sechuana Reader in International Phonetic Orthography with English Translations (Padisi ya dinaane Tsa Batswana)*. London: University of London Press, 1916.

Schalkwyk, David and Lerothodi Lapula. 'Solomon Plaatje, William Shakespeare, and the Translations of Culture'. *Pretexts: Literary and Cultural Studies* 9, no. 1 (2000): 9–26.

Seddon, Deborah. 'Shakespeare's Orality: Solomon Plaatje's Setswana Translations'. *English Studies in Africa* 47, no. 2 (2004): 77–95.

Seddon, Deborah. 'Written out, Writing in: Orature in the South African Literary Canon Author(s)'. *English in Africa* 35, no. 1 (May, 2008): 133–50.

Seddon, Deborah. 'The Colonial Encounter and *The Comedy of Errors*: Solomon Plaatje's *Diphoshophosho*'. In *The Shakespeare International Yearbook: Volume 9*, edited by Graham Bradshaw and Tom Bishop, 66–86. London: Routledge, 2016.

Shakespeare, William. *The Comedy of Errors*. Translated by Sol Plaatje, *Diphoshophosho*. Morija: Morija Press, 1930.

Shakespeare, William. *Julius Caesar*. Translated by Sol Plaatje, *Dintshontsho Tsa Bo-Juliuse Kesara*, Johannesburg: University of the Witwatersrand, 1937.

Starfield, Jane. 'The Lore and the Proverbs: Sol Plaatje as Historian'. Paper presented to the African Studies Seminar, University of the Witwatersrand, 26 August 1991.

Thorpe, Andrea Susan. 'Cosmos in London: South Africans Writing London after 1948'. PhD diss. University of London, 2016.

Wade, Michael. *Peter Abrahams*. London: Evans, 1972.

Willan, Brian. *Sol Plaatje: A Biography*. Johannesburg: Wits University Press, 1984.

3

Dislocation in Ahmad Saadawi's *Frankenstein in Baghdad* and Hassan Blasim's *The Madman of Freedom Square*

Tasnim Qutait

إنني أؤمن بمستقبل الشعر العربي إيماناً حاراً عميقاً. أؤمن أنه مندفع بكل ما في

صدور شعرائه من قوى ومواهب وإمكانيات، ليتبوأ مكاناً رفيعاً في أدب العالم

— نازك الملائكة 'شظايا ورماد

In the introduction to her collection *Shaẓāyā wa-ramād* (Splinters and Ash, 1949), the Iraqi poet Nazik al-Malaika states that she 'believe[s] in the future of Arabic poetry fervently and deeply, and that it will propel itself forward, through the poets' power, talent, and abilities, to achieve an elevated place in the literature of the world'.[1] A proponent of the free verse movement, al-Malaika presents the future of poetry as phoenix-like, emerging from splinters and ash to orient itself towards the future, in this case associated with an orientation to the wider world. Al-Malaika's term is *adab al-'ālam*, literally 'the world's literature', which suggests the maximalist definition of world literature as 'all of the world's literature, without pronouncing on questions of quality and influence'.[2] Yet al-Malaika's belief that Arabic poetry will one day achieve an elevated place suggests that she sees this poetry travelling beyond a particular location to become *adab 'alamī*, or globally recognized literature. The claim to worldliness here positions itself within a particular geographical context while expressing an orientation outward, aspiring to a literature recognized as *'alamī* (global), which is not always distinct from the literature of *'awlama* (globalization, literally one-worlding).[3]

---

[1] Nazik al-Malaika, *Shaẓāyā wa Ramād*, 1949 (Beirut: Dār 'Awdah, 1971), 27.

[2] Theo D'haen, César Domínguez and Mads Rosendahl Thomsen, *World Literature Reader* (New York: Routledge, 2012), xi.

[3] Marie Thérèse Abdelmessih discusses this terminological tension in *Al-thaqāfa al-qawmiyya bayn al-'ālamiyya wa al-'awlama* (National Culture between Worldiness and Globalisation, 2006).

As this volume explores, the co-constitutive terms 'location' and 'orientation' are bound up with the uneven flows and disparities in cultural capital that construct the 'world' in world literature. Seven decades on from al-Malaika's prediction, Arabic literature is still peripheral in most accounts of world literature, if seen through David Damrosch's definition of world literature as 'literary works that circulate beyond their culture of origin'.[4] Though it would no longer be accurate to claim, as Edward Said did in 1990, that Arabic literature is 'embargoed',[5] the number of Arabic texts that achieve international prominence remains limited. The dilemma for the study of postcolonial literatures in a global context is, as May Hawas describes it, that 'the more postcolonial paradigms are widened, the less definitional force they have; and the more World Literature paradigms are generalised, the less political capacity it has'.[6] Recent critiques of 'comparative literature in its globalizing guise' [7] have noted how Eurocentric taxonomies such as the focus on a (single) national language highlight the inherent limitations of macro models. This production of the world in the image of globalization, the 'unworlding of the world'[8] in Pheng Cheah's phrase, underlines the need to theorize the term 'world' in world literature differently.

This chapter applies the conceptual pair orientation–location to an examination of how literary texts refer to temporal and geographical scales beyond the locations they represent: in laying claim to and representing one place, that place invariably becomes attached to locations elsewhere. Literature might therefore be described as a 'locality-producing activity' which, in Arjun Appadurai's description, is 'not only context-driven but also context-generative'.[9] The chapter examines two texts by contemporary Iraqi writers, Ahmed Saadawi's *Frankenstein in Baghdad* (2018)[10] and Hasan Blasim's short story collection *The Madman of Freedom*

---

[4] David Damrosch, *What Is World Literature?* (Princeton: Princeton University Press, 2018).

[5] See also, Hosam Aboul-Ela, 'Challenging the Embargo: Arabic Literature in the US Market', *Middle East Report*, no. 219 (2001): 42–4, https://doi.org/10.2307/1559255; Mustapha Marrouchi, 'Introduction: Embargoed Literature: Arabic', *College Literature* 37, no. 1 (2010): 1–10; Robyn Creswell, 'Is Arabic Untranslatable?', *Public Culture* 28, no. 3 (2016): 447–56.

[6] May Hawas, *Politicising World Literature: Egypt, Between Pedagogy and the Public* (New York: Routledge, 2019), 1.

[7] Karima Laachir, Sara Marzagora and Francesca Orsini, 'Multilingual Locals and Significant Geographies: For a Ground-up and Located Approach to World Literature', *Modern Languages Open* (September 2018): 19.

[8] Pheng Cheah, *What Is a World?: On Postcolonial Literature as World Literature* (Durham, NC: Duke University Press, 2015), 193.

[9] Arjun Appadurai, *Modernity at Large: Cultural Dimensions of Globalisation* (Minneapolis: University of Minnesota Press, 1996).

[10] Ahmed Saadawi, *Frānkishtāyn fī Baghdād: riwāyah* (Beirut: Manshurat al-Jamal, 2013).

Square (2009),[11] which both claim a communicable sense of place and generate orientations beyond their boundaries. Saadawi's title relocates the monster from Mary Shelley's *Frankenstein* to Baghdad in the aftermath of the 2003 invasion, while Blasim combines elements of magical realism and metafiction to represent the dislocating force of violence, war and dictatorship. Both writers juxtapose vernacular and cosmopolitan modes, introducing cosmopolitan non-mimetic genres and tropes to represent the dislocation of familiar geographies. These are texts which represent particular locations, often using vernacular language, a function of literature oriented towards local audiences. However, they are also texts about place becoming other, representing a location transforming and mutating, ranging far afield in order to produce an emotionally resonant map of dislocation. Through combining vernacular forms of language and style with cosmopolitan references, the writers generate a variety of orientations that I argue have been a factor in allowing these Arabic-language texts to travel beyond the region.

Arabic literature in the Anglosphere

The limited frameworks through which non-Western texts become intelligible as world literature can be elaborated through two frequently cited examples of Arabic literature entering the Anglosphere. The first is Abdelrahman Munif's *Cities of Salt* in 1988, which John Updike deemed 'insufficiently Westernised to produce a narrative that feels much like what we call a novel'.[12] This line is often quoted as an example of anodyne globalism suppressing local literary traditions, and remains relevant in a context where Arabic, as Shaden Tageldin suggests, has become an 'avatar of untranslatability'[13] for comparative studies. If Munif represents a text deemed too located to travel, the case of Alaa Al-Aswany's *The Yacoubian Building* (2002)[14] is an example of 'the emergence of Arabic bestsellers',[15] which impacts and is impacted by what is translated into the global anglophone market.

---

[11] Hassan Blasim, *Majnūn sāḥat al-ḥurrīyah: qiṣaṣ qaṣīrah* (Beirut: al-Mu'assasah al-'Arabīyah lil-Dirāsāt wa-al-Nashr, 2012).

[12] John Updike, 'Satan's Work and Silted Cisterns', *The New Yorker*, 17 October 1988, 117.

[13] Shaden Tageldin, 'Untranslatability', in *Futures of Comparative Literature: ACLA State of the Discipline Report*, ed. Ursula K. Heise (New York: Routledge, 2017), 234.

[14] 'Alā' Aswānī, *Imārat Ya'kūbiān* (*The Yacoubian Building*) (Cairo: Mīrīt lil-Nashr wa-al-Ma'lūmāt, 2002).

[15] Tetz Rooke, 'The Emergence of the Arabic Bestseller: Arabic Fiction and World Literature', in *From New Values to New Aesthetics. Turning Points in Modern Arabic Literature*, ed. Stephan Guth and Gail Ramsay (Wiesbaden: Harrassowitz, 2011), 201–14.

As Mourid Barghouthi describes it, 'in these strange days, the Arab writer chases after the opportunity to be translated so that his local value rises, as though he wants to be read by the English to be known by the Arabs'.[16] As this statement suggests, there are competing and entangled cosmopolitanisms involved in this process. Writers continue to aspire to wider regional readership within the Arabic literary cosmopolis, where, as Alexander Beecroft has discussed, Arabic has been preserved as 'a unified written language, based on the cosmopolitan language, valuing transnational solidarity over particularist nationalism'.[17] Understanding the value of the distribution channels of global publishing houses does not replace this regional cosmopolitan readership; instead, translation into English is assumed to have an amplifying effect on the regional level, as writing with an orientation towards the Anglosphere is a strategy to circumvent a sometimes inefficient Arabic publishing system.

The reconfiguration of contemporary Arabic literature under the pressures of globalization is impacted by two seemingly contradictory but in fact often complementary trends: on the one hand, the awareness that a certain level of familiarity helps to sell non-Western literature to a global audience, and on the other, a perceived need to defamiliarize the conventions of Arabic literary writing in order to speak to regional political and social realities. Hassan Blasim posits a particular sense of misalignment resulting from this political context in the following rhetorical question: '[h]ow can I write like [the medieval Sufi poet] Ibn Arabi about car bombs?'[18] This question reprises a long-standing debate about the effects of using the standard written forms of Arabic rather than vernacular forms (*ammiyya*) in literary writing, the critique being that the orientation back to classical forms and styles involves a distancing effect from the localities depicted.

Taking into account these developments, there has been a recent move in Arabic literary criticism against homogenizing representations of Arabic as 'a single language, spoken by one supra-nation, implementing a revered heritage'.[19] The attempt to redefine the field as inherently comparative seeks to renegotiate

---

[16] Mourid Barghouthi, *Ra'aytu Rām Allāh* (I Saw Ramallah) (al-Dār al-Bayḍā': al-Markaz al-Thaqāfī al-'Arabī, 2011), 144 (my translation).

[17] Alexander Beecroft, *An Ecology of World Literature: From Antiquity to the Present Day* (New York: Verso, 2015), 143.

[18] Marcia Lynx Qualey, 'Iraqi Novelist Defies Arab Critics', *Al Jazeera*, 27 May 2014, www.aljazeera.com/opinions/2014/5/27/iraqi-novelist-defies-arab-critics/

[19] Marie Thérèse Abdelmessih, 'Rethinking Critical Approaches to Arabic Comparatively, in a "Post" Colonial Context', *Interventions* 20, no. 2 (17 February 2018): 205.

the paradigms of comparative and world literature in relation to the regional context. This shift from the macro-language level of Arabic as a cosmopolitan unified language to a more located emphasis on the multicultural dimensions and particularities of language raises methodological questions, as Ayman El-Desouky among others has pointed out, about 'the circulation of concepts as analytic tools beyond (but also bringing along with them) their hermeneutic provenances'.[20] For example, Samia Mehrez's translation of Franco Moretti's genre-mapping into Arabic[21] invites us to think about how far the injunction to '[t]ake a form, follow it from space to space, and study the reasons for its transformations'[22] takes account of the alterity of language development, and how far the recognizability of genre defines intelligibility across borders. In the cases examined in this chapter, the use of genre becomes a strategy to represent the transformations of localities, referring to and thereby generating orientations to the world beyond. In what follows, I will first discuss how transcultural tropes of horror, a genre of mass consumption, have been used tactically in contemporary Arabic literature both to disguise political critique and, as a reviewer of Blasim's work puts it, to represent 'lived horror' (الرعب المُعاش [23]). I will then examine how the use of non-mimetic cosmopolitan modes has allowed Arabic literature to travel as examples of fiction that combine familiar genre forms and foreign content, and analyse how Saadawi and Blasim represent the consequences of war through a kind of affective realism, drawing on syncretic horror tropes to represent the dislocating and disorienting force of violence.

Global horror as dislocation

Postcolonial horror is constituted by its borrowings from global tropes, where symbols which may be semiotically overused in one context are repurposed in another. Horror as a mode is itself, as Ken Gelder describes, 'fascinated by circulation: one thing passing into another, mutating, even melting, identities

[20] Ayman A. El-Desouky, 'Beyond Spatiality: Theorising the Local and Untranslatability as Comparative Critical Method', in *Approaches to World Literature*, ed. Joachim Küpper (Munich: De Gruyter, 2013), 60.
[21] Samia Mehrez, 'خارطة الرواية: فرانكو موريتي وإعادة رسم التاريخ الأدبي' (Mapping the novel: Franco Moretti and the remaking of literary history), *Alif: Journal of Comparative Poetics* 34 (2014): 67–92.
[22] Franco Moretti, *Graphs, Maps, Trees: Abstract Models for Literary History* (New York: Verso, 2007), 90.
[23] Mustafa Deeb, 'نصوص مشبعت من الانتهاك (texts saturated with violation), *Ultrasawt*, 27 September 2017, https://www.ultrasawt.com/

along the way'.[24] While realism has been the dominant mode in contemporary Arabic fiction, writers have often turned to the fantastical as a mode of estrangement and as a disguise in contexts where writing which might be deemed political is risky. For example, Muhsin al-Musawi has discussed how Arab writers strategically use ambiguity to free expression, as 'the search for adequate strategies and models for characterization has to take into account the need to dupe or evade the censor'.[25] Referring to Musawi's work, Ferial Ghazoul reads the uncanny and the unhomely in Iraqi short stories which span half a century as 'both an aesthetic quest and a political camouflage'.[26] Horror, as Gelder notes, has a particular valence 'as a *critical* form … not always progressive, but nevertheless critically motivated (since something must always be "wrong" for horror to come into being)'.[27] In their analysis of peripherality in the world-literary system, the WReC argue that 'irrealist or catachrestic features' register 'the violent reorganisation of social relations engendered by cyclical crisis'.[28] Using irrealist modes, and in particular horror tropes, allows writers to represent the 'wrongness' of such violence while also having the benefit of disguising their critique of those in power.

When such irrealist forms travel beyond their contexts, their strategic defamiliarization through the use of non-mimetic genres can become a helpful marker of familiarity on the international stage. Too much familiarity in the postcolonial adaptation of 'low-brow' popular global culture is often seen as marking the loss of autochthonous modes, casting forms that are too recognizable as (doubly) minor, derivative and sensationalist.[29] However, familiar forms and genres can help texts circulate due to 'denationalised content [which] can be absorbed without any risk of misunderstanding'.[30] In recent translations of

[24] Ken Gelder, 'Global/Postcolonial Horror: Introduction', *Postcolonial Studies* 3, no. 1 (1 April 2000): 35.
[25] Muhsin Al-Musawi, *Postcolonial Arabic Novel: Debating Ambivalence* (Leiden: Brill, 2003), 258.
[26] Ferial J. Ghazoul, 'Iraqi Short Fiction: The Unhomely at Home and Abroad', *Journal of Arabic Literature* 35, no. 1 (2004): 1–24
[27] Ken Gelder, 'Global/Postcolonial Horror: Introduction', 35.
[28] Sharae Deckard et al., eds., *Combined and Uneven Development: Towards a New Theory of World-Literature*, Postcolonialism across the Disciplines 17 (Liverpool: Liverpool University Press, 2015), 72.
[29] For example, a reviewer of Mohammed al-Ibrahim's *Lockdown: Red Moon Escape* (2012) comments: '[w]hile it is intriguing to see the worldwide domination of the zombie film reach Arab cinema, in truth the region needs no real assistance from Western-orientated horror genres' asking why not instead turn to 'Arab ghosts – Djin'. Mark Adams, 15 April 2012, 'Lockdown: Red Moon Escape', *Screen*, www.screendaily.com/-lockdown-red-moon-escape/5041746.article. On the use of Western horror genres in postcolonial cinema, see Dan Hassler-Forest, *Science Fiction, Fantasy, and Politics: Transmedia World-Building beyond Capitalism* (London: Rowman & Littlefield International, 2016).
[30] Pascale Casanova, *The World Republic of Letters* (Cambridge, MA: Harvard University Press, 2004), 172.

Arabic fiction, there are efforts to adjust this ratio of strangeness and familiarity to facilitate recognizability while suggesting newness. A notable example is Comma Press's translation imprint, which has worked with Arabic short story writers to produce anthologies ranging from Iraqi and Palestinian science fiction to 'banthologies', fiction from the nations under the label 'Muslim ban'. These collections are commissioned by and born straight into the anglophone market, rather than being 'born translated' in Rebecca Walkowitz's sense of writing made for almost simultaneous publication across languages.[31] Translations of shorter texts in particular have paved the way for accessible Arabic fiction through strategic titles, and both Blasim and Saadawi have benefited from a strategy of translating short texts under genre headings. Blasim's first translated story appeared in the Comma Press anthology *Madinah: City Stories from the Middle East* (2008), while Saadawi has a short story in the collection *Baghdad Noir* (2018) from Akashic Books' noir series, and an extract of *Frankenstein in Baghdad* appears in *Beirut 39: New Writing from the Arab World* (2010). As these titles suggest, world literature here is the literature of major cities, locations combined with familiar markers or key words (new writing, city stories, noir) which serves to orient the text towards a Western audience.

The two texts I focus on here emerge from different but overlapping ecosystems, to use Beecroft's terminology.[32] Blasim's unusual route to literary success exemplifies the dynamics of cosmopolitan and vernacular ecologies. Now living in Finland, Blasim first published his stories in Arabic on the website iraqstory. com, where some of his writing is still accessible. Reading through the stories on this website is a reminder of how online spaces can offer alternative platforms for what often falls into an 'analytical vacuum' between heterogeneous cultural forms and 'homogenizing mediations of Arab cultures'.[33] Blasim's writing reacts against the conventions of literary writing, and especially the sustained use of Classical Arabic (CA, *fuṣḥā*), which he regards as too removed for his themes. Although Blasim himself mostly writes in modern standard Arabic (MSA), he also uses elements of *'ammiyya* (vernacular) which are not always restricted to dialogues as conventional.[34] Perhaps even more than the vernacular language,

---

[31]　Rebecca L. Walkowitz, *Born Translated: The Contemporary Novel in an Age of World Literature* (New York: Columbia University Press, 2017).

[32]　Beecroft, *An Ecology of World Literature*.

[33]　Anastasia Valassopoulos et al., *Arab Cultural Studies: History, Politics and the Popular* (New York: Routledge, 2013), 16.

[34]　On *'ammiya* (Arabic dialects) and the vernacular, see Shaden M. Tageldin, 'Beyond Latinity, Can the Vernacular Speak?', *Comparative Literature* 70, no. 2 (2018): 114–31.

however, Blasim's use of unconventional structure and imagery deemed incoherent or vulgar proved an obstacle for Arabic publishing houses.[35] His stories were therefore first published in book form when they were translated into English. Two short story collections, *The Madman of Freedom Square* (2009) and *The Iraqi Christ* (2013), have thus far appeared through Comma Press, and stories from both works were published in the USA as *The Corpse Exhibition* (2014). Since then, two further works have been published in Arabic. However, Blasim remains better known in translation, and the fact that he has been described as 'perhaps the best writer of Arabic fiction alive'[36] indicates a level of unfamiliarity with the Arabic literary scene which decontextualizes his experimental writing. His success suggests the marketability of what is considered subaltern or emergent, in particular when framed as a controversial subversion of local conventions.

Saadawi, as a writer based in Baghdad whose works circulated first in a national ecology, exemplifies the dynamics of world literature as a refracted national literature, with the added familiarity of the horror genre. His novel *Frankenstein in Baghdad* was the first example of genre fiction to win the IPAF (International Prize for Arabic Fiction), achieving a regional audience and guaranteeing its translation into English (access to global audiences being equated primarily to the anglophone market).[37] Saadawi's attention-grabbing title seems to encapsulate a world literature constituted through combining a marker of location with a marker of the text's orientation beyond that location. The novel was shortlisted for the Man Booker international prize and its publication in English was strategically linked to the 200th anniversary of the publication of *Frankenstein* – although, as reviewers of the English translation have almost invariably pointed out, and as I will discuss later, the novel does not provide the retelling it promises.

On the anglophone market, Iraqi literature becomes the 'other side' to Western cultural representations of Iraq in the wake of the 2003 invasion.[38] It is instructive

---

[35] Although since Blasim's collections were published in Arabic, they have mostly received a positive reception, this is not comparable to the attention he has received outside the region. Some of his works have been subject to censorship, in particular the collection *Ṭifl al-Shīʿa al-Masmūm* (The Shia's Poisoned Child).

[36] Robin Yassin-Kassab, 'Beirut 39: New Writing from the Arab World', *The Guardian*, 11 June 2010, www.theguardian.com/books/2010/jun/12/beirut-new-writing-arab-world.

[37] The IPAF, established in 2007, is supported by the Booker Foundation and the Emirates Foundation. Similar to the Saif Ghobash Banipal Prize for Arabic Literary Translation, established in 2005, the IPAF was primarily set up to encourage publishers to translate from Arabic and focuses on contemporary literature.

[38] A recent example of Iraqi locality refracted through a global frame is the film *Mosul* (2019), set during the battle to liberate the city of Mosul from the Islamic State. Produced by the Russo brothers, who also produced *Avengers: Endgame*, *Mosul* was marketed as presenting voices attuned to that location, featuring actors speaking in Iraqi dialects.

to compare the translation sales of *Frankenstein in Baghdad* with the other novel by an Iraqi writer nominated for the IPAF in the same year: *Ṭashshārī* by Inaam Kachachi, which has a title in Iraqi dialect.[39] Kachachi, who lives in France, won the Prix de la Littérature Arabe for this novel, which was translated as *Dispersés* (2016) by François Zabbal. However, by far her most widely translated work is one which signals another geography: *Al-Ḥafīda al-Amīrikīya* (The American Granddaughter, 2010),[40] the story of an Iraqi-American woman returning to her homeland to serve as a military translator during the 2003 invasion. The thematization of translation in this text is connected with its production of location as a site of encounter, set in Iraq but gesturing elsewhere even in its title, which has impacted its translatability.

This framing of Iraqi literature as educating Western readers about Iraqi perceptions of the war extends to publicity events. For example, when Blasim's *The Corpse Exhibition* was published, Blasim was invited to appear in a panel discussion with US Marine veteran and author Phil Klay. Reviews often compare post-2003 Iraqi literature with American fiction about the war. In one case, a review of *Frankenstein in Baghdad* notes the affectless tone of the translation, suggesting turning to 'Kevin Powers' Iraq war novel *The Yellow Birds* for conflict's pity and terror' since Saadawi's novel 'amounts to an appalled and baffled shake of the head.'[41] In the reviewer's account, Saadawi appears to be the more distant observer, while Powers's novel provides the literary exposition of war more familiar to Western readers. There are particular expectations of what an Iraq war novel should look like, and Saadawi's '[a]bsurdist morality fable meets horror fantasy'[42] does not fully meet those expectations in that its tone fails to conform to established associations relating to the pity and terror of war. Instead, the expected affects are located in Saadawi's use of the horror genre.

In order to succeed on the international market, it seems, translated Iraqi fiction about the war must promise a certain emotional register. Literary texts from Iraq are eased into global circulation through connecting affect and genre, as is exemplified by this blurb to the anthology *Iraq + 100*, which was edited by Blasim:

---

[39] *Ṭashshārī* (Beirut: Dār al-Jadīd), 2014. As the IPAF website defines it, Tashari is 'an Iraqi word referring to a shot from a hunting rifle which is scattered in several directions. Iraqis use it as a symbol of loss and being dispersed across the globe', www.arabicfiction.org/en/Tashari

[40] Inaam Kachachi, *Al-Ḥafīda al-Amīrikīya* (Beirut: Dār al-Jadīd, 2008).

[41] Sarah Perry, '*Frankenstein in Baghdad* by Ahmed Saadawi Review – Strange, Violent and Wickedly Funny', *The Guardian*, 16 February 2018, www.theguardian.com/books/2018/feb/16/frankenstein-in-baghdad-by-ahmed-saadawi-review.

[42] Perry, '*Frankenstein in Baghdad*'.

> In a calm and serene world, one has the luxury of imagining what the future might look like. Now try to imagine that future when your way of life has been devastated by forces beyond your control. *Iraq + 100* poses a question to Iraqi writers (those who still live in that nation, and those who have joined the worldwide diaspora): What might your home country look like in the year 2103, a century after a disastrous foreign invasion? Using science fiction, allegory, and magical realism to challenge the perception of what it means to be "The Other", this groundbreaking anthology edited by Hassan Blasim contains stories that are heartbreakingly surreal, and yet utterly recognizable to the human experience.[43]

Here the text's accessibility beyond its location is identified with its thematization of violence as dislocation, alongside genre markers guaranteeing the themes the Western cosmopolitan reader might expect. When Blasim's *Corpse Exhibition* is blurbed as a 'pageant of horrors', the label 'horror' signals not only genre but the themes expected from contemporary Iraqi literature. In the context of an endless war on terror and ever-impending ecological crisis, the rapid expansion of critical work relating to insecurity, vulnerability and precarity has provided a theoretical toolbox to engage with these issues. Terms relating to insecurity are replacing, or combining with, the terms which constitute what Waïl Hassan has called a 'canon of postcolonial-literature-as-world-literature' which 'inscribes "writing back", Diaspora, migrancy, border-crossings, inbetweenness, and hybridity as the defining features of the "postcolonial condition".[44] Blasim's migrant horror stories and Saadawi's Iraqi retelling of *Frankenstein* converge in occupying an overlapping area between these frameworks. While they offer the reader an insight into the particularities of the locations they represent, their use of non-mimetic modes borrowing from horror and dystopia represents an orientation outward. For an international readership, the use of familiar genre tropes may reinforce expectations about an already anarchic world, confirming the idea of post-2003 Baghdad as already dystopian, staging the extremes of anarchy experienced elsewhere across the globe. However, for regional readers, the departure from conventional realism approximates rather a sudden dislocation from normality, breaking apart a coherent sense of locality through multiple, contradictory reference points to elsewhere.

The multiple cultural references in these texts return us to Blasim's question about the misalignment of Arabic literary conventions and the dislocating force of violence. While years of dictatorship has meant that violence is a pervasive

[43] *Iraq + 100: Stories from a Century after the Invasion* (Manchester: Comma Press, 2016).
[44] Valassopoulos, *Arab Cultural Studies*.

theme in modern Arabic literature, narratives about Iraq after the occupation have been particularly concerned with the inadequacy of mimetically-oriented narratives to represent and claim a once familiar location. Many Iraqi writers have therefore turned to the most located form, the body, as a terrain for exploring geopolitical forces that act on and through location. For example, Haytham Bahoora has discussed how 'the body's violent dismemberment and mutilation' becomes a way for Iraqi writers to 'narrat[e] a terrain of unspeakable violence'.[45] Similarly, Ikram Masmoudi discusses how 'the Iraqi novel has become a representation of the manifestation of sovereign power':

> one is struck by the references to death, killing, madness and loss, all in connection with Iraq itself – for example, *Amwāt Baghdād* (The Dead of Baghdad), *Mashraḥat Baghdād* (The Morgue of Baghdad), *Frānkishtāyn fī Baghdād* (Frankenstein in Baghdad), *Majānīn Būkā* (The Madmen of Camp Bucca), *al-Minṭaqa al-Khaḍrā* (The Green Zone), *Qatala* (Killers), *Ḍayāʿ fī Hafir al-Bāṭin* (Loss in Hafr al-Bāṭin) and many others ... Iraq and especially Baghdad appear to be a death world where thanatopolitics, war and killing are omnipresent.[46]

These novels locate their topics in their titles, many claiming a specific geographic territory. However, that specific location expands outward, spatially and temporally, through universal terms which interlink place with its loss, with madness and death. As Elaine Scarry describes, '[w]ar is relentless in taking for its own interior content the interior content of the wounded and open human body'.[47] In contemporary Iraqi fiction, the impact of war is represented through non-mimetic forms which convey the destruction of coherence of location and, concomitantly, of where the text orients itself. In Diaa Jubaili's novel *Márquez's Curse* (2007), for example, a draft of a novel is found written in code in the ruins of a post office, ready to be posted, but without address or recipient: in other words, the unreadable text is found in a destroyed location and lacks any perceivable orientation. As the title suggests, Jubaili, like Blasim, turns to magic realism in

[45] Haytham Bahoora, 'Writing the Dismembered Nation: The Aesthetics of Horror in Iraqi Narratives of War', *Arab Studies Journal* 23, no. 1 (Fall 2015): 184–5.

[46] Ikram Masmoudi, *War and Occupation in Iraqi Fiction* (Edinburgh: Edinburgh University Press, 2015), 2.

[47] Elaine Scarry, *The Body in Pain: The Making and Unmaking of the World* (Oxford: Oxford University Press, 1985), 81. This strategy of embodied horror, its abstraction and translatability, is evident also in recent translated Syrian fiction: compare Iraqi poet Dunya Mikhail's collection *The War Works Hard* (2005) with Syrian writer Khaled Khalifa's *Death is Hard Work* (2016). Embodied horror does not necessarily provide enough ambiguity for the censors however: Aḥmad Zaʿtari's *al-Inḥināʾ ʿala juththat ʿAmmān* (Bowing over the corpse of Amman, 2014), was banned for some time in Jordan for supposedly inciting violence.

this novel in order to convey the destruction of coherence, using the symbolism of the destroyed post office and the unaddressed letter to speak in metafictional terms about the inability to represent the scale of destruction in Iraq.

There is a recognition on the part of Iraqi writers that the use of such non-mimetic forms might be understood as a conscious orientation beyond the region. For example, Blasim has addressed the issues of style and genre and their implications for audiences, reporting that when he is told "'[y]our style is magical realist like Marquez'", he replies: "'No, I write nightmare realism.' And they nod, mm-hmm, and write in the newspapers: "nightmare realism'".[48] Here, Blasim reflects somewhat ironically on the need for epistemic frames in order to translate the culturally other. As I will discuss in more detail later, the strategic use of magic realism in Blasim's writing is interrelated with his thematization of violence, which invites critical readings using conceptual frameworks of biopolitics and ecocriticism,[49] as well as madness and trauma.[50] Saadawi's text meanwhile has been read as representing the unliveable lives created through 'combined and uneven development'[51] and inverting US narratives of biomedical salvation.[52] These readings demonstrate how non-Western texts can acquire relevance through connecting localized crises to a globalized sense of insecurity. As I now turn to the texts, I will discuss how Blasim and Saadawi's use of these non-mimetic modes becomes a strategy to represent dislocation: how, in other words, their representation of the coherence of location falling apart is made possible through an orientation outward.

Relocating *Frankenstein* into Baghdad

Frankenstein in Baghdad is set between 2005 and 2006 and opens with the scene of a car bombing 'swallowing up the surrounding cars and the bodies inside them, cutting electricity lines and killing birds, shattering glass and collapsing doors, cracking the walls of nearby homes and collapsing the old roofs of al-Batawin,

---

[48] Johanna Sellman and Margaret Litvin, 'Hassan Blasim: Interview for Tank Magazine', *Tank Magazine* 8, no. 9, https://tankmagazine.com/issue-69/talk/hassan-blasim

[49] Rita Sakr, 'The More-than-Human Refugee Journey: Hassan Blasim's Short Stories', *Journal of Postcolonial Writing* 54, no. 6 (2018): 766–80.

[50] Khaled Al-Masri, 'An Enchanted Ring and a Dung Beetle: Contaminated Borders in Hassan Blasim's Nightmarish Narratives', *Middle Eastern Literatures* 21, no. 2–3 (2018): 115–33.

[51] Sinéad Murphy, '*Frankenstein in Baghdad*: Human Conditions, or Conditions of Being Human', *Science Fiction Studies* 45, no. 2 (2018): 273–88.

[52] Annie Webster, 'Ahmed Saadawi's *Frankenstein in Baghdad*: A Tale of Biomedical Salvation?', *Literature and Medicine* 36, no. 2 (2018): 439–63.

all in one moment.'[53] Following this scene of carnage, the novel departs from verisimilitude as though this undoing of location cannot be contained in a mimetic frame. Frankenstein in Saadawi's rendering is the junkdealer Hadi al-Attag. Hadi visits bombing sites, picking up body parts which he then reconstructs into a body 'so it wouldn't be treated as rubbish ... and given a proper burial.'[54] After the corpse is assembled, the monster is reanimated during a storm and disappears into the city where he proceeds to seek vengeance for the victims/body-parts that construct his body. The rest of the novel is loosely structured around the security services hunting down the monster, who is absent for much of the text. Instead, the narrative follows subplots involving various characters from the elderly 'madwoman' Elishva, whose son disappeared during the Iran–Iraq war; the real estate agent Faraj, busy profiteering from property abandoned during the war; and Mahmoud al-Sawadhi, a journalist working to determine the cause of the latest spate of brutal killings. The narrative tension expected of a horror novel frequently dissipates in metaphysical conversations between the monster and the symbolic accomplices who aid his mission. In an interview with France 24 Arabic, Saadawi describes how he built the novel on five layers of political realism, horror, detective fiction, fantasy and metaphysical narrative.[55] Saadawi describes this last aspect as central, however the symbolic references around the saviour figure is also the layer that proved the most untranslatable, involving religion and narratives tied to location which are in tension with the more globally familiar genres.

Saadawi's use of different genres creates a somewhat disjointed narrative only loosely held together by the use of Frankenstein's monster as an allegory for the fragmented national body. The monster is initially unnamed, until Elishva calls him Danyal, mistaking him for her returned son. At this point, he is reanimated, resurrected as a composite of fragments which makes him the 'first true Iraqi citizen.'[56] This use of the monster as a symbol to think with is also metafictionally embedded in the text. As Saadawi explains, his intention was not a retelling but rather to invoke 'the vast cultural space that is called "Frankenstein".'[57] In fact, the title shifts during the novel from the paratextual level to a recognizable name to the rumours about such a monster. The creature is renamed Frankenstein's

[53] Ahmed Saadawi, *Frankenstein in Baghdad* (New York: Penguin Books, 2018), 25.
[54] Saadawi, *Frankenstein in Baghdad*, 25.
[55] France Arabic 24, أحمد السعداوي: نحن جميعا مساهمون بالقتل (We are all contributing to the killing), 25 October 2016, Youtube Video, 8:59, www.youtube.com/watch?v=DJJMciOsW30
[56] Saadawi, *Frankenstein in Baghdad*, 147.
[57] Marcia Lynx Qualey, 'Baghdad Writes!', *ArabLit* (blog), 30 April 2014, https://arablit.org/2014/04/30/baghdad-writes/.

monster by the media; a German journalist comments that Hadi had 'stolen his story from a Robert de Niro film'[58] referencing Kenneth Branagh's 1994 adaptation. The monster is therefore not only derivative, but removed from the original, a recycling of an overused symbol. The name Al-Attag (pedlar or junk dealer) suggests this recycling of material. However, this meaning is contrasted with Hadi's first name, meaning the guide/saviour, who joins discarded parts into a new whole. This suturing of parts onto one another is also the work Saadawi himself is performing in bringing together genres, splicing horror onto thriller onto metaphysical religious narratives to tell his story.

When Hadi speaks about the monster he created, he is referred to as 'playing the role of the old storyteller'.[59] Significantly, Saadawi uses a specifically Iraqi term, *alqaṣkhūn*,[60] to refer to the dying profession of the storyteller (referred to elsewhere in the region as the *ḥakawātī*). The vernacularization of Shelley's text is embedded in the language: while the international media sees the monster as a borrowed *Frankenstein* story, Hadi has his own name for his creation, calling him *shesma*, (شسمه) a contracted dialect word for an object whose proper name is forgotten (literally 'what-is-his-name'; Jonathan Wright translates this as 'whatsitsname', perhaps with Rushdie's *Midnight Children* in mind). According to Saadawi, this (un)naming signifies the monster as an amalgam or everyman representing national complicity in the post-invasion violence. The monster, already unnamed in Shelley's text, here becomes named as unnameable, a thing whose proper name is forgotten, which speaks to the need to find new names to represent the remains left after the carnage. By the end, the monster has taken to random killings to reconstitute his own disintegrating body, an imbrication in the violence that complicates the symbolism of a cosmopolitan monster recast as postcolonial or vernacular avenging figure. The novel relocates a monster from the Western canon to represent a Baghdad that has become unrecognizable to its inhabitants. Notably, Saadawi's recycling of Frankenstein's monster, and its reconfiguration as the *shesma*, proved to have regional resonance. The author has described how 'after many Arab readers read it, they said Frankenstein in Damascus, Frankenstein in Sanaa, Frankenstein in Cairo'.[61] The juxtaposition of a global horror icon and the city in the title clearly contributed to the novel's

---

[58] Saadawi, *Frankenstein in Baghdad*, 19.
[59] Saadawi, *Frankenstein in Baghdad*, 112.
[60] *Frānkishtāyn fī Baghdād*, 131.
[61] France Arabic 24, ‏نحن جميعا مساهمون بالقتل‎ :‏أحمد السعداوي‎ (Ahmed Saadawi: We are all contributing to the killing), 25 October 2016, Youtube Video, 6:00, https://www.youtube.com/watch?v=DJJMciOsW30

regional circulation, suggesting that cosmopolitan modes do not necessarily subsume the national.

While the title locates the novel in Baghdad, most of Saadawi's novel is more specifically set in Bataween, a working-class, multi-religious and ethnically diverse neighbourhood, once home to migrants especially from Sudan and Egypt. The text includes real aspects of the urban landscape, and the translator has described using Google Maps to ensure an accurate portrayal. Saadawi details the demographic and structural changes Batawween underwent in the first few years after the war, including the return of 'dead people … emerg[ing] from the dungeons of the security services'.[62] The allegory of a monster returning from the dead plays out in this real space and time of rapid transformation.

Saadawi's use of *Frankenstein* is interlinked with his representation of how violence transforms location, using Hadi's monstrous creation to represent a compression of time and space. Notably in the final act of renaming, the monster is identified as 'Criminal X' by authorities located within the Green Zone. Within this microcosm of globalization, the feasibility of the nation is rearticulated, and the aspects which mark the failed state, such as informal structures and dysfunctional institutions, serve to consolidate the power of the elite. Once the journalist Mahmoud is able to access the secluded world beyond the Green Zone walls, he 'look[s] at himself in the mirrors that were everywhere' only to acknowledge that his reflection is in fact his own irrelevance in the larger scheme of things: 'what he saw meant nothing. All he saw was [his editor's] network of relationships'.[63] The novel is also then in part a reflection on how power is reconstructed under globalization, remapping the hierarchies of national structures in favour of global networks. In the terms of Saadawi's allegory, Iraq is reassembled into a new monstrous form, its localities reconstituted into the body-parts of a global monster.

Opening with the car-bomb scene which obliterates location, Saadawi's novel ends on the indeterminacy of Iraq's future orientation. The final paragraphs of the novel are set in an abandoned hotel, which is now also unnamed: '[s]ince Faraj had taken down the sign outside, the hotel hadn't had a name. It was no longer the Orouba Hotel, and it hadn't yet become the Grand Prophet Hotel, as Faraj had been planning to call it'. Following the shift away from Orouba (عروبة signfiying pan-Arab ideology), but not yet given a name appropriate for a Shia-

---

[62] Saadawi, *Frankenstein in Baghdad*, 235.
[63] Saadawi, *Frankenstein in Baghdad*, 271–2.

majority religious state, the unnamed hotel becomes the home of the monster who looks out from its windows at the ongoing 'festival of ruin and destruction'.[64]

In the translation, the relocation of *Frankenstein* into Baghdad 'provides ... relief from the limited way Iraq is traditionally represented',[65] as one reviewer has it. However, the coherence of this intertext is confused through the multiple names for the monster, whose identity shifts between Elishva's resurrected son Danyal, Hadi's forgotten object (*shesma*), the media's borrowed *Frankenstein* story, and the security state's Criminal X. When Hadi is arrested on suspicion of himself being the monster, the confusion between creator and creation further complicates the story through metafictional commentary on the role of the storyteller. Through these various renamings, the intertextual reference becomes less accessible. The narrative does not ultimately provide the promised coherence of a cosmopolitan retelling from the periphery. Instead, the title and the cover promise the coherence of a retelling which disintegrates into an absurd, fragmentary tale, finally eroding the structural sympathy of allegory.

Reorienting realism in Hassan Blasim

While Saadawi invokes a globally familiar image of corporeal dismemberment in order to interrogate the dissolution of location, Blasim uses metropolitan horror tropes, dream logic and magical realism to examine the complex relationship between storyteller and audience, between the text's laying claim to certain locations and generating different orientations. In a discussion of Blasim's play *Digital Hats*, Margaret Litvin and Johanna Sellman point out that Blasim is working 'under an added weight of audience preconceptions about what kind of theatre to expect from immigrants, warzone witnesses and Arab Muslims'.[66] The significance of audience expectations is evident in Blasim's work, from 'The Corpse Exhibition' in which an apprentice assassin discusses how to artistically stage corpses, to 'The Song of the Goats', a game show where contestants compete to tell the most horrific anecdote.[67] In most of Blasim's stories, there are frame

---

[64] Saadawi, *Frankenstein in Baghdad*, 27.

[65] Alexandra Alter, 'Middle Eastern Writers Find Refuge in the Dystopian Novel', *The New York Times*, 29 May 2016, https://www.nytimes.com/2016/05/30/books/middle-eastern-writers-find-refuge-in-the-dystopian-novel.html.

[66] Margaret Litvin and Johanna Sellman, 'An Icy Heaven: Arab Migration on Contemporary Nordic Stages', *Theatre Research International* 43, no. 1 (March 2018): 46.

[67] Blasim's short story is reminiscent of the story of the contest which inspired Shelley's *Frankenstein*.

narratives and writer-narrators discussing how fiction might 'try through meagre words to express its anger and interest in human terror at the same time'[68] while being aware of orientation as a problematic factor, in the 'Third World clichés which try to appeal to the sentiments of Western audiences'.[69] Blasim's short stories are almost invariably shot through with such comments on the dangers of clichés, but also, often just as insistently, on the magic of stories and their capacity to relate particularity to a universal human experience.

'The Market of Stories' is a case in point, opening with a quote by Béla Hamvas about the possibility of knowing the world while at home. This quote is offered as a justification by the protagonist, the writer Khalid al-Hamrani, to explain why he 'had never left his home town', and 'had not written a single story that did not take place around the street market close to his house':

> In a curious interview with him in one of the local newspapers, [Hamrani] said: 'You can turn the woman who sells fish in the market into a spaceship lost in the cosmos ….' Asked if his stories were much alike and boring because the market alone was their 'magic box', he spoke straight: 'What I detest is looking for new experiences and places in order to say the same thing.'[70]

This passage points to a tension between location and literary 'magic'. The narrator informs us that Hamrani's work 'transport[s] the reader to another world', shifting from the (realist, limited) scale of the market to the cosmos.[71] However, given the irrealism of his style, the narrator also informs us that Hamrani's stories 'were not very interesting to most readers', in what we might take as a comment on Blasim's own difficulties in having his work accepted by Arabic publishing houses. In the next story in the collection, 'Ali's Bag', the narrator remembers Hamrani as a cautionary tale, not wishing to be like the writer who 'killed himself, leaving six collections of stories, all of them about the world of the market'[72] after the single setting of his stories, the marketplace, is finally demolished. In these linked stories, the writer-figure Hamrani is at once too located, limiting his world to the location of the market, and also too esoterically cosmopolitan, quoting Hamvas and thinking about the cosmos and spaceships. He is unable to reorient his writing for readers who, '[s]ince the fall of Saddam Hussein' demand writing that is 'intelligible, realistic, factual

---

[68] Hassan Blasim, *The Madman of Freedom Square* (Manchester: Comma Press, 2009), 61.
[69] Blasim, *The Madman of Freedom Square*, 61.
[70] Blasim, *The Madman of Freedom Square*, 51.
[71] Blasim, *The Madman of Freedom Square*, 55.
[72] Blasim, *The Madman of Freedom Square*, 60.

and pragmatic.'[73] In failing to subscribe to the expected conventions, Blasim's writer-figure Hamrani represents a dysfunctional relationship between audience and writer, an orientation out of sync with location.

At times, Blasim deliberately invokes the familiarity of magic realism in order to make a point about reader expectations, such as with the invocation of the Mexican novelist Carlos Fuentes in 'The Nightmares of Carlos Fuentes'. The story opens with the protagonist Salim, a street-sweeper in Baghdad assigned to cleaning up after explosions, who steals a ring from a dismembered finger 'after an oil tanker had exploded nearby, incinerating chickens, fruits and vegetables and some people.'[74] As in Saadawi's text, Blasim is concerned with the devaluing of human life: here, the landscape of destruction has become so routine that the reference to 'some people' reads like an afterthought. Salim later leaves Iraq, changing his name to one chosen from a newspaper (which happens to be Carlos Fuentes). However, once relocated in the Netherlands, Salim/Carlos is not able to forget his former life. The stolen ring comes to represent both his guilt for leaving and his inability to begin a new life, despite his efforts. In a series of nightmares, Carlos re-encounters his former self. In one dream, Salim speaks to his employer in an Iraqi dialect. In another, he is in a courtroom, accused of planting a car bomb in Amsterdam. This time he is told not to speak in Dutch, even though the translator is unable to understand his Iraqi dialect, leaving him without language. At the end of the story, and in the final dream, the doubleness of Salim/Carlos is resolved in Carlos killing his former self. The final paragraphs relate the body's posthumous relocation:

> Perhaps Fuentes would have forgiven the Dutch newspapers, which wrote that an Iraqi man had committed suicide at night by jumping from a sixth-floor window, instead of writing that a Dutch national had committed suicide. But he will never forgive his brothers, who had his body taken back to Iraq and buried in the cemetery in Najaf.[75]

The story of Salim/Carlos speaks to the limits of recognizing what is strange through a more familiar framework. That Salim takes the name Carlos (whether or not the character recognizes the name of the author) is analogous to Blasim's 'nightmare realism' doubling, registering or disguising itself as magical realism. By the end, however, this attempt at a reorientation is limited, since Salim's identity remains territorially inscribed within the nation state.

---

[73] Blasim, *The Madman of Freedom Square*, 54.
[74] Blasim, *The Madman of Freedom Square*, 75.
[75] Blasim, *The Madman of Freedom Square*, 82.

Several of Blasim's stories are set in constrained spaces, both metaphorical (a borrowed identity, a nightmare) and literal (a refugee centre, a truck), where magical/macabre bodily transformations capture uncanny dislocation. In 'The Truck to Berlin' the shift from realism to phantasmagoria is mapped onto physical movement, promising a linear journey to a location but never arriving at its destination. The story begins with a frame narrative where the narrator is planning to continue his migratory journey, after 'fear of the unknown helped obliterate the sense of belonging to a familiar reality'.[76] The narrator is discouraged from choosing the 'truck route' after being told a story about traffickers who abandoned a locked truck in the Serbian forest. The story then shifts into the embedded tale, a retelling of Ghassan Kanafani's canonical text 'Rijāl fi al-Shams' (Men in the Sun), a short story about Palestinian migrant workers who suffocate inside a truck on the way to Kuwait. Blasim's story, however, extends the ending. While Kanafani's text famously ends by questioning the silent suffocation of the Palestinian workers, part of the horror of Blasim's story is its graphic description of the migrants' deaths, including their screams (the narrator at the outset comments that 'the story would make a good experimental radio piece'). In the final sentences, the story switches to the horror genre through a supernatural twist: when the police open the truck, the one survivor who emerges 'started to run on all fours, then turned into a grey wolf', disappearing into the forest.[77] This story is described at the outset as 'a modest allegory', with the narrator posing questions about staging. As the narrator reminds us, there are 'many similarly tragic stories … focused first and foremost on migrants drowning' which have no apparent impact.[78] Rewriting Kanafani's canonical story using the tropes of global horror, Blasim transfigures migrant into werewolf, testing the cultural representations of violence that register on a global stage.

Blasim's concern with the limits of representation and the problems of expectation are again the theme in 'The Reality and the Record', where an asylum seeker's memories of Baghdad are set against the expectations of his audience. Nadia Atia points out that the Arabic title is 'the reality and the archive', and I would highlight the significance of *arshif* as a transliteration from *archive* in relation to this story, which thematizes the problems of recording and archiving traumatic experiences. The question of what is true is described as

[76] Blasim, *The Madman of Freedom Square*, 67.
[77] Blasim, *The Madman of Freedom Square*, 73.
[78] Blasim, *The Madman of Freedom Square*, 67.

almost incidental, as the anonymous speaker instead provides the migration officer with a confusing, impossible story, concluding '[w]hat I am saying has nothing to do with my asylum request. What matters to you is the horror'.[79] There is a double-edged aspect to this accusation, a suggestion that the speaker will provide what the migration officer (and the reader) already anticipate. Here and elsewhere, Blasim's multilayered short stories incorporate an awareness of the expectation to read about lived horror. The extra-diegetic narrators convey being 'of the world', while also discussing in metafictional terms how literatures become relevant at the global level, as reports of the difficult realities of life elsewhere which serve to augment the 'archive' of world literature.

This functional use of literature is exemplified by a story from Blasim's second collection *The Iraqi Christ*, 'Why Don't You Write a Novel', where the narrator is given the suggestion that he should write in a more expansive form 'instead of talking about all these characters – Arabs, Kurds, Pakistanis, Sudanese, Bangladeshis and Africans' since each of these characters 'would make for mysterious, traditional stories'.[80] Beyond the preference for the novel form, this question speaks to the expectation that 'world' literature will provide the reader with a window onto elsewhere. Since there are so many characters, their stories cannot be amenable to the compressed form, and therefore the narrator must justify '[w]hy [he] cram[s] all these names into one short story'.[81] Implicitly however, the reader will recognize that the limited space of the form mirrors the setting in the quarantine section of a reception centre, which, the narrator states, is 'crowded with Afghans, Arabs, Kurds, Pakistanis, Sudanese, Bangladeshis, Africans and some Albanians'.[82] These characters, like the monster in Saadawi's novel, remain nameless, reduced to national and regional markers, the constrained (narrative and physical) space leaving no room for the unfolding of their stories in an expansive representation which would allow the reader 'to get a grip on some reality'.[83]

In the textual worlds Blasim creates, the narrators think constantly about representation as a form of fabulation, producing rather than reflecting the world. Transcultural modes of worlding, according to Rogan Ghosh, are 'not about going beyond the global or reducing the local to a form of representation or

---

[79] Blasim, *The Madman of Freedom Square*, 9.
[80] Hassan Blasim, *The Iraqi Christ* (Manchester: Comma Press, 2013), 97.
[81] Blasim, *The Iraqi Christ*, 97.
[82] Blasim, *The Iraqi Christ*, 93.
[83] Blasim, *The Iraqi Christ*, 98.

meaning-formation' but rather 'a way of providing a sense of a totality, a world-wide-forming totality, whose access is not always in accessibility'.[84] In Blasim's short stories, locations are claimed and represented in very particular terms: rather than offering unimpeded access to the places represented, verisimilitude and vernacular modes (the potential of mysterious, traditional stories) are disrupted through cosmopolitan, non-mimetic modes and references. In other words, the worlding in Blasim's works is precisely about the precarious attempt to avoid the reduction of the local to a single meaning, refusing to offer a comprehensible representation of a locality, turning Iraq's war stories into versions of global horror culture and spin-offs to magic realism as nightmare realism.

Portable words and dislocated worlds

Speaking at a translation workshop entitled 'The Bearer-Beings: Portable Stories in Dislocated Times' in 2016, the poet Tamim Barghouti discussed his book-length poem entitled *Maqām 'Irāq*[85] written in the wake of the 2003 invasion. The word *maqām*, which means place, position or location, references melodic modes in Arabic music. Barghouti uses the word in his poem to signal his concern with form and with its relationship to place. The poem begins, in elevated language, by stating that the traditional poetic form of *rithā'* (elegy/requiem) is inadequate to the context:

كفو لسان المراثي إنها ترف
عن سائر الموت هذا الموت يختلف
...
ظل الكلام وظل المهتدون به
إن الصفات خيانات لما تصف

'Silence the tongue of requiems/This death is different ... Language is lost and lost are those who seek its guidance/Descriptions are betrayals of what they describe.' Like Blasim questioning the viability of 'writ[ing] like Ibn Arabi about car bombs', these lines challenge the conventions of Arabic literature in the context of the violence unleashed in post-2003 Iraq, suggesting that responses to these conditions of location need to develop modes of writing which do not

---

[84] Ranjan Ghosh. 'More than Global', In *Thinking Literature across Continents*, ed. Ranjan Ghosh and J. Hillis Miller (Durham, NC: Duke University Press, 2016), 113.

[85] Tamim Barghouti, *Maqām 'Irāq: qaṣīdat kuffū lisān al-marāthī* (Cairo: Aṭlas lil-Nashr wa-al-Intāj al-I'lāmī, 2005).

(only) orient themselves back to the classical forms and styles. Barghouti reflects on the need to break conventional forms to reflect a sense of unworlding, which is particular in the case of Iraq, given its standing in Arabic literary imagination. As Barghouti puts it, 'the names Baghdad, Kufa, Basra … come with images of decorations on mosques and palaces, sounds of poetry, rules of grammar'. The connotations around these city names change under the impact of the war, and this transformation of location means 'formative images being violently changed and altered':

> you want to save whatever you can save, to salvage. To take a snapshot of time and space, because everything you see is temporary; the building that now is there will not be there tomorrow. So look at it, keep it in memory, codify it somehow and do that in language, because language is the most portable form.[86]

The title of the workshop at which Barghouti was speaking is taken from lines in Wallace Stevens's 'An Ordinary Evening in New Haven': '[s]o much ourselves, we cannot tell apart/The idea and the bearer-being of the idea'.[87] The notion of a 'bearer-being' suggests that ideas and the forms through which they travel are intertwined: here to 'salvage' memories, and to 'codify' place in language creates a portable world.

To return to al-Malaika's term, *adab al-'ālam* (the world's literature) is not only dependent on the portability of language across locations, but also what is produced, the generative and speculative quality of writing. Thinking of literature as a locality-producing activity involves reflecting on the semiotics of place as always involving other locations, becoming other in its representation depending on style and form and references. That is, producing locality in fiction perhaps goes beyond the stability of a geographical terrain, *'ālam,* or world, to instead approximate the construction of the world as *dunyā*, a temporal category emerging from the verb *danā* (to bring near). Writing of one location 'brings near' the world, orienting the writing to various elsewheres through various forms of intertextuality, references and resemblances.

The texts I have been discussing in this chapter exemplify wider trends across the region, adapting literary cosmopolitan tropes and genres to represent the upheaval of the political order, and thereby adapting cosmopolitan non-mimetic modes to new uses. Saadawi's *Frankenstein in Baghdad* narrates the impact of

---

[86] Tamim al Barghouti, 'The Bearer-Beings': Portable Stories in Dislocated Times. Youtube, uploaded by The Weidenfeld-Hoffmann Trust, 13 July 2016, https://www.youtube.com/watch?v=dHiY2XAKEGE.

[87] Wallace Stevens, *The Collected Poems of Wallace Stevens* (New York: Alfred A. Knopf, 2011), 466.

the US-led invasion of Iraq through the relocation of a globally recognized text, a departure from the coordinates of realism which conveys the tenuousness of locality and portrays the characters' sense of inhabiting a place that is being unmade and remade. Blasim's stories, meanwhile, contort conventional realism by incorporating fantastical modes and metafictional devices. The author acknowledges his orientation towards a primarily Western audience while addressing the assumption that literature ought to provide a window onto an unfamiliar world.

The works of Saadawi and Blasim may fail to evoke the kind of affective response expected of war literature, given these juxtapositions of cosmopolitan modes and vernacular traditions, and the multiple local and global conventions and expectations involved. However, this chapter has argued that these texts are less about representing the war than they are about the dissolution, transformation and mutation of localities under the pressures of globalization and the paradoxical reality of violent crises becoming routine. The porous boundaries of reality represent the instability of location under these conditions, introducing the terrain of global horror and magic realism into the representation of place as a strategy to capture such dislocation.

Bibliography

Abdelmessih, Marie Thérèse. 'Rethinking Critical Approaches to Arabic Comparatively, in a "Post" Colonial Context'. *Interventions* 20, no. 2 (2018): 192–209. https://doi.org/10.1080/1369801X.2017.1403348.

Aboul-Ela, Hosam. 'Challenging the Embargo: Arabic Literature in the US Market'. *Middle East Report*, no. 219 (2001): 42–4. https://doi.org/10.2307/1559255.

Al-Malaika, Nazik. *Shaẓāyā wa Ramād*. 1949. Beirut: Dār ʿAwdah, 1971.

Al-Masri, Khaled. 'An Enchanted Ring and a Dung Beetle: Contaminated Borders in Hassan Blasim's Nightmarish Narratives'. *Middle Eastern Literatures* 21, no. 2–3 (2018): 115–33.

Al-Musawi, Muhsin Jassim. *The Postcolonial Arabic Novel: Debating Ambivalence*. Leiden: Brill, 2003.

Alter, Alexandra. 'Middle Eastern Writers Find Refuge in the Dystopian Novel'. *The New York Times*, 29 May 2016. www.nytimes.com/2016/05/30/books/middle-eastern-writers-find-refuge-in-the-dystopian-novel.html.

Appadurai, Arjun. *Modernity at Large: Cultural Dimensions of Globalization*. Minneapolis: University of Minnesota Press, 1996.

Ashfeldt, Lane. 'Literary Defiance: An Interview with Hassan Blasim'. *World Literature Today* 89, no. 1 (2015): 10–12.

Atia, Nadia. 'The Figure of the Refugee in Hassan Blasim's "The Reality and the Record"'. *The Journal of Commonwealth Literature* 54, no. 3 (2019): 319–33.

Bahoora, Haytham. 'Writing the Dismembered Nation: The Aesthetics of Horror in Iraqi Narratives of War', *Arab Studies Journal* 23, no. 1 (Fall 2015): 184–5.

Barghouthi, Mourid. *Ra'aytu Rām Allāh*. Al-Dār al-Bayḍā': al-Markaz al-Thaqāfī al-'Arabī, 2011.

Beecroft, Alexander. *An Ecology of World Literature: From Antiquity to the Present Day*. New York: Verso, 2015.

Blasim, Hassan. *The Madman of Freedom Square*. Manchester: Comma Press, 2009.

Blasim, Hassan. *The Iraqi Christ*. Manchester: Comma Press, 2013.

Casanova, Pascale. *The World Republic of Letters*. Cambridge, MA: Harvard University Press, 2004.

Cheah, Pheng. *What Is a World?: On Postcolonial Literature as World Literature*. Durham, NC: Duke University Press, 2015.

Creswell, Robyn. 'Is Arabic Untranslatable?' *Public Culture* 28, no. 3 (2016): 447–56.

Damrosch, David. *What Is World Literature?* Princeton: Princeton University Press, 2018.

Deeb, Mustafa. 'كاهتنالا نم تعبش صوصن,' [texts saturated with violation] *Ultrasawt*, 27 September, 2017. https://www.ultrasawt.com/ثقافة/أدب-ديب حسن-بلاسم-في-طفل-الشيعة-المسموم-نصوص-شبعت-من-الانتهاك/مصطفى

D'haen, Theo, César Domínguez and Mads Rosendahl Thomsen. *World Literature Reader: A Reader*. New York: Routledge, 2012.

El-Desouky, Ayman A., 'Beyond Spatiality: Theorising the Local and Untranslatability as Comparative Critical Method'. In *Approaches to World Literature*, ed. Joachim Küpper, 59–84. Munich: De Gruyter, 2013.

Gelder, Ken. 'Global/Postcolonial Horror: Introduction'. *Postcolonial Studies* 3, no. 1 (2000): 35–8.

Ghazoul, Ferial J. 'Iraqi Short Fiction: The Unhomely at Home and Abroad'. *Journal of Arabic Literature* 35, no. 1 (2004): 1–24.

Ghosh, Ranjan and J. Hillis Miller. *Thinking Literature across Continents*. Durham, NC: Duke University Press, 2016.

Hassler-Forest, Dan. *Science Fiction, Fantasy, and Politics: Transmedia World-Building beyond Capitalism*. London: Rowman & Littlefield International, 2016.

Hawas, May. *Politicising World Literature: Egypt, Between Pedagogy and the Public*. New York: Routledge, 2019.

Kachachi, Inaam. *Al-Ḥafīda al-Amīrikīya*. Beirut: Dār al-Jadīd, 2008.

Kachachi, Inaam. *Ṭashshārī*. Beirut: Dār al-Jadīd, 2014.

Laachir, Karima, Sara Marzagora and Francesca Orsini. 'Multilingual Locals and Significant Geographies: For a Ground-up and Located Approach to World Literature'. *Modern Languages Open* 19, no. 1 (2018). https://www.modernlanguagesopen.org/collections/special/comparative-literature-section-launch-issue/

Litvin, Margaret, and Johanna Sellman. 'An Icy Heaven: Arab Migration on Contemporary Nordic Stages'. *Theatre Research International* 43, no. 1 (2018): 45–62.

Marrouchi, Mustapha. 'Introduction: Embargoed Literature: Arabic', *College Literature* 37, no. 1 (2010): 1–10.

Masmoudi, Ikram. *War and Occupation in Iraqi Fiction*. Edinburgh: Edinburgh University Press, 2015.

Mehrez, Samia. 'خارطة الرواية: فرانكو موريتي وإعادة رسم التاريخ الأدبي' (Mapping the novel: Franco Moretti and the remaking of literary history). *Alif: Journal of Comparative Poetics* 34 (2014): 67–92.

Moretti, Franco. *Atlas of the European Novel, 1800–1900*. New York: Verso, 1998.

Moretti, Franco. *Graphs, Maps, Trees: Abstract Models for Literary History*. New York: Verso, 2007.

Murphy, Sinéad. '*Frankenstein in Baghdad:* Human Conditions, or Conditions of Being Human'. *Science Fiction Studies* 45, no. 2 (2018): 273–88.

Perry, Sarah. '*Frankenstein in Baghdad* by Ahmed Saadawi Review – Strange, Violent and Wickedly Funny'. *The Guardian*, 16 February 2018. www.theguardian.com/books/2018/feb/16/frankenstein-in-baghdad-by-ahmed-saadawi-review.

Qualey, Marcia Lynx. 'Baghdad Writes!' *ArabLit* (blog), 30 April 2014. https://arablit.org/2014/04/30/baghdad-writes/.

Qualey, Marcia Lynx. 'Iraqi Novelist Defies Arab Critics'. *Al Jazeera*, 27 May 2014. www.aljazeera.com/opinions/2014/5/27/iraqi-novelist-defies-arab-critics/

Rooke, Tetz. 'The Emergence of the Arabic Bestseller: Arabic Fiction and World Literature'. In *From New Values to New Aesthetics: Turning Points in Modern Arabic*. Vol. 2. *Postmodernism and Thereafter*, edited by Stephan Guth and Gail Ramsay, 201–14, Wiesbaden: Harrassowitz, 2011.

Saadawi, Ahmed. *Frankenstein in Baghdad*. New York: Penguin Books, 2018.

Said, Edward. 'Embargoed Literature', *The Nation* 251, no. 8, (17 September 1990): 280–85.

Sakr, Rita. 'The More-than-Human Refugee Journey: Hassan Blasim's Short Stories'. *Journal of Postcolonial Writing* 54, no. 6 (2018): 766–80.

Scarry, Elaine. *The Body in Pain: The Making and Unmaking of the World*. Oxford: Oxford University Press, 1985.

Sellman, Johanna, and Margaret Litvin. 'Hassan Blasim: Interview for Tank Magazine', *Tank Magazine* 8, no. 9 (2016). https://tankmagazine.com/issue-69/talk/hassan-blasim

Stevens, Wallace. *The Collected Poems of Wallace Stevens*. New York: Alfred A. Knopf, 2011.

Tageldin, Shaden. 'Untranslatability'. In *Futures of Comparative Literature: ACLA State of the Discipline Report*, edited by Ursula K. Heise et al., 234–6. New York: Routledge, 2017.

'Tageldin, Shaden. M. 'Beyond Latinity, Can the Vernacular Speak?', *Comparative Literature* 70, no. 2 (2018): 114–31.

Updike, John. 'Satan's Work and Silted Cisterns'. *The New Yorker* (17 October 1988): 117–21.

Valassopoulos, Anastasia. *Arab Cultural Studies: History, Politics and the Popular*. New York: Routledge, 2013.

Walkowitz, Rebecca L. *Born Translated: The Contemporary Novel in an Age of World Literature*. New York: Columbia University Press, 2017.

Warwick Research Collective (WReC). *Combined and Uneven Development: Towards a New Theory of World-Literature* (Liverpool: Liverpool University Press, 2015).

Webster, Annie. 'Ahmed Saadawi's *Frankenstein in Baghdad*: A Tale of Biomedical Salvation?', *Literature and Medicine* 36, no. 2 (2018): 439–63.

Yassin-Kassab, Robin. 'Beirut 39: New Writing from the Arab World, Book Review'. *The Guardian*, 11 June 2010. https://www.theguardian.com/books/2010/jun/12/beirut-new-writing-arab-world.

4

Locating the literature of Hawai'i

Sally Anderson Boström

'The air was still, and the high, clear sound wound like a ribbon around the island. It was, I know it, the island, the voice of the island singing … the voice of our island singing.'[1] So writes Maxine Hong Kingston in *Hawai'i One Summer*, a collection of personal essays recording the author's life during the summer of 1978.[2] Though the title seems to indicate a short sojourn on the isles, Kingston lived in Honolulu for nearly two decades. In the 'Preface to the Paperback Edition', written in 1998, she recalls: 'I wrote these essays during the middle of our seventeen-year stay in Hawai'i.'[3] Ever careful in her diction, Kingston does not call Hawai'i home. Relegating seventeen years to a 'stay' she implies that despite this length of time and being endowed a 'Living Treasure of Hawai'i' in 1980,[4] she was only ever a visitor.

Kingston's trepidation around her status on the islands reflects how the literature of Hawai'i operates within a dichotomy of exclusion and inclusion. Questions of who gets to write this literature, where it is written, and what language it is written in, dominate debates that began in the mid-twentieth

---

[1] Maxine Hong Kingston, *Hawai'i One Summer* (Honolulu: University of Hawai'i Press, 1998), 33.

[2] The revival of the study of Hawaiian language and literature has witnessed increased attention to accurate spellings of Hawaiian words, including the use of the *kahakō* or macron to indicate a long vowel sound and the *'okina* or glottal stop signified by ʻ. Out of respect for contemporary concerns around Hawaiian language, I use these two symbols in the spelling of Hawaiian words. The *'okina* is used in the place name 'Hawai'i' but omitted for Anglicized words such as 'Hawaiian' and in citations where the writer does not use such spellings. Kingston uses the *'okina* in the Paperback Edition of *Hawai'i One Summer*, but not in the original *New York Times* column. Maxine Hong Kingston, 'Hers', *The New York Times*, June–July 1978, ProQuest Historical Newspapers: The New York Times with Index.

[3] Kingston, *Hawai'i One Summer*, xi.

[4] The Living Treasure of Hawai'i has been awarded to several recipients every year since its inauguration in 1976. Inspired by a similar award that began in Japan in the same year, it is bestowed by the Buddhist Honpa Hongwanji Temple in Honolulu, which largely serves the Japanese American community. The temple states that the award 'recognizes and honors individuals who have demonstrated excellence and high achievement in their particular field of endeavor, and who, through continuous growth, learning, and sharing, have made significant contributions toward enriching our society'. 'Living Treasures', *Honpa Hongwanji Mission of Hawaii* (blog), https://hongwanjihawaii.com/living-treasures/

century and continue today. Central to the question of who can lay claim to the islands' literature and thus a symbolic claim to the islands themselves, is the contention surrounding what it means to be 'local' and the place of Hawai'i Creole English (HCE) in that debate.[5] This conflict is further complicated by a growing awareness of and sensitivity to Hawai'i's indigenous culture and language, as well as a move away from reading the cultural production of Hawai'i solely in relation to the United States.

This chapter compares Kingston's writing about Hawai'i with that of Lois-Ann Yamanaka, specifically how the two authors locate the islands in their work. Despite these authors' differing orientations of writing about Hawai'i from within as an 'insider' (Yamanaka) or from the ambiguous position of 'visitor' (Kingston), place-based identity and local place descriptions remain prevalent throughout their work. Looking at *Hawai'i One Summer* (1978) and *Blu's Hanging* (1997) alongside several contemporaries in the literature of Hawai'i, I explore questions of location and orientation within the matrix of the cosmopolitan–vernacular exchange.[6] I provide some background to *Hawai'i One Summer* before going into an overview of the literature of Hawai'i and where Kingston and Yamanaka fit within this literary landscape. The second half of this chapter constitutes close readings from *Blu's Hanging* and *Hawai'i One Summer*, analysing how descriptions of place and the use – or absence – of HCE, position these authors vis-á-vis the cosmopolitan, which in the case of Hawai'i is epitomized as the mainland United States.

Hawai'i One Summer first appeared as a column for *The New York Times* entitled 'Hers'.[7] In 1987, the essays were published together as a limited fine-

---

[5] Despite its continued popular use, scholars in Hawai'i have problematized the term 'local'. Candace Fujikane identifies 'local' emerging in the 1970s as a rallying cry for the working class, used to signify 'resistance against forces of commercial, suburban, and resort development'. Fujikane and Okamura, *Asian Settler Colonialism*, 26. But at the same time, 'local' was being used in the emerging literature of Hawai'i that sought to define itself as distinct from American literature, often written in the local language, HCE. To Fujikane, positive understandings of 'local' conceal the way particular ethnic groups in Hawai'i, namely Asians, have abused the term to claim solidarity with the Native population, thus asserting Asian Settler social and political power. Similarly, Haunani-Kay Trask has declared 'local' to be a gloss for 'settler'. This disparity highlights the ongoing debate over who can lay claim to place-based identity in Hawai'i.

[6] Here I am referring to ideas set forth in the General Introduction to *World Literatures, Exploring the Cosmopolitan Vernacular Exchange*, where Stefan Helgesson asserts that the vernacular and the cosmopolitan should not be considered opposites but rather as two vectors of literary worldliness 'that may interact, merge or contest each other'. I use them here heuristically as relational terms, much like orientation and location; one cannot discuss one aspect of the dichotomy without the other. Stefan Helgesson, 'General Introduction', in *World Literatures: Exploring the Cosmopolitan-Vernacular Exchange*, ed. Stefan Helgesson et al. (Stockholm: Stockholm University Press, 2018), 1–11, https://doi.org/10.16993/bat, 2.

[7] All ten essays appeared in *The New York Times* except for 'Lew Wlech: An Appreciation'.

print edition – 150 copies printed on rice paper from Korea in handset type with woodblock prints and a handsewn binding. Upon their release, one copy in a slipcase sold for $500. As Kingston herself acknowledges, they were for 'art collectors not for readers'.[8] This early publication history emphasizes the question of who gets to write about Hawai'i and who gets to read it. Published in the decade that the literature of Hawai'i was coming of age, the fact these essays were published in *The New York Times*, for a mainland audience, is problematic enough. Moreover, the possessive pronoun in the title of the *NYT* column stresses a double ownership – Kingston's possession over her personal stories, but also a possession of the isles she was writing from and about.

The paperback edition of *Hawai'i One Summer* appeared two decades after the original column. It was published by The University of Hawai'i Press, which is significant as this Hawai'i based publisher arguably has a more local audience than *The New York Times*. This edition also appeared the year after Yamanaka's *Blu's Hanging*, making the comparison of the two works quite compelling. There are numerous moments in Kingston's 'Preface to the Paperback Edition' that show an increased awareness and political sensitivity to writing about Hawai'i, one clear example being the inclusion of the 'okina, absent in earlier publications. But it is also possible to read this second preface as a belated attempt to repackage the original text for a changed political climate. Here Kingston writes:

> The literary community in Hawai'i argues over who owns the myths and stories, whether the local language and writings should be exported to the Mainland, whether or not so and so is authentic, is Hawaiian. For me, Hawai'i is a good place for writing about California and China, and not for writing about Hawai'i.[9]

Despite this disclaimer, Kingston's collection does indeed include writing about Hawai'i. This is evident in the opening quote of this chapter, where Kingston calls Mokoli'i – a small islet off the coast of O'ahu – 'our island'. Here, and in numerous instances in *Hawai'i One Summer*, Kingston declares a literary ownership of Hawai'i that is not without contention.

The first essay in the collection discusses Kingston's process of buying a property in Hawai'i. While signing papers at the escrow office, Kingston and her husband discover that their new home is on a Royal Hawaiian Land Grant. Her husband worries they do not belong on the land, but Kingston reasons: 'No matter what year you claim it, the property belongs to a former owner who has

---

[8] Kingston, *Hawai'i One Summer*, xvi.
[9] Kingston, *Hawai'i One Summer*, xi–xii.

good moral reason for a claim. ... Also, doesn't the average American move every five years? We just keep exchanging with one another.'[10] Despite her husband's reservations, Kingston's easy reassurance exposes a lack of knowledge and sensitivity to Hawaiian history. The Native Hawaiian land that Kingston buys was parcelled out and sold to white settlers in the 1840s when King Kamehameha III was forced to adopt private ownership in hopes of preserving national sovereignty against increasing encroachments from the United States and other foreign interests. In *Aloha Betrayed, Native Hawaiian Resistance to American Colonialism*, Noenoe K. Silva explains how in actuality these grants led to the slow erosion of sovereignty, leading to the illegal overthrow of Queen Lili'uokalani in 1893, the United States annexation of Hawai'i in 1898, and the eventual incorporation of Hawai'i as America's fiftieth state in 1959.[11] Moreover, Kingston's categorical use of 'American' ignores the endeavours of the Hawaiian Sovereignty Movement to be seen as culturally and politically distinct from the United States. Kingston's failure to acknowledge these facts, and what some may see as her happy squatting on native lands, puts her at odds with the debate over who can write the literature of Hawai'i.

The literature of Hawai'i

Kingston's collection of essays emerged at a critical moment in Hawai'i's literary history. The 1970s were marked by a growing political and cultural resistance to the United States as a colonial power in Hawai'i that included early strides in the Sovereignty Movement and the foundations of the Second Hawaiian Renaissance. In the literary community, the Talk Story Conference of 1978 would be the watershed event for how the literature of Hawai'i was viewed as well as written. The conference took place during the very summer Kingston wrote these essays – in fact, Kingston was invited and relays the experience in this collection. The organizers of Talk Story describe it as a conference aimed to demonstrate the 'richness of Hawaii's literary heritage', the Modern Hawaiian Literary Tradition 'that recognized "Hawaii's writers as legitimate artists"'.[12]

[10] Kingston, *Hawai'i One Summer*, 6.
[11] Noenoe K. Silva, *Aloha Betrayed: Native Hawaiian Resistance to American Colonialism* (Durham, NC: Duke University Press, 2004).
[12] Eric Chock and Jody Manabe, *Writers of Hawaii: A Focus on Our Literary Heritage* (Honolulu: Bamboo Ridge Press, 1981), Preface.

Now seen as the first attempt to define local literature in Hawai'i, the conference challenged outsiders such as James Michener whose blockbuster novel *Hawaii* (1959) overshadowed local voices. During a speech at Talk Story, Hawai'i-born author O. A. Bushnell stated:

> 'outsiders' as such are not to be despised. An outsider may be a good writer; indeed, he can write a good novel about Hawai'i. Some outsiders have done so. But the very fact that he is an outsider, a haole in the original sense of the word's meaning a 'stranger', makes him – by definition – one who cannot be fully acquainted with the subtleties of our island scene.[13]

Kingston recalls this speech, writing directly after the conference: 'Ozzie . . . said that if "us local kids" don't write the Hawai'i novel, then the outsider will do it. I guiltily identified with this "outsider".[14] In this perplexing move, Kingston identifies with Bushnell's phrase 'us locals' as well as 'the outsider' – a paradox found throughout her essays.[15]

The fact that the title of the conference was not Standard English, but an expression in HCE is significant. Many of the writers invited were experimenting with writing in HCE, resisting notions that the language was 'broken English' and therefore lacked the sophistication for nuanced expression.[16] Using HCE in the conference title can be understood as a move to elevate the status of HCE but perhaps also designated an inclusion, which by its very nature excluded those who did not understand the expression. Simply put, 'talk story' is an informal chat with

[13] Quoted in Seri Luangphinith, 'Beyond Solitary Confinement: Rethinking the Sociopolitical Context of Local Literature in Hawai'i', in *The Cambridge History of Asian American Literature*, ed. Rajini Srikanth and Min Hyoung Song (New York: Cambridge University Press, 2015), 398.

[14] Kingston, *Hawai'i One Summer*, 47.

[15] During the 1960s and 70s the term 'local' was beginning to designate native born, often nonwhite, residents of Hawai'i. Keiko Ohnuma states that 'local' was used to express 'resistance to growing outsider influence, especially by mainland whites' and was 'an assertion of multiculturalism also formed in reaction to the growing Hawaiian sovereignty movement of the 1970s, which barred non-Natives from identifying as "Hawaiian"'. Keiko Ohnuma, '"Aloha Spirit" and the Cultural Politics of Sentiment as National Belonging', *The Contemporary Pacific* 20, no. 2 (1 August 2008): 365–94, https://doi.org/10.1353/cp.0.0005, 375.

[16] Today Hawai'i Creole English, known locally as 'pidgin', is spoken by over a million people, yet it continues to lack a standard orthography, official status and is highly stigmatized. Attitudes towards HCE in both native speakers and speakers of Standard American English still reflect beliefs that it is broken English and it is actively discouraged in formal settings including the workplace and schools. Advocacy in recent decades has begun to change this, and HCE is slowly starting to be seen as a language in its own right. In 2015, the US Census counted HCE as one of the major languages in Hawai'i but it is still not regarded as an official language. State of Hawaii, 'Demographic, Social, Economic, and Housing Characteristics for Selected Race Groups in Hawaii' (Research and Economic Analysis Division, March 2018). Mikaela L. Marlow and Howard Giles, '"We Won't Get Ahead Speaking like That!" Expressing and Managing Language Criticism in Hawai'i', *Journal of Multilingual and Multicultural Development* 31, no. 3 (1 May 2010): 237–51.

friends, which, to use Bushnell's expression, an 'outsider' may find hard to partake in since it is marked by banter about the past, local places and collective stories. Kingston does not use any HCE in *Hawai'i One Summer*. She mentions its use at the Talk Story conference, writing that Bushnell's speech in 'both standard English and pidgin' left her feeling 'scolded, a Captain Cook of literature'.[17] Reading Kingston's reflections on the Talk Story Conference, we are reminded that vernaculars reflect orientation, perhaps even more so than location. The move towards using HCE in local literature was a move away from the mainland United States, a way of identifying with Hawai'i and claiming as space for 'Hawaii's writers as legitimate artists'. Kingston continues her reflection on the conference by saying she fears she is 'distorting the landscape with a mainland – a mainstream – viewpoint',[18] a fear emphasized by her ambiguous outsider/insider position as well as the fact that her writings do not orient inwards to Hawai'i but outwards to the mainland United States. This is apparent in her physical points of reference to the mainland, her political subjectivity, as well as her use of Standard English.

The Talk Story Conference emerged in resistance to earlier anglophone attempts at defining a 'Hawaiian literary canon' that excluded local and indigenous voices. From the 1940s to 1960s, Carl Stroven and A. Grove Day edited a series of anthologies of Pacific Island literature, beginning with *The Spell of the Pacific*, followed by *A Hawaiian Reader*, and the *Spell of Hawai'i*, which attempted to create a canon of what they called 'Hawaiian literature'. The book jacket for *A Hawaiian Reader* boasts a 'colorful treasure house of the best writings of Hawaii from Captain Cook's arrival to the year of statehood'.[19] Following the influence of F. O. Matthiessen's *American Renaissance* (1941), the trend of attempting to create an American literary canon was in full bloom by the 1950s. Day and Stroven's anthologies are emblematic of nation formation and the geopolitical ethos of the time; they exhibit a desire to create a 'Hawaiian literature' in relation to American literature – an effort of cultural production inextricable from the imagining of a US history and its expanding empire. The 1970s movement of creating a local literature in Hawai'i worked against these cultural formations of an American, and more specifically, American Pacific canon.

Attempts at defining the literature of Hawai'i have continued to come under scrutiny since its departure from these earlier collections. Questions of ownership and authority are weighted with historical cause and cultural sensitivity to

[17] Kingston, *Hawai'i One Summer*, 47.
[18] Kingston, *Hawai'i One Summer*, 47.
[19] A. Grove Day and Carl Stroven, eds., *A Hawaiian Reader*, Paperback (Honolulu: Mutual Publishing, 1961).

Hawai'i's indigenous population. The literature of Hawai'i is not to be confused, as it often is, with indigenous Hawaiian literature, *mo'olelo Hawai'i*. Literary scholar and Hawaiian language activist ku'ualoha ho'omanawanui asserts that this misuse of terms denies Native Hawaiians' long history of oral and written literature. She argues that Hawaiian literature has suffered reduced visibility since it is often in *'ōlelo Hawai'i*, the native language of Hawai'i, which was 'nearly extinguished by the hegemony of English'.[20] Since the arrival of Captain Cook, Native Hawaiians have faced subjugation and persecution that led to the near-disappearance of their people, culture and language. In the decade following US statehood (1959), Hawai'i saw a resurgence of indigenous activism. This so-called Second Hawaiian Renaissance revived Hawaiian cultural practices as well as the Hawaiian language.[21] This revival helped formulate definitions of Hawaiian literature as separate from the relatively recent anglophone tradition. In a now foundational essay, 'Decolonizing Hawaiian Literature', Haunani-Kay Trask states: 'Hawaiian literature is that which is composed by Hawaiians' – by which she means Native Hawaiians alone.[22] Thus, discussions of what constitutes the literature of Hawai'i must begin by observing its distinction from indigenous Hawaiian literature.

An understanding of Hawai'i's literary history is incomplete without acknowledging America's colonial oppression of the islands and what Trask and others (Fujikane et al.) have called Asian Settler Colonialism. Trask declares Hawai'i to be a settler state where, 'an immigrant/settler consciousness is attempting to dispossess our Native people through the backdoor of identity theft'.[23] While it is debatable whether Hawai'i is a colonial or settler state, in the decades since Trask's essay, the binary of Native/Settler continues to appear in contemporary scholarship. It is with Trask's 'backdoor of identity theft' metaphor in mind that I explore how Kingston and Yamanaka navigate local identity and place. It is necessary to mention here that both writers fall into the category Trask

---

[20] ku'ualoha ho'omanawanui, 'He Ahu Mo'olelo: E Ho'okahua i Ka Paepae Mo'olelo Palapala Hawai'i: A Cairn of Stories: Establishing a Foundation of Hawaiian Literature', *Palapala* 1 (2017): 51–100, 51.

[21] The first Hawaiian Renaissance occurred in the nineteenth century while Hawai'i was still an independent kingdom as an attempt to preserve traditional culture, such as the hula banned by American missionaries, and revive oral myths and legends. The illegal annexation of Hawai'i by the United States in 1896 suppressed public displays of indigenous cultural practice and instituted a ban on speaking Hawaiian that was not officially lifted until the 1980s. In 1983, activist Larry Kimura estimated that there were only fifty speakers of Hawaiian under the age of eighteen. Larry Kimura, 'The Hawaiian Language', in *Native Hawaiians Study Commission Report*, vol. 1 (Washington, DC: U.S. Department of the Interior, 1983), 173–203. Today, the language is still classified as endangered but there are Hawaiian language immersion schools and Master's and PhD programmes offered in Hawaiian at the University of Hawai'i.

[22] Haunani-Kay Trask, 'Decolonizing Hawaiian Literature', in *Inside Out: Literature, Cultural Politics, and Identity in the New Pacific*, ed. Vilsoni Hereniko and Rob Wilson (Lanham: Rowman & Littlefield, 1999), 168.

[23] Trask, 'Decolonizing Hawaiian Literature', 169.

and others call 'Asian Settlers' – people of Asian descent that move to, or are born in, Hawai'i. This label is used in contrast to Native, a binary whose functionality in Hawai'i I question, since many residents of the islands share Asian and Hawaiian ancestry and arguments about genealogy quickly become tenuous.[24]

Da mainland to me

Following Day and Stroven's anthologies, scholars and writers in Hawai'i have critiqued how the cultural production of Hawai'i has primarily been read in relation to the United States.[25] Several writers have dramatized the very act of positioning Hawai'i from the perspective of, and in relation to, the mainland. These attempts at reorientation illustrate the political and literary landscape of contemporary Hawai'i. Honolulu poet Wing Tek Lum writes:

> O
> East is East
> and
> West is West.
> but I never did
> understand
> why
> in Geography class
> the East was west
> and
> the West was east
> and that no
> one ever
> cared about the difference.[26]

---

[24] This is not to disregard the centrality of genealogy in Native Hawaiian tradition, such as the sacred practice of *mele inoa*, the chanting of one's ancestry. Rather, I believe that while the binary of 'Asian Settler' may serve to highlight Hawaiians loss of land and sovereignty to colonial and settler forces, it serves to further divide the current population of Hawai'i, many of whom share a complex and difficult history of US oppression.

[25] See Haunani-Kay Trask's *From a Native Daughter: Colonialism and Sovereignty in Hawai'i*, which argues against America's illegal takeover of Hawai'i and the importance of preserving indigenous language and literature. Noenoe K. Silva's *Aloha Betrayed: Native Hawaiian Resistance to American Colonialism* offers a corrective to the English-language accounts of Hawai'i's history with a study based on thousands of pages of texts written in Hawaiian. See Paul Lyons's *American Pacificism: Oceania in the U.S. Imagination* for a detailed analysis and critique of American representations of Oceania.

[26] Wing Tek Lum, 'East/West Poem', *Hawai'i Review* 10 (spring/fall 1980): 140. Poem reprinted in full by permission of the author.

In this rather innocent yet provocative questioning of the world map, the poetic I imagines Hawai'i at the centre with the USA to the East and Asia to the West. The effect of this poem is twofold; at once exposing the powers at play in mapmaking while also pointing to Hawai'i's lack of agency on the world stage. The lines 'and that no/one ever/cared about the difference' signal a submissive acceptance of dominant powers, colonial education, and the displacement of Hawai'i as part of the periphery. Rob Wilson reads Lum's 'East/West Poem' as interrogating Hawai'i's unstable position of centre and periphery – where in one moment Honolulu is a capitalist centre only to be overridden in another by Tokyo or Los Angeles that dwarf island economics.[27] What I see as so captivating about Lum's poem, is that rather than orienting from one of these capitalist, and arguably cosmopolitan, centres, he turns inward, asking us instead to orient from the perspective of the islands. By doing so, he aligns himself with a new generation of writers actively resisting the US-centric tendency seen in Day and Stroven's American Pacific canon.

In 'Da Mainland to Me', Hawai'i-born poet Joe Balaz uses a dialogue between two locals to highlight the geopolitical imbalance between Hawai'i and the United States:

Eh, howzit brah,
I heard you going mainland, aah?
　　No, I going to da continent.
Wat? I taught you going California
foa visit your braddah?
　　Dats right.
Den you going mainland brah!
　　No, I going to da continent.
Wat you mean continent brah?!
Da mainland is da mainland,
dats wheah you going, aah?!
　　Eh, like I told you,
　　dats da continent-
　　Hawai'i
　　is da mainland to me.[28]

[27] Rob Wilson, *Reimagining the American Pacific: From South Pacific to Bamboo Ridge and Beyond* (Durham, NC: Duke University Press, 2000), 128.

[28] Joe Balaz, *Pidgin Eye* (Honolulu: Ala Press, 2019), 156. Poem reprinted in full by permission of Ala Press.

Here, the second speaker resists the comparison of Hawai'i to the USA while playing with the prefix 'main' in mainland to stress Hawai'i's centrality. Written in conjunction with the growing Sovereignty Movement, this poem can be read as a political statement declaring Hawai'i as independent from the United States.[29] Defining Hawai'i as the 'main' land, the speaker, who has the last word in the dialogic poem, decentralizes the USA and disrupts the first speaker's geopolitical tautology. Contrary to popular conceptions, the second speaker imagines a Hawai'i that *is* extricable from the imagining of a US history and its empire. The fact that the conversation takes place in HCE is significant: the poem claims a central space not only for Hawai'i but also for its local language. I read 'Da Mainland to Me' as a powerful example of what Sheldon Pollock defines as the moment when vernacular literary cultures are 'initiated by the conscious decisions of writers to reshape the boundaries of their cultural universe by renouncing the larger world for the smaller place'.[30] This decision, however, does not hold uniformly across the literature of Hawai'i. *Hawai'i One Summer* reveals a consistent orientation towards the mainland in its literary language, place description, and publication history. Yamanaka, on the other hand, explicitly uses the vernacular to distinguish her work from American, or even Asian American literature. Yamanaka's use of HCE and the way she describes the islands declares a literary space decidedly distinct from that of the continental USA.

Yamanaka stands with Balaz and Lum as examples of writers in Hawai'i who attempt to locate and relocate the islands into the centre point of orientation. Their work began the process of reimagining, contesting and constructing cultural production from Hawai'i. Yet Wilson, writing in 2000, argues these ideas need to be carried forward into the 'postplantation and tourist-centered economy' of the twenty-first century.[31] In an interrogation of what is 'local' in Hawai'i, Wilson asserts that given contemporary transformations to place, region and community, people in Hawai'i are no longer asking, 'Who am I? What is my origin? but rather, Where are we? or Where are we going? as a community

[29] This poem has been cited in various discussions of relational discourse, most recently in *Archipelagic American Studies*, where the editors use it to emphasize the importance of 'decontinentalizing' – to reorient from the space of the island to avoid continental bias and open new perspectives for scholarly inquiry. Brian Russell Roberts and Michelle Stephens, 'Archipelagic American Studies and the Caribbean', *Journal of Transnational American Studies* 5, no. 1 (1 January 2013): 1–20, 13.

[30] Sheldon Pollock, 'Cosmopolitan and Vernacular in History', *Public Culture* 12, no. 3 (1 September 2000): 591–625, 591.

[31] Wilson, *Reimagining the American Pacific*, xviii.

with a disintegrating ethos of the tactile, natural, vernacular and near."[32] In a post-Marxist turn, Wilson asserts that the 'local' risks being dismantled in its encounters with the 'global' (and here we could read cosmopolitan) – where local cultural production is exploited for capitalist gain. To Wilson, defining local identity requires 'a boundary-bashing world system' that dismantles nation states, asserts transnationality, but also risks ignoring cultural and political difference.[33] Thus, questions of what is local need to be articulated in conjunction with thinking through dominant configurations of the global. Wilson suggests that the way forward for local politics in the Pacific is a move away from fixed ideas of cultural purity and towards a plurality of cultures and language. This move, however, has been blasted by scholars such as Candace Fujikane and Jonathan Okamura who say describing Hawai'i as 'panethnic' or 'multicultural' is to 'ignore Hawaiians' ongoing struggle for self-determination as well as the tremendous political power some Asian groups have used against Hawaiians."[34] Such dispute reveals the complexity of the cosmopolitan–vernacular exchange where understandings of the global and the local are compounded with indigenous rights and desires for sovereignty.

In their rather controversial collection, *Asian Settler Colonialism*,[35] Fujikane and Okamura state that any potentially romantic notions of plurality subsumed under the category of the 'local' are demonstrative of 'ideological communities with white settler colonial historiography."[36] Fujikane asserts that as the first people of Hawai'i, only Native Hawaiians can claim ownership over its lands.[37] Drawing on Trask and anthropologist Patrick Wolfe, Fujikane claims that the failure to identify immigrants in Hawai'i as settlers leads to the fallacy that Hawai'i is a 'multiracial nation."[38] Thus, according to Fujikane, celebration of cultural pluralism in Hawai'i ignores the struggles of the indigenous population and the fight for sovereignty. The disagreement over who is 'local' and who can lay claim to the islands point to the crux of contention in contemporary

[32] Wilson, *Reimagining the American Pacific*, 138.
[33] Wilson, *Reimagining the American Pacific*, 138.
[34] Candace Fujikane and Jonathan Y. Okamura, *Asian Settler Colonialism: From Local Governance to the Habits of Everyday Life in Hawai'i*(Honolulu: University of Hawai'i Press, 2008), 3.
[35] For critical responses to this collection and its earlier form as a special edition of *Amerasia Journal*, called 'Whose Vision? Asian Settler Colonialism in Hawai'i' see Wilson's *Reimagining the American Pacific*, Seri Luangphinith's 'Beyond Solitary Confinement: Rethinking the Sociopolitical Context of Local Literature in Hawai'i', and Lori Pierce's review of *Asian Settler Colonialism*.
[36] Fujikane and Okamura, *Asian Settler Colonialism*, 3.
[37] Fujikane and Okamura, *Asian Settler Colonialism*, 11.
[38] Fujikane and Okamura, *Asian Settler Colonialism*, 11.

literary scholarship in Hawaiʻi. If one follows Fujikane's logic, neither Yamanaka or Kingston have the right to call themselves 'local' nor can they be read as writing the literature of Hawaiʻi. Yet, as we will see, this does not stop them from claiming a literary ownership of the islands.

Poetics of place: *Blu's Hanging* and Molokaʻi

Between Oʻahu and Maui is the lesser-known island of Molokaʻi. Home to indigenous Hawaiians for over a millennium, the island was developed for pineapple plantations during the nineteenth century. From 1865 to 1969, Molokaʻi served as a leprosy colony with lifetime involuntary isolation. Many of the patients were Hawaiians; some were plantation workers from other islands sent to Molokaʻi by managers fearful of contaminating their labour force. Many were children. Healthy children born to infected parents in the colony were separated against the family's will and sent to adoptive parents.[39] This darker part of Hawaiʻi's history, left out of tourist brochures and mainland representations of Hawaiʻi as a tropical paradise, is the foundation for Lois-Ann Yamanaka's second novel *Blu's Hanging*.

The novel tells the story of twelve-year-old Ivah, a *sansei* forced to care for her two younger siblings after her mother dies and her father, Poppy, must take on an extra job working the night shift at the Dole pineapple factory.[40] Poppy is rarely home and his grief makes him all the more absent. It is not until midway through the novel that Ivah learns her parents met as children in the leprosy settlement Kalaupapa. After years of confinement, they were released as healthy adults but Ivah's mother, Ella, continued to take her medication. In the words of Poppy: 'I told your madda take the sulfones only when she flare up. Bumbye she get immune, but she no listen. She no listen. She no like *eva* get leprosy again. And the bugga been eat up her kidneys.'[41] Ella continued to take her medication

---

[39] 'Leprosy and the Family', International Leprosy Association – History of Leprosy, https://leprosyhistory.org/impact/leprosy-and-the-family. For first-hand accounts, see Anwei Skinsnes Law's *Kalaupapa: A Collective Memory* (Honolulu: University of Hawaiʻi Press, 2012), which combines interviews with archival documents, including more than 300 letters and petitions written by the earliest residents of Kalaupapa. For a historical analysis of how Molokaʻi's leprosy colony contributed to colonization of Hawaiʻi, see R. D. K. Herman's 'Out of Sight, out of Mind, out of Power: Leprosy, Race and Colonization in Hawaiʻi', *Journal of Historical Geography* 27 (1 July 2001): 319–37.

[40] A *sansei* is third-generation Japanese immigrant. The distinctions *nisei* (second generation), *sansei*, and *yonsei* (fourth generation) are used prevalently in Hawaiʻi. Yamanaka herself is a *sansei*, born on the island of Molokaʻi to a family of plantation workers and raised on the Big Island in the working-class town of Pahala.

[41] Lois-Ann Yamanaka, *Blu's Hanging* (New York: Harper Collins, 1997), 144.

out of fear of falling ill again and out of fear of losing her children, 'she wen kept taking the sulfones so she would neva have to go back there without you kids, so that she neva abandon her kids like her family abandon her'.[42] Nevertheless: 'The thing wen' kill her slow. And she abandon us anyway. Was love wen' kill my Ella. Love for *you*.'[43] Ivah shoulders this charge and does her best to mother her younger siblings. But her brother Blu's desperate search for love repeatedly puts him in dangerous situations. The novel culminates with Blu being raped at the age of ten by their Filipino neighbour, Uncle Paulo. The story is harrowing, depicting Moloka'i's poverty and dark history of leprosy and the plantation against the backdrop of tropical flora and red dirt roads.

Early in her career, Yamanaka was heralded for her honest portrayal of the islands and use of HCE, winning several awards including the Pushcart Prize for poetry in 1993. *Blu's Hanging* was bestowed with the Association for Asian American Studies' (AAAS) Fiction Award in 1997, only to have it quickly rescinded following claims that depictions of its characters were racist. Racial tensions do exist in the novel, often reflecting the racial hierarchy instigated by the plantation system that continues to reverberate in modern Hawai'i. In Poppy's words: 'All the lunas all haole before on the sugar plantation – they mean sunnavabitches with bullwhips for hit the kids and all'.[44] Poppy describes the plantation's racial structure to Ivah, with the whites, *haoles*, at the top, followed by Portuguese, then Japanese, with Filipinos and Hawaiians at the bottom. Hawaiians are almost excluded from the novel entirely, their absence common in the literature of Hawai'i at this time, the majority of which focused on the Asian American experience.[45] Critics of *Blu's Hanging* claimed that it reinforced negative stereotypes of racial groups in Hawai'i, particularly Filipinos. Jonathan Okamura declared he was 'deeply offended and outraged by the portrayal of Filipino Americans'.[46] Candace Fujikane wrote to the *Hawaii Herald* reiterating

---

[42] Yamanaka, *Blu's Hanging*, 145.

[43] Yamanaka, *Blu's Hanging*, 145.

[44] Yamanaka, *Blu's Hanging*, 58.

[45] 1985 marked the centennial arrival of Japanese immigrants to work on sugar plantations in Hawai'i and the years that followed saw an increase in publications dedicated particularly to the Japanese immigrant experience, and later Asian Americans in Hawai'i more generally. The interest catapulted several careers such as Milton Murayama's, who struggled to get his first novel, *All I Asking for Is My Body*, published in the 1960s and finally self-published in 1978, only to have it republished by The University of Hawai'i Press in 1988 with an afterword by Asian American historian and Professor of Ethnic Studies at University of Hawai'i, Franklin Odo. Continuing on this streak of success, Murayama received the Hawai'i Award for Literature in 1991and went on to publish three more novels: *Five Years on a Rock* (1994) *Plantation Boy* (1998) and *Dying in a Strange Land* (2008), all published by University of Hawai'i Press.

[46] Quoted in Jamie James, 'This Hawaii Is Not for Tourists', *The Atlantic*, February 1999.

these concerns, arguing that the novel did not 'help others' and that literature should serve to uplift the spirit, asking: 'Do we speak out about our experiences of pain only to create new pain for someone else?'[47] A year later Fujikane wrote a piece entitled, 'Sweeping Racism under the Rug of "Censorship": The Controversy over Lois-Ann Yamanaka's *Blu's Hanging*' in which she asserted the media spun a story 'consistent with the state's denial of racial inequalities' focusing on the sensationalism of the controversy rather than telling the story of 'local Japanese racism and political dominance in Hawai'i'.[48] This idea is congruent with her later sentiments about the abuse of power by Asian Settlers in Hawai'i. The controversy over *Blu's Hanging* underlines ruptures within Hawai'i over who, and how, one can lay claim to the islands' literature.

When the award for *Blu's Hanging* was presented at the AAAS Conference in Honolulu, members of the audience stood up and turned their back to the stage. Wing Tek Lum, former AAAS prize-winner and friend of Yamanaka, said: 'The ethnic-studies people hijacked the conference and imposed mob rule' (quoted in James). The dispute, or 'brouhaha' as Luangphinith has called it,[49] appeared in *The Los Angeles Times*, *Newsweek* and *The Atlantic* under the headlines: 'Authentic Characters or Racist Stereotypes?', 'Trouble in Paradise: A Hawaiian Novelist Sparks a P.C. Protest' and 'This Hawaii Is Not for Tourists'. The latter two titles serve as a reminder of the reductive views of Hawai'i as paradise or tourist playground shared by mainland readers of these publications, suggesting that they expect the literature of the islands to perpetuate these fantasies and an interest in this novel simply because it did not. The controversy over *Blu's Hanging* both on the islands and as depicted in mainland media, reveals that the novel engages the dynamic between a location and orientations beyond that location. The local and national interest in this dispute points to the fact that the novel had a readership on both island and mainland but the reactions in each location display differing orientations of looking at the literature of Hawai'i from within or from afar. More broadly, the controversy over *Blu's Hanging* highlights how disputes over the right to claim a place can play a role in the reception of a literary work and thus underscores the importance of reckoning with location and orientation in literary study.

[47] Quoted in James, 'This Hawaii Is Not for Tourists'.
[48] Candace Fujikane, 'Sweeping Racism under the Rug of "Censorship": The Controversy over Lois-Ann Yamanaka's *Blu's Hanging*', in *The Japanese American Contemporary Experience in Hawai'i*, ed. Jonathan Y. Okamura (Honolulu: University of Hawai'i Press, 2002), 36–72, 38.
[49] Luangphinith, 'Beyond Solitary Confinement: Rethinking the Sociopolitical Context of Local Literature in Hawai'i', 389.

In an essay for the *Asian Settler Colonialism* collection, entitled 'This Land Is Your Land, This Land Was My Land' ku'ualoha ho'omanawanui writes about *Blu's Hanging*. She does not aim to add to the AAAS debate but rather reads the novel from a Native Hawaiian perspective. She lambasts, and rightly so, mainlanders who have called Yamanaka 'Native Hawaiian' and one reviewer who called her the 'first talented Hawaiian writer of fiction'.[50] Yamanaka is not Native Hawaiian and there are centuries of talented writers and storytellers in Hawai'i that predate her work. Yet ho'omanawanui seems to read Yamanaka's very decision to write about Moloka'i as an assault on Hawaiian literature, or *mo'olelo Hawai'i*. In a comparison of descriptions of *'āina* in Native Hawaiian and Asian 'settler' texts, ho'omanawanui concludes that differences in representation are indicative of the writer's position of power in Hawai'i. English words used by settlers, such as 'landscape', 'geography' and 'environment', 'connote a Western-based understanding of what land is, terms that overshadow and negate Native understandings of land as 'āina'.[51] She claims that in *Blu's Hanging*, Yamanaka describes Moloka'i in exclusively negative terms that disregard the spiritual significance of the island to Kānaka Maoli. She refers to Ivah's description of her hometown Kaunakakai:

> It's so hot in this town that babies wear diapers only, men go without shirts, windows and doors stay wide open, and people seek out the shade of a mango tree, or a lanai where there's a breeze. Inside, ceiling fans whir and standing fans with blue-cool plastic blades collect oily dust in a blue-gray blur. That's why Mama said steam, don't fry – it's so hot here that when you're standing over a pan of bubbling oil, your sweat rolls off your eyebrow, lands in the hot oil, and wham, it shoots you right in the face.[52]

To ho'omanawanui, Ivah only depicts the island as a place one wants to escape, which perpetuates 'colonial views of immigrants trying to find their place in America rather than connecting to the 'āina as a place of nourishment and sustenance'.[53] Such criticism, however, ignores the poverty and dire straits the character Ivah finds herself in – where struggling to feed her siblings and protect her brother from sexual abuse takes precedence over appreciating the

[50] ku'ualoha ho'omanawanui, '"This Land Is Your Land, This Land Was My Land": Kanaka Maoli versus Settler Representations of 'Āina in Contemporary Literature of Hawai'i', in *Asian Settler Colonialism*, ed. Candace Fujikane and Jonathan Y. Okamura (Honolulu: University of Hawai'i Press, 2008), 116–54, http://www.jstor.org/stable/j.ctt6wr0h6.13, 135.

[51] ho'omanawanui, '"This Land Is Your Land, This Land Was My Land"',188.

[52] Yamanaka, *Blu's Hanging*, 65.

[53] ho'omanawanui, '"This Land Is Your Land, This Land Was My Land"', 136.

island's natural beauty. While Yamanaka has been praised for being 'willing to go places no writer of Hawai'i imagined before',[54] ho'omanawanui maintains that Yamanaka's work displays disconnection from the land. She juxtaposes Yamanaka's descriptions of Moloka'i with those in Kanaka Maoli poetry, which celebrate Moloka'i as a place of beauty and as home. This argument runs a dangerous course of suggesting that one person's depiction of home is more valuable than another's, in this case, privileging a person of Native Hawaiian descent over an 'outsider' even if that outsider has been born on the island, like Yamanaka herself, or the several thousand leprosy patients forced to call Moloka'i home. My point here is not *who* can call Moloka'i home but the implications of a literary work that does so.

ho'omanawanui goes on to read *Blu's Hanging* as an example of local literature that, seemingly 'embraces a mixture of regionally based writing and ethnic or culturally based writing' but in actuality is just a novel set in Hawai'i with characters that uphold American values.[55] She claims the novel reveals a 'bias toward O'ahu', reading Ivah's aspiration to go to a private school in Honolulu as a desire to 'pursue the American dream'.[56] Yet this conflation of O'ahu and the mainland is erroneous. While seeming to be in line with the argument for putting Hawai'i at the centre and moving away from American politics at large, ho'omanawanui misses the fact that Yamanaka's novel is an important reorientation *away* from the mainland. Rather than making O'ahu a centre analogous to the mainland, *Blu's Hanging* puts Moloka'i at its centre. The entirety of the novel plays out on this 'peripheral' island with the exception of one visit to the Big Island. Rather than glorify the mainland, or even O'ahu, the novel focuses on the quotidian lives of Moloka'i. Yamanaka clearly claims the island as the centre of this literary world, where characters orient from the perspective of Moloka'i. References to O'ahu and the mainland are minor and, rather than revealing 'American values', serve to accentuate the characters' location on, and orientation from, Moloka'i. As seen with Lum's and Balaz's poems, this seems to be another instance of 'renouncing the larger world for the smaller place'.[57] *Blu's*

54 Marie Hara, quoted in ho'omanawanui, "'This Land Is Your Land, This Land Was My Land'", 136.
55 She goes on to attack the major publisher of 'local' literature in Hawai'i: 'Bamboo Ridge claims to be a literary journal for Hawai'i writers' but 'what it has actually become is a literary journal run by Asian American settlers publishing (mostly) other Asian American settlers who trace their "island roots" back to Hawai'i's sugar plantations and no farther'. ho'omanawanui, "'This Land Is Your Land, This Land Was My Land'", 136.
56 ho'omanawanui, "'This Land Is Your Land, This Land Was My Land'", 137.
57 Sheldon Pollock, 'Cosmopolitan and Vernacular in History',*Public Culture*12, no. 3 (1 September 2000): 591–625, 591.

Hanging, however, is a deviation in the literature of Hawai'i where characters moving to the mainland in search of the American dream is a common trope.

Milton Murayama's Oyama tetralogy is exemplary of the fictional formula found in the literature of Hawai'i. His novels follow the life of Kiyo Oyama who is born on a sugar plantation in Maui but thanks to the GI Bill moves to the mainland after the Second World War. Despite longing for the islands and retaining the language of his home, Kiyo chooses the mainland over what he sees as the provinciality of the islands. Kiyo's brother Tosh stays in Hawai'i but torments himself with comparisons to family members on the mainland and spends his life trying to prove himself more successful. Ultimately, he succeeds by becoming an architect on O'ahu and building the new American Hawai'i. Capitalizing on statehood and the tourist industry, Tosh goes from 'plantation boy' to millionaire, attaining the quintessential American rags-to-riches dream.[58]

The majority of Murayama's tetralogy is written in Standard English. The use of HCE is relegated to dialogue between Kiyo and his siblings or Tosh and his childhood friends. By contrast, Yamanaka privileges HCE in all her work.[59] In *Blu's Hanging*, HCE dominates the dialogue and punctuates the first-person narration, so much so that when characters speak in Standard English, it is presented as a deviation from the norm and is marked by phrases like: 'The guy speaks such good English, it's disgusting.'[60] In a parent-teacher conference between Ivah and her sister's teacher, Ivah says: '"My fadda no can come ever 'cause he got work."' To which the teacher from the mainland replies: '"Well, *dear*, we need to speak in standard English for the duration of this conference. I find the pidgin English you children speak to be so limited in its ability to express fully what we need to cover today. Am I clear?"'[61] The condescending nature of the teacher's remark reflects attitudes about HCE congruent with the novel's period, as well as the power dynamic between the mainland and the islands. Here a teacher from Minnesota is brought to Moloka'i with a certain cultural and linguistic authority by which she asserts the power of Standard English over the vernacular. In *Blu's Hanging*, Yamanaka creates a self-conscious articulation of the vernacular's literary value, which emerges in relation to the literary culture and language of the US mainland and Standard English. Following Alexander

---

[58] Milton Murayama, *Dying in a Strange Land* (Honolulu: University of Hawai'i Press, 2008).
[59] HCE is most dominant in Yamanaka's poetry, see for example *Saturday Night at the Pahala Theatre*, Bamboo Ridge Press, 1993.
[60] Yamanaka, *Blu's Hanging*, 35.
[61] Yamanaka, *Blu's Hanging*, 59–60.

Beecroft, who writes that historically the world's cosmopolitan languages were Sanskrit and Latin and today are predominantly (Standard) French and English, we may see the teacher's authority as cosmopolitan.[62] Beecroft asserts that vernacular literatures emerge as a self-aware response to the cosmopolitan and that dominant language. Even without the obvious exchange between Ivah and her teacher, *Blu's Hanging* makes us aware of the cosmopolitan pole in its conscious choice to privilege the vernacular. In this student–teacher exchange, Ivah resists the teacher's mainland authority and ignores her request to speak Standard English, and instead speaks 'pidgin' for the duration of the meeting.[63]

In Hawai'i, the decision to write in vernacular reveals more than a distinction from the cosmopolitan. By using HCE in *Blu's Hanging*, Yamanaka claims a literary space for this vernacular form. Her depictions of Moloka'i also stake a claim on the island as a non-Hawaiian, non-white 'local'. The fact that the main character is a *sansei* is important in a space where ethnicity and duration of residency on the islands repeatedly arise in assertions of local identity and local literature. *Blu's Hanging* is part of the literary movement responding to previous anglophone depictions of Hawai'i, the majority of which were written by white, American males. Pre-dating *Blu's Hanging*, literary depictions of Moloka'i in English were scant but included those by Jack London and Robert Louis Stevenson. Despite being horrified by the presence of leprosy on the island, both London and Stevenson describe it as one of the world's last remote paradises. London even goes as far as to designate the island a sanctuary for lepers, writing the 'Settlement of Molokai enjoys a far more delightful climate than even Honolulu'.[64] Rod Edmond has written that both Stevenson and London saw Moloka'i as the paradise Hawai'i used to be, a 'flawed remnant of the hedonistic communities that once typified Polynesian culture'.[65] Such are the narratives that Yamanaka strives, and succeeds, to write against. Yamanaka's use of HCE and her focus on Moloka'i's working-class population, destabilizes mainland expectations of literature about Hawai'i. The novel provides a new literary landscape separate from that seen in Day and Stroven's 'Hawaiian literature' as well as in the tradition of the *mo'olelo Hawai'i*. Rather, *Blu's Hanging* claims the islands as a literary space that engages the dynamics of its location with its vernacular language and inward orientation.

[62] Alexander Beecroft, *An Ecology of World Literature: From Antiquity to the Present Day* (London: Verso Books, 2015).
[63] Yamanaka, *Blu's Hanging*, 60.
[64] Jack London, *The Cruise of the Snark* (The Floating Press, 1911), 97.
[65] Rod Edmond, 'Leprosy and Colonial Discourse: Jack London and Hawaii', *Wasafiri* 12, no. 25 (March 1997): 78–82, 79.

Poetics of place: *Hawai'i One Summer* and Mokoli'i

Not to be confused with Moloka'i, Mokoli'i is a small islet off O'ahu's windward coast accessible by canoe, surfboard, swimming, or even wading at low tide. The view of the basalt islet is striking, as it rises out of the Pacific in a black conical peak. In Hawaiian mythology, Pele's younger sister, Hi'iaka, killed a giant lizard, or *mo'o*, and tossed it into the ocean. According to the legend, the islet is the lizard's tail rising out of the water, thus giving it its name: *moko* (an older form of *mo'o*) and *li'i*, meaning small, or tiny.[66] Colloquially, however, the island is referred to as Chinaman's Hat. In an essay with this title in *Hawai'i One Summer*, Kingston writes: 'I had a shock when I heard it was called Chinaman's Hat ... I had never heard "Chinaman" before except in derision when walking past racists.'[67] She continues, 'I did not call it Chinaman's Hat, and no one calls it Mokoli'i Island, so for a long time I didn't call it anything.'[68] Here, in her initial resistance to the vernacular place name, Mokoli'i becomes nameless. This reluctance displays Kingston's unfamiliarity with the different uses of the term 'Chinaman' in Hawai'i and the mainland. As with many English words in HCE, their usage is different than in Standard English.[69] Her misunderstanding of 'Chinaman's Hat' reveals an orientation towards Hawai'i from the mainland where the word is historically derogative. 'Chinaman' does not have the same discriminatory weight in Hawai'i, where the Chinese, the first immigrant labourers brought to work on the plantations and today a large percentage of the islands' population, use the phrase self-reflexively. Kingston eventually becomes aware of these different uses. In the later essay on the Talk Story Conference, she acknowledges, though is surprised by, 'the speakers' proud use of the word "Chinaman"'.[70] In the essay 'Chinaman's Hat' we see her slowly grow accustomed to the name: 'At first I watched expressions and tones of voice for a snide reference to me. But the locals were not yelling at me or spitting at me or trying to run me down with a bike

---

[66] ho'omanawanui, '"This Land Is Your Land, This Land Was My Land"', 133.

[67] Kingston, *Hawai'i One Summer*, 29.

[68] Kingston, *Hawai'i One Summer*, 30.

[69] The lexifier or superstrate of HCE is English, but many words from the English language are used differently, for example, *alphabet* is used to designate one letter in the alphabet and *cockaroach*, means both the insect and a verb to steal or sneak away with something. Kent Sakoda and Jeff Siegel, *Pidgin Grammar: An Introduction to the Creole Language of Hawaii*, Bilingual edition (Honolulu: Bess Press Inc, 2003), 16.

[70] Kingston, *Hawai'i One Summer*, 49. The speakers she is referring to are Jeff Paul Chan and Shawn Wong, Chinese-American editors of the anthology *Aiiieeeee! An Anthology of Asian-American Writers* (1974). Arguably these writers were vying for a re-appropriation of the term Chinaman, but this is not discussed in Kingston's essay.

saying, "Chinaman."'[71] After this comment, Kingston uses the colloquial name for the rest of the essay, a shift suggesting she learns the vernacular.

The opening lines of 'Chinaman's Hat' clearly position Kingston as a visitor to Hawai'i unaccustomed to island spaces: 'Living on an island, I miss driving, setting out at dawn and ending up five or six hundred miles away – Mexico – at nightfall. Instead, we spin around and around a perimeter like on a race track.'[72] In this first sentence, Kingston's point of reference is the mainland, chiefly California. She describes travel as something continental, where one has the possibility of reaching new countries without ever crossing water. It is on one of these drives around the 'race track' of O'ahu that Kingston sees Mokoli'i and decides, despite not being a strong swimmer, to venture out. The islet is described a luscious, magical, something separate and unknown from the mainland or even O'ahu. She describes fish and fauna as though enchanted:

> We swam through spangles of silver white fish. I hovered in perfect suspension over forests, flew over spring forests, and winter forests. … Sometimes the sun made golden rooms, which we entered from dark hallways. Specks of sand shone like gold and fell like motes, like the light in California. Sea cucumbers rock from side to side.[73]

Her choice of simile 'like the light in California' displays her constant comparison of Hawai'i to the mainland. But there is also a reverence here for what is new, separate from the mainland, or land at all. Her descriptions reach a transcendental peak when she writes: 'Lying in a tide pool, I saw nothing but blue sky and black rock; the ocean spit cold now and again. The two friends with us stood in a blowhole and said wedding vows while the ocean sprayed rainbows around their heads.'[74] At the day's end, 'we pulled ourselves up on the land, lay with our arms open holding on to Oahu. We were grateful to return, relieved we had made it back alive.'[75] Later, 'our friend who got married in the blowhole, often broke into hysterics, and she and her husband returned to the cool northern Californian woods.'[76] These hysterics are not explained, though Kingston seems to imply a psychological apposition between mainland and island wherein the psyche of one used to living on a continent is challenged by

[71] Kingston, *Hawai'i One Summer*, 30.
[72] Kingston, *Hawai'i One Summer*, 29.
[73] Kingston, *Hawai'i One Summer*, 30–31.
[74] Kingston, *Hawai'i One Summer*, 31.
[75] Kingston, *Hawai'i One Summer*, 31.
[76] Kingston, *Hawai'i One Summer*, 32.

living on an island. This may explain her own relief to reach the larger island of O'ahu. She embraces the 'land' with open arms, an expression of gratitude but perhaps also an attempt to 'hold on' to her sanity.

It would be an exaggeration to say Kingston does not use any vernacular in this collection of essays. As mentioned, she does eventually use the name Chinaman's Hat but clearly does not speak HCE. She seems to hold the language at a distance, marvelling at its presence at the Talk Story Conference; in the 'Preface to the Paperback Edition' she confesses she did not know 'how to teach standard English to students who speak pidgin without offending or harming them'.[77] Yet the vernacular does appear in her work, if in subtle and ambivalent ways. Hawaiian words are scattered throughout her narration, mostly in place names, but she uses the terms *haole* and *aloha* without italics and they fit rather seamlessly into her writing. Arguably these are two of the most common Hawaiian words used by locals and tourists alike but Kingston does seem to understand the complex meaning of *aloha* when she signs the Preface to the Paperback Edition, 'Ke aloha nō! Aloha!' This unglossed salutation is concluded with the designation, 'Mainland, 1998'.[78] While it is not uncommon to sign a letter with a place name, it is noteworthy that she does not write San Francisco or California but rather 'Mainland', as if in opposition to Hawai'i. The inclusion of this valediction signals that while it may not be clear in the essays, by the paperback edition Kingston recognizes the tensions between island and mainland and can locate herself in that dialectic.

Conclusion: Vernacular as home

In the year following the publication of *Blu's Hanging*, Yamanaka declared a commitment to writing in HCE, saying in an interview: 'I am devoted to telling stories the way that I experience them – cultural identity and linguistic identity being skin and flesh to my body'.[79] Milton Murayama has also written on the importance of including HCE in his work, stating: 'The aim of writing is to get as close as possible to the experience and if the experience is in dialect, you write in dialect'.[80] Joe Balaz's poem, 'The History of Pidgeon' can easily be read

---

[77] Kingston, *Hawai'i One Summer*, xiii.

[78] Kingston, *Hawai'i One Summer*, xv.

[79] Renee H. Shea, 'Pidgin Politics and Paradise Revisited', *Poets and Writers* 26, no. 5 (1998): 32–9, 32.

[80] Milton Murayama, 'Problems of Writing in Dialect and Mixed Languages', *MELUS* 4, no. 1 (1977): 7–9, https://doi.org/10.2307/763423, 7.

as a defence of HCE: 'Like different kine words/da world wuz full of different kine birds/ ... I guess wit such wun wide blue sky/everything deserves to fly.'[81] And yet hoʻomanawanui staunchly declares: 'the authentic sound and voice of Hawaiʻi is ʻōlelo Hawaiʻi, the Hawaiian language, not HCE.'[82] Protecting the use of Hawaiian as the indigenous language of Hawaiʻi is imperative and such struggle is deeply correlated to the Hawaiian Sovereignty Movement, and yet, stressing its value over HCE is precarious as such a discourse on authenticity quickly becomes essentialist and exclusionary.

To hoʻomanawanui however, it is most imperative that literature written in Hawaiʻi display reverence for *ʻāina*. She criticizes 'the world of "local" literature' where '"local" is being defined through a linguistic rather than physical "landscape"'.[83] While it is true that a commitment to HCE courses throughout the literature of Hawaiʻi, I argue that the linguistic landscape does not take precedence over the physical but rather the two are intertwined. The main character, Lovey, in Yamanaka's first novel expresses this well:

> I can't talk the way that he wants me to. I cannot make it sound his way, unless I'm playing pretend-talk-haole. I can make my words straight, that's pretty easy if I concentrate hard. But the sound, the sound from my mouth, if I let it rip right out the lips, my words will always come out like home.[84]

Here Lovey asserts the connection between home and language, and for many in Hawaiʻi 'pidgin' is inseparable from place. In the dialogue between Ivah and her teacher, Ivah's refusal to speak Standard English resists the teacher's mainland authority and claims HCE as the language of their location on Molokaʻi. When Kiyo in Murayama's tetralogy picks up the phone in San Francisco to call his brother Tosh in Honolulu, HCE serves as the literal link to home.[85] By contrast, Kingston's lack of HCE in *Hawaiʻi One Summer*, reveals that despite living nearly two decades on the islands, they were never home. Rather, seventeen years is relegated to a 'stay', her place descriptions are in Standard English and often use the mainland as a point of comparison.

In all the examples used in this chapter, descriptions of physical landscape are essential to the way these writers attempt to lay a literary claim to the islands. But these descriptions also situate the authors within larger debates on local politics

---

[81] Balaz, *Pidgin Eye*, 11–12.

[82] hoʻomanawanui, '"This Land Is Your Land, This Land Was My Land"', 139.

[83] hoʻomanawanui, '"This Land Is Your Land, This Land Was My Land"', 138.

[84] Lois-Ann Yamanaka, *Wild Meat and the Bully Burgers* (New York: Picador, 1996), 14.

[85] Murayama, *Dying in a Strange Land*.

and the vernacular. In *Hawai'i One Summer*, Kingston tries to maintain distance, treading carefully around HCE and never calling the islands home. As opposed to the authors who associate HCE with home, Kingston's use of Standard English and comparisons to California suggest homesickness. On her journey to Mokoli'i, however, her place descriptions reveal a reverence for the islands' natural beauty and a connection so strong she declares she can hear (with the possessive pronoun) 'the voice of our island singing'.[86] Later publications of the collection point to Kingston's ambivalence over who has the right to write about Hawai'i. In a preface from 1984, she states: 'It is very difficult to capture Hawai'i. Whose point of view among all of Hawai'i's peoples is the right way of seeing?'[87] This chapter has shown there are a multitude of ways. Hawai'i exists within a complex matrix of indigeneity and migration, local and global, sovereign and colonial. Kingston's aim to have 'incidentally described her [Hawai'i] piece by piece, and hope that the sum praises her',[88] is not Kingston's accomplishment but that of all literature from the islands. What distinguishes these literary works from each other is not whether the author is Hawaiian, local, or *haole*, but how these authors locate the islands in their work and the language they choose to do so in. This in turn reveals an orientation towards or away from the islands. Reading the literature of Hawai'i with this location–orientation perspective allows us to see the political and linguistic complexities implicit in claiming the islands as a literary space.

Bibliography

Balaz, Joe. *Pidgin Eye*. Honolulu: Ala Press, 2019.

Beecroft, Alexander. *An Ecology of World Literature: From Antiquity to the Present Day*. London: Verso Books, 2015.

Chock, Eric and Jody Manabe. *Writers of Hawaii: A Focus on Our Literary Heritage*. Honolulu: Bamboo Ridge Press, 1981.

Day, A. Grove and Carl Stroven, eds. *A Hawaiian Reader*. 1959. Honolulu: Mutual Publishing, 1961.

Day, A. Grove and Carl Stroven, eds. *The Spell of Hawaii*. New York: Meredith Press, 1968.

Day, A. Grove and Carl Stroven, eds. *The Spell of the Pacific: An Anthology of Its Literature*. New York: MacMillan, 1949.

---

[86] Kingston, *Hawai'i One Summer*, 33.
[87] Kingston, *Hawai'i One Summer*, xviii.
[88] Kingston, *Hawai'i One Summer*, xviii.

Edmond, Rod. 'Leprosy and Colonial Discourse: Jack London and Hawaii'. *Wasafiri* 12, no. 25 (March 1997): 78–82.

Foot, Donna. 'Trouble in Paradise: A Hawaiian Novelist Sparks a P.C. Protest'. *Newsweek*, 17 August 1993.

Fujikane, Candace. 'Sweeping Racism under the Rug of "Censorship": The Controversy over Lois-Ann Yamanaka's *Blu's Hanging*'. In *The Japanese American Contemporary Experience in Hawaiʻi*, edited by Jonathan Y. Okamura, 36–72. Honolulu: University of Hawaiʻi Press, 2002.

Fujikane, Candace and Jonathan Y. Okamura, eds. *Asian Settler Colonialism: From Local Governance to the Habits of Everyday Life in Hawaiʻi*. Honolulu: University of Hawaiʻi Press, 2008.

Helgesson, Stefan. 'General Introduction'. In *World Literatures: Exploring the Cosmopolitan–Vernacular Exchange*, edited by Stefan Helgesson, Annika Mörte Alling, Yvonne Lindqvist and Helena Wulff, 1–11. Stockholm: Stockholm University Press, 2018. https://doi.org/10.16993/bat.

Herman, R. D. K. 'Out of Sight, out of Mind, out of Power: Leprosy, Race and Colonization in Hawaiʻi'. *Journal of Historical Geography* 27 (1 July 2001): 319–37.

Honpa Hongwanji Mission of Hawaii. 'Living Treasures'. https://hongwanjihawaii.com/living-treasures/

hoʻomanawanui, kuʻualoha. '"This Land Is Your Land, This Land Was My Land": Kanaka Maoli versus Settler Representations of ʻĀina in Contemporary Literature of Hawaiʻi'. In *Asian Settler Colonialism*, edited by Candace Fujikane and Jonathan Y. Okamura, 116–54. From Local Governance to the Habits of Everyday Life in Hawaiʻi. Honolulu: University of Hawaiʻi Press, 2008. http://www.jstor.org/stable/j.ctt6wr0h6.13.

hoʻomanawanui, kuʻualoha. 'He Ahu Moʻolelo: E Hoʻokahua i Ka Paepae Moʻolelo Palapala Hawaiʻi: A Cairn of Stories: Establishing a Foundation of Hawaiian Literature'. *Palapala* 1 (2017): 51–100.

International Leprosy Association – History of Leprosy. 'Leprosy and the Family'. https://leprosyhistory.org/impact/leprosy-and-the-family

James, Jamie. 'This Hawaii Is Not for Tourists'. *The Atlantic*, February 1999, 90–94.

Kimura, Larry. 'The Hawaiian Language'. In *Native Hawaiians Study Commission Report*, 1:173–203.Washington, DC: U.S. Department of the Interior, 1983.

Kingston, Maxine Hong. 'Hers'. *The New York Times*, June–July 1978. ProQuest Historical Newspapers: The New York Times with Index.

Kingston, Maxine Hong. *Hawaiʻi One Summer*. Honolulu: University of Hawaiʻi Press, 1998.

Law, Anwei Skinsnes. *Kalaupapa: A Collective Memory*. Honolulu: University of Hawaiʻi Press, 2012.

London, Jack. *The Cruise of the Snark*. The Floating Press, 1911.

Luangphinith, Seri. 'Beyond Solitary Confinement: Rethinking the Sociopolitical Context of Local Literature in Hawaiʻi'. In *The Cambridge History of Asian American*

Literature, edited by Rajini Srikanth and Min Hyoung Song, 389–405. New York: Cambridge University Press, 2015.

Luangphinith, Seri. 'The View from Another Shore: An Island-Specific Approach to Literary Criticism'. In *Oxford Research Encyclopedia of Literature*. Oxford University Press, 29 July 2019. https://doi.org/10.1093/acrefore/9780190201098.013.843.

Lum, Wing Tek. 'East/West Poem'. *Hawai'i Review* 10 (spring/fall 1980): 140.

Lyons, Paul. *American Pacificism: Oceania in the U.S. Imagination*. New York: Routledge, 2006.

Marlow, Mikaela L. and Howard Giles. '"We Won't Get Ahead Speaking like That!" Expressing and Managing Language Criticism in Hawai'i'. *Journal of Multilingual and Multicultural Development* 31, no. 3 (1 May 2010): 237–51.

Murayama, Milton. 'Problems of Writing in Dialect and Mixed Languages'. *MELUS* 4, no. 1 (1977): 7–9. https://doi.org/10.2307/763423.

Murayama, Milton. *All I Asking for Is My Body*. Honolulu: University of Hawai'i Press, 1988.

Murayama, Milton. *Five Years on a Rock*. Honolulu: University of Hawai'i Press, 1994.

Murayama, Milton. *Plantation Boy*. Honolulu: University of Hawai'i Press, 1998.

Murayama, Milton. *Dying in a Strange Land*. Honolulu: University of Hawai'i Press, 2008.

Ohnuma, Keiko. '"Aloha Spirit" and the Cultural Politics of Sentiment as National Belonging'. *The Contemporary Pacific* 20, no. 2 (1 August 2008): 365–94. https://doi.org/10.1353/cp.0.0005.

Pierce, Lori. Review of *Asian Settler Colonialism: From Local Governance to the Habits of Everyday Life in Hawai'i*, by Candace Fujikane and Jonathan Y. Okumura. *Journal of American Ethnic History* 31, no. 2 (2012): 150–52. https://doi.org/10.5406/jamerethnhist.31.2.0150.

Pollock, Sheldon. 'Cosmopolitan and Vernacular in History'. *Public Culture* 12, no. 3 (1 September 2000): 591–625.

Roberts, Brian Russell and Michelle Stephens. 'Archipelagic American Studies and the Caribbean'. *Journal of Transnational American Studies* 5, no. 1 (1 January 2013): 1–20.

Sakoda, Kent and Jeff Siegel. *Pidgin Grammar: An Introduction to the Creole Language of Hawaii*. Bilingual edition. Honolulu: Bess Press, 2003.

Seo, Diane. 'Authentic Characters or Racist Stereotypes?' *Los Angeles Times*, 23 July 1998. www.latimes.com/archives/la-xpm-1998-jul-23-ls-6201-story.html.

Shea, Renee H. 'Pidgin Politics and Paradise Revisited'. *Poets and Writers* 26, no. 5 (1998): 32–9.

Silva, Noenoe K. *Aloha Betrayed: Native Hawaiian Resistance to American Colonialism*. Durham, NC: Duke University Press, 2004.

State of Hawaii. 'Demographic, Social, Economic, and Housing Characteristics for Selected Race Groups in Hawaii'. Research and Economic Analysis Division, March 2018.

Stevens, Tom. 'The Meaning of Kama'aina'. *Maui Nō Ka 'Oi Magazine*. 1 September 2010. www.mauimagazine.net/the-meaning-of-kamaaina/.

Trask, Haunani-Kay. 'Decolonizing Hawaiian Literature'. In *Inside Out: Literature, Cultural Politics, and Identity in the New Pacific*, edited by Vilsoni Hereniko and Rob Wilson, 167–82. Lanham: Rowman & Littlefield, 1999.

Trask, Haunani-Kay. *From a Native Daughter: Colonialism and Sovereignty in Hawai'i*. Honolulu: University of Hawai'i Press, 1999.

Wilson, Rob. *Reimagining the American Pacific: From South Pacific to Bamboo Ridge and Beyond*. Durham, NC: Duke University Press, 2000.

Yamanaka, Lois-Ann. *Wild Meat and the Bully Burgers*. New York: Picador, 1996.

Yamanaka, Lois-Ann. *Blu's Hanging*. New York: Harper Collins, 1997.

5

Sites of solidarity and circuits of Second World reading: Ralph de Boissière's *Crown Jewel* and the locations of the proletarian novel

Bo G. Ekelund

Introduction: *Crown Jewel* as 'world literature', the Caribbean as world

'This extraordinary novel is one of the lost masterpieces of world literature.' Those are the words with which the 1981 re-publication of Ralph de Boissière's *Crown Jewel* was promoted, on the front flap of the dustjacket. The publisher's hyperbole may be standard marketing, but the claim that the novel belongs to world literature is worth taking seriously, if only to ask what world and what world literature we need to reckon with. It could also be argued that the novel is still 'lost', although critical attention has grown steadily.[1] This chapter will look into some of the paths along which the novel was lost and found, to make an argument about proletarian cosmopolitanism, as constituted by the literature of workers' struggles, circulating from the Third World to the Second World and back. The relative absence of this cosmopolitanism in the 'age of the globalized world' then becomes an important critical category for current discussions of world literature. As I will argue, it marks the disappearance of a particular horizon of orientations.

---

[1] Critical works that I am indebted to include Reinhard W. Sander, *The Trinidad Awakening: West Indian Literature of The 1930s* (New York: Greenwood, 1988); Robert Carr, *Black Nationalism in the New World: Reading the African-American and West Indian Experience* (Durham, NC: Duke University Press, 2002); Mike Walonen, 'Resistance, Oil, and Awakening: Textual Responses to the Butler Strike and Its Aftermath', *Ariel: A Review of International English Literature* 44, no. 2–3 (2014): 59–84; Elizabeth McMahon, *Islands, Identity and the Literary Imagination* (London: Anthem Press, 2016); Michael Niblett, '"It's the Mass that Counts": Striking Energies in Working-Class Fiction', *Journal of Postcolonial Writing* 53, no. 3 (2017): 303–15; and Jak Peake, *Between the Bocas: A Literary Geography of Western Trinidad* (Oxford: Oxford University Press, 2017).

I will suggest that de Boissière's novel forms an exemplary instance of this particular form of world literature by its use of a vernacular form of narrative that claims its location as a typological one, thus aligning itself with countless similar locations in their orientation towards international solidarity. The 'vernacular' tendency here is one determined by class and class struggle; it is the pole at which the social capital of autochthony – those social resources that are based on local relationships – enables an international orientation.[2]

For a keynote to that argument, look at how the novel shows us its black workers' leader, Ben Le Maître, gathering support for the cause: "'Comrades', Le Maître would say, lapsing into Creole, which bound the workers to him at once. "I ehn come to talk to all-you 'bout Gawd, nuh? It's food I come to talk about, how you and me eatin'".[3] Le Maître brings everything down from the beyond to the here and now of material needs and, most importantly, to dialogue, talk, and as we see, down to a particular sociolect that de Boissière presents as Creole.[4] Le Maître's code-switching places him in a linguistic and social position as mediator and 'leader' but only because a bond is granted to him.[5] In this polyphonic novel, various forms of speech, ranged along the vernacular–cosmopolitan pole, are set in dialogue and in conflict within an overall struggle over Trinidad as location. The use of the vernacular has not been given much attention in the scholarship on de Boissière, but it is, I will argue, central to how the novel claims its location, the Trinidad of the workers, the people.

The Caribbean is a distinctive region with regard to vernacular and cosmopolitan orientations. The languages spoken by the forty-five million or so inhabitants of the Caribbean islands are alien to the land, as it were: imperial languages and languages formed in subordination to and as insubordination to those languages. When Caribbean writers make literary claims to places and territories, their relationship to their linguistic resources are inherently conflicted, as Le Maître's 'lapsing into Creole' shows. One might plausibly claim that the

[2] See Fabrice Ripoll and Sylvie Tissot, 'La dimension spatiale des ressources sociales', *Regards sociologiques* 40 (2010): 5–7; and Nicolas Renahy, 'Classes populaires et capital d'autochtonie: Genèse et usages d'une notion', *Regards sociologiques* 40 (2010): 9–26.

[3] Ralph de Boissière, *Crown Jewel* (London: Allison & Busby, 1981), 95. The 1952 edition has almost exactly the same wording, with some minor alterations of the 'creole' and 'the people' instead of 'the workers'. Ralph de Boissière, *Crown Jewel* (Melbourne: Australasian Book Society, 1952), 70. Henceforth, the 1981 version will be referenced as *Crown* 1981 and the 1952 version as *Crown* 1952. The 1956 version has very few changes compared to the 1952 original, but will be referenced as *Crown* 1956.

[4] Elsewhere in the novel, there is also the term '*patois*', with reference to the black heroine Cassie's singing, explained in a footnote in *Crown* 1952 as 'Broken French' (124) which the East German edition emends to 'Provincial French', *Crown* 1956, 147.

[5] De Boissière removed responses by the workers when he revised the novel. The original better captures the dialogic principle of this encounter.

imperial languages of education – English, French, Spanish and Dutch – feed into cosmopolitan forms of writing, while the Creoles and patois of the street provide a vernacular means of addressing readers, but things are not so simple.

While linguistic discussions about a creole continuum point to a reality in which creole vernaculars shade into 'standard', normative forms of language use, literary forms cannot be assumed to follow the same logic. The various properties displayed along such a continuum are the raw materials that literary writing converts into the forms that can be recognized as literary. Those literary forms, in turn, will be recognized for their valence within the continuum, or, in the foundational terms of this volume, the cosmopolitan–vernacular dynamic. In the example we started with, de Boissière relies on one of the key effects of the creole continuum. Since every speaker 'represents not a single point but a span on this continuum', it is always possible to move from one end of that span to the other, the strategy we know as code-switching.[6] Le Maître can switch from the 'standard' English in which he converses with the middle-class protagonist André to the Creole that his worker comrades will recognize as appropriate. That is to say, also, that de Boissière can avail himself of that linguistic movement for certain literary effects.

The use of Creole, and the use of 'Creole', however, is not a stable indicator that a vernacular orientation towards the smaller world (drawing mainly on autochthonous capital) is at work. Charles Stewart provides a lucid discussion of the history of the concept.[7] Paradoxically, some theories of creolization place it as one of the characteristics of globalization or at least of a transnational and transcultural force. Noting the increasing generalization of 'creole concepts', Ulf Hannerz suggests that the late twentieth century 'world of movement and mixture is a world in creolization'.[8] In a similar formulation, the *Creolité* advocates point to 'a world evolving into a state of Creoleness', while Édouard Glissant speaks of the 'cultural creolization of the world'.[9] We may add James Clifford's oft-quoted appropriation of Caribbeanness as a universal state of affairs: 'We are

[6]   David DeCamp, 'Social and Geographical Factors in Jamaican Dialects', in *Proceedings of the Conference on Creole Language Studies Held at the University College of the West Indies, March 28–April 4, 1959*, ed. Robert Le Page (London: Macmillan, 1961), 82.
[7]   Charles Stewart, 'Creolization Historicized', in *Creolization: History, Ethnography, Theory* (London: Routledge, 2016), 1–20.
[8]   Ulf Hannerz, 'The World in Creolisation', *Africa* 57 (1987): 551.
[9]   The Creolité group, quoted in Stewart, 'Creolization Historicized', 3. The idea of cultural creolization is fundamental to Glissant's thinking, as in *Poetics of Relation* (Ann Arbor: University of Michigan Press, 1997), 34, but the quote itself is from a web interview, quoted in Mylène Priam, 'Antillanité', *The Oxford Encyclopedia of African Thought*, Volume 1, ed. Abiola Irele and Biodun Jeyifo (Oxford: Oxford University Press, 2010), 82.

all Caribbeans now ... in our urban archipelagos.'[10] As Stewart observes, critics of this tendency, such as Sidney Mintz, Aisha Khan, Mimi Sheller and Stephan Palmié, argue that creoleness and Caribbeanness are not concepts that can be lifted from their ground of emergence, but rather terms that denote highly specific qualities bound up with the particular histories of the plantation societies on Caribbean islands. The academic debate over the term 'creole' is thus itself a case of the vernacular–cosmopolitan dynamic manifesting itself.

My own theoretical preferences here will be to tread lightly among and at the side of the various positions while adhering to sociological principles of understanding. The literary and scholarly uses of linguistic forms that can be recognized as belonging to a creole continuum will be analysed in a strong contextual way: they adopt available social modes of expression to address particular audiences. Within a study of locations and orientations, these uses can be analysed for their attempts to inhabit and claim space. While this chapter will not engage with the theoretical discussions of creolization directly, it should be clear that the creole continuum allows those who speak Creole and those who speak about it to affirm vernacular or cosmopolitan orientations. However, for the Caribbean writer, creole forms do come with a primary association with the vernacular, with street rather than school, with the people rather than the elites. This is how Le Maître's 'bond' with the workers is established.

That association means that the creole vernacular has a class dimension. Not that other vernaculars do not, but the seminal formulations of the creole continuum were singularly stark in their sociolinguistic logic. In David DeCamp's 1961 paper, this 'linguistic continuum [ranged] from the speech of the most backward peasant or labourer all the way to that of the well-educated urban professional', and ten years later he described it as 'ranging from the "bush talk" or "broken language" of Quashie to the educated standard of Philip Sherlock and Norman Manley'.[11] The greater concreteness of the latter formulation is interesting, precisely because the social logic only allows one part of the continuum individual speakers.[12] The Quashie end of the creole continuum is

---

[10] James Clifford, *The Predicament of Culture* (Cambridge, MA: Harvard University Press, 1988), 173.

[11] DeCamp, Social and Geographical Factors, 82; David DeCamp, 'Towards a Generative Analysis of a Post-Creole Continuum', in *Pidginization and Creolization of Languages*, ed. Dell Hymes (Cambridge: Cambridge University Press, 1971), 350.

[12] Claude McKay's early poems give to his various speakers, one of them named 'Quashie', a distinctiveness and demotic force that turns the table on such distributions of individuality. See the 'Songs of Jamaica' and the 'Constab Ballads' sections in the *Complete Poems* (Urbana: University of Illinois Press, 2004).

where the vernacular meets the vulgar, where the 'social life of the verbal sign' is instantly classifiable by the sociolinguist as rural or proletarian backwardness.[13] The class character of Creole serves notice that the cosmopolitan–vernacular dynamic is one in which class is always active, although in misrecognizable forms. That is, literary forms are always refracted forms of class language.[14] For a 'world literature' like de Boissière's, the attempt to speak of class struggle in Trinidad involves a set of contradictions. As I will try to show in what follows, the proletarian novel is a form that depends on an appreciation of the vernacular forces from beneath while taking those forces as a means to produce its own brand of cosmopolitanism: that of international solidarity. In the cultural and linguistic pushing and jostling that the form absorbs, moreover, place is essential: class struggle is about who controls the places of production and reproduction, but also the places of public and political representation. As we will see, de Boissière claims a set of key Trinidad locations by modulating vernacular and cosmopolitan forms across a large span of the creole continuum, but those local, vernacular claims are oriented towards the horizon of universal class struggle and solidarity. This orientation is then to a certain extent realized in the circulation of this novel in the Second World in the late fifties and sixties through a series of translations into mainly East European languages, until its final republication in the metropolitan centre, in London, in 1981, as 'one of the lost masterpieces of world literature'.

World literature is a matter of the different worlds in which literature circulates, but also a matter of the world-orientation of given literary texts. *Crown Jewel* is a text that took shape and reached readers over much of the period that Michael Denning has termed the 'Age of Three Worlds', and we may legitimately ask whether it has any significance in the age of the one, but unequal world of globalized capital (or alternatively, the age of the one, capitalocene world).[15]

In the following analysis, I will first present the novel's production, and then analyse how it claims different locations that make up the typical proletarian space of Trinidad of the mid-1930s. From that literary construction of location/

---

[13] The quoted phrase is from V. N. Voloshinov, *Marxism and the Philosophy of Language* (Cambridge, MA: Harvard University Press, 1986), 21. In that light, it is difficult to assent to the parallel made by Gayatri Spivak when she claims that Dante's preferred Italian vernacular was a Creole, more precisely an 'aristocratic ("curial") political Creole' (Gayatri Chakravorty Spivak, 'World Systems and the Creole', *Creolizing Europe: Legacies and Transformations*, ed. Encarnación Gutiérrez Rodríguez and Shirley Anne Tate (Oxford: Oxford University Press, 2015), 26).

[14] Voloshinov, *Marxism*, 23.

[15] Michael Denning, *Culture in the Age of Three Worlds* (London: Verso, 2004).

orientation, I will then show how the text entered a circulation that is anticipated by its internal orientation. As a way of conclusion, I will show that the general implications of these readings for a study of the vernacular–cosmopolitan dynamic are rather straightforward: the class dimension of this dynamic matters a great deal, and must be given its due.[16]

Ralph de Boissière, from Port-of-Spain to Melbourne, the Beacon group to the Realist Writers' group

Ralph de Boissière's *Crown Jewel* is a peculiar case in many ways, but its peculiarity is exemplary rather than eccentric. It raises questions about the proletarian novel as world literature; it also shows how such a novel must necessarily construct a social space marked by a local distribution of symbolic and material goods, while its success as a proletarian world novel rests on showing the universal implications of that space. In laying its literary claim for the value of Port-of-Spain, Fyzabad, Carenage and other parts of Trinidad, the novel necessarily draws on cultural and linguistic resources that are more or less vernacular, more or less cosmopolitan. For the proletarian writer, these are particularly vexed choices, and especially when the class identity of the author is itself ambiguous, as was the case with Ralph de Boissière.

De Boissière was born in Trinidad in 1907, of a prominent French Creole family, but in an off-shoot of its less legitimate branch.[17] He grew up feeling he did not quite fit into the social circles of Port-of-Spain. After graduating from Queens Royal College, he worked as a salesman for a bakery, in which capacity he travelled all over the island. Taking up writing in the late 1920s, de Boissière fortuitously entered the highly charged intellectual milieu around the journal *The Beacon*. By a chance encounter with William 'Sonny' Carpenter, he was introduced to Alfred Mendes and C. L. R. James, and later to Albert Gomes.[18]

---

[16] My argument is closely aligned with Sonali Perera's analysis of working-class literature that insists on including 'the world as written from locations of peripheral labor' in *No Country: Working-Class Writing in the Age of Globalization* (New York: Columbia University Press, 2014), 3.

[17] My account will largely rely on Ralph de Boissière, *Life on the Edge: The Autobiography of Ralph de Boissière*, ed. Kenneth Ramchand (Melbourne: Lexicon, 2010) and Reinhard W. Sander's contribution, 'Ralph de Boissière', in *Fifty Caribbean Writers: A Bio-Bibliographical Critical Sourcebook*, ed. Daryl Cumber Dance (New York: Greenport, 1986), 151–9.

[18] There is something marvellous about the coincidences that determined de Boissière's literary fate: the chance encounter with Sonny Carpenter on the Port-of-Spain Savannah, here, and twenty years later his running into the leftist Australian writer Frank Hardy in a street in Melbourne. The chronotope of the encounter in public space is central to *Crown Jewel*, but also in the real life of the author.

This small group of men played an outsize role in the history of the beginnings of West Indian writing.[19] It is clear that *Trinidad* and *The Beacon* served significant pioneer roles, and in that light, the coming-together of these men with highly disparate trajectories is worth attention. More importantly, their collaboration affected de Boissière's complicated sense of his own intellectual place, feeding into *Crown Jewel*'s configuration of intellectual orientations. De Boissière's own description of the principals is fascinating, with its admiration for C. L. R. James's historical understanding of issues and ideas that the two others treated more breezily.[20] Alfred Mendes belonged to a 'rich, long-established Portuguese merchant family' and had been educated in England.[21] Albert Gomes's Madeiran family, on the other hand, 'lived among the poor' but Gomes had the advantage of a recent stay in New York.[22] From de Boissière's perspective, Mendes's 'spontaneous enthusiasms' contrasted with James's careful balancing of historical perspectives, while he saw Gomes as 'wallowing in ideas' rather than grasping their meaning.[23] These judgements come from someone who consistently sees himself as a secondary actor, dependent on the intellectual energies of the three other men, whose wide reading and, in the case of Mendes and Gomes, metropolitan experience, made him feel ignorant and provincial. On the other hand, his sceptical assessment of the superficiality of the way Gomes and Mendes flaunted their intellectual prowess and his admiration for James's historically based weighing of perspectives show us a writer looking for a form of literary expression that might balance the biases of metropolitan ideas. The meetings in Mendes's book-lined study helped de Boissière take the measure of that distance, and returned him to his own 'little world':

> we needed to discuss what bedevilled our little world that had been fashioned by British hands both indifferent and purposeful; and on such afternoons we realized ourselves and flourished as Alfie and Nello James with their rich reading rolled back the curtains of our narrow colonial education to reveal a great world that was not England. Trinidad was simmering, and London was too far

---

[19] See Sander, *The Trinidad Awakening*, and Kenneth Ramchand, *The West Indian Novel and Its Background* (London: Faber, 1970). See also de Boissière's own account in *Life on the Edge*, 57–66. Leah Reade Rosenberg's *Nationalism and the Formation of Caribbean Literature* (New York: Palgrave, 2016) revises the picture with attention paid to a larger set of actors.

[20] The *roman à clef* elements of *Crown Jewel* have been picked up by various commentators. We may add the scene in which Joe Elias marvels at the self-assurance of Le Maître, an assurance 'rooted in history', using almost exactly the same terms with which de Boissière describes James in his autobiography (*Crown* 1981, 110; *Life on the Edge*, 58.)

[21] Boissière, *Life on the Edge*, 57.

[22] Boissière, *Life on the Edge*, 64.

[23] Boissière, *Life on the Edge*, 64.

away to see it. Even had London seen that simmering it would have surpassed their understanding. The Beacon group was one of the many little bubbles that coalesced to create the uprising in the oil fields in 1937.[24]

De Boissière's description of these discussions point to three important elements: first, the 'little world' that is shaped by colonial forces and its distance to the colonial centre; second, the 'great world *that was not England*' – that is, a sense of a cosmopolitan orientation that might bypass the false cosmopolitanism of the colonial metropolis; and third, the image of the many bubbles that combine to produce a political event.

That political eruption would furnish de Boissière with the pivot of the novel he was working on at the time. It is there in the dedication of *Crown Jewel* to 'the workers of Fyzabad, ... without [whose] struggle in 1937 this novel would not have been conceived'. And in his autobiography, we can read a conversion narrative that includes the 'lightning' that struck not only the oilfields, but de Boissière's literary consciousness, making him abandon his 'semi-autobiographical tale of early youth' with its basis in the 'sycophancy of little colonial minds'.[25] Instead, in the 'most important decision' of his literary development, he would take the 'point of view ... of working folk' although, importantly, he would keep much of his material 'about middle-class existence'.[26]

This rewriting would keep de Boissière busy for many years to come. An early version of the novel was rejected by Knopf in 1944. Two years later, he left Trinidad for a course in car mechanics in the USA, and then continued to permanent exile in Australia. There he joined a group of socialist writers, the 'Realist Writers' Group', formed in 1944, determined to rework his material with an enlarged 'understanding of life in Trinidad and of the inner worlds of its people'.[27] Narrating this writing process in retrospect, de Boissière keeps framing his development in terms of worlds: 'The West Indian Writer who had not lived in the larger world could not see beyond his small island's mental and spiritual confines that made him little'.[28] On the other hand, the truth of the novel that was now finding its form lay in 'the spirit, the inner world that arose and took shape for a little while only' in the heroes that marched and gave speeches.[29]

---

[24] Boissière, *Life on the Edge*, 66.
[25] Boissière, *Life on the Edge*, 104.
[26] Boissière, *Life on the Edge*, 105.
[27] Boissière, *Life on the Edge*, 169.
[28] Boissière, *Life on the Edge*, 170.
[29] Boissière, *Life on the Edge*, 171.

His relocation to a country with a 'conscious' working class directed him to the truth of the innermost kernel of his own country. Resisting the doctrines of socialist realism, he was prompted by them to see more clearly the necessity of holding on to the experiences of his 'tiny island'.[30] We see de Boissière writing and revising his story of middle-class origins and working-class struggle in a drawn-out process given fuel by locations and dislocations: the book-filled study of Alfred Mendes, a series of workplaces, the moves from Trinidad to Chicago to Melbourne, the meetings of the Realist Writers' Group. Finally, in 1952, by one of those coincidences typical of de Boissière's life, *Crown Jewel* was published by the Australasian Book Society, the first title from this publishing venture started by the Realist Writers to bring to print the writing of Australian workers. As John McLaren says in his book on literature and politics in post-war Australia, *Crown Jewel* was 'a strange choice for a society trying to cultivate an interest in Australian literature among a public scarcely knowledgeable about their own writers, let alone those from exotic cultures'.[31] However, the point to be made is that the idea of a proletarian perspective in literature must be seen as the expression of an international culture, or at least expressing a vision of a culture that is shared across all locations where workers work, struggle and die. De Boissière's 'inner world' was expected to speak to 'a greater world that was not England' in a language that could claim Trinidad's place in that world. That greater world would, in the actual facts of book circulation, turn out to be the countries of Eastern Europe, in a series of materializations that served to animate different conceptions of the 'colonial world'.[32]

We will turn now to *Crown Jewel*'s fictional world, and more particularly, the way it musters spatial and linguistic resources to claim a location.

Claiming Trinidad: The worlding of *Crown Jewel*, raw space through the refinery

By using the term 'spatial resources', I mean to indicate a general hypothesis that space and place in novels from the peripheries of the world system – which includes areas and sectors within the putative centres or cores of the system –

---

[30] Boissière, *Life on the Edge*, 173.
[31] John McLaren, *Writing in Hope and Fear: Literature as Politics in Postwar Australia* (Cambridge: Cambridge University Press, 1996), 35–6.
[32] Publisher's foreword, *Klejnot korony* (Warsaw: Czytelnik, 1953), 6. Such 'world-norms' are not necessarily the norms of the world of the novel, but that latter world is, as Eric Hayot says of aesthetic worlds in general, 'always relations to and theories of the lived world'. 'On Literary Worlds', *Modern Language Quarterly* 72, no. 2 (June 2011): 137.

enter a kind of extractive economy. Like the crude oil pumped up in the oil fields of southern Trinidad, or the cane sugar and cocoa exported by the thousands of tonnes from the island in the heyday of those crops, its raw spaces, like any raw space of any area of the globe, must be refined into the form that can gain literary recognition. De Boissière's tortured wrestling with the value of the inner world, manifested by his characters and their actions as something that will transcend the 'small island's mental and spiritual confines', is testimony to that process of extraction and refinement. While it is a quirk of the dictionary that the word 'refinement' applies in different semantic fields to crude oil as well as to 'manners, feelings, or taste' (OED), it speaks quite logically to the process of working up a raw material into a form that will have value on a particular social market.

De Boissière's intense modelling of Trinidadian space depends on, and reproduces, the power-geometry of class society, while expressing forms of solidarity and love that might escape this geometry. In fact, the novel uses courtship and solidarity-building as a way of claiming a Trinidadian location whose orientation points towards other sites of a globe structured in domination, and towards the possibility that social space may be rendered more equal. Crucial for this spatial claim is the dynamics of vernacular and cosmopolitan forms: linguistic forms, certainly, but also the social configuration of characters with diverse orientations.

What the novel does first is to deal with one of the most powerful ideological oppositions in cultural imaginings of space: that between history and an unchanging nature. In *Caribbean Discourse*, Édouard Glissant emphasizes the 'creative link between nature and culture' and gives the writer the task of reestablishing a 'dialectic ... between nature and culture in the Caribbean'.[33] What is meant here is not to give some pristine nature its due, but precisely to see nature as history, history as nature. De Boissière starts his novel with a 'Prologue' that takes us back to 1498 and Columbus first catching sight of the island he baptized Trinidad, thus transfiguring the three mountain tops from topographical materiality into ideological form. The Prologue evokes

> a lovely land, full of sparkling streams, and broad savannahs where the wild deer roamed; and the woods abounded in meat and fruit and were bright with the flight and scream of birds.[34]

---

[33] Édouard Glissant, *Caribbean Discourse* (Charlottesville: University of Virginia Press, 1989), 65.
[34] *Crown* 1981, 1. *Crown* 1952 is slightly different, the last phrase reading 'and the sounds of a thousand different birds', vii.

In just three pages the history of Trinidad is recounted: the near-annihilation of the indigenous Arawaks, the arrival of French planters, of English imperialists, African slaves and Indian indentured labourers, the schooling of the freed slaves into the imperial ideology, so that the 'sons of Africa … went out of the school doors into the world with England's greatness like a noose about them'.[35] The prologue then ends with a return to that image of natural beauty: 'But had Columbus returned to Cairi in 1935 he would have found her still beautiful as on that July day four hundred years before': red monkeys, humming-birds, ibises, the sunset and the stars.[36] We are neatly moved to the present, 1935, and we are given, it seems, an image of largely unchanged natural beauty. What follows is a careful booby-trapping of the trope of nature as an unmediated source of beauty. The latter-day reader may think we are meant to perform the very misrecognition of persistent beauty ascribed to a Columbus returning to the island, until we carefully register the jolt of turning the page to the next scene. Here, we are thrown into the midst not so much of things as of work or working men, *in medias labores* rather than *res* as it were: 'They gripped the spokes of the two-wheeled timber cart and threw their bodies forward./"Heave! … And again! … *And* again!"'[37]

It will turn out that the cart is delivering floorboards to a supplies shop owned by Dollard & Company, a figure in the novel for British economic dominance of trade in Port-of-Spain, 'Dollard' capturing both the dollar, with the USA's increasing economic influence, and the dullard of one-dimensional economic man. With the timber cart, we are instantly disabused of Columbus's ability to see natural beauty while looking for gold: the red monkeys are retreating as the extractive economy grows. When we enter Dollard & Company's lumberyard, we are taken into a site of labour, action and language. The prologue of the 1952 version spells out the indoctrination of the island inhabitants into English perspectives on the world, singling out the mimic men:

> So the little handful who could afford it sent their children to England, taught them to speak with English accents and married them to English women. "Representatives of the people" though they might be, they gave blessing in the English accents to the wishes of Oil and Sugar, for they would have all men know that they were not what they seemed.[38]

---

[35] *Crown* 1981, 3. *Crown* 1952, x, but with the 'people' of Cairi rather than 'sons of Africa'.
[36] *Crown* 1981, 3; *Crown* 1952, x–xi.
[37] *Crown* 1981, 4. Elisabeth McMahon notes of this sequence that it 'juxtaposes the gazing apprehension of the island as fetish object with the experience of being in the island immersed in labour'. *Islands*, 189.
[38] *Crown* 1952, x.

The 'English accents' introduce the sociolinguistic structuring of the novel's world, and in the 1952 version they are explicitly tied to the extractive economy of oil and sugar. That association will be established in the 1981 version as well, but another change made in the early part of the novel is more important, and underlines the multi-accentuality, or creole continuum, of the novel's construction of space: it immerses the reader directly in the scene of labour, punctuated by the speech of the labourers pulling the cart. The 'English accents' are absent, while the workers' vernacular, in the voice of the helmsman Jacob, takes us through the first page: 'Heave! … And again! … *And* again! … Swing you' swing! … Now, all-you! … Lordy, Lordy … I nearly piss meself laughin'. … Ah! That nice, that good!'[39] Taking pride of place among the many speakers and points on the creole continuum, the vernacular, here in full vulgar regalia, dominates the first scene, linking labour, extractive economy and characters. It is an important revision, reinforcing the heteroglossic patterning of the novel. The other key revision in the first scene is the complete removal of André de Coudray, de Boissière's rather transparent highly educated alter ego, so that the span in the creole continuum extends no further than to the middle-class voice of Joe Elias and the intermediary voice of the Venezuelan clerk, Luna Popito, who next enter the scene. Elias's speech is often marked by the dropped g at the end of present participles, Popito likewise, but as an intermediary the latter switches to more clearly marked vernacular speech when, in a later scene, he speaks to Jacob alone.

Presently, two Englishmen are introduced: Dollard himself, the owner, and Brassington, the manager of the Hardware department and Popito's boss. While Dollard humours his subordinates, Brassington is irked by any sign of disorderliness. This disposition is used by de Boissière to set up another linguistic encounter, in which Popito deliberately intrudes on the orderliness of Brassington's domain with his blustering style of speech – 'He could talk if he liked, couldn't he?' – prompting a reprimand from his superior: 'Must you make such a noise?' Tensions build up until Popito butts Brassington out of the blue, 'in the best Creole style'.[40] This leads to Popito getting fired and excluded from employment.

Within the Dollard company timber yard and its Hardware store, then, de Boissière draws on the continuum to mark out the social coordinates of this location, thus presaging the method by which the entire novel will draw in an expanding social universe corresponding to southern Trinidad, with Port-of-

---

[39] *Crown* 1981, 4.
[40] *Crown* 1981, 8. In *Crown* 1952, 24, this altercation is slightly delayed.

Spain and Fyzabad the two geographical poles. Styles of speech become styles of taking up space and, almost inevitably, styles of violence. These are aligned with racial and ethnic identifications – the black labourers, the Syrian merchant's son, the Venezuelan immigrant, the two English bosses. The novel will fill in the whole creole continuum in due course, and will sometimes be very explicit about the finer shadings. While the French Creole scion André was removed from the first chapter for the 1981 edition, he will still play an important role in the novel, as the young bourgeois who gains a social consciousness of class injustices. This key trope in many proletarian novels is carefully made likely by André's placement within the continuum. Alone among the children of Henri de Coudray, André had not been 'finished.' The finishing involves

> to mix with men and women who knew what was "the thing" and when to do this thing, and who spoke with English accents – above all, the accent. It was as if a stamp "Made in England" had to be acquired before Mr. de Coudray and his fellow West Indians could consider themselves other than "cha-cha" – of no account.[41]

André finds himself without the linguistic stamp that would save him from being regarded as inferior, and is thus predisposed to embrace other social positions, even to disinherit himself completely (as in fact he will). In addition, he is conscious of the family secret of black blood from his great-grandmother Rosette whose mother was a slave and who was, in his Aunt Clotilde's account, 'very uneducated, a mere peasant, hail-fellows-well-met with all the [n-word], talking just like them'.[42] Thus, this key character is suspended between the ends of the creole continuum, the English accent and black peasant speech. He is also placed between the cosmopolitanism of the metropolis, with its linguistic 'finishing', and the cosmopolitan solidarity of 'the people'.

While André embodies this social and linguistic tension, and while Ben Le Maître draws on the possibilities of the continuum, other characters display more static linguistic identities, such as the confident weight of Judge Osborne, moving within an 'impenetrable shell' of imperial traditions, 'large with the authority derived from a foreign land'.[43] Others yet start from being identified with their use of the socially

---

[41] *Crown* 1981, 131. The term 'cha-cha' is recorded as meaning poor whites of French descent in the Virgin Islands, especially St. Thomas, memorably in a weird tale by Henry S. Whitehead, from 1931, where it is explained as deriving from 'the peculiar sneezing nasality with which these French poor-whites enunciate their Norman French'. Henry S. Whitehead, 'Hill Drums', reprinted in *Tales of the Jumbee and Other Wonders of the West Indies* (Cabin John: Wildside Press, 2009), 140.

[42] *Crown* 1981, 133.

[43] *Crown* 1981, 161–2.

least commanding vernacular, and take that speech into situations where it rings out with power, as in the figure of the all but destitute servant Cassandra. In short, *Crown Jewel* takes a panoply of characters from different social stations, exhibiting different forms of speech, and by a series of encounters in socially significant locations the novel subjects them all to the pressure of class conflict.

The worlding of the novel takes as its principle the deep connection between place and social forms of action, most importantly speech. This connection, I suggest, is typological in character. This category invokes both Georg Lukács and Jane Tompkins, critics concerned with the political or cultural work carried out by novels, and it seems a helpful category for saying what a novel like *Crown Jewel* does with space.[44] The Dollard lumber yard and supplies shop is a concrete place in the extensional universe of the novel, but it is also a type of place, or typical place, in the world space of class struggle. The dining room at the Judge Osborne house has a similar typological role. For a typological reading of places, de Boissière shows us that it cannot limit itself to the empirical perception of place nor its symbolic meaning (directed by imaginary identifications) but must move on to its insertion into a constellation of places and concrete situations that is repeated across locations in world space.

Courtship and solidarity in *Crown Jewel*

A full account of the novel's vernacular claim on Trinidad would analyse all those concrete situations. It must be enough here to point to the underlying logic of the novel's shuffling of characters and places, and to identify those arrangements as an extended use of the courtship plot. In fact, the novel has numerous scenes of courtship, traditionally understood, but beyond those recognizable romantic conventions, the novel consistently stages meetings of characters in which other sympathies and antipathies are at work. Courtship in *Crown Jewel* thus works as a typological device that serves to mobilize common vernacular forces (or their opposite, as may be the case). In my reading, courtship extends beyond what readers would spontaneously identify as such.[45] What we see is a basic type

---

[44] See George Lukács on historical-social types and typification, *The Historical Novel* (Lincoln: University of Nebraska Press, 1962): 34–5; Jane Tompkins on typological structures in nineteenth-century narratives, *Sensational Designs* (Oxford: Oxford University Press, 1985).

[45] Both Carr and Niblett note that the romantic plotlines of *Crown Jewel* are politicized. Carr, *Black Nationalism*, 114; Niblett, 'It's the Mass that Counts', 312.

of situation: characters engaging with one another to win sympathy, support or erotic mutuality within a typological framework, and, more importantly for my argument, within the use of spatial divisions and unities. The romantic courtships parallel the other meetings in which social bonds are strengthened or weakened, and contrast with the meetings in which no bonds, only implacable distance, is confirmed. The latter is typified by Popito's initial act of violence against his English superior, after which he is driven from place to place, finding there is 'no place' for him in Port-of-Spain.[46] Similarly, the courtships drive people across a physical topography, which is also social, in order that they meet with other people to find a 'place' of possible conviviality.

The courtship-plot logic distinguishes two cases. The conservative courtship is precisely about conserving social relationships and maximizing social profit from the existing relationships. It implies a rigid upholding of all the principles of vision and division that sustain the status quo of social space. It can be engaged in without the discomfort of disturbing that space: like speaks to like.

The progressive courtship, on the other hand, takes its chances that the social order may change, as illustrated admirably by the scenes in which Popito 'woos' the labour leader Ben Le Maître. After Popito's failed rounds of courting prospective employers, he has fallen into despondency and drinking. A visit to Jacob, the timber cart worker, shows him his future social fate in the barrack-yards,[47] but coming out of the slums into Charlotte Street, a revelation is waiting for him:

> Suddenly he saw the crowd as it went past the side street, and at the head of it – Le Maître! Alarm and gladness seized Popito. ... His one desire was to keep abreast of Le Maître. The latter attracted all eyes with his big voice, masterful bearing and determined, firm steps. ... 'How well he marches', Popito thought, longing to walk beside Le Maître at the head of that militant-looking crowd. ... 'Le Maître, that's Le Maître! Damn good man!' cried Popito, ready in his excitement to vouch to everyone for Le Maître.[48]

Popito walks alongside the marchers, among the shop clerks on the sidewalk who have come out to observe: 'When Le Maître said, "Join us!" Popito itched to do so but hung back, remembering he was a clerk, and looking among the marchers for others like himself.' But then Le Maître is jolted and drops his placard, and Popito

---

[46] *Crown* 1981, 9.
[47] Here, de Boissière revisits the archetypal setting of the barrack-yard narratives of his peers, such as C. L. R. James's 'Triumph' and *Minty Alley*, implying the need to move out of this type of miserabilist account to the street of protest, agency and change. *Crown* 1981, 75–7.
[48] *Crown* 1981, 79.

runs in to grab it from a worker who has stopped to pick it up, and presents it to
Le Maître, offering to carry it and march alongside Le Maître.[49] Soon, Le Maître
asks why Popito does not join the Negro Welfare, and Popito takes him to be
asking 'Is it that you think yourself too white for us?' He responds, 'I am ready to
join now.'[50] The movement from the sidewalk to the middle of the street propels
Popito across physical, social and racialized boundaries.

Popito joining Le Maître during this march through Port-of-Spain is a
typological event, and so is the march itself and the way that it traverses urban
space stitching together disparate social spaces, taking over public spaces in the
name of the people. Principles of spatial division are reimposed at the end of
the march, when only Le Maître and one more participant is allowed into the
Government House to speak with the Governor, but the struggle over public
space is then taken further as Le Maître's followers gatecrash a meeting held
by the reformist politician Boisson in Woodford Square. This sequence of sites
and conflicts over the right to inhabit and dominate them takes in many of the
landmarks of Port-of-Spain, allowing the novel a claim on actual, urban space.

The larger, expanding sympathies invoked by the class-crossing courtships
contribute to a general pattern of exploding the existing structure of social space
and expanding the principles of comradeship. While Carr argues that the novel
mainly attempts to ground national consciousness, it seem clear that the expansive
movement is larger than this. For example, in one of the street meetings in which
Le Maître attacks the white reformist leader, Boisson, who has taken it upon
himself to represent the black workers, the invasion of Abyssinia is held up as
guaranteeing a different kind of bond than the vertical one between parliamentary
representative and voters. The fawning for the English royalty on the part of Boisson
is the occasion for Le Maître's rebuke: 'They are spending millions of pounds on
the coronation, entertaining the fascists, the very beasts who are slaughtering the
Abyssinians, our people.'[51] This is greeted with approval by the crowd: 'In Port-
of-Spain they had marched in protest to the Italian Consul, Thousands expressed
their sympathy for their African brothers by holding meetings and cabling protests
to Mussolini.'[52] The street is the space for building the national movement, but also
for building international solidarity, for an orientation from one 'peripheral' site
to another that rejects the metropolitan orientation.

[49] *Crown* 1981, 80.
[50] *Crown* 1981, 82.
[51] *Crown* 1981, 309.
[52] *Crown* 1981, 309.

Solidarity as it is expressed here is, among other things, a principle for rearranging social space, for new ways of using space. That kind of solidarity takes one step beyond Durkheim's notion of solidarity as a principle of cohesion across the division of labour, a network of social interaction apart from those of economic exchange, since it prefigures a society in which the division of labour and economic exchange are subordinated to social bonds of sympathy, of social love as it were. The courtship patterns and the claiming of space and spatial connections are meant to build movements that dissolve the boundaries in urban and geographical space that mirror the existing divisions of labour.

The progressive courtship elements – romantic and political – are balanced by conservative matches in the novel, and, more importantly, by the aggressive policing of boundaries. The colonial status quo guarantees the hierarchy built on racialized and ethnified class distinctions, expressed as points in the creole continuum, and smoothed over by political 'concessions'. It preserves an extractive location, whose orientation is determined by capital in the form of crude exports and profits to the economic core sites. When that location is imagined instead as one of solidarity with other peripheral sites, the colonial structuring of space is challenged.

As we have already seen, this space connects different peripheries, such as Trinidad and Abyssinia, in the name of black solidarity. Two centres of colonial extraction, Trinidad and South Africa, are also connected, but by means of what we might call a solidarity of oppressors. In a climactic scene staging the policing of boundaries, the readiness to resort to racist violence is shown to be shared across continents and sites of extraction. When the oil workers approach the gates to the Point Fortin Refineries they find them guarded by a group of armed men, chief among them a major Bullen in the Volunteers, a South African. Speaking to one of his West Indian subordinates, Jake Lorrimer, Bullen says 'I've seen this sort of thing in South Africa. You've got to deal with them very firmly.'[53] This is the overture to the build-up of racial-sexual fantasies in the mind of Lorrimer, whose subsequent action is overdetermined by the various components of the boundary work that seeks to maintain economic, political, racial and sexual hierarchies. Dealing with 'them' firmly means, in Trinidad as in South Africa, lethal violence. De Boissière carefully lays out the conditions and mechanisms behind the shooting of the protesting workers that inevitably follow, using free indirect discourse to pierce the mentality of Bullen, Lorrimer, the workers, the

[53] *Crown* 1981, 330.

agitator Clem Payne, and then releasing the abrupt explosion of the tension up to the melodramatic final sentence, 'The last man to be killed was Clem Payne.'[54]

In this scene of overt violence, the key issue is access to a place, and the overall formation of the novel's aesthetic world draws our attention again and again to struggles over the right to inhabit and claim places. The large set pieces, when the masses take over public spaces are the most striking in this regard: the march down Charlotte Street, the showdown between Le Maître and Boisson in Woodford Square, the hunger march from Fyzabad to Port-of-Spain. But the council meetings, and the meeting of the committee for the minimum wage supply similar scenes of confrontation, as linguistic markets on which different forms of social speech disrupt the normal price formation for linguistic capital. In addition, there are the fraught moments when the division of space is defended with main force. These public spaces are claimed by the novel as arenas in which the people challenge an oppressive order by means of moving bodies, physical violence, and not least by language, dialogic or confrontational. At the end of the novel, Trinidad has not been transformed into a location belonging to the people, but the claim has been made, and the mechanisms that refuse the claims have been analysed.

Read typologically, the novel's realist analysis of social affinities and antagonisms that are animated by a major proletarian uprising can be added to a literature that spanned the globe from the 1920s and into the 1960s. The sites of solidarity shaped in key scenes produce an orientation towards an international conception of struggles over space. In other words, the novel had an intrinsic orientation towards an international audience, towards a dialogue between Trinidad and Abyssinia, Point Fortin and South Africa, Port-of-Spain and Russia. This inner-textual orientation was to be realized in the international circulation of books after de Boissière's highly contingent move to Australia and his contacts with socialist writers there.

The Second Worlding of *Crown Jewel*

Boissière's unusual trajectory from Trinidad to Melbourne made him a different kind of exile writer than the majority of West Indian writers in his generation, who went to England. In an interview a long time later, de Boissière claims that

---

[54] *Crown* 1981, 334. This martyr's death is an interesting tribute to the real Clem Payne, a labour organizer and friend of de Boissière's, who died after collapsing in the midst of agitating. Boissière, *Life on the Edge*, 107.

he 'could not go there' because of his intense dislike of the British, an aversion that also played a part in his love of Russian literature, with its more universal compassion.[55] A chance meeting with Frank Hardy, a socialist and the author of *Power without Glory* (1950), led de Boissière into the Realist Writers' Group.[56] One of the original members, Stan Robe, suggested that de Boissière submit his novel to the Polish publisher Czytelnik. The acceptance letter came the same year that the Australasian Book Society published *Crown Jewel* as its first novel in 1952.[57] It was the first of a series of translations:[58]

1. *Klejnot korony* (Polish, 1953. With a publisher's Foreword).
2. *Kronjuwel: Roman* (German, 1954).
3. *Giuvaerul coroanei* (Romanian, 1955. With a substantial foreword by George Macovescu).
4. *Korunní Klenot* (Czech, 1956).
5. *Crown Jewel* (A new edition of the English original published in Leipzig, 1956. With notes on author and work).
6. *Жемчужина короны* (Russian, 1958. With a foreword by de Boissière and a lengthy afterword by the literary scholar Evgenyia Galperina).
7. 王冠上的宝石 (Chinese, 1958. With a translator's foreword).
8. *Бисер от короната* (Bulgarian, 1960).
9. *Krunski dragulj* (Serbo-Croatian, 1961. With a note by the translator).
10. *Margaritari i kurorës* (Albanian, 1971).

This chain of translations constitutes an instance of a parallel cosmopolitanism whose circuits bypassed or only briefly passed through the centres of the advanced capitalist literary markets in the Northern Atlantic zone. Whatever the contingencies and coincidences involved in the case of *Crown Jewel*, the novel had properties that allowed for those happenstances to propel it into this circuit, and to land it, many years later, as that forgotten piece of world literature. As we have seen, it claims literary value for its peripheral-colonial location and its vernacular forms, while it is typologically oriented towards other, distant sites of struggle for equality and dignity. By looking at the paratexts of the Second World translations, we can see how these properties were then mediated into the various target cultures.

[55] Allan Gardiner, 'Comrades in Words', interview with Ralph de Boissière, *Kunapipi* 15, no. 1 (1993): 36.
[56] Ian Syson, 'Out From the Shadows: The Realist Writers' movement, 1944–1970, and Communist Cultural Discourse', *Australian Literary Studies* 15, no. 4 (October 1992): 333–51.
[57] Boissière, *Life on the Edge*, 180–1.
[58] For bibliographical documentation, see the bibliography.

The most substantial paratext, according to every measure, is the Soviet translation's afterword by a scholar who had pioneered the study of African literature in the USSR. Its title, 'Trinidad Takes Its Place in Literature',[59] seems to emphasize the fact that each translation is evidence of that claim. Generally, the paratextual comments on the novel and its author support such a claim, but in different ways and focusing on different aspects of the novel. The transmission of *Crown Jewel* into the Second World negotiate a number of issues, all in the service of a target audience legibility: the author's trajectory towards class consciousness; the West Indian setting's distance and proximity; the history of colonial oppression and anti-colonial struggle, and the international solidarity emerging from it; the artistic achievement of this novel (often bound up with the other elements).

The figure of the author is an important feature in the paratexts accompanying *Crown Jewel*, from the original Australian publication onwards. It is also an important device for the 'Second Worlding' of the novel: the author must be shown to display certain traits that are legible within the typology of proletarian literature. Katerina Clark outlines the shifts in the Soviet debate over working-class literature from the Revolution to the stagnation years in the Brezhnev and post-Brezhnev era, pointing out an early and enduring tension between 'the educated intellectual and the proletarian'.[60] In de Boissière's personal circumstances, the paratexts find an ideal compromise that also includes the added value of the victim of colonial oppression and fighter in the anti-colonial struggle.

As an author with a bourgeois background, de Boissière's trajectory presents itself as a conversion narrative, explaining his development of a different class consciousness, and thus his access to a cosmopolitanism from below. A note on 'The Author' in the 1952 book's back matter, mostly quoting de Boissière himself, presents his itinerary as a worker and writer, from the 'jolt' of unemployment in 1939, the 'stifling atmosphere of intellectual submission' that drove him from the island, and the profound effect of 'the struggles of the militant Australian workers' on his world view, causing him to revise the novel.[61] These notes reappear in the Leipzig edition and then, partly in direct translation, in the Chinese foreword and the Croat translator's note. The fact that de Boissière has experienced the

---

[59] Evgenyia Galperina, '[Trinidad Takes Its Place in Literature.]' Жемчужина Короны (Moscow: Izd-vo Innostran. Lit.-ry, 1958): 377–84. The literal translation is Trinidad enters literature, but its meaning is precisely that Trinidad is given a place within what counts as capital 'L' literature.

[60] Katerina Clark, 'Working-Class Literature and/or Proletarian Literature: Polemics of the Russian and Soviet Literary Left', in *Working-Class Literature(s): Historical and International Perspectives*, ed. John Lennon and Magnus Nilsson (Stockholm: Stockholm University Press, 2017), 2.

[61] *Crown* 1952, 432.

workers' struggle in two different theatres is clearly an important facet of his formation as a writer. Having absorbed these collective experiences, he is able to represent his people, but also to 'put his talent at the service of mankind's main cause' as the Romanian foreword has it.[62]

In the Soviet translation, de Boissière gets the opportunity to address his Russian-language readers in an author's note. He repeats the main stations of the conversion narrative, from his middle-class education to serving the cause of liberation, but he adds a note about discovering, in Australia, the periodical *Soviet Literature*, and learning about socialist realism.[63] His autobiography has an eye-opening discussion of his encounter with literary dogmatism, in discussions with the socialist writers' group, which qualifies this bland statement a great deal – in effect, rejecting the tenets of socialist realism – but the Soviet paratext ensures that *Crown Jewel* enters that world on the accepted terms.

The author's movement in a world of different national class struggles, and his coming into contact with 'vanguard' ideas delineates a trajectory from the local to the international. Something similar can be seen in how Trinidad is given a literarized place in the Second World. A rhetorical move that is repeated across the paratexts is to start with the beauty and natural wealth of the island, and then go from there to the exploitation of this wealth.

The Chinese preface starts from the island as 'a scenic place, rich in cocoa, sugar cane and oil', while the Croat translator invokes 'this very beautiful island, full of sugar cane plantations, cocoa, oil and especially asphalt' before turning to the exploitation of these riches.[64] The Romanian foreword is especially poetic in this regard, as it speaks about The 'beauties and riches of this well-endowed corner of the Earth':

> Nature is generous, vegetation is lush, the earth is fertile and in its deeps lie hidden precious metals and crude oil, the surrounding waters harbor rare fish species, and the sea beds hide pearls ... On these islands grow aromatic tobaccos and coffee more fragrant than in Brazil, the air is heavy with the aroma of exotic fruit and of the flowers which bedeck the landscape in all seasons, while sky-blue waters roll off blood-red rocks.[65]

[62] George Macovescu, 'Foreword', *Giuvaerul coroanei* by Ralph de Boissière (Bucharest: Editura pentru Literatură şi Artă, 1955), 11.
[63] Ralph de Boissière, '[From the Author]', Жемчужина Короны (Moscow: Izd-vo Innostran. Lit.-ry, 1958), 5.
[64] Shi Xianrong, '[Translator's Foreword]', [Jewel in the Crown] by Ralph de Boissière (Shanghai: [New Literature Press], 1958), I; Josip Matijaš, [A Note on the author and the work], *Krunski dragulj* by Ralph de Boissière (Zagreb: Zora, 1961), 472.
[65] George Macovescu, '[Foreword]', *Giuvaerul coroanei* by Ralph de Boissière (Bucharest: Editura pentru Literatură şi Artă, 1955), 5–6.

This is in fact a more lyrical image than anything the novel musters. Galperina, in the Russian afterword, makes a very interesting point in this regard, after having noted 'how the fabulous "hummingbird island" Trinidad encountered by Columbus was transformed into a land of severe suffering and harsh social conflicts under the yoke of colonialism'.[66] She points out that de Boissière is 'frugal in his description of his country's beauty. This asceticism is emphatic and polemical. It stands in stark contrast against the exoticism and the "prettiness" found in bourgeois literary descriptions of tropical lands'.[67] Galperina believes this asceticism belongs to an early stage of progressive literature, noting that more recently the foremost authors in Africa, the Antilles and Latin America have shown a penchant for underlining the poetical beauty of their countries while linking that beauty to the complex struggle for national liberation.

The poetical beauties and natural riches are specific to Trinidad, the extraction and exploitation bring the island into the imperialist world history that makes the narrative's setting something more than an exotic tropical island. That world history is one of extraction, exploitation and colonial oppression, which becomes the general background for the narrative of rising class consciousness that the substantial paratexts all point to. Faced with the 'greediest type of capitalism, snaring the worker masses in its claws', suffering under 'the iron yoke of English imperialism', and living under a double, social and ethnic oppression, the workers develop a political consciousness and join together in a struggle whose temporary defeat is less significant than the collective transformation of these ethnically divided workers.[68] Overcoming such divisions is also a contribution to a larger sense of the common cause. De Boissière says in the Russian edition that the story 'will not appear strange' to readers who have memories themselves of living under colonial oppression.[69]

The mixture of a strangeness that is superficial and the common bonds of people struggling against exploitation and oppression is how *Crown Jewel* is offered to readers in the Second World. Trinidad is made a literarized part of the world for the readers of Eastern Europe and China by being made legible as both exotic – stressing its vernacular dimension – and as adhering to a historical development that is directly relevant for the political claims to the world that go back to the Russian Revolution – a cosmopolitan orientation.

---

[66] Galperina, 'Trinidad', 379.
[67] Galperina, 'Trinidad', 380.
[68] Macovescu, 'Foreword', 6.
[69] Boissière, '[From the Author]', 5.

In the comments that relate to the novel's artistic achievement, this relevance, at once political and aesthetic, is spelled out in more and less dogmatic ways. Only in de Boissière's foreword to the Soviet edition and in the Chinese translator's foreword is 'socialist realism' explicitly mentioned, but an admiration for the realism of the novel and its truthfulness forms a chorus in these paratexts.[70] The German dustjacket copy text claims that de Boissière has 'excelled in communicating a true-to-life image of his homeland and people in a captivating story'.[71] This relation to 'life' is highlighted in the Romanian foreword, too: 'it is life penetrated in its deeps, examined and exposed in its most essential details'.[72] This richly realistic examination is evoked by means of the trope of the removed wall, reminiscent of the spirit that removes the house-tops in Dickens's *Dombey and Son*: 'As with a block of flats whose frontal wall has been detached through extraordinary circumstances, one is able to see the compartments of a society brought to boil.'[73] In the Soviet edition, too, the success of the realistic reflection of life and 'great historical events' is noted, and Galperina is careful to point out how de Boissière has avoided the pitfalls of the heroic stereotype in his portrayal of the workers' leader Le Maître, a creation which 'differs advantageously from the many failed schematic portraits of workers' leaders by having real national characteristics and a truth to nature'.[74] More generally, de Boissière is credited with an artistic sensibility that avoids schematic solutions, refusing to iron out the wrinkles from his characters, who often fail to find their way and end up in cul-de-sacs.

In their general appreciation of the rich gallery of characters created by de Boissière, the two most substantial paratexts, the Romanian from 1955 and the Soviet from 1958, make cogent points about the typological force of de Boissière's handling of character. In the Romanian foreword this is quite explicit: 'The people in the novel *Crown Jewel* are alive, they live because they are typical of their society and they are typical because the author knew how to represent life in a truthful manner.'[75] Galperina, too, points to de Boissière's use of types or prototypes, based on real personages in the workers' movement in Trinidad.[76] To bind typicality

---

[70] Boissière, '[From the Author]', 5; Shi Xianrong, '[Translator's Foreword]', III.
[71] Dustjacket flap, *Kronjuwel*, translated by Eva Schumann (Berlin: Verlag Volk und Welt, 1954).
[72] Macovescu, '[Foreword]', 10.
[73] Macovescu, '[Foreword]', 7.
[74] Galperina, 'Trinidad', 381.
[75] Macovescu, '[Foreword]', 10.
[76] Galperina, 'Trinidad', 379.

to vivid and truthful representation expresses an essential aesthetic principle for the realist novel, as understood in the Marxist tradition, and it is one of the ways that the 'literature of a world' – a world that is in essence vernacular – can be taken up in 'a world literature'. Types ensure a particular kind of legibility across national or language borders, since they create an association between characters and a historical moment that is registered globally. That legibility does not imply a formulaic treatment – the type is not a stereotype – which is why Galperina praises de Boissière's non-schematic creation of vivid characters. It does imply, however, a mode of reading that invests hope in a common world being shaped by historical forces and collective struggles to which the readers are not strangers.

For the commentators overseeing its transmission to the Second World, the typological thrust of *Crown Jewel* places it among a wave of novels that represent the anti-colonial, decolonizing movement worldwide. Galperina identifies *Crown Jewel* and its sequel, *Rum and Coca-Cola*, as belonging to a form of narrative that became common in many countries after the Second World War, an epic type of literature that sought to recreate the life and struggles of whole peoples. She points to Mohammed Dib, Louis Aragon, George Lamming and Jacques Stephen Alexis, with the last two serving as instances of a literature of national liberation in the West Indies.[77] Josep Matijaš, in the Serbo-Croatian edition's afterword, notes that de Boissière should be placed alongside authors like Mohammed Dib, Amos Tutuola and Ferdinand Oyono who have gained recognition outside their own borders and whose books 'have made their way out into the rest of the world precisely thanks to the struggle of their peoples'.[78] The point made here is that the literature of these 'nations' gain literary recognition only by virtue of the more or less successful struggles for national independence: the claim for a literary value of its locations is dependent on the struggle for the territory itself. The literary claims to a place are added to political claims for a national space, which are all seen in the light of a common fate for struggling workers. Typicality translates into a solidarity that bridges geographical separation:

> The distance between us and the island in the West Atlantic is measured in thousands of kilometers, but the concerns of the people toiling there are not far from our understanding, they cannot remain foreign to us, because they are part of the common cause, of our cause, the cause of all of us dreaming and working for the new world, the one in which man is proudly conscious of being man.[79]

[77] Galperina, 'Trinidad', 377–8.
[78] Josip Matijaš, ['A Note'], 471.
[79] Macovescu, 'Foreword', 9.

Having achieved translocal recognition, *Crown Jewel*'s claim to a local space in the colonized Third World becomes utopian in its Second World circulation. The 'cause' is nowhere achieved: none of the paratextual commentaries imply that the orientation of *Crown Jewel* has been fulfilled by the conditions attained in Romania, the USSR or Yugoslavia. Its horizon is rather to be located in the future, as in the evocative phrase that ends the Panther Books edition, and is incorporated by the Serbo-Croatian translator, about its narrative being 'planted deep in the rich, ripe earth but reaching out toward the future victory of Man'.[80] As Darko Suvin argued, the proletarian novel's orientation is thus always utopian. As the characters of the novel move into new spaces or as they appropriate spaces they were symbolically barred from, they perform that movement from the 'locus' of the 'rich, ripe earth' to the horizon of that 'not-yet-manifest type of human relationships' that the 'future victory' holds out.[81]

This figure of thought – the seed in the fecund soil – posits a rich but narrow location with an orientation that is both geographical and temporal. It is also curiously extractive: the Trinidad location is metaphorically using the source domain of agriculture, while the orientation is aligned with struggles and war. And no doubt there is an extractive dimension at work in the circulation of *Crown Jewel* in the Second World: the literature of the Third World becomes ripe for literary recognition when anti-colonial struggles can be harvested to nourish the putative future orientation of the de-Stalinizing Soviet sphere, or of Tito's Yugoslavia, almost forty years after the October Revolution and in the midst of the Cold War.

Conclusion: Becoming a lost masterpiece in London

It was not until 1981 that de Boissière first novel finally achieved publication in London, announced as the 'lost masterpiece of world literature' on the dustjacket. The publishing company of Allison & Busby had by then established itself as a successful publisher of a variety of fiction and non-fiction, but was especially remarkable for its focus on writers from all over the African diaspora.

---

[80] 'Briefly, about the Book', *Crown Jewel* by Ralph de Boissière, 2nd ed. (Leipzig: Panther Books, 1956), Front matter; Josip Matijaš, ['A Note'], 473, and also on dustjacket flap.
[81] Darko Suvin, 'Locus, Horizon, and Orientation: The Concept of Possible Worlds as a Key to Utopian Studies', *Utopian Studies* 1, no. 2 (1990): 79.

In addition, they had a sideline of books on socialism and Eastern Europe.[82] Margaret Busby was recognized at the time as a major innovator and the first black publisher in London, and has since become, as a recent heading in *Black History Magazine* put it, the 'doyenne of Black British Publishing'.[83] With Clive Allison, Busby had published African-American, Black British, African and Caribbean writers such as Sam Greenlee, Ishmael Reed, Buchi Emecheta, Roy Heath, C. L. R. James, George Lamming, Andrew Salkey and Nuruddin Farah. *Crown Jewel* fits very well into that profile, and the copy text celebrates the novel's qualities, noting its original publication by a 'small Australian book club' and its translation into eight languages (actually nine), all leading up to the astonished observation that it has never before been published in Britain or America. To the extent that the copy text recognizes place, it does so not in the form of an exotic, tropical island, but in the shape of social contradictions, very much in line with de Boissière's own treatment. The front flap concludes with a reference to two of de Boissière's favourite authors, saying that his 'vision of people in society ... has earned him comparison with Tolstoy and Turgenev and the European masters'. Those references might then help us place the conception pushed here of the 'world literature' of which *Crown Jewel* is a 'lost masterpiece'. Complicating the identification of that world is the lack of comment about the eight languages of translation. There is no doubt that Allison & Busby, with their rich backlist of political books about socialism and Eastern Europe, knew exactly how *Crown Jewel* had made its way from Australia to nine other national book markets, but they want their readers to see it as forming part of a literary tradition that happens to be political, rather than as part of a politically conditioned circulation of a literary work. It would seem accurate to say that it is both, and to emphasize that the novel's claim to a place for Trinidad in literature is successful politically to the extent that it succeeds as literary valorization of place.[84]

The world literature that *Crown Jewel* belongs to, then, is that of 'the age of three worlds', which complicates any present identification of its status. It

---

[82] For example, their publications include books by Henre Lefebvre, Agnes Heller and C. L. R. James. For Eastern Europe, examples include Hilda Scott, *Women and Socialism: Experiences from Eastern Europe* (1976); Andras Hegedus, *The Humanisation of Socialism: Writings of the Budapest School* (1976); William Lomax, *Hungary 1956* (1976); and Mark Rakovski, *Towards an East European Marxism* (1978).

[83] John Stevenson, 'Margaret Busby: Doyenne of Black British Publishing', *Black History Month Magazine*, 7 March 2019, www.blackhistorymonth.org.uk/article/section/bhm-firsts/margaret-busby-doyenne-black-british-publishing/

[84] See Bo G. Ekelund, 'Dots on the Literary Map?: Literary Valorizations of Place, the Wealth of Earl Lovelace's Trinidad, and Geometric Data Analysis', *Ariel* 49, no. 2–-3 (2018): 1–36.

may seem a straightforward case to make that *Crown Jewel* is an instance of world literature in the Damroschian sense, since it circulated 'beyond [its] culture of origin'.[85] On the other hand, that understanding of a 'culture' with a particular origin seems to fit this case badly: de Boissière's 'culture' is not that of Trinidad, or of the beneficiary of British colonial education, or of postcolonial hybridity. Rather it is all those ordered within an emergent culture defined by an orientation towards a socialist horizon in a world divided into political blocs of shifting certainties. That orientation is supported, confirmed and sustained by the reproduction of the novel in the forms presented and analysed above.

The particular way that *Crown Jewel* claims its Trinidadian location made it legible within a widespread, transnational culture of reading in which highly vernacularized narratives were oriented towards a horizon of solidarity. Arguments will continue about how to conceive of novels with this legibility within the tradition broadly framed as working-class literature or proletarian literature. Michael Denning sees it as forming an 'international of the novel' in a particular period, under specific conditions. Sonali Perera, on the other hand, seizes on this 'changing *formation*' as an 'interminably provisional and shifting terrain' that extends past Denning's periodization, and beyond any academic pigeonholing by virtue of its relation to class.[86]

Seeing *Crown Jewel* as a particular case of the proletarian or working-class novel written from a site marked by anti-colonial and anti-capitalist struggles, this chapter has highlighted how de Boissière's novel claims a location – Trinidad as a community in the making – by means of a refunctioned courtship structure that allows for dialogic encounters of voices on the creole continuum. The vernacular invades public and official spaces, while official colonial language seeks to fend it off. As streets and open urban spaces are taken over by 'the people', vectors of solidarity are established that link up with Ethiopia, South Africa and with the workers' movements in the metropolis. The novel ends, in its original edition, with the scion of an old French Creole planter's family and the daughter of a Venezuelan migrant seamstress marvelling at the leadership qualities of Cassie, a black servant girl. In the last lines of the novel, they pledge their own membership among the Trinidadian people, turning the story sharply inwards to the island's struggles.[87] However, as a typological figure, this inward orientation offers itself to be read as having the world as its horizon. The circulation of the novel in the

---

[85] David Damrosch, *What Is World Literature?* (Princeton: Princeton University Press, 2003), 4.
[86] Perera, *No Country*, 78.
[87] *Crown* 1952, 431.

Second World takes this figure as a given, extracting the Trinidadian struggle for readers who are invited to share that orientation.

Ralph de Boissière's novels have not been republished after the UK editions of the early 1980s, when *Crown Jewel* was announced as a lost masterpiece of world literature. That is quite simply because it belonged to another 'world literature' than the various formations that now pass under that name. It is a masterpiece, perhaps, of a lost world literature which contributed to a world whose contours are difficult to discern under the waves of globalization. Its particular combination of location and orientation and its quirky trajectory as a book should not make us miss its typicality, registering the cosmopolitan hopes of vernacular struggles.

Bibliography

Ralph de Boissière's *Crown Jewel*: Editions, translations, and paratexts in chronological order.

Boissière, Ralph de. *Crown Jewel*. Melbourne: Australasian Book Society, 1952.

Boissière, Ralph de. *Klejnot korony* [Crown jewel]. Trans. Janusz Grabowski. Warsaw: Czytelnik, 1953.

Publisher's foreword. *Klejnot korony*. Trans. Janusz Grabowski. Warsaw: Czytelnik, 1953. 5–6.

Boissière, Ralph de. *Kronjuwel* [Crown jewel]. Trans. Eva Schumann. Berlin: Verlag Volk und Welt 1954.

Boissière, Ralph de. *Giuvaerul coroanei* [Crown jewel]. Trans. Madeleine Scarlat. Bucharest: Editura pentru Literatură și Artă, 1955.

Macovescu, George. 'Foreword'. Boissière, Ralph de. *Giuvaerul coroanei*. Bucharest: Editura pentru Literatură și Artă, 1955. 5–11.

Boissière, Ralph de. *Crown Jewel*. 2nd ed. Leipzig: Panther Books, 1956.

'Briefly, about the Book'. *Crown Jewel* by Ralph de Boissière, 2nd ed. Leipzig: Panther Books, 1956. Front matter.

Boissière, Ralph de. *Korunni Klenot* [Crown jewel]. Trans. Ota Beck and Pavel Stránský. Prague: Nakladatelstvi, 1956.

Boissière, Ralph de. Жемчужина Короны [Zhemchuzhina korony, The pearl in the crown]. Trans. Tatiana Shinkar. Moscow: Izd-vo Innostran. Lit.-ry, 1958.

Boissière, Ralph de. '[From the Author]'. Жемчужина Короны. Moscow: Izd-vo Innostran. Lit.-ry, 1958. 5–6.

Galperina, Evgenia. 'В литературу входит Тринидад [Trinidad Takes Its Place in Literature]'. Жемчужина Короны Moscow: Izd-vo Innostran. Lit.-ry, 1958. 377–84.

Boissière, Ralph de. 王冠上的宝石 [Jewel in the Crown]. Trans. 施咸荣 [Shi
  Xianrong]. Shanghai: 新文艺出版社 [New Literature Press], 1958.
Shi Xianrong. '[Translator's Foreword]'. Boissière, Ralph de. 王冠上的宝石 [Jewel in the
  Crown]. Shanghai: 新文艺出版社 [New Literature Press], 1958. i–iv.
Boissière, Ralph de. Бисер от короната. [Biser ot koronata, The jewel of the crown].
  Trans. Todor Vălčev. Sofia: Narodna kultura, 1960.
Boissière, Ralph de. *Krunski dragulj* [Crown jewel]. Trans. Josip Matijaš. Zagreb: Zora,
  1961.
Josip Matijaš, [A Note on the author and the work]. *Krunski dragulj* by Ralph de
  Boissière Zagreb: Zora, 1961. 471–3.
Boissière, Ralph de. *Margaritari i kurorës* [The pearl in the crown]. Trans. Mina T
  Qirici. Tirana: Shtëpia botuese 'Naim Frashëri', 1971.

Bibliography

Boissière, Ralph de. *Life on the Edge: The Autobiography of Ralph de Boissière,* edited by
  Kenneth Ramchand. Melbourne: Lexicon, 2010.
Carr, Robert. *Black Nationalism in the New World: Reading the African-American and
  West Indian Experience.* Durham, NC: Duke University Press, 2002.
Clark, Katerina. 'Working-Class Literature and/or Proletarian Literature: Polemics
  of the Russian and Soviet Literary Left'. In *Working-Class Literature(s): Historical
  and International Perspectives*, edited by John Lennon and Magnus Nilsson, 1–30.
  Stockholm: Stockholm University Press, 2017. https://doi.org/10.16993/bam.b.
Clifford, James. *The Predicament of Culture.* Cambridge, MA: Harvard University Press,
  1988.
Damrosch, David. *What Is World Literature?* Princeton: Princeton University Press,
  2003.
DeCamp, David. 'Social and Geographical Factors in Jamaican Dialects'. In *Proceedings
  of the Conference on Creole Language Studies Held at the University College of the
  West Indies, March 28–April 4, 1959*, edited by Robert Le Page, 61–84. London:
  Macmillan, 1961.
DeCamp, David. 'Towards a Generative Analysis of a Post-Creole Continuum'. In
  Pidginization and Creolization of Languages, edited by Dell Hymes, 349–70.
  Cambridge: Cambridge University Press, 1971.
Denning, Michael. *Culture in the Age of Three Worlds.* London: Verso, 2004.
Donnell, Alison. *Twentieth-century Caribbean Literature: Critical Moments in
  Anglophone Literary History.* London: Routledge, 2006.
Ekelund, Bo G. 'Dots on the Literary Map?: Literary Valorizations of Place, the Wealth of
  Earl Lovelace's Trinidad, and Geometric Data Analysis'. *Ariel* 49, no. 2–3 (2018): 1–36.

Gardiner, Allan. 'Striking Images: Ralph De Boissiere's Australian Socialist Realism'. In *Rereading Global Socialist Cultures after the Cold War*, edited by Dubravka Juraga and M. Keith Booker, 165–82. Westport: Praeger, 2002.

Gardiner, Allan. 'Comrades in Words'. Interview with Ralph de Boissière. *Kunapipi* 15, no. 1 (1993): 32–41.

Glissant, Édouard. *Poetics of Relation*. 1990. Trans. Betsy Wing. Ann Arbor: University of Michigan Press, 1997.

Glissant, Édouard. *Caribbean Discourse*. Charlottesville: University of Virginia Press, 1989.

Hannerz, Ulf. 'The World in Creolisation'. *Africa* 57 (1987): 546–59.

Hayot, Eric. 'On Literary Worlds'. *Modern Language Quarterly* 72, no. 2 (June 2011): 129–61.

Lukács, George. *The Historical Novel*. Lincoln: University of Nebraska Press, 1962.

McKay, Claude. *Complete Poems*, edited by William J. Maxwell. Urbana: University of Illinois Press, 2004.

McLaren, John. *Writing in Hope and Fear: Literature as Politics in Postwar Australia*. Cambridge: Cambridge University Press, 1996.

McMahon, Elizabeth. *Islands, Identity and the Literary Imagination*. London: Anthem Press, 2016.

Priam, Mylène. 'Antillanité', in *The Oxford Encyclopedia of African Thought*, Volume 1, edited by Abiola Irele and Biodun Jeyifo, 80–83. Oxford: Oxford University Press, 2010.

Niblett, Michael. '"It's the Mass that Counts": Striking Energies in Working-Class Fiction'. *Journal of Postcolonial Writing* 53, no. 3 (2017): 303–15.

Peake, Jak. *Between the Bocas: A Literary Geography of Western Trinidad*. Oxford: Oxford University Press, 2017.

Perera, Sonali. *No Country: Working-Class Writing in the Age of Globalization*. New York: Columbia University Press, 2014.

Pollock, Sheldon. *The Language of the Gods in the World of Men: Sanskrit, Culture, and Power*. Berkeley: University of California Press, 2006.

Ramchand, Kenneth. *The West Indian Novel and Its Background*. London: Faber, 1970.

Ripoll, Fabrice and Sylvie Tissot, 'La dimension spatiale des ressources sociales'. *Regards sociologiques* 40 (2010): 5–7.

Renahy, Nicolas. 'Classes populaires et capital d'autochtonie: Genèse et usages d'une notion'. *Regards sociologiques* 40 (2010): 9–26.

Rosenberg, Leah Reade. *Nationalism and the Formation of Caribbean Literature*. New York: Palgrave, 2016.

Sander, Reinhard W. 'Ralph de Boissière'. In *Fifty Caribbean Writers: A Bio-Bibliographical Critical Sourcebook*, edited by Daryl Cumber Dance, 151–9. New York: Greenport, 1986.

Sander, Reinhard W. *The Trinidad Awakening: West Indian Literature of The 1930s*. New York: Greenwood, 1988.

Spivak, Gayatri Chakravorty. 'World Systems and the Creole'. In *Creolizing Europe: Legacies and Transformations*, edited by Encarnación Gutiérrez Rodríguez and Shirley Anne Tate, 26–37. Oxford: Oxford University Press, 2015.

Stevenson, John. 'Margaret Busby: Doyenne of Black British Publishing'. *Black History Month Magazine*. 7 March 2019. www.blackhistorymonth.org.uk/article/section/bhm-firsts/margaret-busby-doyenne-black-british-publishing/

Stewart, Charles, ed. *Creolization: History, Ethnography, Theory*. London: Routledge, 2016.

Stewart, Charles. 'Creolization historicized'. In *Creolization: History, Ethnography, Theory*, 1–20. London: Routledge, 2016.

Suvin, Darko. 'Locus, Horizon, and Orientation: The Concept of Possible Worlds as a Key to Utopian Studies'. *Utopian Studies* 1, no. 2 (1990): 69–83.

Syson, Ian. 'Out From the Shadows: The Realist Writers' Movement, 1944–1970, and Communist Cultural Discourse'. *Australian Literary Studies* 15, no. 4 (October 1992): 333–51.

Tompkins, Jane. *Sensational Designs*. Oxford: Oxford University Press, 1985.

Voloshinov, V. N. *Marxism and the Philosophy of Language*. Trans. Ladislav Matejka. Cambridge, MA: Harvard University Press, 1986.

Walonen, Mike. 'Resistance, Oil, and Awakening: Textual Responses to the Butler Strike and Its Aftermath'. *Ariel: A Review of International English Literature* 44, no. 2–3 (2014): 59–84.

Whitehead, Henry S. 'Hill Drums', *Tales of the Jumbee and Other Wonders of the West Indies*. Cabin John: Wildside Press, 2009. Story originally published in *Weird Tales*, 1931.

6

Core: Ecologies of Muslim-American writing

Adnan Mahmutović

بِسْمِ اللَّهِ الرَّحْمَنِ الرَّحِيمِ

At the core of this analysis is the notion that world literature, here Muslim-American writing in particular, can be defined in terms of its way of working with(in) the dynamic between location and orientation. After 11 September 2001, Martin Amis argued, 'all the writers on earth were reluctantly considering a change of occupation'. In his view, the very *raison d'être* of literature was brought into question. There is no doubt that this infamous event has had global significance, but to ascribe a veritable global existential crisis to global writers says more about Amis's location in certain literary ecologies than world literature as such. Such a crisis could perhaps be identified in the American literary ecology in the years that followed, for instance in the discourse developed by Richard Gray and Michael Rothberg.[1] However ridiculous Amis's generalization may appear at first sight, there is, in my view, a truth in it that can help us approach what I have called Muslim-American writing, which indeed seems to have arisen from such a crisis, or an imposition of such a crisis through the escalation of the propaganda against Muslims in much Western media and the treatment of citizens of Islamic faith in most Western countries. Here we find authors such as Mohsin Hamid, Michael Muhammad Knight, Khaled

---

[1] Richard Gray, 'Open Doors, Closed Minds: American Prose Writing at a Time of Crisis', *American Literary History* 21, no. 1 (2008).

Hosseini, Mohja Kahf, G. Willow Wilson and others.[2] Their diverse works, often produced as some form of response to post-9/11 historical developments, stage a particular dialectic between the cosmopolitan notions of flexible world citizen (Ong) and location within national borders.[3] Muslim-American writing in this reading contains two movements elaborated in the critical dialogue between Gray and Rothberg: 'centripetal' globalization and a complementary centrifugal mapping that charts 'the prosthetic reach of [the US] empire into other worlds'.[4] In contrast to the pervasive domestication of change in post-9/11 American literary ecology, which is not only visible in a lack of *formal* innovation but also in a failure to engage the *global* dimensions of that change, Muslim-American writing does not exhibit Gray's 'imaginative paralysis'.[5] What is more, the fact that this writing is read across multiple ethnoscapes, to use Arjun Appadurai's term,[6] and that it often inspires change in different demographics, is an example of an ongoing oscillation between location and a strong need for cosmopolitan orientation. Often using distinct American locations, Muslim-American writing seems to utilize an orientation towards cosmopolitanism as a way of showing hitherto unrepresented characteristics of those locations. Notable examples are Knight's Muslim-punk house in Buffalo, Hamid's New York with its gateways to locations around the globe, Kahf's Muslim missionaries in Indiana, and Willow Wilson's American-Pakistani Superhero in New Jersey.[7] Location here entails a combination of several things, such as geographic place, social space, language, literary history, etc. While they are all important, in any given narrative, they may be more or less important. Location as such is mainly defined through a

---

[2] In contrast to globally popular ways of disseminating categories and discussing literature, the tag 'Muslim' does not appear much in critical reception (including reviews and interviews). A notable exception is for instance the work of Rehana Ahmed et. al. Rehana Ahmed, Peter Morey and Amina Yaqin, *Culture, Diaspora and Modernity in Muslim Writing* (New York: Routledge, 2012). Dealing with Muslim-related, often controversial subjects such as terrorism does boost sales and international distribution. Besides Mohsin Hamid's and Khaled Hosseini's work, we see this all over the world with for example Tabish Khair's *How to Fight Islamic Fundamentalism from the Missionary Position* (Northampton, MA: Interlink Publishing Group, 2013) and *Just Another Jihadi Jane* (Northampton, MA: Interlink Publishing Group, 2016). Works by, for instance, Leila Aboulela, which are more character driven, subtle stories of identity crises, do not reach the required heights of global literary markets to make any significant impact on the different ecologies.

[3] Aihwa Ong, *Flexible Citizenship: The Cultural Logic of Transnationality* (London: Durham University Press, 1999).

[4] Michael Rothberg, 'A Failure of the Imagination: Diagnosing the Post-9/11 Novel: A Response to Richard Gray', *American Literary History* 21, no. 1 (2009): 153.

[5] Rothberg, 'A Failure of the Imagination', 135.

[6] Arjun Appadurai, *Modernity at Large: Cultural Dimensions of Globalization* (Minneapolis: University of Minnesota Press, 1996).

[7] Mohja Kahf, *The Girl in the Tangerine Scarf* (New York: Carroll & Graf Publishers, 2006).

sense of limitations that these factors impose on individuals and communities. Orientation, in contrast, is an active attempt to look beyond those limitations as a way of (re)shaping any given location.

If Alexander Beecroft is correct in claiming that *a* literature is made mainly through the ways readers make connections between works – as well as authorial intentions in cases where writers aim to produce a particular type of literature – it is possible to speak of Muslim-American writing as *a* literature that simultaneously belongs to different literary ecologies: vernacular, national and cosmopolitan (given its dissemination, translatability and accessibility).[8] Muslim-American writing may not only find itself pulled in several directions through the workings of literary markets and diverse audiences, but also deliberately, through form and content, orient itself towards different ecologies. This is the main feature I see as defining Muslim-American writing. It is the kind of writing that can be, at the same time, firmly located in American national literature but oriented towards other national literatures and cosmopolitan and global literary ecologies.

What we gain from seeing Muslim-American writing in terms of literary ecologies is an expanded sense of diversity and cross-pollination that explain certain defining features that pull together sets of works into a category which yields itself to analysis.[9] The label 'Muslim-American' pulls together often very idiosyncratic works on the basis of interrelated sets of concerns as well as the fact that it is tied to and strongly defined by the American literary markets. To only locate certain writing in a national literary ecology and deem it niche would, for Muslim-American writing, effectively stage a forgetting of the cosmopolitan heritage of Islam, which informs this writing and de facto produces its particular dynamic between location and orientation. Indeed, Muslim-American writing is a product not only of our time but strongly informed by the continuous, fourteen-centuries-long form of what Alex MacGillivray calls 'archaic globalization',[10] which includes the history of Muslim expansion and its economic and cultural impact on the world.

---

[8] Alexander Beecroft, *An Ecology of World Literature: From Antiquity to the Present Day* (London: Verso, 2015). In his identification of basic types of ecologies – epichoric, panchoric, cosmopolitan, national, vernacular, global – Beecroft looks at the following factors: the linguistic situation, economy, the political world, religion, cultural politics and technologies of distribution.

[9] Beecroft's model is useful because literature must 'be understood as being in an ecological relationship to other phenomena – political, economic, sociocultural, religious – as well as to the other languages and literatures with which it is in contact', *An Ecology of World Literature*, 19. An ecological lens helps us understand processes 'of survival and recognition' (20).

[10] Alex MacGillivray, *A Brief History of Globalization* (London: Robinson, 2006), 15.

Moreover, we must not forget the notion of the Muslim Ummah as an early form of cosmopolitan consciousness, which strongly affects the very conceptualization of location–orientation of/in Muslim-American writing. Indeed, by positing itself as a global project, Islam not only achieved a transcontinental reach centuries before European colonialism and industrialization but continues to be an essential part of current globalization processes the effects of which are felt in world literature, especially the types of works produced by those for whom Muslim identity is at stake. Just looking at a recent anthropological study of South-East Asia by Khairudin Aljunied, we see how a spread of contemporary Muslim cosmopolitanism arises from a long history of Islamic expansionism through merchants and preachers which, 'propagated a universalist rather than a communalist conception of Islam'.[11] Critiquing 'theorists who have attributed the development of religious cosmopolitanism principally to the forces of European globalisation and technological revolutions', Aljunied shows 'religious cosmopolitanism that includes both "elite" and "subaltern" as well as "official" and "vernacular" Muslim cosmopolitanisms'. Such 'Muslim cosmopolitanism can emerge both "bottom up" and "top down" from within individuals, communities and activists, just as emerging global factors can aid in the process of sharpening cosmopolitan outlooks in a particular setting'.[12] Although his argument focuses on South-East Asia, it seems to me that the history of Islam has countless examples where the cosmopolitan project of Islam has thrived despite 'spectres of secular fundamentalism, nationalist particularism, religious fundamentalism and state intolerance'.[13] This is why, in this analysis, I pay particular attention to Michael Muhammad Knight, who offers, in my view, perhaps the unique and rawest literary response.

Born Irish Catholic, Knight converted to Islam as a sixteen-year-old and went straight to what he called a hardedge Saudi Islam that is commonly associated with fundamentalism. This type of Islam drives a hardline, singular view of a few key issues in both the faith itself (*Al-Deen*) and practice (*Al-Islam*) with a particular focus on what is allowed (*halal*) and what is forbidden (*haram*).

[11] Khairudin Aljunied, *Muslim Cosmopolitanism: Southeast Asian Islam in Comparative Perspective* (Edinburgh: Edinburgh University Press, 2017), xx.
[12] Aljunied, *Muslim Cosmopolitanism*, xvi. Furthermore, he writes: 'Muslim cosmopolitanism in Southeast Asia is a style of thought, a habit of seeing the world and a way of living that is rooted in the central tenet of Islam, which is that everyone is part of a common humanity accountable to God and that we are morally responsible towards one another. To embrace Muslim cosmopolitanism is to exhibit a high degree of receptiveness to universal values that are embedded within one's own customs and traditions (*adat*)', xix.
[13] Aljunied, *Muslim Cosmopolitanism*, xxiv.

Believing that the fundamentalist movements suffocate the original potential of Islam, Knight sought a way to release the positive energies of Islam and highlight its heterogeneity. Knight's development as a young and troubled convert, which includes all manner of ideological and emotional jumps, is well covered in his fictional and non-fictional work, for instance *Blue-eyed Devil*[14] and *The Five Percenters*.[15] His first novel, *Taqwacores*,[16] tells a story of Muslim punk rockers in a house in Buffalo who are trying to coexist and deal with their Muslim identity. The house represents the troubled house of Islam (*Dar Al-Islam*) in a modern age, fighting to keep the core of its cosmopolitan project in the face of fundamentalism, sectarianism, nationalism, etc. As such, it presents a strong dynamic between location and orientation, both in terms of its form-content and as a cultural product of the post-9/11 era.

The very labelling of *Taqwacores* as 'The Catcher in the Rye for young Muslims' and 'The Hunter S. Thompson of Islamic Literature' (on the cover) firmly situates the novel in the ecology of American national literature. The original nature of its distribution, as if it were some bootleg edition or DIY-zine, reinforces certain American cultural stereotypes of underground writing and the avant garde. It spread through niche venues, creating not only readers, but also followers, movements, and only much later, a film adaptation, which in turn led to new cultural phenomena. In *Taqwacores*, Knight reworks narrow understandings of Muslim identity by inventing a community of Muslim punks. He makes a vibrant synthesis of two *seemingly* opposed ideas: Islam as 'submission' (represented by *taqwa*, that is, God consciousness) and the hardcore rebelliousness of the punk movement. The members of the motley community are both highly individualized in their understandings of faith and religious practice, and partly representative of existing Muslim groups (e.g. sunni, shia, sufi, selefi, etc.). Their Islamic identities, in public and private spheres, often differ so much that it appears as if they do not adhere to one and the same religion. The signifier 'Islam' borders on being empty or very elastic. In this way, Knight attempts to explore a range of modern variations of Islam, or maybe even a post-modern Islam. He goes against the still operative East–West binary, but also the old binary that was created politically in the centuries following Muhammad's message:

---

[14] Michael Muhammad Knight, *Blue-eyed Devil: A Road Odyssey Through Islamic America* (New York: Autonomedia, 2006).

[15] Michael Muhammad Knight, *The Five Percenters: Islam, Hip-hop and the Gods of New York* (New York: One World Publications, 2008).

[16] Michael Muhammad Knight, *Taqwacores* (New York: Soft Skull Press, 2004).

Dar Al-Islam (the abode/house of Islam, that is, societies in which Muslims are secure) and *Dar Al-Harb* (the abode of war, that is, societies in which Muslims are not secure). To begin with, we can argue that Knight represents a tendency in contemporary Muslim discourses to see oneself as both a part of the American society and an alien in it, both a citizen and an illegal, like we see in for instance Hamid's *The Reluctant Fundamentalist*.

While it would be easy to identify the house as *Dar Al-Islam* and boil down the problematic to the post-9/11 discrimination against Muslims in the USA, Knight shows that many Muslims also see certain things as dangerous for their Muslim identity (alcohol, music, sex). The main character is sent to this house because his parents thought this house, this *Dar Al-Islam* is going to protect him, socially speaking, from the dangers of American social life. The house turns out to be the microcosm of everything they consider horrendous. Knight's allegorical house of Muslims, as a location, is hardly a safe space because the ideological differences between the variegated Muslims are often causes of conflict. By creating a fake bubble, a location within a location (a house of Islam in the house of the American nation), Knight shows that which Tariq Ramadan points out in *Western Muslims and the Future of Islam*: 'There is no longer a place of origin from which Muslims are "exiled" or "distanced", and "naturalized", "converted" Muslims – "Western Muslims" are at home, and should not only say so but feel so.'[17] This is how the narrator of *Taqwacores* relates this insight:

> I stopped trying to define Punk around the same time I stopped trying to define Islam. They aren't so far removed as you'd think. Both began in tremendous bursts of truth and vitality but seem to have lost something along the way – the energy, perhaps, that comes with knowing the world has never seen such positive force and fury and never would again. Both have suffered from sell-outs and hypocrites, but also from true believers whose devotion had crippled their creative drive. Both are viewed by outsiders as unified, cohesive communities when nothing can be further from the truth … You cannot hold Punk or Islam in your hands. So what could they mean besides what you want them to?[18]

In many ways, *Taqwacores* is an American story about young people trying to find their way in *their* nation, but despite all the particularity of American culture, the location appears transnational. It is a petri dish of variegated religious dogma and global youth culture. Knight uses the typical metaphor

---

[17] Tariq Ramadan, *Western Muslims and the Future of Islam* (Oxford: Oxford University Press, 2004), 53.
[18] Knight, *Taqwacores*, 7.

of a microcosm containing the macrocosm to present both intra-religious and intra-national dynamics. The local here is therefore ultimately national and global. This metaphoric character of the house effectively situates Islam in the USA as part and parcel of the nation and, despite the sense of national claustrophobia, creates a centrifugal orientation towards the imagined global community of Muslim Ummah. What keeps the youth together is both the fact that they are American and that they are Muslim. Since Muslim Ummah has never been, at its core, homogenous, the house introduces a problematic of containing such a cosmopolis (of Islam), which acknowledges no borders, within the nation state. Every single aspect of the Muslim youth in the confines of this American house points to the core of that which they have in common: an orientation. However strange it may look, this house in Buffalo may be a hyperbolic metaphor for a mosque in its original meaning/intention, that is, not just a devotional place but a place where both spiritual and profane needs are addressed, a place of learning and politics, a place of the projection of 'the cosmopolitan temperaments' (Aljunied). If it were not for this orientation out, that is, this implied consciousness of a cosmopolitan project of Islam, the novel would have a very local, practically vernacular character (aesthetically and in terms of the content). In order to highlight and examine the novel's oscillation between location and orientation, I will focus on three things from Beecroft's model: language, content and dissemination.

Language: The making of a global vernacular

Linguistically speaking, though the core language of *Taqwacores* is the current global lingua franca English, whose literary history affects its craft (in particular American literature), the novel features a unique kind of translingualism which gives its language a vernacular character. It belongs to new types of writing which, according to Michael Boyden and Eugenia Kellbert 'allow their language of writing to be cross-fertilized by idioms, dialects, and literary traditions that most would consider alien to it'.[19] Knight's discourse seems to posit a practically existential need to let other languages, most dominantly Arabic, seep into and

---

[19] Michael Boyden and Eugenia Kelbert, 'Introduction: The Theory Deficit in Translingual Studies', *Journal of World Literature* 3 (2018): 127. For Boyden and Kellbert, although 'translingualism is now a commonly accepted label, it has to compete with many other, overlapping terms such as multilingual, exophonic, other-language, heteroglossic, hybrid, and accented literature' (131).

form his American English. This language is an attempt to represent, if not necessarily create, some form of a global vernacular that arises at the meeting of two cosmopolitan languages. Arabic is significant because, according to Beecroft, it 'perhaps uniquely, remains extant as a literary cosmopolis today'.[20] In other words, the cosmopolitan or global orientation is, language-wise, created not solely because English is a global lingua franca, but because of the previously mentioned global spread of Islam. Arabic is de facto a default language of Islamic practice and the official language of the Muslim Ummah. More specifically, it is not simply Arabic, but rather a particular Qur'anic Arabic mainly tied to its liturgic use and cultural significance. That is, given our contemporary 'postmonolingual condition',[21] which implies serious challenges to the 'myth of monolingualism',[22] when we speak of English and Arabic as cosmopolitan languages, we must do so in the plural: Englishes and Arabics (a consequence of being cosmopolitan or global). The English of *Taqwacores* is often skilfully broken up and stitched together with such liturgic Arabic to the point of appearing as some form of global vernacular that caters to global Muslims more than general American readership and yet it is also a lingo that, because of its local character, is bound to create cultural opacity for global audiences. While similar translingualism can be found in many national languages, this case is different because the discourse results from an interplay between two cosmopolitan languages. In contrast, for instance, in the Bosnian language (my own mother tongue), the slavic dialect was reshaped by Arabic, Turkish, Farsi, Russian and German. It is thus an official national language (with a literature) that is operative in a locality. For instance, Bosnians, like Turks, call the daily prayers 'namaz' (Farsi) and not 'salat' (Arabic). This would not happen, or even be possible in a work such as Knight's even with Iranian characters because the implied readership would be much more confined to certain localities and lose some cosmopolitan aspirations.

Although there are plenty of interesting examples of Knight's type of (cosmopolitan/global) vernacularization, I will only focus on the opening sentence because it represents, principally, what he does in general throughout the novel (and his oeuvre). The opening, 'Bismillahir, Rahmanir *and so on*',[23] speaks volumes. It consists of two distinct parts, the first in Arabic, transcribed

---

[20] Beecroft, *An Ecology of World Literature*, 143.

[21] Yasemin Yildiz, *Beyond the Mother Tongue: The Postmonolingual Condition* (New York: Fordham University Press, 2012).

[22] Liesbeth Minnaard and Till Dembeck, eds. *Challenging the Myth of Monolingualism* (Amsterdam: Rodopi, 2014).

[23] Knight, *Taqwacores*, 5.

in his own way, and the second in English.[24] The first part is a segment from the most uttered Islamic phrase – Bismillahi-rRahmani-rRahim (in the name of God, most Gracious, most Compassionate) – which opens every (except one) *surah* (section) of *The Qur'an*, and which you can see in Arabic at the beginning of this chapter. It is also a phrase that is uttered by Muslims before any action as an affirmation that it is done in the name of God (before meals, before work, and even before sexual intercourse). On the surface this could be rather basic code-switching in a translingual text, but stylistically, unlike many other works with foreign terms, in particular those written by Muslims or with Muslim characters, the Qur'anic phrase is used as if it were entirely natural in English, like 'once upon a time' or 'in the beginning there was'. A Muslim reader would know that the Bismillah-opening is obligatory for any type of halal work, that it would signal the narrator's intent (automatically reliable) and also that the narrator addresses a community (location and orientation). The second part, *'and so on'*, is in italics as if that was the foreign segment, that is, as if Arabic was primary and English secondary.

This *'and so on'*, at first sight, also appears disrespectful because the narrator does not complete the entire phrase by rote (missing 'Rahim'), as Muslims always do, but this speaking-by-rote of the phrase is implied.[25] It is the very relaxed way of translingual exchange or play that makes the language appear at the same time both very local and global (because it speaks to Muslims globally and most such passages would be entirely obscure to readers who do not know anything about Islamic practices). The fact that the novel opens with this phrase, albeit incomplete, is no doubt a statement of faith, but the omission with the partly mocking *'and so on'* seems to immediately cut at the heart of the ritual. In other words, with this translingual gesture, Knight forges *taqwa* and punk, as promised in the novel's title. Given the general anti-religious sentiment in the punk movement, this linguistic gesture may be read while giving primacy to the second half of the line, that is, as a form of negation of the first half.

---

[24] There are many ways to do a transcription from Arabic بِسْمِ اللهِ الرَّحْمَنِ الرَّحِيمِ to English, and other languages, because one attempts to represent sounds as well as reading rhythms (merging of words in reading). There is no consensus on this, though with time certain patterns have emerged as more popular.

[25] A possible interpretation of the missing second word may be related to the original meanings of the double name of God (Allah), that is Rahman الرَّحْمَن and Rahim الرَّحِيم. Rahman comes from the root R-H-M which means womb and is supposed to refer to God's relationship to His creation in this world, something which can be given and also taken away. Rahim, on the other hand, has the same root but it refers to God's relationship to those who are in Paradise, that is an unchanging relationship. One could speculate that the exclusion of Rahim, from the POV of the character, either makes him doubt he will actually receive R-H-M or, given his devotion, it is because God is above all things gracious/merciful/forgiving/loving, the forgiveness of this trespassing is implied/guaranteed anyway.

However, this is not the case. Both parts are in fact affirmed and negated and this is where Knight seems to find the drive for an otherwise plotless narrative. Tension and conflict are created. Neither side is supposed to take over but bring out, or tease out, the other's full potential. This is in keeping with what Knight states in the documentary *Taqwacore: The Birth of Punk Islam* (2009), that both Islam and punk are movements with great potential that is far from realized in the twentieth and the twenty-first centuries. It is important to keep in mind this mutual coexistence of two ways of thinking especially when the characters' actions appear to be blasphemous in the narrow religious sense of the word or are too religious from a punk point of view.

Knight's American vernacular arises at the meeting of two cosmopolitan languages and thus serves as a shifting marker of value. It is true that there is no language called 'the vernacular' – a term originally used in imperial Rome to designate the language of the 'house-born slave' – yet almost any language can be *positioned* as a vernacular. In the world of literary publishing and reception, this relational understanding of the vernacular is self-evidently true, given that print cultures always entail stratification, specialization and standardization, rendering variations deviant or exotic. If language can be defined as 'a dialect with a literature',[26] then print literature is a key factor behind what has been called the 'monolingual paradigm' (Yildiz 2012 and Anderson 1983) and the ensuing positioning of certain usages and modes of speech as vernacular. Value-coding of expressions and styles undergoes transformation. In the transcontinental marketing and importation of books, new juxtapositions of languages and linguistic registers can change local categories of value. Amelié Hurkens and Pieter Vermeulen point out how 'a world literary vernacular is a vernacular that is not just defined through its resistance to global circulation ... but participates in that circulation, and would be unthinkable without it'.[27] For Aamir Mufti, the global spread of English did not replace the vernacular, but rather enabled vernacularization and thus the vernacular became an effect of the dialectic of vernacularization and cosmopolitanization.[28]

What we have in this example, in some way, is a cosmopolitan or global language which creates rich signification for Muslims regardless of their ethnicity,

[26] Beecroft, *An Ecology of World Literature*, 6.
[27] Amélie Hurkens and Pieter Vermeulen, 'The Americanization of World Literature? American Independent Publishing and the World Literary Vernacular', *Interventions* 22, no 3. (2020): 437.
[28] Aamir Mufti, *Forget English! Orientalisms and World Literature* (Cambridge, MA: Harvard University Press, 2016), 96.

nationality, particularity of religious practice and dogma, etc. While a vernacular would, according to Beecroft, prevent wider distribution of the work, the novel's outward orientation makes us revise this analysis. Disregarding its potentially controversial content, this novel would be highly accessible to a Muslim readership around the globe while at the same time also quite obscure for both national (American) and most global audiences which do read in English. In other words, it is defined by the dynamic it creates between its American location and (a particularized) cosmopolitan orientation. The fact that a global Muslim audience would be able to appreciate Knight's language produces a rather unusual situation within and across literary ecologies (especially national and cosmopolitan).

Another reason I call Knight's language a global vernacular is the argument by Tim Parks, in 'The Dull New Global Novel', that a perception of an 'ultimate audience as international rather than national', mostly changes the character of writing.[29] Using Kazuo Ishiguro's notes about trying to make his translator's life easier, Parks traces 'a tendency to remove obstacles to international comprehension'. Consequently, since authors deploy 'highly visible tropes immediately recognizable as "literary" and "imaginative", [is] analogous to the wearisome lingua franca of special effects in contemporary cinema', what is 'doomed to disappear, or at least to risk neglect, is the kind of work that revels in the subtle nuances of its own language and literary culture'. *Taqwacores*, in many ways, creates a private lingo that only the characters in the house can understand and that makes them even more isolated from their American location. As mentioned before, many scenes are not even connected to each other (plotlessness) and remain quite obscure even when little Arabic is employed. This is because they are written as some form of Socratic dialogues on specific ideological or political notions that are of concern for particular kinds of people undergoing identity crises: terrorism, gender trouble, economy, morality, etc. While one could argue that the issues they deal with are bound to their American, post-9/11 location, we know from global discourses that they have the same spread and become concerns for Muslims worldwide. As such, though the book caters to an envisioned global audience of Muslims, *Taqwacores* often satisfies the criteria for a local, culturally specific work, yet can feel obscure even for this implied audience. It evinces great awareness of both locality and globality, obscurity and presumed universality.

---

[29] Tim Parks, 'The Dull New Global Novel', *The New York Review Blog*, 9 February 2010, www.nybooks.com/daily/2010/02/09/the-dull-new-global-novel/.

This is where we can trace the theological, Islamic, notions of location and orientation as an influence. *The Qur'an* says: 'And God's is the east and the west: and wherever you turn, there is God's countenance' (2.115).[30] The omnipresence of God in Islam is stressed through the act of turning. Turning, or orientation, is primary in Islam and as such defines both human agents and places. Thus a Muslim praying in Buffalo must not just turn to Mecca in prayer (which is a location symbolizing God's singularity) but also always be oriented towards (turned to) God. Mecca as such, as a location, is also a point of orientation. It is not just, or really, Mecca, as a city, as a cartographic node, one turns to but the *house* of Abraham called Kaaba. Thus we have youngsters located in a house in Buffalo oriented to a house in Mecca. This orientation is both physical/geographic and symbolic, just as their American location is physical and symbolic. Kaaba is not just a real place that exists right now, but a place of the past and the envisioned future. Turning towards Kaaba entails certain atemporality. This means that because Islam is a part of their being, there can never be a location without an orientation (even when they are not in prayer). It is a default mode of being of any Muslim: orientation to God and orientation to Muslim Ummah as a concept of being-in-community. *Bismillah* as a liturgic phrase is the ultimate act of orientation. Now, the broken-ness of it with the added '*and so on*' signals a particularity of their American location. This '*and so on*' linguistically and in terms of character-attitude, locates the characters in Buffalo, America. This is a strategy which Knight uses throughout the book both in terms of language and content. He will typically lay out a scene which will treat some key part of Islamic theology or ritual, thus signalling an orientation, and then add or remove something, which will in turn give a unique character to the situation and the characters. The effect is the reshaping of a location by means of messing with the orientation, and the emphasis on the orientation by messing with the location. This supports Stefan Helgesson and Christina Kullberg's claim that translingualism, in contrast to heterolingualism, can offer 'a broader canvas against which the literary uses of language can be assessed and actualized in reading'.[31] Indeed, considering a 'staging of language',[32] we could see how 'literary language may ultimately be read outside of identity and difference as a constantly adaptable assemblage of vernacular and cosmopolitan, private and public,

---

[30] Muhammad Asad, *The Message of Qur'an* (Bristol: The Book Foundation, 2003).
[31] Stefan Helgesson and Christina Kullberg, 'Translingual Events: World Literature and the Making of Language', *Journal of World Literature* 3 (2018): 138.
[32] Helgesson and Kullberg, 'Translingual Events', 138.

conventional and transgressive vectors'.[33] Thus, 'different languages at play in politically charged colonial and postcolonial translingual contexts are certainly identifiable, but their meaning will vary depending on perspective, voice, mode, medium, and address'.[34] It is clear in Knight's work that we have a strong sense of locality but not a local language that is shaped and policed in the way some other (even translingual) dialect may be. Knight's imagined lingo is shaped, at its core, through an orientation to an envisioned global Muslim audience (Ummah). No doubt, while Knight's global practice still happens locally, his use of a global vernacular, shows a need for a more dynamic sense of language practices.

Content: Global liturgic practice goes local

The previously analysed example of language-use already pointed us in the direction of the content, the matters of religious identity and liturgy. The dynamic between location (vernacularization) and orientation (cosmopolis) is stressed in many scenes where liturgy is changed, where it is made local and often individualized. Some scenes, such as the very first scene, contain a small plot in their own right that restates, or dramatizes the more abstract point I highlighted in the opening line. This scene is almost entirely a dialogue between two unnamed characters who are discussing a third character (no direct relation to a plot of any sort). This is what they say:

> 'He lost his right index finger in a bet.'
> 'Are you fuckin' kidding? What was the bet?'
> 'That he wouldn't chop off his finger.'
> 'So he won the bet.'
> …
> 'Yeah but when he's in salat and it comes the time for the Tashahud, instead of the index he has to bob his *middle* finger up and down. It's like he flips himself off every time he prays.'[35]

I first want to point out that this already suggests that these characters live in some form of community and that they are extremely different from each other, that they affirm their differences, that they are partly judgemental, but most

[33] Helgesson and Kullberg, 'Translingual Events', 139.
[34] Helgesson anda Kullberg, 'Translingual Events', 151.
[35] Knight, *Taqwacores*, 5.

importantly that these differences have not driven them away from each other. Second, as a connection to the previous section on language coding, I need to point out that Knight does not italicize 'Tashahud' and 'salat' but does the word 'middle'. This is immensely significant because it signals that the author does not care to fully explain the discourse to an American audience, or global readers of English (thus satisfying Park's preferences), practically assuming that this situation is just a part of everyday (American) life. In other words, an Islamic practice is fully naturalized and does not show awareness of possible outsiders/ onlookers who do not understand what they are talking about. To understand the full brunt of this exchange in terms of location and orientation we need to grasp 'salat' (صلاة) and 'Tashahud' (تَشَهُّد). Salat is a Muslim prayer, performed at five prescribed times each day (morning, noon, afternoon, dusk and night). Each of the five prayers has an established ritual structure in which the recitation of Qur'anic verses is combined with specific bodily movements. After every two 'rakats' (ركعة),[36] and the very end of the prayer, there is a sitting when the person utters prescribed words and one of the smaller gestures done during the sitting is Tashahud (the witnessing), when the person bobs the right index finger up and down, uttering *La ilaha il-Allah* (There is no other divinity but God).[37] In Knight's novel, the unnamed character had lost his index finger and could not perform this gesture, but he still wanted to conform to the ritual, that is follow the Prophet's sunna (example), and decided to bob his middle finger, which entails an entirely different symbolism in the American location, as if he is giving the finger to his own religious drive. The character is therefore positioned between utter conformism to form and a sort of anti-conformist gesture (punk). The same gesture becomes both affirmative and negating at one and the same time. As before in the case of 'Bismillah', in the interpretation of this scene, it would be easy to reduce the reading to some simple anti-religious gesture, rather typical of many works in the American literary ecology. However, what the character gives the finger to is not really his faith but the notion of ritual for the

---

[36] A 'rakat' ركعة is a segment of a prayer 'salat' صلاة consisting of: 1. Qiyam قيام: standing and reciting, 2. Ruku ركوع: bowing down, 3. Sujuud سجود: prostration.

[37] While there is no singular explanation for this gesture (and many do not bob the finger but merely raise it), the most common is that it symbolizes monotheism. It is a gesture ascribed to the Prophet s.a.w.s. One can see for instance how the four major schools of Islamic jurisprudence interpreted how it should be done. So for instance the Hanafi school states that the finger should be raised when saying *laa* ('no') in the phrase *Esh-hedu en laa ilaahe ill-Allah* (I bear witness that there is no god except Allah), and it should be lowered when saying *ill-Allah*. The Shaafi say that it should be raised when saying *ill-Allah*. The Maaliki would argue that it should be moved right and left until one finishes the prayer. According to the Hanbali school one should point with the finger when saying the name of Allah, without moving it.

sake of ritual. The ritual is important, but only in the sense that the character must be fully aware of its implications. This essential paradox is crucial to Knight's entire novel, and it is not a disturbing middle zone that must be resolved by choosing a side between conformity and nonconformity or by creating a bogus synthesis. Knight wants to keep the two opposed elements at work, unresolved, feeding each other, emphasizing the importance of faith for the character, but also the importance of constant individual choice in how the faith is understood and practiced in a particular location. This seems to be the basic principle of 'taqwacore'. As such, this gesture is extremely individual and localized (in some cultures the middle finger has no significance or has a different one), but at the same time this scene, and this gesture, can only be fully understood if we think of it in terms of location and orientation.

What Knight brings about within variegated American mediascapes, to use Appadurai's term, are heterogeneous Islamoscapes.[38] The house may look like 'W. had bombed the hell out of it looking for evildoers',[39] but it is a place with extreme vitality. All characters, without exception, are portrayed as exhibiting contradictions in terms of what they say and do. Even the supposedly hardedge Umar, who is the only one in the house besides the protagonist Yusuf Ali who does not drink or have extramarital sex, swears a lot when he is angry with others when they disrespect the rules he adheres to. Just like the other youngsters, Umar too has unconventional ways of expressing his faith, such as tattoos, 'big black "X" on the back of each hand, star-and-crescent on outer right of forearm, Muhammad's name … in Arabic on outer left forearm, and … right on his throat, a green 2:219', which refers to chapter and verse in *The Qur'an*.[40] There is much in this supposedly fundamentalist character (named after the second righteous Khalifa) that one could criticize from a theological point of view. Then there is Amazing Ayyub, 'the bone-thin Iranian smack-head in tight blue jeans and no shirt and a huge KARBALA tattooed in Old English letters just below his collarbone, dancing like a bald idiot on the porch and hollowing'.[41] The Shia and Sunni split between Ayyub and Umar is immediately obvious. In time for prayer, Yusuf Ali sees Fasiq Abasa sitting on the edge of the roof, smoking narcotics and reading *The Qur'an*. When Jehangir Tabari is introduced

---

[38] While Appadurai speaks of 'ethnoscapes', this term is limiting in the discourse I analyse. Islamoscapes, however strange it may sound, denotes social formation related to but not limited by the religion of Islam, which cross through any number of ethnoscapes.

[39] Knight, *Taqwacores*, 7.

[40] Knight, *Taqwacores*, 11.

[41] Knight, *Taqwacores*, 10.

he is playing 'an electric-guitar adhan': the call for prayer.[42] He 'stood statuesque with foot-high yellow Mohawk thick and bristly like the brush on an old Roman soldier's helmet'.[43] He gives the protagonist 'a sensation entirely new: a surging resonance of hope, a vibrant six-string promise that Islam's glory days were not the sole property of Abbasids and Fatimids but could be our days here, now, if we had the spirit to claim them'. Jehangir's unconventional behaviour is not met with fear for the faith, the way a fundamentalist would react, but with hope, even when Jehangir after the adhan says 'Fuck', thus 'returning us to Earth'.

Among the male characters, there is a single woman, and for Yusuf Ali she may be the most unconventional Muslim there is:

> Rabeya sat content knowing that none of my existing scripts for male–female interaction, mumin or kafr gave me any frame of reference for dealing with her. … While Rabeya was as staunch a Muslim as anyone there, it remained her own Islam as she saw fit to live it. This was the girl who jumped in front of the microphone at last night's party through her niqab singing slow and spooky-like Iggy Pop's withered Old Man Mortality voice – 'I want to fuck her on the floor, among my books of ancient lore' – the same girl who stood in front of our baseball-bat-through-the-wall-mihrab on Fridays to give khutbah and circulated handwritten rants on the sexism of both hemispheres in her self-published zine *Ayesha's Hymen*.[44]

Again, the coexistence of religious terms 'mumin', 'kafr', 'mihrab' and 'khutbah' with popular culture (Iggy Pop and baseball) produce the tension and significance of the content, and thus also an extreme particularity, which gives the book its highly local character while it stages and maintains an ongoing dialogue with an imagined readership that is global Ummah. Before becoming the only woman preaching to men, as Umar informed him, Rabeya lived 'downstairs' and had her own entrance and no man could use the kitchen unless she was away:

> She knew her stuff more than any of us, used books for furniture in her room – guests sitting on stacks of Betty Freidan and Simone de Beauvoir and Fatima Mernissi and Leila Ahmed and Amina Wadud and what-not – and gave everything she had, every stupid second of her life, to that Islam. But I felt like there was nowhere else in the world that she could give khutbah to men, and for that maybe we would be the vanguard of something new.[45]

[42] Knight, *Taqwacores*, 12.
[43] Knight, *Taqwacores*, 13.
[44] Knight, *Taqwacores*, 8–9.
[45] Knight, *Taqwacores*, 19.

The emphasis on individualism tied to a locality (often seen as Western) does not seem to go against a sense of communal bonding (seen as Eastern).[46] Going against Serge Latouche's dictum that 'Whatever is Western is Anti-Islamic', Tariq Ramadan argues,

> more and more young people and intellectuals are actively looking for a way to live in harmony with their faith while participating in the societies that are their societies ... constructing a 'Muslim personality' that will soon surprise many of their fellow citizens. Far from media attention. Going through the risks of a process of maturation that is necessarily slow, they are drawing the shape of European and American Islam: faithful to the principles of Islam, dressed in European and American cultures, and definitively rooted in Western societies. This grassroots movement will soon exert considerable influence over worldwide Islam.[47]

Although I doubt Ramadan would approve of intoxication and many other acts from the story (tattooes, sex, music, etc.), the point he makes is related to the way location in one place with an orientation out can actually create a healthy oscillation that has, and will continue to, (re)define Muslim Ummah. This is exactly what happens as Knight tries to cope with his complex identity. However extreme examples he may give (on-stage oral sex by a radical feminist in a burka spitting semen on the audience), what is interesting is that the *taqwacore* of Knight's imagination found resonances in the real sociopolitical life of Muslim-Americans. The phrase 'taqwacore' became an unintentional name for these silent processes that Ramadan assumes are in the workings, but which no one can actually predict or determine in advance. While Ramadan opposes Latouche's view that Islam has nothing in common with the West, for Knight it is not so much a question whether or not anything Western has a place in the reform of Islam, but more importantly, the place of Islam in the change of the West. This is why the firm location of his work in American literary ecology is so important in dialogue with its cosmopolitan aspirations. It is possible to dislocate fundamentalism by showing how it creates effects locally and globally, while not belonging anywhere, while trying to sell itself as universal. The political import of Knight's novel is that it dismantles both this modern binary and the potential misconception of what diversity entails within Islamic communities. Not only is there a much wider variety of Muslim expression,

---

[46] Communal prayers carry the value of twenty-seven prayers in solitude, according to recorded sayings by the Islamic Messenger Muhammad s.a.w.s., and what is more, the verses commonly recited in prayers are usually in the plural, such as the opening surah of *The Qur'an*, Al-Fatiha, 'You alone we worship, to You alone we turn for help' (1.4). Asad, *The Message of Qur'an*.

[47] Ramadan, *Western Muslims and the Future of Islam*, 4.

but neither has primacy over the other. Fundamentalist jihadists are just as modern a phenomenon as punk Muslims and any other formation because most of them define their particular standpoints from historically very specific socio-political space, or location, while also attempting to universalize the experience through cosmopolitan orientation and reaction to globalization.

Dissemination: Creating welcoming spaces

In the end, I want to highlight a few points regarding dissemination. It is not the movement of the text itself that defines it, that is the distribution and the sales of books, but ultimately the reception and the *taqwacore* effect: for instance, the creation of Muslim punk bands and other such alternative music scenes among Muslim youth. In other words, the content of the novel, though fictional, inspired a great deal of transnational movement among Muslims (LeVine[48]; Fiscella[49]). The increased demand led to distribution by the publishers (Alternative Tentacles and then Autonomedia). Asra Nomani has credited the novel as the source of the idea for woman-led prayer, which took place on 18 March 2005 with Amina Wadud acting as imam. Another example, from the previously mentioned documentary, is the performance of a taqwacore band at the ISNA (Islamic Society of North America) convention in Chicago. The band members that arrived with Knight expected a negative response due to the conventional connotations of loud music, female singers and dancing, all of which were against ISNA regulations. While the organizers pointed out the inappropriateness, the members of the audience seemed overwhelmingly positive. One woman said she found the performance fresh and used the expression 'mashallah', usually used in reaction to any positive thing. Moreover, one of the organizers commented on the importance of diversity within the convention.

Speaking with this band on a tour from Boston to Chicago, after their complaints about the misrepresentations in the media, Knight says that the media cannot understand that they can be a community and have no firm ideological ground, that some of them are interested in spirituality, some have a lot of faith

---

[48] Mark LeVine, *Heavy Metal Islam: Rock, Resistance, and the Struggle for the Soul of Islam* (New York: Broadway Books, 2008).

[49] Anthony T. Fiscella, 'From Muslim Punks to Taqwacore: An Incomplete History of Punk Islam', *Contemporary Islam* 6, no. 3 (2012) and Anthony T. Fiscella, 'Michael Muhammad Knight – An Interview', http://vimeo.com/11294095.

and some little, some drink and some abstain, that they have different political views and values, different tastes. They are as heterogeneous a community as it can be, and there is no political language for this type of personal expression. In fact, in an interview on QTV, Knight stated that he refrains from even calling taqwacore a movement because a movement implies that everyone should be on the same page.[50] He does not want to see himself as a representative of taqwacore because that would mean that he speaks for everyone. In other words, he has no desire to be an imam in such a hybrid and changing house as taqwacore. In the same interview, the director of the documentary, Omar Rajid argued that taqwacore is a name without a fixed essence. Its essence is its malleability. Their music may be a true attempt, albeit somewhat clichéd, to establish new possible mediascapes in which Homi Bhabha's notion of 'difference' can be articulated.

I have quoted Ramadan as claiming that much of the ongoing revolutions within variegated Islamic communities take place in silence. The reason for this, to go back to the comments on the media attention, is that the existing mediascapes cannot digest the heterogeneity of these revolutions. The taqwacore expressions are in a way producing possible mediascapes that can reach out across the boundaries of different ethnoscapes. What is important to note is that the taqwacore expressions of identity, albeit necessarily filtered through different media, do not seem to primarily seek media outlets. Fame is not an issue nor is it a goal. What they do is primarily turned towards the reform of themselves. In this way, they have, perhaps unconsciously or even deliberately, avoided the Baudrillardian dictum of postmodern hyperreality in the sense that they do not primarily seek to be media-people, that they instinctively react against being-a-copy, and they do not want their Islam, whatever it may be in the final account, to be a simulacrum of yet another media defined thing.

However, since their responses are indeed conditioned by the simulacra of Muslim realities represented in the media, taqwacore Islam too is partly a hyper-Islam, as much as it goes against the hyper-Islam of the media. If these two premises seem to stand in opposition, one being positive in the Romantic sense of the return to origins and the other negative in the sense that nothing is ever original and authentic, this contradiction is not a negative synthesized premise itself. Just as the phrase 'taqwacore' entails a creative contradiction, so does this double relationship to Islam and punk. The taqwacore people who have

[50] Michael Muhammad Knight, "'The Taqwacores" on Q TV', www.youtube.com/watch?v=RKx2pvkD5Jw.

a relationship with Islam, be it as religion or faith or culture, seem to suggest that the only way to be respectful is to be partly disrespectful. In an interview during his visit to Sweden, Knight argued that the reason he imagined such a motley community is because he felt a need to remain a Muslim while being free to be honest about the elements of Islam he could not cope with, and that the only way he could remain a Muslim was to be creative about his approach to the faith and religion.[51] This attitude is political in that it asks for active participation within the national and religious confines, and the right to try to reform both at the same time. The point is not to merely survive or be tolerated in a benevolent system, and thus affirm the system through a passive attitude, but to affirm it through participating in its reform. The importance of Knight's work is that it stresses a need to a form of affirmative unfaithfulness. This unfaithfulness is not a simple apostasy, or simplistic rebellion, but a need to produce a political and social space from which to speak with honesty in relation to oneself and community/nation.

Knight's imagination, which moves quite freely through Islamic history, seems to play with Al-Ghazali's notion of *dihliz* (threshold), which Ebrahim Moosa explains as 'the critical intermediary space between outside and inside, between exoteric (*zahir*) and esoteric (*batin*) … a welcoming space', which allowed Ghazali to deal with conflicting discursive traditions.[52] At the same time as he may be using such philosophical notions – especially in relation to the character of Jehangir, who embodies such locality where conflicts can take place as well as overlapping concerns and beliefs – Knight is aware of the wild directions interpretation processes can take. At times it appears that the characters interpret Western cultural influences in terms of Islam to reconcile the two, as when Rafiq reads the lyrics by Iggy Pop to entail a notion of spiritual transformation, and considers Iggy Pop a Muslim Sufi. In a sense, at the moment when Knight seems to endorse a simplified idea that anything goes, he finds it necessary to also state the opposite, there are limits to what a cultural text may mean, but it is important to maintain social imagination that can answer the question what it means to be a Muslim today, how to remain true to ones principles and generate a social capital that cuts across boundaries. To use Amyn B. Sajoo's words, '[i]n the bid for legitimacy, political and religious, where each side portrays the other as betraying modernity and

---

[51] Incidentally, in this interview, Knight wore a T-shirt with Derrida's picture and the famous term 'deconstruction' above the print.

[52] Ebrahim Moosa, *Ghazali and the Poetics of Imagination* (NC & London: Chapel Hill, 2005), 48.

tradition, the fertile middle ground best found in the *imaginaire* of ordinary citizens, which rarely sits at either extreme'.[53]

Conclusion

I have argued that Muslim-American writing can be defined in terms of its particular way of working with(in) the dynamic between location and orientation, between rootedness in American National literary ecology and a cosmopolitan orientation towards the Muslim Ummah. The example of *Taqwacoes* shows a particular way of treating this dynamic in terms of form and content, as well as through the book's place and role in contemporary youth culture. A unique feature of Knight's work is that it uses Islamic theology to shape the concepts of location and orientation and show how they work in terms of language, content and dissemination. This entails that the specific location is always subsumed to the social space that the characters create in relation to the Islamic notion of the global Ummah. This results in a general tendency to approach location allegorically more than in terms of the material conditions. Orientation, as the factor which infuses the local social space with allegoricity, can seem the more dominant part in the dynamic binary but this is not the case. The specific American location, with all the elements it brings to the discourse of identity formation, reshapes the very character of the orientation the characters envision. This is, I argue, perhaps most prominent in the use of a global vernacular language which is at the same time very much American and yet contains elements which suggest that it is directed to imagined global Muslim Ummah that would best understand it. What is more, having also looked at dissemination and the effects of the novel in youth culture, I find that an analysis of *Taqwacores* supports Helgesson and Kullberg's argument that 'world literature can be explored … as uneven translingual events in which linguistic tensions are manifested either at the micro level of the individual text or at the macro level of publication and circulation – or both'.[54] A truly dynamic relationship between location and orientation becomes a general strategy of identity production and as such, in the post-9/11 era of global identity crises, the identifying feature of Muslim-American writing in general.

---

[53] Amyn B. Sajoo, ed. *Muslim Modernities: Expressions of the Civil Imagination* (London: I.B. Taurus, 2008), 14.

[54] Helgesson and Kullberg, 'Translingual Events', 137.

Bibliography

Ahmed, Rehana, Peter Morey and Amina Yaqin. *Culture, Diaspora and Modernity in Muslim Writing*. New York: Routledge, 2012.

Aljunied, Khairudin. *Muslim Cosmopolitanism: Southeast Asian Islam in Comparative Perspective*. Edinburgh: Edinburgh University Press, 2017.

Appadurai, Arjun. *Modernity at Large: Cultural Dimensions of Globalization*. Minneapolis: University of Minnesota Press, 1996.

Asad, Muhammad. *The Message of Qur'an*. Bristol: The Book Foundation, 2003.

Beecroft, Alexander. *An Ecology of World Literature: From Antiquity to the Present Day*. London: Verso, 2015.

Boyden, Michael and Eugenia Kelbert. 'Introduction: The Theory Deficit in Translingual Studies'. *Journal of World Literature* 3 (2018): 127–35.

Fiscella, Anthony T. 'From Muslim Punks to Taqwacore: An Incomplete History of Punk Islam'. *Contemporary Islam* 6, no. 3 (2012): 255–81.

Fiscella, Anthony T. 'Michael Muhammad Knight – An Interview'. http://vimeo.com/11294095.

Gray, Richard. 'Open Doors, Closed Minds: American Prose Writing at a Time of Crisis'. *American Literary History* 21, no. 1 (2008): 128–51.

Helgesson, Stefan and Christina Kullberg. 'Translingual Events: World Literature and the Making of Language'. *Journal of World Literature* 3 (2018): 136–52.

Hurkens, Amélie and Pieter Vermeulen. 'The Americanization of World Literature? American Independent Publishing and the World Literary Vernacular'. *Interventions* 22, no. 3 (2020): 433–50.

Kahf, Mohja. *The Girl in the Tangerine Scarf* (New York: Carroll & Graf Publishers, 2006).

Khair, Tabish. *How to Fight Islamic Fundamentalism from the Missionary Position*. Northampton, MA: Interlink Publishing Group, 2013.

Khair, Tabish. *Just Another Jihadi Jane*. Northampton, MA: Interlink Publishing Group, 2016.

Knight, Michael Muhammad. *Taqwacores*. New York: Soft Skull Press, 2004.

Knight, Michael Muhammad. *Blue-eyed Devil: A Road Odyssey Through Islamic America*. New York: Autonomedia, 2006.

Knight, Michael Muhammad. *The Five Percenters: Islam, Hip-hop and the Gods of New York*. New York: One World Publications, 2008.

Knight, Michael Muhammad. '"The Taqwacores" on Q TV'. www.youtube.com/watch?v=RKx2pvkD5Jw.

LeVine, Mark. *Heavy Metal Islam: Rock, Resistance, and the Struggle for the Soul of Islam*. New York: Broadway Books, 2008.

MacGillivray, Alex. *A Brief History of Globalization*. London: Robinson, 2006.

Minnaard, Liesbeth and Till Dembeck, eds. *Challenging the Myth of Monolingualism*. Amsterdam: Rodopi, 2014.

Moosa, Ebrahim. *Ghazali and the Poetics of Imagination*. NC & London: Chapel Hill, 2005.

Mufti, Aamir. *Forget English! Orientalisms and World Literature*. Cambridge, MA: Harvard University Press, 2016.

Ong, Aihwa. *Flexible Citizenship: The Cultural Logic of Transnationality*. London: Durham University Press, 1999.

Ramadan, Tariq. *Western Muslims and the Future of Islam*. Oxford: Oxford University Press, 2004.

Rothberg, Michael. 'A Failure of the Imagination: Diagnosing the Post-9/11 Novel: A Response to Richard Gray'. *American Literary History* 21, no. 1 (2009): 152–8.

Sajoo, Amyn B. ed. *Muslim Modernities: Expressions of the Civil Imagination*. London: I.B. Taurus, 2008.

Parks, Tim. 'The Dull New Global Novel'. *The New York Review Blog*, 9 February 2010. www.nybooks.com/daily/2010/02/09/the-dull-new-global-novel/

Yildiz, Yasemin. *Beyond the Mother Tongue: The Postmonolingual Condition*. New York: Fordham University Press, 2012.

7

Locations, orientations and multiple temporalities in the contemporary, 'global' Latin American novel

Jobst Welge

Orientations of the Latin American novel as world literature

The tension between the pressure to identify itself as local and to reach for universal significance has characterized modern Latin American literature from its inception. In Latin America, the genre of the novel has played a central role in this negotiation of cosmopolitan values. In his book *Cosmopolitan Desires*, Mariano Siskind has introduced the simple, yet suggestive distinction between two interrelated phenomena; what he calls 'the globalization of the novel', on the one hand, and the 'novelization of the global', on the other.[1] The first category prompts the question how the form of the novel is part and parcel of the process and the discourse of globalization. Concerning Latin America, Siskind writes the following:

> Because of the kind of experiences that the novel afforded to the readers of the colonial and semi-colonial peripheries, Latin American intellectuals immediately realized the important role that the consumption, production, and translation of novels could play in the process of socio-cultural modernization. … Through processes of formal and thematic imitation, importation, translation, and adaptation, the institution of the novel grew roots in Latin America during the nineteenth century, and towards the 1880s novelistic production and consumption had become well established.[2]

[1] Mariano Siskind, *Cosmopolitan Desires: Global Modernity and World Literature in Latin America* (Evanston: Northwestern University Press, 2014), 31.
[2] Siskind, *Cosmopolitan Desires*, 31.

The novel, as Siskind writes, is a 'universal aesthetic form of modernity', and its adaptation in nineteenth-century Latin America is not so much indicative of cultural imperialism, but rather of the active *desire* to participate in cultural modernity.

Turning to the epoch of globalization, in his study *An Ecology of World Literature* Alexander Beecroft has included a brief discussion of how the post-Boom Latin American novel has eschewed a previous focus on national identity and self-exoticization ('Magical Realism') in favour of a new sense of geographical interconnectedness that is in turn echoed by the narrative technique of *entrelacement* (a 'multi-strand narration, as a means of narrating the experience of globalization'), a tendency shared with other instances of the contemporary 'global' novel.[3] In this regard, the paradigmatic Latin American novel briefly discussed by Beecroft is, naturally, Roberto Bolaño's *2666* (2004), which indeed has been canonized as a watershed event in the way in which Latin American literature positions itself in global networks, including the global market of the novel.[4] As critics have variously recognized, Bolaño's work generally harbours a 'translocal aesthetic potential',[5] and it is distinguished by a 'permanent transgression of national, continental contexts, with concentrated images of the global history of the world and of literature'.[6] Beecroft's sense of 'ecological' interconnectedness suggests the relation between spatial movement (in global space), and hence the multiplication of locations as well as the sequential connection between different narrative strands. In other words, 'interconnectedness' operates on various levels, but basically in the sense of *horizontal* relays between the various threads of the narrative.

Yet, as I will argue in the following, the contemporary global Latin American novel connects not only different geographical spaces through different narrative lines; it also juxtaposes different temporalities as they emerge from specific places. For my own purposes, and with regard to the framing concepts of this volume, I suggest, moreover, that the relational

[3] Alexander Beecroft, *An Ecology of World Literature: From Antiquity to the Present Day* (London: Verso, 2015), 283.
[4] Roberto Bolaño, *2666* (Barcelona: Anagrama, 2004).
[5] Siskind, *Cosmopolitan Desires*, 3.
[6] Benjamin Loy, 'Deseos de mundo. Roberto Bolaño y la (non tan nueva) literatura mundial', in *América Latina y la literatura mundial: mercado editorial, redes globales y la invención de un continente*, ed. Gesine Müller and Dunia Gras Miravet (Frankfurt am Main: Vervuert, 2015), 281. Cf. Stefano Ercolino, *The Maximalist Novel: From Thomas Pynchon's Gravity's Rainbow to Roberto Bolaño's 2666* (New York: Bloomsbury, 2015), 40. Unless otherwise noted, all translations into English are my own.

dialectic between cosmopolitan and vernacular tendencies[7] is precisely what distinguishes such novels, conceiving 'vernacular' here as a sort of local/regional residue or specificity that coexists with and modifies the globalizing aspects and effects of these works. As Hector Hoyos has argued, the recent tendencies and orientations of the Latin America novel do not end up in the rootless idea of the vaguely global, but their worlding function emerges from concretely situated lifeworlds, so that what he calls the 'global Latin American novel' simultaneously resonates within a global and a continental, or regional ('Latin American') circumference. Specifically, Hoyos has cautioned against the totalizing, abstract and systemic assumptions underlying some of the current theorizations of world literature and urged us to start instead from the worlding practices imbued in the literary texts themselves: 'We imagine the global as we imagine everything else: through metaphor, narrative, image, and related means. Therein lies the renewed interest in the practice of close reading',[8] namely to trace the consciousness and the 'emplotment of globalization'[9] within the text itself (as opposed to theories of distant reading embodied by Franco Moretti and Pascale Casanova). In the following I want to adapt Hoyos's model to novels that explore the relation between local and transnational aspects, vernacular and cosmopolitan orientations; in the second part of the chapter I will focus especially on novels that engage in this sense the hemispheric interrelation and the border between the Americas. Moreover, I intend to identify those intrinsic features of these novels that invoke a global imaginary or interpellate a potentially global readership. I argue that this sense of a broader orientation is achieved not only by spatial relations, but also by the orientation towards different temporalities.

Thus, in her study *Ghost-Watching American Modernity* (2012) María del Pilar Blanco has argued that while the categories of the Fantastic, as well as Magical Realism and American Gothic are highly significant and symptomatic for the hemispheric literary field of the Americas, they are ultimately insufficient, or too narrow to do justice to the multiple dimensions of supernatural or trans-real occurrences in literature. A broader concept, she argues, is supplied by the

[7] Stefan Helgesson, 'General Introduction: The Cosmopolitan and the Vernacular in Interaction', in *World Literatures: Exploring the Cosmopolitan-Vernacular Exchange*, ed. Stefan Helgesson, Annika Mörte Alling, Yvonne Lindqvist and Helena Wulff (Stockholm: Stockholm University Press, 2018), 1–11.

[8] Hector Hoyos, *Beyond Bolaño. The Global Latin American Novel* (New York: Columbia University Press, 2015), 21–2.

[9] Hoyos, *Beyond Bolaño*, 1–2.

idea of *haunting*, which she understands as a 'disquieting experience of sensing a collision of temporalities or spaces' in either urban or desert regions of the Americas.[10]

In a related, yet somewhat different context, Kaisa Kaakinen has recently shown that the modernist and the contemporary novel make use of techniques such as historical analogy and narrative parataxis in order to interrelate the present with multiple dimensions of the historical imaginary. Kaakinen insists that such novelistic representations of untimeliness may not only involve a post-traumatic sense of haunting but may even involve the dimension of futurity and possibility, and hence have not only a world-reflecting but a world-creating function: 'Untimely temporal figures in literary texts may open up new possibilities for conceiving historical relations, without ignoring historical factuality or specific real-world events.'[11] For Kaakinen, this sense of multiplication, or of the 'heterogeneity' of the present is typical for 'our current historical moment characterised by the co-presence of heterogeneous global reading contexts'[12] – which precisely do not eschew historical or geographical specificity but open it up towards multiple constellations. This approach, while primarily developed from the European novel, complements Pilar Blanco's conception of a present-progressive concept of haunting in the hemispheric American scene of modernity, as distinguished by multiply layered and simultaneous landscapes.[13]

Therefore, I have selected a number of recent novels that deliberately *multiply* the senses of (concrete, given) locations and (potential, multiple) orientations. If we understand 'location' with regard to the novelistic representation of space *and* time (where and when a novel's plot is set), we recognize also the multiple orientations that tend to branch out from the specificity of place(s). Furthermore, if we take into account the fact that the emergence and development of Latin American literature has been accompanied by what Siskind has called its 'cosmopolitan desire', we may also ask whether and how the contemporary version of this desire to inscribe oneself within international, world (literary) space and multiple

---

[10] María del Pilar Blanco, *Ghost-Watching American Modernity: Haunting, Landscape, and the Hemispheric Imagination* (New York: Fordham University Press, 2012), 182.

[11] Kaisa Kaakinen, *Comparative Literature and the Historical Imaginary: Reading Conrad, Weiss, Sebald* (New York: Palgrave Macmillan, 2017), 19.

[12] Kaakinen, *Comparative Literature*, 219.

[13] Pilar Blanco, *Ghost-Watching*, 7. Cf. Caio Yurgel, *Landscape's Revenge: The Ecology of Failure in Robert Walser and Bernardo Carvalho* (Berlin, Boston: De Gruyter, 2019), 45–6.

readerships[14] retains or remobilizes vernacular traditions and traces that belong to (Latin) American physical locations or (Latin) American literary landscapes. It goes without saying that contemporary novels emphasize and participate in these multiple orientations to different degrees and in different ways. My following reflections will therefore merely explore some possible constellations on the contemporary scene.

Local hauntings, historical orientations

The work by the Colombian author Juan Gabriel Vásquez is a good example of the cosmopolitan orientation of locally grounded narratives. Vásquez's cosmopolitan poetics is expressed by his programmatic essay 'The Art of Distortion',[15] in which he models the figure of the writer on the position of the 'inquilino' (tenant), meaning a concept of authorship that conceives 'exile' as something other than a pragmatic or political distance from one's country of origin.[16] His novels all delve into different aspects of the extremely violent history of his home country Colombia (to which he has returned in recent years). Among these novels, the most recent one, *La forma de las ruinas* (The Shape of the Ruins, 2015)[17] is especially significant with regard to the multiple orientations (biographical, national, global) generated from a symbolic event of *national* history. The historical centre of this novel is the political murder of the liberal politician Jorge Eliécer Gaitán (9 April 1948), which had provoked an orgy of destruction in Bogotá, known as 'Bogotazo'. The evocation of this civil-war-like violence is framed by the documentary endeavours of a homodiegetic, auto-fictional narrator who is marked by several biographical references, including the seemingly off-hand, but in fact highly significant remark that it was in 1999 that he first discovered the 'very strange' work of W. G. Sebald. The reference to Sebald (discussed by Vásquez in some of his essays) is suggestive because the German author (who had lived in self-imposed exile in England) has produced a body of work (including the novel *Austerlitz*, 2001) in which historical scenarios branch off in multiple, global directions and allow for

---

[14] Rebecca L. Walkowitz, *Born Translated: The Contemporary Novel in an Age of World Literature* (New York: Columbia University Press, 2015), 220.

[15] Juan Gabriel Vásquez, *El arte de la distorsión* (Madrid: Alfaguara, 2009).

[16] Vásquez, *El arte de la distorsión*, 22–3. Vásquez invokes the transnational paradigms of authors such as J. Conrad, V. Nabokov, or V. S. Naipaul.

[17] Juan Gabriel Vásquez, *La forma de las ruinas* (Madrid: Alfaguara, 2015).

productive, if highly melancholic juxtapositions.[18] And indeed Vásquez takes up this idea of the novel not as an instrument of historical reproduction, but as a vehicle for exploring historical possibility and hypothetical speculation.[19] In fact, the novel elaborately juxtaposes the murder of Gaitán not only with the previous murder of the Colombian presidential candidate Rafael Uribe Uribe (1914) but also with the internationally much more widely known murder of John F. Kennedy (1963) – the last event alone is discussed for about forty pages. Therefore, Vásquez intends to place this traumatic event of Colombian history, as well as the literary text, within a larger hemispheric context, as evidence of an entire era of political murder. Moreover, the narrator moves through the streets of Bogotá in a multiply haunted, historical palimpsest of violence, as filtered through the Borgesian tale of 'Death and the Compass'[20]; that is, the assassination of Gaitán calls up previous and subsequent violent deeds of Colombian history, including the drug-related violence of recent memory.

Even as the novel features characters that promote conspiracy theories as a problematic way to link these different events,[21] it is driven by the intent to show the recurrence of political violence in a specific urban location. At the same time, the juxtaposition with the notorious and highly mediatized Kennedy murder helps international readers to establish a comparative, more global frame of reference.[22] Vásquez also implies a parallel between his own novel and the postmodern classic *Libra* (1988) by Don DeLillo, an author cited by Vásquez as one of the greatest influences he has received from North American literature. Even if Vásquez is concerned here with a symbolic *lieu de mémoire* of Colombian history, the novel uses various strategies to open up the historical and specific urban location to anthropological speculation and global orientations as well as extended historical comparisons and analogies.[23]

Among the auto-/meta-fictional episodes we also find a central scene of authorial repentance. The narrator/author began his literary career from a

---

[18] Kaakinen, *Comparative Literature*, 282–4.

[19] Hanna Meretoja, *Ethics of Storytelling: Narrative Hermeneutics, History and the Possible* (Oxford: Oxford University Press, 2017), 34.

[20] Vásquez, *La forma de las ruinas*, 115.

[21] The novel is thus illustrative of what Beecroft identifies as 'the paranoiac interconnectedness of life in a globalized era', *An Ecology of World Literature*, 115; cf. Ercolino, *The Maximalist Novel*, 105–107.

[22] This might be compared to the concept of 'multidirectional memory', as introduced by Michael Rothberg, *Multidirectional Memory: Remembering the Holocaust in the Age of Decolonization* (Stanford: Stanford University Press, 2009).

[23] Kaakinen, *Comparative Literature*, 18–19. The global, multidirectional orientation of Vásquez's novel includes, for instance, references to J. F. Kennedy, Shakespearean tragedy, enigmatic photographs in the manner of Sebald.

position of hyper-cosmopolitanism. While being a resident of Belgium, Vásquez wrote elegant love stories set in the Belgian Ardennes,[24] which completely abstracted from any sense of Latin American identity. In an essay on the relation between history and literature, Vásquez similarly reflects on his (re-)turn to the subject of episodes of Colombian history in his subsequent literary works, raising the question of how the violent events are relevant for those who have 'inherited' them.[25] He thus conceives his work as speaking both to local/national and global audiences.[26]

Locations of the vernacular/cosmopolitan writer figure

Another, if stylistically very different, example for such a co-presence of different temporalities and a self-conscious inscription of the figure of the cosmopolitan Latin American writer is Valeria Luiselli's debut novel *Los ingrávidos* (2011; translated as *Faces in the Crowd*).[27] Luiselli is the daughter of a Mexican ambassador, has grown up in eight different countries, resides in New York and has established herself as a bilingual writer. Her first novel, written in Spanish, is a partly auto-fictional narrative of a young woman residing in Mexico City recalling her days as a literary scout in New York, searching in vain for a sort of 'next Bolaño', while discovering unpublished work by the scarcely known Mexican avant-garde poet Gilberto Owen (1904–1952), who had lived in New York during the 1920s Harlem Renaissance, and who was in contact with, for instance, Federico García Lorca. The auto-fictional narrator presents a faked 'translation' and simulacra of Owen's poetry to the American publisher she is working for, which will finally be discovered. As the novel progresses, the narrator becomes more and more obsessed with Owen, who haunts her with his ghostly presence in subways and the streets of Harlem. The novel thus reads the city of New York as being haunted by the spectres of Latin American literature, of an international avant-garde that prefigures the scene of contemporary cosmopolitanism. The novel may thus be read as a self-inscription of the

---

[24] Juan Gabriel Vásquez, *Los Amantes de Todos los Santos* (Madrid: Alfaguara, 2001).

[25] Vásquez, *Viajes con un mapa en blanco* (Madrid: Alfaguara, 2018), 132–3.

[26] For an extended analysis of this novel, see Jobst Welge, 'Historical Reference and Self-Reflection in Recent Latin American (Auto)Fiction', in *Fictionality, Factionality, and Reflexivity Across Discourses and Media*, ed. Erika Fülöp, with Graham Priest and Richard Saint-Gelais (Berlin: De Gruyter, 2021), in print.

[27] Valeria Luiselli, *Los ingrávidos* (Mexico: Sexto Piso, 2011).

contemporary Latin American writer, as a figure that typically faces situations of displacement, (voluntary) exile, loss and migration.[28] The narrator's phantasmatic experience of Owen's ghostly presence in the urban spaces of New York and her sensation of feeling 'inhabited by another possible life',[29] suggests not only a sense of analogy between the historical avant-garde and the 'global' writer of the present, a fictionally engendered solidarity between the two expatriate writers in their respective solitudes; it also erases the boundaries between past and present, since the 'undead' poet Owen is said to have plans for a novel that strangely resembles the circumstances of the very novel we are reading:

> I know that I want to write a novel that takes place in a big house in Mexico City and in the New York of my youth. All the characters are dead, or in shock, but they don't know it. Salvador Novo told me that there is a young writer in Mexico who is doing something similar.[30]

Moreover, the historical figure of Owen worked as a diplomat and thus embodies a cultural mediation between anglophone and hispanophone cultures that resonates with Luiselli's own bilingual, cross-cultural, translational practice and poetics.[31] Through various references to both Spanish and North American poetry, the novel suggests a programme of hemispheric cultural exchange and translation. By way of the narrator's role as literary scout and translator it also explicitly addresses the issue of *gringo* (and potentially also global) expectations regarding a consumable, exportable Latin American literature. Notably, we read about the publisher: 'White was sure that after Bolaño's success in the gringo market more than five years ago, there would be a next Latin American boom.'[32] The phantasmatic poetics of the novel is explored through various intersections of the world of the dead and the living, through the co-presence of different temporalities. Indeed, this aspect is self-consciously addressed, as when the narrator befriends a student of philosophy, who studies precisely this

---

[28] Cecily Raynor, 'Place-Making in the Solitude of the City: Valeria Luiselli's *Los ingrávidos*', in *Urban Spaces in Contemporary Latin American Literature*, ed. José Eduardo González and Timothy Robbins (London: Palgrave Macmillan, 2018), 147.

[29] The original reads: 'habitada por otra posible vida'. Luiselli, *Los ingrávidos*, 33.

[30] The original reads: 'Sé que quiero escribir una novela que sucede en una casona en la ciudad de México y en el Nueva York de mi juventud. Todos los personajes están muertos, o afantasmados, pero no lo saben. Me contó Salvador Novo que hay un joven escritor en México que está haciendo algo parecido'. Luiselli, *Los ingrávidos*, 136.

[31] Ilse Logie, '¿Escritos en la traducción y para la traducción? Dos ejemplos: Valeria Luiselli y Mario Bellatin', in *Literatura latinoamericana mundial. Dispositivos y disidencias*, ed. Gustavo Guerrero, Jorge L. Locane, Benjamin Loy and Gesine Müller (Berlin: De Gruyter, 2020), 210.

[32] The original reads: 'White estaba seguro de que, trás el éxito de Bolaño en el mercado gringo hacía más de un lustro, habría un siguiente boom latinoamericano'. Luiselli, *Los ingrávidos*, 24; cf. 36.

aspect of analytical philosophy: 'Vagueness and fuzzy time limits.'[33] Luiselli's meta-fictional novel inscribes the authorial persona into a self-consciously marginal, yet at the same time cosmopolitan paradigm of the historical movement of the avant-garde and carves out a literary space that seeks to mediate between the local and the global. While the novel's cultural and (meta-)literary references certainly privilege the hemispheric axis between the two Americas, there is also a sense that the auto-fictional author, through her identification with Owen and *his* contact with the Spanish poet García Lorca (*Poeta en Nueva York*, 1940) associates herself with a yet broader geo-cultural frame. I can't develop this here in any detail, but the urban poetics of the novel appears also to be influenced by the Spanish novelist Enrique Vila-Matas or the Russian-American poet Joseph Brodsky, about whom Luiselli has written admiringly in her essayistic work.[34] While exploring 'local' Mexican-American relations and displacement, Luiselli also self-consciously inscribes herself in the tradition of the radical cosmopolitanism embodied by the Mexican writer Sergio Pitol (1933–2018).[35]

Novels on the border I: Analogies, multiple orientations

The problems associated with the Mexican–American border have become a central issue of hemispheric relations and a recurring topic in recent fiction, not least in Bolaño's *2666* (2004). Insofar as the literary representation of the border region emphasizes a sense of layered temporalities, such a practice has been anticipated by the hugely influential Mexican classic *Pedro Páramo* (1955), by Juan Rulfo, which features the uncanny emergence of the voices of the dead in the barren landscape of the Mexican desert. This novel, significantly, operates within the broader field of a modernist Latin American regionalism, and is therefore emphatically bound up with local specificity and vernacular traditions, even as they are subsumed by an archaic universalism.[36] As Pilar Blanco has shown, Rulfo's novel may be said to prefigure a prominent tendency of the contemporary Latin American or hemispheric novel, namely

---

[33] The original reads: 'Vaguedad y límites temporales difusos.' Luiselli, *Los ingrávidos*, 21.

[34] Valerisa Luiselli, *Papeles Falsos* (Madrid/Mexico: Sexto Piso, 2010), ch. 1.

[35] Valeria Luiselli, 'Sergio Pitol/Best Untranslated Writers', *Granta* (2013), https://granta.com/best-untranslated-writers-sergio-pitol/

[36] Paulo Moreira, *Modernismo Localista das Américas. Os contos de Faulkner, Guimarães Rosa e Rulfo* (Belo Horizonte: UFMG), 40.

its 'increasing awareness of simultaneous landscapes and simultaneous others living within unseen, diverse spaces in the progressively complicated political and cultural networks of hemispheric modernization'.[37] In fact, contemporary Mexican-American literature has explored the border region between Mexico and the United States not only as a geographical limit or contact zone, but also as a space of layered, deep temporalities.

For instance, Yuri Herrera's short novel *Señales que precederán al fin del mundo* (Signs Preceding the End of the World, 2009) subtly suggests that the itinerary of a woman named Makina, in search of her brother across the border to the North, corresponds with mythological conceptions of the pre-Hispanic, Aztec underworld of Mictlán. In addition, the name of Makina serves as an allusion to the historical figure of Malinche, Hernán Cortés's lover and interpreter, a cultural go-between who has become a foundational figure for hybrid Mexican identity. In fact, Makina works as a local switchboard operator and a messenger of sorts, and she is translating between a local vernacular, English and Spanish. Her perception of urban spaces suggests a mythical deep time beyond and below surfaces: 'lost cities within lost cities, … the vague memories of a less cynical time, the villages emptied of men'.[38]

On the one hand, and similar to *Pedro Páramo* – although Herrera himself downplayed the significance of this particular influence[39] – the novel entirely eschews concrete place names and thus evokes a mythical, universal aura. On the other hand, the frequent use of the neologism 'jarchar' (translated by Lisa Dillman in her English translation as 'to verse'),[40] meaning something like 'to cross' or 'to move', is related to the term 'jarcha', which refers to a genre of Spanish medieval poetry written in Arabic; it specifically refers to the last lines of these poems, written in Mozarabic, which is a 'disappeared Romance language employed by Christians living in Muslim territories of the Iberian peninsula', usually requiring oral performance.[41] Through this linguistic connotation, the key word 'jarcha' refers to an extremely transitional, vernacular form of language, and thus 'widens the reader's perspective on the idea of human beings in movement well beyond the Mexico-

---

[37] Pilar Blanco, *Ghost-Watching*, 7.
[38] The original reads: 'ciudades perdidas dentro de otras ciudades perdidas … los recuerdos vagos de un tiempo menos cínico, los pueblos vaciados de hombres'. Yuri Herrera, *Señales que precederán al fin del mundo* (Cáceres: Periférica, 2015), 35.
[39] Aaron Bady, 'The Mexican novelist Yuri Herrera talks about the first English translation of one of his novels, the Mexican afterlife, and Dante', *The Nation*, 2 December 2015.
[40] Bady, 'The Mexican novelist'.
[41] Nathan Richardson, 'Reading Makina/Makina Reading in Yuri Herrera's *Señales que precederán al fin del mundo*', *Ciberletras* 41 (2019): 19.

United States context'.[42] The term therefore highlights the vernacular dimension of language, yet not as an obvious Mexicanism but as a broader, or displaced signifier of the vernacular that has to be filled in by the reader – and for which translators of the novel have to find their own solutions.[43] While these mythological and linguistic references are culturally specific and refer to local cultures, they are simultaneously literary means of alienation and transfiguration that suggest the text's multiple, palimpsest-like orientations and universalizing strategies.

Another case in point is Luiselli's recent novel *Lost Children Archive* (2019). In contrast to her previous work in Spanish, this is her first novel written in English, thus furthering her stance of cultural mediation between the Americas and her inscription into a contemporary world literature ('in English').[44] The novel involves partly what is apparently an auto-fictional scenario, since Luiselli draws here on her experiences as a volunteer interpreter in New York City's federal immigration court, where she worked with undocumented refugee children who had fled from Central American countries across Mexico over the North American border. Luiselli had already published a short documentary-interventionist essay on this politically urgent subject matter, *Tell Me How It Ends: An Essay in Forty Questions* (2017), in which she muses on her interviews with Latin American children facing deportation, and thus critically interrogates the (nowadays rather shaken) American self-image as a safe haven for immigrants. Particularly, she insists that the causes driving these children across various countries and borders are frequently ignored, even though they are 'deeply embedded in our shared hemispheric history'.[45] The essay also refers to a family road trip during which the parents tell their children about the (Mexican) history of the old American Southwest, including the so-called Indian Removal Act. The Chiricahua 'finally surrendered in 1886 and were "removed" to the San Carlos Reservation – in southern Arizona, toward which we are now driving. It's curious or perhaps just sinister, that the word "removal" is still used to refer to the deportation of "illegal" immigrants'.[46] The essay suggests that this sort of 'deep' history is essentially connected to the border landscape.

---

[42] Cecilia Alvstad, 'Anthropology over Aesthetics: On the Poetics of Movement and Multilingualism in Three Translations of Yuri Herrera's *Señales que precederán al fin del mundo*', in *Literatura latinoamericana mundial. Dispositivos y disidencias*, ed. Gustavo Guerrero, Jorge L. Locane, Benjamin Loy and Gesine Müller (Berlin, Boston: De Gruyter, 2020), 229.

[43] Alvstad, 'Anthropology over Aesthetics', 228–9.

[44] Cf. Walkowitz, *Born Translated*.

[45] Valeria Luiselli, *Tell Me How It Ends: An Essay in Forty Questions* (Minneapolis: Coffee House Press, 2017), 85.

[46] Luiselli, *Tell Me How It Ends*, 17.

Lost Children Archive, then, is a highly self-reflective 'novelization' of this documentary, essayistic material. The theme of child refugees is here approached from the perspective of an auto-fictionally inflected American road novel (in the tradition of Vladimir Nabokov's *Lolita* and Jack Kerouac's *On the Road*), which involves a family vacation trip from New York City to Arizona in the year 2014. The four-person family includes 'mom' and 'dad', a ten-year-old 'boy' (the father's son from another marriage) and a five-year-old 'girl' (the female narrator-mother's daughter, also from another marriage).

The road trip takes the family from New York City to Cochise County, Arizona, at the Mexican border. While they are driving through Oklahoma, they hear on the radio the news of unaccompanied refugee children crossing the border. The autobiographical constellation (Luiselli making the trip with her former husband, Álvaro Enrigue, and their respective children) is fictionalized insofar as the anonymous parents are not presented as writers but as sound documentarians of sorts: she is working on a sound documentary on the children's refugee crisis, while he is making an 'inventory of echoes' about 'the ghosts of Geronimo and the last Apaches'.[47] These fictional documentary projects evidently resonate with the respective literary projects of Luiselli and Enrigue, apparently resulting from this common road trip. The emphasis on 'sounds' suggests a literary dedication to the documenting of the voices of others, while also alluding to invisible presences in a haunted landscape. The auditory dimension extends to the echo of literary voices, especially since the narrator comments on the various audiobooks played during the drive: Cormac McCarthy's *The Road*, William Golding's *Lord of the Flies* and Juan Rulfo's *Pedro Páramo*. As James Wood has observed in a perceptive and balanced review for *The New Yorker*, these novels work as 'a troika of patron texts', alluding to lost children and, in the case of Rulfo, to the ghosts of the dead.[48] Moreover, it's a British-American-Mexican 'troika', and Rulfo's novel provides an important precedent for the idea of a desert landscape marked by different temporalities and the history of violence, as we have seen.

The family's use of a polaroid camera leads to reflections about Man Ray's 'rayographs' as traces of absent objects, which is in turn understood as informing the (novelist's) practising of archive work and documentation.[49]

---

[47] Luiselli, *Lost Children Archive*, 21.

[48] James Wood, 'Writing about Writing about the Border Crisis', www.newyorker.com/magazine/2019/02/04/writing-about-writing-about-the-border-crisis.

[49] On photographs as 'modern paradigms of the archive', see Patricia López-Gay, *Ficciones de verdad. Archivo y narrativas de vida* (Frankfurt am Main: Vervuert, 2020), 50–53.

These photographs/rayographs are said to be 'like the ghostly traces of objects no longer there, like visual echoes, or like footprints left in the mud by someone who'd passed by long ago'.[50] Furthermore, the narrator's voice also reflects on the 'visual echoes' of American cultural history, as they impinge on, and predetermine her own perception:

> I know, as we drive through the long, lonely roads of this country – a landscape that I am seeing for the first time – that what I see is not quite what I see. What I see is what others have already documented: Ilf and Petrov, Robert Frank, Robert Adams, Walker Evans, Stephen Shore – the first road photographers and their pictures of road signs, stretches of vacant land, cars, motels, diners, industrial repetition, all the ruins of early capitalism now engulfed by future ruins of later capitalism.[51]

This sense of a landscape as a palimpsest of ruins and the co-presence of different materials from the cultural archive is reflected by the novel's collage-like assembly of different textual forms, media, so-called boxes (belonging to different family members) with lists of literary and historical parallels and influences, as well as by the (sometimes overly explicit) philosophizing by the narrator, who senses an 'absence of future, because the present has become too overwhelming, so the future has become unimaginable. And without future, time feels like only an accumulation'.[52] The idea of an unlimited contemporaneity, the limitless availability of the past in a 'broad present' has indeed been identified as typical for our time's experience of temporality.[53] Arguably, within this undifferentiated realm of the present, novels may take on the function to make visible its heterogeneity, as sedimented in seemingly 'empty' landscapes. Luiselli's novel repeatedly uses especially childrens' imagination, their naivety and their fascination with adventure stories to question the foreclosed sense of history, and to imagine alternative histories and different positions of historical agents:

> We realize then that they in fact have been listening, more attentively than we thought, to the stories of Chief Nana, Chief Loco, Chihuahua, Geronimo – the last of the Chiricahuas – as well as to the stories we are all following on the news,

---

[50] Luiselli, *Lost Children Archive*, 56. In this sense, the photographs, also reproduced in the novel, are reminiscent of W. G. Sebald's use of photography in his novels. I'm grateful to Bo G. Ekelund for reminding me of this.

[51] Luiselli, *Lost Children Archive*, 102.

[52] Luiselli, *Lost Children Archive*, 103.

[53] Hans Ulrich Gumbrecht, *Our Broad Present: Time and Contemporary Culture* (New York: Columbia University Press), 207; Aleida Assmann, *Ist die Zeit aus den Fugen? Aufstieg und Fall des Zeitregimes der Moderne* (Munich: Hanser, 2013), 250–52.

about the child refugees at the border. But they combine the stories, confuse them. They come up with possible endings and counterfactual histories.

What if Geronimo had never surrendered to the white-eyes?
What if he'd won that war?
The lost children would be the rulers of Apacheria![54]

The dangerous fate of the refugee children is juxtaposed with the personal crisis of a family, whose two children – even as they don't fully understand what their parents have been trying to document – tentatively and 'playfully' (fictionally) try to put themselves into the place of their less fortunate peers. The latter part of the novel even imagines a sort of stream of consciousness by the family's boy, as he and the girl get lost in the desert and re-enact scenes the older boy had been reading and hearing about, namely the refugee childrens' journey on the train ('the Beast') towards the border. The text from which they heard about the childrens' fate is said to be by an Italian writer named Ella Camposanto, an entirely fictional writer from whose book excerpts are reproduced in the latter part of the novel. As the boy navigates between the place names of Echo (!) Canyon and Bowie (Fort Bowie in Southeastern Arizona, an outpost of the US Army during the nineteenth century), he addresses his younger sister in the following way:

So then I said, remember …Bowie is the author of our favorite song … So then I told you the only thing I actually knew, which was that Bowie was the place where Geronimo and his band were forced to get on a train that deported them someplace far away, and Pa had told us about it.[55]

Whether this and similar passages are a convincing mimesis of a child's train of thought, and whether the locution that 'our children disappeared'[56] might be forced or not, is open to discussion. The inherent ethical problematics of this form of identification and empathy, as well as the general question of literature's capability to intervene politically and ethically, is in fact thematized by the novel itself.[57] The novel also embodies world-reflecting and world-creating functions in the direction of what Hanna Meretoja has called a 'sense of the possible', which is to say the analysis of a given historical context as a space of possibilities that

[54] Luiselli, *Lost Children Archive*, 75.
[55] Luiselli, *Lost Children Archive*, 291.
[56] Luiselli, *Lost Children Archive*, 299.
[57] On the question of ethics and affective identification, see Ilse Logie, '*Los niños perdidos*, de Valeria Luiselli: el intérprete ante las vidas 'dignas de duelo', *Iberoamericana* 75 (2020): 103–116.

'encourages certain modes of experience, thought, and action, and discourages and disallows others'.[58] Still, I think the novel is at times somewhat over-explicit and uni-directional, if we compare it with the practice of (historical) juxtapositions and parallels discussed by Kaakinen in the works of Peter Weiss and W. G. Sebald.[59] Yet *Lost Children Archive* is certainly suggestive in its use of the border landscape as a space that evokes a mobile sense of history and opens up the possibility for identification with others. In this sense we might say that the novel, just like *Los ingrávidos*, is not so much 'set' in a location, but rather emphasizes the connection between space and imaginary projection and identification. In contrast to the earlier novel, *Lost Children Archive* seeks to appeal to the reader's *ethical* response to an intra-American human tragedy. All of the members of the family have their own ways to re-embody and re-narrate the haunted history and present of a landscape. The 'archive' of the title clearly refers not to a sense of stable depository, but to the activity of producing and selecting a fragmentary and mobile archive, steered by subjective and partial desires and perspectives.[60] Therefore, the novel also raises more general questions about the relation between art, imagination and ethics in a globalized world; it embodies the global novel's tension between geopolitical referentiality and a more open sense of orientation, namely how humans can inhabit the space of others through their imagination.

Novels on the border II: A common history, multiple orientations

Álvaro Enrigue's most recent novel, *Ahora me rindo y esto es todo* (Now I give up and that's all, 2018) is similarly concerned with the Mexican–American border landscape. *Ahora me rindo* is a more directly meta-historiographical work, concerned with the disappearance of the historical Apache territory, as it has been subsumed and eradicated by both the United States and Mexico. Previous novels by Enrigue, most importantly perhaps *Muerte súbita* (Sudden Death, 2013), have already demonstrated the novelist's interest in an

---

[58] Meretoja, *Ethics of Storytelling*, 18.
[59] Kaakinen, *Comparative Literature*, 20: 'Weak analogies are largely paratactic, because they leave the suggested relationship undetermined.'
[60] See the excellent discussion of the semantic re-evaluation of the archive in recent times by López-Gay, *Ficciones de verdad*, 71–2.

encyclopedic, open approach to the historical archive as an echo chamber for concerns of the present.[61]

As has already become apparent, the novels by Luiselli and Enrigue explicitly intersect with each other, and the auto-fictional narrators include references to the other's real name and respective literary projects,[62] so that both novels may be seen as outcomes of the same, common journey. In terms of literary form, Enrigue seeks here to blend the atmosphere of the American Western with metanarrative and epic traditions known from modern Latin American literature (Borges, Fuentes, García Márquez). His novel is an example of a 'postgenocidal, transnational historical narration' in the context of hemispheric relations.[63] The historical fulcrum of the novel, emblematized by its title, concerns 4 September 1886, when the Indian chief Goyahkla, better known as Geronimo, surrendered, together with his last thirty-six warriors, to general Nelson A. Miles. This capitulation marked the end of the so-called Indian Wars in the border region between Arizona and New Mexico, where the Chiricahua Apaches had vigorously defended their land against the settlers in Northern Mexico and Southern Arizona, in a region where a treaty of 1882 had allowed both countries to hunt down the Apaches even into the territory of the neighbouring state. Previously, the warlike Apaches had been working strategically with permanent crossings of the border line, thus extending their radius to New Mexico and Arizona in the United States as well as Sonora and Chihuaha on the Mexican side.[64]

The novel interweaves the story of the mestiza woman Camila, who has been kidnapped by men belonging to the Apache chief Mangas Coloradas and is now tracked by the lieutenant Zuloaga of the Mexican army. To his astonishment, Zuloaga discovers that Camila has voluntarily decided to remain the wife of the Apache chief. In his rewriting of the documented history[65] Enrigue stresses this tendency to cross cultural boundaries. Camila's way into cultural transformation is reminiscent of the story of Malinche, frequently invoked in Enrigue's previous novel *Muerte súbita*.[66] As in the previous novel,

---

[61] Enrigue's historically encyclopedic, Borgesian, rather than psychological approach to the form of the novel, has been pointed out in a review by Carlos Fonseca (2018): https://elroommate.com/2018/11/09/carlos-fonseca-resena-la-ultima-novela-de-alvaro-enrigue-mexico/.

[62] Cf. Enrigue, *Ahora me rindo*, 297.

[63] Kaakinen, *Comparative Literature*, 21.

[64] Aram Mattioli, *Verlorene Welten. Eine Geschichte der Indianer Nordamerikas 1700–1910* (Stuttgart: Klett-Cotta, 2017), 289; Jeanette Erazo Herzfelder, *Welcome to Borderland: Die US-mexikanische Grenze* (Berlin: Berenberg, 2018), 138–9.

[65] The narrative is partly based on the account that the old Geronimo gave to a journalist in 1905. Cf. Herzfelder, *Welcome to Borderland*, 138; Enrigue, *Ahora me rindo*, 59.

[66] Álvaro Enrigue, *Muerte súbita* (Barcelona: Anagrama, 2013).

Enrigue inserts the anecdotal fragments into a longer history, suggesting both continuities (with the history of the conquest) and parallels, such as the suggested comparison between Geronimo and Pancho Villa, famed general and outlaw of the Mexican Revolution.[67]

Enrigue's saga of the Apache ruler Geronimo's last stand and the various battles and border-crossings between Mexico and the United States is interspersed with metanarrative and meta-historiographical reflections on the author's own sense of a liminal, beleaguered sense of national belonging, as he is awaiting Green Card formalities. The text, again, suggests 'anachronistic' parallels between the present, autobiographical situation and the historical subject matter:

> But I'm not quite there where I live and my bureaucratic status weighs on me. I never wanted to be anything more than what I am: Mexican. The things of the world, the fear of living like an Apache, have put me, however, in a benumbed mood.[68]

The novel, then, suggests the multidirectional implications and resonances of the American Indians' dispersal and defeat, including references to the battle of Tenochtitlán in the year 1521, as another, earlier case of American Indians' resistance against colonial conquest,[69] or the anthropological studies of the descendants of the Apaches during the 1930s.[70] Moreover, when the auto-fictional narrator finds himself in Berlin, his wife being invited there to give lectures as an artist in residence, he comments tongue-in-cheek that 'Berlin will soon have more Latin American writers and artists than Latin America'[71] – thus acknowledging the typical topos of displacement and cosmopolitanism of the Latin American writer. The novel is indeed insistently concerned with questions of displacement, travel, transnational contact and bilingualism (including the case of the narrator's own children),[72] thus creating a circuit of multiple orientations between past, present and the personal. The novel explores Mexican–American relations with regard to the specific location and the specific identities it produces, namely the trans-American borderland, which is in turn

---

[67] Enrigue, *Ahora me rindo*, 328.
[68] The original reads: 'Pero no estoy del todo donde vivo y mi estatus burocrático me pesa. Nunca quise ser nada más que lo que soy: mexicano. Las cosas del mundo, el miedo a vivir como un apache, me han puesto, sin embargo, en un ánimo claudicatorio.' Enrigue, *Ahora me rindo*, 38.
[69] Enrigue, *Ahora me rindo*, 44, 60.
[70] Enrigue, *Ahora me rindo*, 53.
[71] The original reads: 'pronto Berlín va a tener más escritores y artistas latinoamericanos que Latinoamérica'. Enrigue, *Ahora me rindo*, 50.
[72] Enrigue, *Ahora me rindo*, 103.

temporally and culturally layered, with ruins and traces pointing to the Indian past, the Spanish empire, the first Mexican Republic, and so forth.[73]

Yet another thread of the topic concerns the question of cultural appropriation, in the form of voyeuristic exhibitions of the Native American legacy, a topic that has been imaginatively explored in a recent novel on Buffalo Bill's Wild West shows by the French writer Éric Vuillard (*Tristesse de la Terre*, 2012).[74] A few years after his surrender and his incarceration, beginning in 1889, at Fort Sill, the Apache leader Geronimo has been conscripted in the theatrical, yet supposedly authentic re-enactment of history in exhibitions and parades, always with the idea that he would play himself.[75] Let us recall that the very notion of the 'Wild West', ever since Buffalo Bill's performances in the 1880s, refers to a location that as such conjoins past and present, a 'transportable conflation of myth and true history', in short, a 'simultaneous landscape'.[76]

At certain points, Enrigue engages in explicit historical comparisons. Thus, the numbers Native Americans had been forced to wear in the Reservation of San Carlos, Florida, are compared to the Jews wearing the yellow star in Nazi Germany.[77] These references, although mostly very brief, underscore the intended sense of a multidirectional memory and interpellate the reader repeatedly to establish or interrogate connections and resonances between the past and the present. For instance, the narrator insists that, in spite of the Apache Indians having become a part of North American national mythology, they have in fact New Mexican roots: 'All spoke Spanish as a second language and none ever learned English; all had the skin colour that half of Americans think will degrade their country if people continue to migrate.'[78]

The narrator repeatedly comments on the ideological 'whitening' of the American racial consciousness and the obliteration of history in the 'ghost towns of Arizona'.[79] Even the official, national landmarks such as Fort Bowie appear to be abandoned[80] and thus require the narrator to 'resurrect' the interrelated

[73] Enrigue, *Ahora me rindo*, 235; cf. José David Saldívar, *Trans-Americanity: Subaltern Modernities, Global Coloniality, and the Cultures of Greater Mexico* (Durham, NC: Duke University Press, 2011).
[74] Éric Vuillard, *Tristesse de la Terre* (Arles: Actes Sud, 2012).
[75] Vuillard, *Tristesse de la Terre*, 64.
[76] Pilar Blanco, *Ghost-Watching*, 69.
[77] Enrigue, *Ahora me rindo*, 81.
[78] The original reads: 'Todos hablaban español como segunda lengua y ninguno aprendió nunca inglés; todos tenían el color de piel que la mitad de los estadounidenses piensa que va a degradar su país si se sigue permitiendo la migración de gente de México y Centroamérica.' Enrigue, *Ahora me rindo*, 66.
[79] Enrigue, *Ahora me rindo*, 235.
[80] Enrigue, *Ahora me rindo*, 246.

histories that foreground the often neglected Mexican implications in this 'American' history of violence and genocide. At the same time, the sense of transcultural, transnational passing, explored on the level of the novel's episodes and form, brackets the idea of nationhood in favour of the understanding of a nationally intertwined history and present. Yet this history is presented as an imaginary one that extrapolates from the sources and then reverts back to their mediatic character. For instance, for the description of the Native Americans the narrator immerses the reader in the immediacy of the historical present and their world view, even as he underlines that he 'imagines'[81] that things have happened in a particular way and puts emphasis on the perspective of hindsight, the historical record, or the remaining material traces the author/narrator has actually witnessed during the road trip: 'Yusn was a generous god, he must have listened to Nana's plea, he must have told her something and offered her, also, some guarantee, because the son of a bitch lived thirty years more. He went all the way to Oklahoma to die – we saw his grave a few days ago.'[82]

The reconstruction of historical scenes in the second and middle part of the novel, entitled 'Album', amounts to a polyphonic representation of the multiple viewpoints and positions, giving voice to various military officers from both sides of the border, involved in the campaigns to capture Geronimo in the Mexican Sierra Madre. However, the focus on the various historically documented figures is always accompanied by the meta-historical perspective of the narrator, who repeatedly foregrounds the resonances across the 'deep time' of Mexican–American relations:[83] 'Lawton and his men should have noticed the brilliant irony that everyone present was armed with American guns: politics, then as now, runs everywhere, but money has always flowed in one direction.'[84]

Enrigue's and Luiselli's novels, both engaging with a common experience of an American, transcultural border landscape and hemispheric literary traditions, may indeed be seen as complementary. Where Luiselli relates the contemporary migration scenario to private repercussions and the 'deep time'

[81] Enrigue, *Ahora me rindo*, 209.
[82] The original reads: 'Yusn era un dios generoso, debe haber atendido a la súplica de Nana, le debe haber dicho algo y le habrá ofrecido, también, alguna garantía, porque el hijo de la chingada vivió treinta años más. Se fue hasta Oklahoma a morir – vimos su tumba hace unos días.' Enrigue, *Ahora me rindo*, 210.
[83] Cf. Wai Chee Dimock, *Through Other Continents. American Literature Across Deep Time* (Princeton: Princeton University Press, 2006).
[84] The original reads: 'Lawton y sus hombres tendrían que haber notado la genial ironía de que todos los presentes estaban armados con fusiles estadounidenses: la política, entonces como ahora, corre para todos lados, pero el dinero ha fluido siempre en una sola dirección.' Enrigue, *Ahora me rindo*, 332.

of Native American displacement, Enrigue presents a painstakingly researched, if sometimes prolix meta-historical novel that opens up towards the experience and politics of the (Inter-)American present. Both novels are highly self-reflective contributions to a hemispheric concern with desert landscapes, which are far from being untroubled, yet allow for possibilities of renewal. They may be cast as the 'unseen space of an ongoing modernity'.[85] The foregrounding of the border landscape corresponds not only to the inherently transnational concerns of these novels: the anthropological and topographical specificity of the landscape, combined with the documentary gesture, speaks also to the desire of contemporary writers to anchor their narratives not only in global, multiple reading contexts, but also in a local credibility and concreteness that complements the cosmopolitan orientations.

Conclusion

The novels briefly discussed here exhibit cases of transnational relations and historical analogies which require a world literary approach that is hesitant in applying abstract models of world literary circulation. As Benjamin Loy, drawing partly on Hoyos, has recently proposed: 'Instead of succumbing to the illusory description of world literature as an always necessarily vast compound of texts and practices, a solution to this problem might consist in abandoning this Hegelian line and to turn our attention to the various forms to "read the world" by way of different metaphors and in specific historical and geo-cultural contexts'.[86] Instances of the 'global' Latin American novel, by engaging in temporally and spatially heterogeneous constellations of the present, may be understood as modelling an alternative to the prevailing 'temporal regime of modernity' (Assmann) and may be read as supporting the notion of a 'broad present' (Gumbrecht) from which different temporalities come into view.

Furthermore, the novels considered here exhibit a propensity for what has sometimes been called 'hypermodernity', that is, 'a re-emergence of the subjective function and the re-negotiation between *fiction* and *non-fiction*'.[87]

[85] Pilar Blanco, *Ghost-Watching*, 68.
[86] Benjamin Loy, 'Historia literaria en la edad global: una lectura crítica desde América Latina', in *Aspectos actuales del hispanismo mundial*, edited by Christoph Strosetzki (Berlin, Boston: De Gruyter, 2018), 196.
[87] Raffaele Donnarumma, *Ipermodernità. Dove va la narrativa contemporanea* (Bologna: Il Mulino, 2014), 18.

The incorporation of historical facts and characters, of photographs, relics and autobiographical details into a literary work may be understood as a 'resistance against referential dissolution' in the age of post-postmodernism.[88] These novels intertwine historical reference with a subjective search, partly adopting such techniques and genres as auto-fiction, bio-fiction and historiography.[89] As Beecroft has remarked, the cosmopolitanism of Latin American literature, the reaching towards a potentially global readership does not mean that authors will forgo 'modernist linguistic experimentation' and 'local cultural references' altogether.[90] The novels discussed in this chapter suggest indeed that these tendencies and multiple orientations – the present and the past, the vernacular and the cosmopolitan, local/hemispheric reference and an inscription into global world literature – may be experienced simultaneously.

Bibliography

Alberca, Manuel. '¿Existe la autoficción hispanoamericana?' *Cuadernos del CILHA* 7/8 (2006): 115–27.

Alvstad, Cecilia. 'Anthropology over Aesthetics: On the Poetics of Movement and Multilingualism in Three Translations of Yuri Herrera's *Señales que precederán al fin del mundo*'. In *Literatura latinoamericana mundial. Dispositivos y disidencias*, edited by Gustavo Guerrero, Jorge L. Locane, Benjamin Loy and Gesine Müller, 223–42. Berlin, Boston: De Gruyter, 2020.

Assmann, Aleida. *Ist die Zeit aus den Fugen? Aufstieg und Fall des Zeitregimes der Moderne*. Munich: Hanser, 2013.

Bady, Aaron. 'The Mexican novelist Yuri Herrera talks about the first English translation of one of his novels, the Mexica afterlife, and Dante'. *The Nation* 2 December 2015. www.thenation.com/article/border-characters/.

Beecroft, Alexander. *An Ecology of World Literature: From Antiquity to the Present Day*. London: Verso, 2015.

Bolaño, Roberto. *2666*. Barcelona: Anagrama, 2004.

Dimock, Wai Chee. *Through Other Continents: American Literature Across Deep Time*. Princeton University Press, 2006.

Donnarumma, Raffaele. *Ipermodernità. Dove va la narrativa contemporanea*. Bologna: Il Mulino, 2014.

---

[88] Donnarumma, *Ipermodernità*, 32.

[89] Alberca, '¿Existe la autoficción hispanoamericana?'

[90] Beecroft, *An Ecology of World Literature*, 280. Cf. Walkowitz, *Born Translated*.

Enrigue, Álvaro. *Ahora me rindo y eso es todo*. Barcelona: Editorial Anagrama, 2018.

Enrigue, Álvaro. *Muerte súbita*. Barcelona: Anagrama, 2013.

Ercolino, Stefano. *The Maximalist Novel: From Thomas Pynchon's* Gravity's Rainbow *to Roberto Bolaño's* 2666. New York: Bloomsbury, 2015.

Fonseca, Carlos. Review of Álvaro Enrigue, *Ahora me rindo y eso es todo*. https://elroommate.com/2018/11/09/carlos-fonseca-resena-la-ultima-novela-de-alvaro-enrigue-mexico/2018.

Gumbrecht, Hans Ulrich. *Our Broad Present: Time and Contemporary Culture*. New York: Columbia University Press, 2014.

Helgesson, Stefan. 'General Introduction: the Cosmopolitan and the Vernacular in Interaction'. In *World Literatures: Exploring the Cosmopolitan–Vernacular Exchange*, edited by Stefan Helgesson, Annika Mörte Alling, Yvonne Lindqvist and Helena Wulff, 1–11. Stockholm: Stockholm University Press, 2018.

Herrera, Yuri. *Señales que precederán al fin del mundo*. Cáceres: Periférica, 2011.

Herzfelder, Jeanette Erazo. *Welcome to Borderland: Die US-mexikanische Grenze*. Berlin: Berenberg, 2018.

Hoyos, Hector. *Beyond Bolaño: The Global Latin American Novel*. New York: Columbia University Press, 2015.

Kaakinen, Kaisa. *Comparative Literature and the Historical Imaginary: Reading Conrad, Weiss, Sebald*. New York: Palgrave Macmillan, 2017.

Logie, Ilse. '¿Escritos en la traducción y para la traducción? Dos ejemplos: Valeria Luiselli y Mario Bellatin'. In *Literatura latinoamericana mundial. Dispositivos y disidencias*, edited by Gustavo Guerrero, Jorge L. Locane, Benjamin Loy and Gesine Müller, 207–222. Berlin, Boston: De Gruyter, 2020.

Logie, Ilse. '*Los niños perdidos*, de Valeria Luiselli: el intérprete ante las vidas 'dignas de duelo'. *Iberoamericana* 75 (2020): 103–116.

López-Gay, Patricia. *Ficciones de verdad. Archivo y narrativas de vida*. Frankfurt am Main: Vervuert, 2020.

Loy, Benjamin. 'Deseos de mundo. Roberto Bolaño y la (no tan nueva) literatura mundial'. In *América Latina y la literatura mundial: mercado editorial, redes globales y la invención de un continente*, edited by Gesine Müller and Dunia Gras Miravet, 273–94. Frankfurt am Main: Vervuert, 2015.

Loy, Benjamin. 'Historia literaria en la edad global: una lectura crítica desde América Latina'. In *Aspectos actuales del hispanismo mundial*, edited by Christoph Strosetzki, 55–71. Berlin, Boston: de Gruyter, 2018.

Luiselli, Valeria. *Papeles falsos*. Madrid/Mexico: Sexto Piso, 2010.

Luiselli, Valeria. *Los ingrávidos*. Mexico: Sexto Piso, 2011.

Luiselli, Valeria. 'Sergio Pitol/Best Untranslated Writers'. *Granta* (2013). https://granta.com/best-untranslated-writers-sergio-pitol/.

Luiselli, Valeria. *Tell Me How It Ends: An Essay in Forty Questions*. Minneapolis: Coffee House Press, 2017.

Luiselli, Valeria. *Lost Children Archive*. New York: Knopf, 2019.

Mattioli, Aram. *Verlorene Welten. Eine Geschichte der Indianer Nordamerikas 1700–1910*. Stuttgart: Klett-Cotta, 2017.

Meretoja, Hanna. *Ethics of Storytelling: Narrative Hermeneutics, History and the Possible*. Oxford: Oxford University Press, 2017.

Moreira, Paulo. *Modernismo Localista das Américas. Os Contos de Faulkner, Guimarães Rosa e Rulfo*. Belo Horizonte: UFMG, 2012.

Pilar Blanco, María del. *Ghost-Watching American Modernity: Haunting, Landscape, and the Hemispheric Imagination*. New York: Fordham University Press, 2012.

Raynor, Cecily. 'Place-Making in the Solitude of the City: Valeria Luiselli's *Los ingrávidos*'. In *Urban Spaces in Contemporary Latin American Literature*, edited by José Eduardo González and Timothy R. Robbins, 138–51. London, New York: Palgrave Macmillan, 2018.

Richardson, Nathan. 'Reading Makina/Makina Reading in Yuri Herrera's *Señales que precederán al fin del mundo*'. *Ciberletras* 41 (2019): 12–23.

Rothberg, Michael. *Multidirectional Memory: Remembering the Holocaust in the Age of Decolonization*. Stanford: Stanford University Press, 2009.

Saldivar, José David. *Trans-Americanity: Subaltern Modernities, Global Coloniality, and the Cultures of Greater Mexico*. Durham, NC: Duke University Press, 2011.

Siskind, Mariano. *Cosmopolitan Desires: Global Modernity and Word Literature in Latin America*. Evanston: Northwestern University Press, 2014.

Vásquez, Juan Gabriel. *Los Amantes de Todos Los Santos*. Madrid: Alfaguara, 2001.

Vásquez, Juan Gabriel. *El arte de la distorsión*. Madrid: Alfaguara, 2009.

Vásquez, Juan Gabriel. *La forma de las ruinas*. Madrid: Alfaguara, 2015.

Vásquez, Juan Gabriel. *Viajes con un mapa en blanco*. Madrid: Alfaguara, 2018.

Vuillard, Éric. *Tristesse de la Terre*. Arles: Actes Sud, 2012.

Walkowitz, Rebecca L. *Born Translated: The Contemporary Novel in an Age of World Literature*. New York: Columbia University Press, 2015.

Welge, Jobst. 'Historical Reference and Self-Reflection in Recent Latin American (Auto) Fiction'. In *Fictionality, Factuality, Reflexivity Across Discourses and Media*, edited by Erika Fülöp, with Graham Priest and Richard Saint-Gelais,122–44. Berlin, Boston: De Gruyter, 2021.

Wood, James. 'Writing about Writing about the Border Crisis'. www.newyorker.com/magazine/2019/02/04/writing-about-writing-about-the-border-crisis

Yurgel, Caio. *Landscape's Revenge: The Ecology of Failure in Robert Walser and Bernardo Carvalho*. Berlin, Boston: De Gruyter, 2019.

8

Ambiguous arrival: Emotions and dislocations in the migrant encounter with Sweden

Helena Wulff

Sweden is relatively new as an immigration country, and there used to be a claim to an ethos of ethnic inclusivity, in policy as well as in informal interaction. With the growth of immigration in the post-Second World War period, however, migrants' experiences of exclusion became more noticeable in society at large. The 1960s saw a peak of migrants arriving on labour recruitment schemes mainly from Italy, Greece, former Yugoslavia and Turkey, as well as Finland. This was followed by war refugees in the 1980s from Iran and Iraq, and in the 1990s from the Balkans. In 2015, when the migration crisis erupted in Europe, more than 160,000 refugees from Syria, Afghanistan and North Africa arrived in Sweden during the course of a couple of months.[1] The migration infrastructure collapsed, as it was not prepared to process this huge number of asylum seekers in such a short period of time.[2] One response to this sudden impact of refugees in Sweden was a growing anti-immigration attitude. This was in line with the agenda of an expanding right-wing party, the Sweden Democrats.

Exclusion, even prejudice and racism, are recurrent topics in fiction and autobiography by a young generation of writers who migrated to Sweden as children.[3] In their fiction they all share a concern with *migrant experiences* that expose cruel conditions, yet often in tandem with instances of integration as a matter of course in residential areas, at places of work, among friends and in

---

[1] See https://www.scb.se/en/finding-statistics/statistics-by-subject-area/population/. In 2019, just over 2 million of the 10 million+ population in Sweden were born abroad, www.scb.se/hitta-statistik/sverige-i-siffror/manniskorna-i-sverige/utrikes-fodda/.

[2] Bruno Meeus, Karel Arnaut and Bas van Heur, eds., *Arrival Infrastructures: Migration and Urban Social Mobilities* (New York: Palgrave, 2019).

[3] Elsewhere the study incorporates writers who were born in Sweden to parents who have migrated there. See for instance, Helena Wulff, 'Writing Truth to Power: Jonas Hassen Khemiri's Work in Stockholm and New York', *Anthropology & Humanism* 44, no.1 (2019): 7–19.

marriages. While their location is Sweden, this can be a contested space for them which is why the notion of *dis*location is more appropriate in their case than location, as their orientation is also towards their country of origin.

My literary anthropological study of migrant writing in Sweden includes three autobiographical stories of arrival in Sweden that I will explore in this chapter in terms of emotions, dislocations and the migrant encounter along a time axis.[4] This will reveal how the stories register the writers' changing emotional orientations to their locations, not only to Sweden, but also to their countries of origin over time. It follows Patrick Colm Hogan's observation that: 'The centrality of emotions to literature and literary experience has been recognized throughout literary history and across literary traditions.'[5] In relation to the remit of this volume, and the idea of location as claimed by cosmopolitan and vernacular strategies, this chapter, again, reveals rather a sense of dislocation. Still, cosmopolitan and vernacular processes are at stake. As to the vernacular, written in Swedish originally (and not always available in translation), migrant writing and literature in Sweden is a form of vernacular literature. It should be pointed out that those writers who have native languages other than Swedish occasionally include a term from this language for non-Swedish food or an expression signalling a significant circumstance. It goes without saying that immigrant background is indicated with the use of, for instance, Persian or Arabic first names of characters in the stories. Jonas Hassen Khemiri (who was born in Sweden to a father from Tunisia and a Swedish mother) even invented a Swedish immigrant dialect identified as 'jubilantly rhythmic and consciously accented Swedish' in his iconic debut novel *One Eye Red* (*Ett öga rött*).[6, 7] The exceptional success of this book – especially among young Swedes from migrant backgrounds, but also among native Swedes – provided its successful entry into the Swedish literary world as a vernacular product. In addition, its story about young people in immigrant suburbs of Stockholm is an example of how the work of these writers is *cosmopolitanizing Sweden from within*.[8] The point is that

[4] See also Wulff, 'Writing Truth to Power'. Helena Wulff, 'Diasporic Divides: Location and Orientations of "Home" in Pooneh Rohi's *Araben*', in *World Literatures: Exploring the Cosmopolitan-Vernacular Exchange*, eds. Stefan Helgesson, Annika Mörte Alling, Yvonne Lindqvist and Helena Wulff (Stockholm: Stockholm University Press, 2018), 119–28. Helena Wulff, 'Diversifying from Within: Diaspora Writings in Sweden', in *The Composition of Anthropology: How Anthropological Texts are Written*, eds. Morten Nielsen and Nigel Rapport (London: Routledge, 2018), 122–36.
[5] Patrick Colm Hogan, *Literature and Emotion* (New York: Routledge, 2018), 1.
[6] All translations of titles and quotes from literary texts and interviews into English are mine.
[7] Jonas Hassen Khemiri, *Ett öga rött* (*One Eye Red*) (Stockholm: Norstedts, 2003), www.khemiri.se/en/books/one-eye-red-ett-oga-rott/.
[8] Wulff, 'Diasporic Divides'; 'Diversifying from Within'.

Khemiri brings the world to his Swedish readership through the experiences of his characters who have come from afar, or whose parents did. This is one part of the idea of a new world literature that Stefan Helgesson and Mads Rosendahl Thomsen make the case for 'because our current historical moment, shaped by migration, digital media and forms of uneven economic globalization, has accelerated the cross-border traffic of (some) literature, genres, writers.'[9]

Before considering the three autobiographical stories on arrival in analytical detail, some contextualization is required. Literature has been one source of cultural knowledge in anthropology to some degree since its inception in the late nineteenth century. With a gradual growth, especially in the last decades, this approach is now established and referred to as literary anthropology. It can be applied in three ways: by referring to literary texts as ethnography, by writing in a literary style and by studying literary culture and production.[10] In *Rhythms of Writing: An Anthropology of Irish Literature*, I combine the use of literary text as ethnography with the study of literary culture and production as I investigate writing in Ireland as craft and career.[11] This combination has also been the methodological procedure in my study of migrant writing in Sweden. As traditional anthropological participant observation does not suffice for this, I have done some participant observation at public events such as literary festivals and book launches, as well as panel discussions and readings by the writers. This is 'interface ethnography', a concept that Sherry Ortner coined for her study of independent filmmakers in Hollywood, as 'most closed communities have events where they interact with the public'.[12] In my study, interviews with writers and close readings of their literary texts as well as media and internet appearances were also crucial. Another methodological feature of this study is that it is a part of the relatively recent tendency in anthropology to research people who in some sense are included in the ethnographer's community of intellectuals.[13] While some of the works of migrant writers are translated into other languages, primarily English which entails a certain international reputation, other writers are mostly known in Sweden only. Researching them all thus entails

9   Stefan Helgesson and Mads Rosendahl Thompsen, 'Introduction: Why World Literature?', in *Literature and the World* (London: Routledge, 2020), 1–23.
10 Ellen Wiles, 'Three Branches of Literary Anthropology: Sources, Styles, Subject Matter', *Ethnography* 21, no. 2 (2020): 280–95.
11 Helena Wulff, *Rhythms of Writing: An Anthropology of Irish Literature* (London: Bloomsbury, 2017).
12 Sherry Ortner, *Not Hollywood: Independent Film at the Twilight of the American Dream* (Durham, NC: Duke University Press, 2013).
13 Douglas R. Holmes and George E. Marcus, 'Cultures of Expertise and the Management of Globalization: Toward the Re-Functioning of Ethnography', in *Global Assemblages: Technology, Politics, and Ethics as Anthropological Problems*, eds. Aihwa Ong and Stephen J. Collier (Oxford: Blackwell, 2005), 235–52.

'studying sideways', as identified by Ulf Hannerz in his investigations into the work of foreign correspondents.[14] Literary scholarship on migrant literature in Sweden also forms a backdrop to my study.[15]

But why this interest in arrival? Apart from being poetic statements of political conflict, what is the analytical significance of this topic for an anthropologist looking at literature? When I started interviewing the writers, I never asked about their arrivals, but they told me at great length about those momentous moments anyway, and when I read their autobiographical accounts, I was struck by the strength of these stories. These real-life dramas that could have gone so very wrong (and, of course, keep going very wrong for masses of people) have stayed with me. Thinking about how to organize my research material – novels and short fiction, interviews, observations – into writing, V. S. Naipaul's acclaimed title *The Enigma of Arrival* occurred to me.[16] Naipaul's title was inspired by the painting *The Enigma of the Arrival and the Afternoon* from 1912, by the surrealist painter Giorgio de Chirico, which is on the front cover of the first editions of his book.[17] This is an autobiography of a writer's journey from Trinidad, then a British colony, to the countryside of England (among other places), and his changing state of mind over the course of twenty years. At one point he finds a book with a picture of de Chirico's painting. This triggers an idea for a story about arrival as a 'scene of desolation and mystery: it speaks of the mystery of arrival'.[18] The story – which is a story-in-the-story of the book – would have a narrator who arrives at this 'port with the walls and gateways like cutouts' and:

> He would walk past that muffled figure on that quayside. He would move from that silence and desolation, that blankness, to a gateway or door. He would enter there and be swallowed by the life and noise of a crowded city … The mission he had come on – family business, study, religious initiation – would give him encounters and adventures. He would enter interiors, of houses and temples. Gradually there would come to him a feeling that he was getting nowhere; he would lose his sense of mission; he would begin to know only that he was lost.

[14] Ulf Hannerz, *Foreign News: Exploring the World of Foreign Correspondents* (Chicago: Chicago University Press, 2004).

[15] See for instance, Satu Gröndahl, 'Identity Politics and the Construction of Minor Literatures: Multicultural Swedish Literature at the Turn of the Millenium', *multiethnica* 30 (2007): 21–9; Magnus Nilsson, 'Swedish "Immigrant Literature" and the Construction of Ethnicity', *TijdSchrift voor Skandinavistiek* 31, no.1 (2010): 199–218; Evelina Stenbeck, *Poesi som politik: aktivistisk poetik hos Johannes Anyuru och Athena Farroukhzad* (Lund: Ellerström, 2017).

[16] V. S. Naipaul, *The Enigma of Arrival* (New York: Alfred A. Knopf, 1987).

[17] In *The Enigma of Arrival*, Naipaul, mentions that it was the poet Guillame Apollinaire who suggested the title of the painting.

[18] Naipaul, *The Enigma of Arrival*, 98–9.

The narrator in Naipaul's imagined story turns back to the quayside, finds the door and thinks with relief that he is saved, but then 'one thing is missing now. Above the cutout walls and building there is no mast, no sail'. The ship is gone. 'The traveller has lived out his life.' This lack of connection and how it lingers on, is what Naipaul grapples with in the book. Writing about his own arrival in Sweden from Southern Africa as a boy, Stefan Helgesson is told that because of family links, this place which seemed foreign to him is in fact his country. This is why he finds a familiarity in Naipaul's depiction of how arrival in a new place 'creates a silence which is mysterious'.[19]

Having your heart in two places

With Naipaul's insights in mind, I now go back to the three autobiographical arrival stories in my study. It is important that they represent different types of migration streams to Sweden over time, from the 1960s labour recruitment scheme to the war refugees in the 1990s and the twenty-first century. The stories reveal the same idea about Sweden as a safe country with opportunities for work and political freedom. They also reveal an acute sense of dislocation. Firstly, there is the autobiographical novel *Foreigners* (*Utlänningar*) by Theodor Kallifatides who came from unemployment and political oppression in Greece in the early 1960s, as a part of a scheme to recruit labourers to Sweden.[20] An acclaimed writer for a long time, Kallifatides is also well known outside the literary world in Sweden: his humble and pleasant ways and storytelling skills work very well in public presentations, whether he performs live on literary panels or is interviewed on television. Secondly, I will discuss two memoirs, both debut books: *The Rain Has No Smell Here: A Family Portrait* (*Regnet luktar inte här: Ett familjeporträtt*) by Duraid Al-Khamisi, and the short booklet titled *The Angel and the Sparrow: Texts by an Unaccompanied Youth on The Run* (*Ängeln och sparven: Texter av en ensam ungdom på flykt*) by Ali Zardadi.[21] Al-Khamisi had to flee from war in Baghdad with his family in 1994. Zardadi came to Sweden from Afghanistan in 2016 as an unaccompanied teenager. By coincidence, all three writers are men,

[19] Stefan Helgesson, *Efter västerlandet: Texter om kulturell förändring* (Stockholm: Natur och Kultur, 2004), 11.
[20] Theodor Kallifatides, *Utlänningar* (Stockholm: Bonniers, 1973).
[21] Duraid Al-Khamisi, *Regnet luktar inte här: Ett familjeporträtt* (Stockholm: Atlas, 2015); Ali Zardadi, *Ängeln och sparven: Texter av en ensam ungdom på flykt* (Gothenburg: Catoblepas förlag, 2017).

as are the writers who make up the comparative cases I use here, except a short section on Pooneh Rohi's work.[22] I should make clear that women writers are the main protagonists elsewhere in my study. None of these three books have been translated into English.

Recalling his arrival in Sweden from Greece several decades ago, Theodor Kallifatides, the pioneering and prominent migrant writer now in his early 80s, told me in an interview:[23]

> You have not really arrived until you are rid of memories from home. As long as memories from home are still a part of everyday life you have not arrived. For me, it took twelve years. It happened when my first child was born.[24]

So not only does a migrant arrival go on for a long time, perhaps forever, emotionally and culturally, it is also morphing into different meanings and phases over time. This can be considered in terms of *multiple arrivals* to a new country, both physically and mentally. Eventually, the political situation in Greece changed, which made it possible for Kallifatides to visit there as he pleases, and then return to Sweden.

In his novel *Foreigners*, Kallifatides has his protagonist describe the very moment of his first arrival[25]:

> Stockholm, June 1964, in the evening. I got off the train slightly confused, tired and worried. It was the first time I arrived somewhere without one single person waiting for me. The Central Station was probably just like many of the other stations I had passed by on my journey, but it still felt different. Here I was going to stay, the Central Station was not a station, it was the end of the journey, and this transformed the station into something secretive and frightening.

Echoing Naipaul's mood above, Kallifatides thus describes how the awareness that he was going to stay 'transformed the station into something secretive and frightening'.[26] There was no passport control at the Stockholm Central Station

---

[22] Wulff, 'Diasporic Divides'.

[23] The interview was conducted in Stockholm on 29 May 2018.

[24] 'Du är inte framme i någon egentlig mening förrän du är av med minnen hemifrån. Så länge minnena är kvar i vardagen har du inte anlänt. För mig tog det tolv år. Det var när mitt första barn föddes.'

[25] Kallifatides, *Utlänningar*, 14: 'Stockholm, juni 1964, på kvällen. Jag steg av tåget lite omtöcknad, trött och orolig. Det var första gången jag kom någonstans utan en enda människa som väntade på mig. Centralen var förmodligen som många av de andra stationerna jag hade passerat på vägen men det kändes ändå annorlunda. Här skulle jag stanna, Centralen var inte en station, den var slutet på resan och detta förvandlade stationen till något hemlighetsfullt och skrämmande.'

[26] Naipaul, *The Enigma of Arrival*, 99. Kallifatides, *Utlänningar*, 14: 'förvandlade stationen till något hemlighetsfullt och skrämmande'.

when Kallifatides got off the train that June evening in 1964. He had already crossed the national border with Denmark, that was open at the time, many hours earlier, as it is located about 600 kilometres south of Stockholm.

Born in 1938 in a village in Greece, Theodor Kallifatides did well at school.[27] He graduated from high school with excellent grades. As expected, he performed outstandingly at the university entrance exam in Athens. Nevertheless, he was rejected on the grounds that his father had been in prison because he was a communist. Denied the university studies he desired, Kallifatides tried to find any kind of job, but failed. He found himself bereft of all opportunities. What to do? Unemployment was widespread in Athens. One afternoon, at the height of political unrest in the early 1960s, Kallifatides and his friends were chased by the police. He took refuge in a cinema where he found himself watching the film *The Virgin Spring* by the Swedish filmmaker Ingmar Bergman. Kallifatides was enthralled by the sound of the Swedish language, identifying it as 'this sparse language', and started to learn Swedish from a Linguaphone record. Incidentally, a friend who was also listening to the Linguaphone records, said: 'This is a language for writing stories!' Kallifatides had made up his mind. Even though he knew next to nothing about Sweden, it was the only country in Europe that was still open to labour migration. He was going to emigrate there. As he said: 'I knew I had to leave my country in order to get a life.' But his sombre advice is: 'Don't do it – until you know that there is no other solution!' His father gave him all his savings, equivalent to 60 euro, and he got on a train to Sweden.

Just like the protagonist in the novel *Foreigners*, Kallifatides' first job was at a restaurant in Stockholm where he became a dishwasher. Later he worked as a newspaper boy, while reading novels by the Swedish author August Strindberg in order to improve his Swedish. One early autumn he brought his high school diploma to the students' entrance office at Stockholm University. The middle-aged lady behind the desk looked bewildered at the diploma and exclaimed: 'But this is pure Greek!' Kallifatides nodded nervously. Then the lady scrutinized him carefully, and demanded: 'Be honest, are these good grades?' Kallifatides was pleased to confirm that they were indeed very good grades. 'Okay', the lady said: 'You can start studying at the University!' Overwhelmed by happiness, Kallifatides studied philosophy, completed a BA and took a job as a schoolteacher.

---

[27] This paragraph is composed of extracts from 'Sommar', a programme broadcast on Swedish Radio, 11 July 2013, with the 2018 interview mentioned above, and Theodor Kallifatides, *Ett nytt land utanför mitt fönster* (*A new country outside my window*) (Stockholm: Bonnier Pocket, 2017), 69–70.

Meanwhile, he was writing poems about the predicament of 'having your heart in two places'. He sent them to Bonniers, the leading publishing house in Stockholm. After a couple of days he received a letter from the editor saying: 'Come and see us soon! To sign the contract!' The editor had found the poems to be of the highest literary quality. They were published as *The Memory in Exile* (*Minnet i exil*) and were very well received.[28] Kallifatides went on to write novels about migrants in Sweden, the history of Greece, and the essence of love, as well as some crime fiction and travel stories, mostly as he got older, including the one about his own journey to Stockholm in 1964, and his first years there.

The autobiographical perspective is even more pronounced in Duraid Al-Khamisi's *The Rain Has No Smell Here*.[29] The year is 1994, the opening scene inside a small fishing boat crammed with panicking refugees in a raging storm on the Baltic Sea, heading for the Swedish island Gotland – but it could have been set recently on the Mediterranean Sea. Al-Khamisi was eight years old and his family (who were Mande, a small Iraqi ethnic group), had left a comfortable upper-class life in Baghdad. Al-Khamisi's father was a highly respected and successful goldsmith, but they had to flee at short notice from Saddam Hussein's oppressive regime. Now they are trapped in the boat for days, before the storm subsides and they are able go up on deck. Even though it is starting to get dark, this is when they spot the shore of Gotland, of Sweden and safety. In order to avoid being discovered by the coastguard, the smugglers will not drive the boat to the shore. The refugees are put into three orange rubber boats. They are all desperate to leave the fishing boat. Close to the shore they get out of the boat and walk in knee-high water to land. Al-Khamisi is soaked and cold. A moment later, he says: 'The following scenes on the pitch dark beach are euphoric. People kiss each other, give thanks to higher powers, lifting us children.' The refugees are taken care of by the Red Cross and stay the night in a hostel. The next day the children get blue bags with 'drawing pad colouring pencils, erasers and a pencil sharpener'. Al-Khamisi adds: 'We got toys. I grabbed a big, red Ferrari car!' So he and his family survived the dangerous journey across the Baltic Sea, but other challenges are now in front of them as they move to a so-called disadvantaged area, a suburb of Stockholm. Al-Khamisi's father remains unemployed, and his mother suffers from loneliness and the dark Stockholm winters, while Al-Khamisi is hanging out with a criminal gang. One night he is in a serious fight in

---

[28] Theodor Kallifatides, *Minnet i exil* (Stockholm: Bonniers, 1969).
[29] Al-Khamisi, *Regnet luktar inte här*, 7–12.

the street and has to go to the hospital as his face is badly hurt. He is bandaged and his lip is sewn up with three stitches. Then he is sent home. The turning point comes when his younger brother (who went on to become a human rights lawyer) is taking him to task for dishonouring their parents, saying 'you are spending time with guys who sell drugs, rob and beat up people. What is wrong with you?' In response to this Al-Khamisi writes[30]:

I was used to the hate from the Swedes. I felt their contempt. But it had never before occurred to me that other immigrants might see me the same way. Look down on me. It began with the teachers, spread to pupils and ended with everyone around me looking down on me. That was enough. I had had enough.

So he took his bag and went to Södertälje, a town south of Stockholm, to live with his uncle. Al-Khamisi was eighteen years old, enrolled in high school with a total focus on getting top grades, which he did. Following his father's advice over the years, he applied to the School of Journalism. He graduated the same year as the Arab Spring flared up. Now he had the tools to tell his stories about the suburb, Swedes and immigrants, and about Iraq both as a place of terror and as a lost home that he keeps missing, not least because, as he told me when we met in December 2018 at a café in Stockholm: 'Writing *The Rain Has No Smell Here* was a way to handle losing a country and all our relatives and friends. So many of my age have died .... Education is important'. He continued empahtically, 'especially for those from the suburbs. They need education and a job'.[31]

Education is a way to build bridges. My hope with *The Rain Has No Smell Here* was to build bridges, that young people would understand their own situation. I wanted to create understanding. But I was shocked by the reactions to it. What happened was that non-white critics did not understand. They just saw me as angry. The book divided the critics.[32]

---

[30] Al-Khamisi, *Regnet luktar inte här*, 106: 'Du hänger med killar som säljer knark, rånar och misshandlar människor. Vad är det med dig?' 'Jag var van vid hatet från svenskarna. Jag kände deras förakt. Men jag hade aldrig förr tänkt på att andra invandrare kunde se mig på samma sätt. Se ner på mig. Det började med lärarna, spred sig till eleverna och slutade med att alla runt omkring såg ner på mig. Jag fick nog. Det räckte.'
[31] The interview was conducted in Stockholm on 8 January 2019. 'Att skriva *Regnet luktar inte här* var ett sätt att hantera förlusten av ett land och alla våra släktingar och vänner. Så många i min ålder har dött.' 'Utbildning är viktigt', han fortsatte, 'speciellt för dem från förorten. De behöver utbildning och job.'
[32] Interview with Al-Khamisi, 2019: 'Utbildning är ett sätt att bygga broar. Min förhoppning med Regnet luktar inte här var att bygga broar, att unga människor skulle förstå sin egen situation. Jag ville skapa förståelse. Men jag var chockad av reaktionerna på den. Det som hände var att icke-vita kritiker inte förstod. De såg mig bara som arg. Boken delade kritikerna.'

The reviews were many, but rather mixed. They did mention Al-Khamisi's anger, as in Ulrika Stahre's description of the book as a story about the journey of a young man who is angry, but moves towards something that resembles peace of mind, while providing an updated picture of Husby (the name of the suburb), of its riots and social bias. It is about life in the suburb as a contrast with life in the city. There is class hate and desire for revenge. Another review, by Bodil Hansson, points out that this is a skilled description of how immensely demanding it is to be young without support, and that there is an expectation of failure. But Al-Khamisi is empowered and gets the energy to get out of that which pulls him down. With education, he is able to create a platform for expressing his experience through words. According to this review:

> This is an important book to read. One should read it if one wants to understand something about what it is like when the rain does not smell. One should read it if one wants to encounter the difficulties many children of refugees have to handle. One should read it if one wants to reflect over what Sweden means to, and does with, our refugees.[33]

Writing stories had been a part of Al-Khamisi's upbringing, as he told me in our interview:

> I have always listened to stories and written stories. I was surrounded by stories when I grew up. My grandmother told morality tales about animals and the devil, aphorisms. My father told stories about heroes, real events, things that had happened, torture and prison. Self-revealing stories, things he remembered about life that he told me straight out, but for no one else.[34]

It is likely that Al-Khamisi acquired storytelling techniques such as suspension and surprise, the use of repetition and rhythm while listening to these stories. His style is quite rhythmical, which might also have something to do with the fact that he often listens to music while writing. He even has a metronome to keep track of different rhythms.

---

[33] Bodil Hansson, 'Om flykt, identitet och saknad', *Litteraturmagasinet*, 12 January 2016: 'Boken är viktig att läsa. Man skall läsa den om man vill förstå något av hur det är när regnet inte luktar. Man skall läsa den om man vill möta de svårigheter som många barn till flyktingar har att bemästra. Man skall läsa den om man vill reflektera över vad Sverige betyder för och gör med våra flyktingar.'

[34] 'Jag var omgiven av berättelser när jag växte upp. Min farmor berättade historier om rätt och fel om djur och jävulen, aforismer. Min pappa berättade historier om hjältar, verkliga händelser, saker som hade hänt, tortyr och fängelse. Självutlämnande historier, saker han kom ihåg om livet som han berättade rakt ut för mig, men inte för någon annan.'

Again, *The Rain Has No Smell Here* was Al-Khamisi's debut book. It did get a lot of attention. He was invited to readings and book signings, and not least to the Swedish literary programme on television called *Babel* where writers of new books are interviewed. This is an influential programme as it sets the status system of the literary world in Sweden. Al-Khamisi told me how pleased he was: 'When they called from *Babel*, I bought a new suit and tie, and went there and talked to Jessika Gedin [who was hosting the programme]. It was mostly about the flight like it always was in interviews, not about the situation in the suburb.'[35]

In his early thirties, Duraid Al-Khamisi is now settled and married, and has a child. He has moved back to the same suburb where he and his family live close to his parents. Writing a new book on 'contemporary Stockholm', he also does freelance jobs as a journalist and helps out in a tobacco shop he bought with his parents. So all is well, yet he told me – much in line with Theodor Kalllifatides' experience of 'having your heart in two places': 'You know, it is easy to be lonely in Sweden. You have to practice to feel at home. A refugee is always missing his country.'[36] A part of this is the particular smell of the rain in Iraq – contrary to the rain in Sweden which has no smell. Iraq consists to a great extent of red desert sand. When there is a storm it whips up a red fog, and Al-Khamisi writes: 'When it later rains the sand goes back down and the loveliest scent I know is released: the smell of kerosene, gas and rain in a tender pairing with the warm scent of jasmin flowers.'[37] This lack of smells in Sweden, especially during winter, comes back in the work of other migrant writers in my study, such as that by Pooneh Rohi.[38] She contrasts Stockholm, 'the city smells of ice', with the memory of Iran and 'the smell of rain that does not cool down, of wet soil and wet stone, a breath of the scent from the rose bushes'. Just like Al-Khamisi, Rohi misses the rain, 'that salty wet air from the sea'. The strong smell of spices and flowers is often missed not least because they indicate what is remembered as a happy childhood.

---

[35] Interview with Al-Khamisi in 2019: 'När de ringde från Babel, köpte jag en ny kostym och slips, och gick dit och pratade med Jessica Gedin (programledaren). Det var mest om flykten som det alltid var i intervjuer, inte om situationen i förorten.'

[36] 'Du vet, det är lätt att vara ensam i Sverige. Man måste öva på att känna sig hemma. En flykting saknar alltid sitt land.'

[37] Al-Khamisi, *Regnet luktar inte här*, 132–3: 'När det sedan regnar lägger sig sanden, och ur den frigör sig den ljuvligaste lukt jag vet: lukten av fotogen, gasol och regnsom ömsint parar sig med den varma doften av jasminblommor.'

[38] Pooneh Rohi, *Araben* (Stockholm: Ordfront, 2013), 9, 77: 'staden doftar av is', 'lukten av regn som inte svalkar, av blöt jord och blöt sten, en fläkt av rosenbuskarnas doft', 'den där salta fuktiga luften från havet.'

Finishing the interview with me, Duraid Al-Khamisi ends on a happy and hopeful note saying that:

> I see a new attitude among the young generation, those who have grown up with immigrants. There are lots of immigrants in Södermalm [a fashionable part of Stockholm] now. Many have done class journeys upwards, many marry each other, are friends with each other, eat each other's food.[39]

Moving on now to the third writer from my study: Ali Zardadi came to Sweden on his own when he was sixteen years old, one among tens of thousands of unaccompanied children and teenagers. Only fifteen months later, his Swedish was good enough for him to write his memoir *The Angel and the Sparrow* (2017). It consists of less than fifty pages, with ten very short stories about his first months in Sweden. As to his actual arrival from Afghanistan, he describes it rather matter-of-factly:

> It was a dark day in winter when I came to Sweden. We went to Malmö first. Stayed one night and then we went to Linköping and had a long journey that day. On the bus we got food and water from the bus staff and I was wondering how to say in Swedish when you want to say thank you.[40]

Ali takes out his mobile phone, and soon finds the word on Google translate: 'Tack'. In Stockholm, the young refugees were taken to the police who wore black uniforms. Ali's experience of the police in Afghanistan makes him frightened of the Swedish police. They start asking questions: 'Are you hungry? Are you tired? Are you cold? Soon you will meet many people who speak your language.'[41] Then Ali and five or six other unaccompanied teenagers were driven to accommodation outside Stockholm. Step by step, he learns Swedish and starts school. He acquires friends, and is planning to become a social worker. But he keeps missing his mother. In his book, in an author biography, he says that he is not a real author. He might well become one, though. Since then he has joined a writer's centre for young people (*Berättarministeriet*) and recently co-published a volume titled *We See, we Feel, we Struggle* together with eight other young people.[42] Ali's chapter is

---

[39] 'Jag ser en ny attityd hos den unga generationen, de som har växt upp med invandrare. Det är fullt av invandrare på Södermalm nu. Det är många som har gjort klassresor, som gifter sig med varandra, äter varandras mat.'

[40] Zardadi, *Ängeln och sparven*, 33–4: 'Det var en mörk dag på vintern när jag kom till Sverige. Vi åkte till Malmö först. Stannade en natt där och sedan åkte vi till Linköping och hade en lång resa under dagen. På bussen fick vi mat och vatten från busspersonal och jag undrade hur man säger på svenska när man vill säga tack.'

[41] Zardadi, *Ängeln och sparven*, 34: 'Är du hungrig?', 'Är du trött?', 'Fryser du?', 'Snart kommer du få träffa många som pratar ditt språk.'

[42] Moa Liem et al., *Vi ser, vi känner, vi kämpar* (Stockholm: BonnierCarlsen, 2018).

on getting your application for asylum rejected, as has happened to a number of his friends. In an online video interview, Ali talks about his writing:

> Through writing you can send your words to others and you can be touched by that. That is why I chose writing as a way to calm down. And to help my friends by being a voice for them.[43]

I learned about Ali Zardadi and his bestselling book *The Angel and the Sparrow* on the news on Swedish television in the summer of 2017 when it had just been published. I have not yet met Zardadi for an interview, but found an interview with him in a local newspaper. It turns out that he had not read novels before, had never seen a library, but in Sweden he had been writing short pieces at school, that his teachers had corrected, about his experience as a refugee. His Swedish 'mother' is his 'angel' for taking care of him, while he himself is the 'sparrow' in the title of the book. It was his Swedish mother who had suggested that he put together the stories into a book. Zardadi had not been thinking about this possibility. But when he posted stories on Facebook, he had a massive positive reaction with so many people asking for them in a book format that they would be able to borrow at the library. They wanted a continuation. This was very inspiring for Zardadi.[44]

He has not seen his real mother since they were torn apart in 2016. Ali, two brothers and their mother had fled from Afghanistan. They were in a big group of about 200 people. Before crossing the border to Turkey, they tried to get some sleep. It was dark. Ali did not know where they were. At dawn he saw mountains. Then he saw Iranian soldiers approaching them. People started to run. A guy took his arm asking him to come with him. Ali hesitated. He did not want to leave his family. But the guy said that his father would take care of them.

At the border he discovered that his mother and brothers were not with them. This made him very sad and worried. 'It was the hardest time in my life.'[45] He was thinking that if he went back, he would not be able to find them. So he came to Sweden on his own. It took him three months to get in touch with his mother again. He does not think his family can come to Sweden. He has a temporary residency at the moment and is waiting for a permanent one. In the meantime,

---

[43] 'Genom att skriva kan man skicka sina ord till andra och man kan bli berörd av det. Så därför valde jag att skriva som ett sätt att lugna ner mina känslor. Och att hjälpa mina vänner genom att vara en röst för dem.' www.selmastories.se/forfattarna/intervju/ali-zardadi/

[44] Frida Wänelöf, 'Ali flyttar saknaden till pappret', *Huddinge Direkt*. 2017, www.stockholmdirekt.se/kultur/ali-flyttar-saknaden-till-pappret/repqcu!c6kYBk3lYDIFi@oud4Mb1A/

[45] Wänelöf, 'Ali flyttar saknaden till pappret': 'Det var den svåraste tiden i mitt liv.'

he has become an award-winning activist for unaccompanied children and teenagers. He writes short articles in newspapers, gives talks and interviews and is involved in the association for unaccompanied young people, organizing get-togethers such as parties and lectures.

Claiming a (contested) space

It is time to move on to an analytical level and compare these three textual arrival stories further. We have already noted that they represent different major migration streams to Sweden over time, from the 1960s labour recruitment scheme to the war refugees in the 1990s and the twenty-first century. The three writers are also at different stages in their life cycles and careers. Both Theodor Kallifatides and Duraid Al-Khamisi were in their mid-twenties when they wrote their respective arrival stories that I have been referring to here. All three stories reveal the same imaginary about Sweden as a country of safety and hope for those fleeing political violence and war. Key to the stories is the ambiguous nature of arrival: a combination of strong contradictory emotions of relief and fright. Even though Helgesson and his family did not have to flee for their lives or for subsistence, he still identifies arrival in a foreign country (which, again, incidentally is also Sweden) in terms of ambiguity, 'the arrival is both delightful and bitter'[46]:

> that which recently filled one's world is still accessible. At the same time one sees another world spreading out, a world where one notices everything that differs from that one has just left. This is a delightful experience ... a feeling of a lightness appears. The world can change!
>
> But the arrival is also bitter. The lightness transforms into rootlessness. Instead of having access to two possible ways of being, you are excluded from both. That which you left is lost and the new place appears incomprehensible, inhospitable, closed.

As the stories of Kallifatides, Al-Khamisi and Zardadi unfold, they are testimonies to emotions of homesickness and loneliness that come with having arrived

---

[46] Helgesson, *Efter västerlandet* 12: 'ankomsten är både ljuv och bitter', 'det som nyss fyllde ens värld känns ännu tillgängligt. Samtidigt breder en annan värld ut sig framför ens ögon, en värld där man lägger märke till allt som skiljer sig från det man just har lämnat. Detta är en ljuv erfarenhet ... En lätthet infinner sig hos jaget. Världen kan förändras! / Men ankomsten är också bitter. Lättheten förbyts i rotlöshet. I stället för att ha tillgång till två möjliga sätt att vara utesluts du från bägge. Det du lämnade bakom dig är förlorat och den nya platsen framstår som obegriplig, ogästvänlig, sluten.'

in a new country as a migrant or refugee. There is also the humiliation that experiences of exclusion and racism produce. During the arrival journeys, the orientation of the migrants and refugees is obviously focused on Sweden. Also, beyond the actual arrival moment of the stories, the dislocation–orientation framework is useful for an analytical understanding of the migrant encounter with Sweden. Even though the three stories vary considerably when it comes to period of time, they obviously share Sweden as a location, but as I have pointed out, it is more appropriate to conceptualize this situation as dislocation even as the stories take place in different settings in Sweden: Kallifatides recalls working-class Stockholm in the 1960s, Al-Khamisi a 'disadvantaged' suburb of Stockholm in the 1990s, and Zardadi another Stockholm suburb in 2017. Despite these different sub-dislocations, the experiences of living in Sweden are strikingly similar, at least in the stories by Kallifatides and Al-Khamisi. This is the case despite the fact that their orientations to a great extent are towards their different countries of origin where the political systems may or may not allow them to return: Greece, Iraq and Afghanistan. These orientations are bound to change over time. This is especially obvious for Theodor Kallifatides, who has spent more than fifty years in Sweden. They all miss their countries of origin, family and friends they have left behind, especially mothers, and the life they led before they had to leave.

The three texts raise the issue of genre and the relationship between fiction and autobiography as they all build on the authors' own experiences of encountering Sweden. Kallifatides' book was marketed as fiction, but based on his own experiences and those of his compatriots. Al-Khamisi's memoir is advertised as 'an honest, furious and vulnerable story about Sweden' on the back cover of the book.[47] The tone is one of reporting, which makes sense as Al-Khamisi also works as a journalist. Zardadi's account is a straightforward story about his experiences of entering into Sweden.

Conclusion

This literary anthropological study of stories of arrival has discussed the ambiguities of these arrivals, which switch between forceful emotions of both relief and fright, but also importantly, as the stories move on, reveal ambiguous

---

[47] Al-Khamisi, *Regnet luktar inte här*: 'en ärlig, rasande och såbar berättelse om Sverige.'

orientations of settling down, coupled with the continued pain of longing for the country of origin and a sense of alienation in Sweden. As migrant writings in general 'educate a mainstream audience in Sweden about the increasing presence of ethnic diversity as a matter of course', these stories specify some of its ambiguities.[48]

The focus here has been on the journeys to Sweden, but what happens after the actual arrival moment? How is the migrant encounter with Sweden in the long run? As the stories of Kallifatides and Al-Khamisi unfold, they convey claims to Sweden that turn out to be a contested space for them: they do not always feel welcome. There are some serious instances of exclusion, on top of homesickness and loneliness that define their dislocation. Zardadi's story is also built around homesickness and loneliness as well as around his longing for his mother in Afghanistan, but it departs from the other two in two ways: firstly, there is no mention of exclusion or racism; secondly, instead, the story is driven by gratefulness for having been received with warmth in Sweden.

In all three stories there is, with time, a sense of some kind of belonging, It should be noted that in migration and refugee studies, the process towards belonging is increasingly connected with the concept of emplacement which is a useful way forward in this analysis too.[49] As Deborah Reed-Danahay points out: '[it] addresses the desire to be emplaced – either not to move at all or to seek emplacement after a geographical move'. Developing Bourdieu's idea of social space, she continues: 'Modes of emplacement or belonging are also modes of positioning in a social space. Migrants bring their dispositions and worldviews with them ... that may or may not be highly valued in the host setting'.[50] And as Kirin Narayan points out, storytelling is an intrinsic part of emplacement 'as an imaginative process, the orienting of self within multiple frameworks of meaning'.[51] The three stories in this chapter are all set in Sweden, yet they differ considerably when it comes not only to period of time, but also type of emplacement process. Despite the different temporalities and sub-

[48] Wulff, 'Writing Truth to Power', 17.
[49] Caroline B. Brettell and Deborah Reed-Danahay, *Civic Engagements: The Citizenship Practices of Asian Indian and Vietnamese Immigrants* (Stanford: Stanford University Press, 2012); Liisa H. Malkki 'Refugees and Exile: From "Refugee Studies" to the National Order of Things', *Annual Review of Anthropology* 24 (1995): 495–523.
[50] Deborah Reed-Danahay, *Bourdieu and Social Space: Mobilities, Trajectories, Emplacements* (Oxford: Berghahn, 2019), 132.
[51] Kirin Narayan, 'Placing Lives through Stories: Second-Generation South Asian Americans', in *Everyday Life in South Asia*, eds. Diane P. Mines and Sarah Lamb (Bloomington: Indiana University Press, 2002), 472.

dislocations, the experiences of living in Sweden in the two stories by Theodor Kallifatides and Duraid Al-Khamisi are on the whole surprisingly similar. While writing the stories is a way to handle their dislocation and at the same time move towards the process of emplacement, they also, importantly, inform a mainstream audience in Sweden about the new ethnic diversity in the country which, like elsewhere across the world, is here to stay and will keep growing.

Bibliography

Al-Khamisi, Duraid. *Regnet luktar inte här: Ett familjeporträtt*. Stockholm: Atlas, 2015.

Brettell, Caroline B. and Deborah Reed-Danahay. *Civic Engagements: The Citizenship Practices of Asian Indian and Vietnamese Immigrants*. Stanford: Stanford University Press, 2012.

Gröndahl, Satu. 'Identity Politics and the Construction of Minor Literatures: Multicultural Swedish Literature at the Turn of the Millenium'. *multiethnica* 30 (2007): 21–9.

Hannerz, Ulf. *Foreign News: Exploring the World of Foreign Correspondents*. Chicago: University of Chicago Press, 2004.

Hansson, Bodil. 'Om flykt, identitet och saknad'. *Litteraturmagazinet*, 12 January 2016. www.litteraturmagazinet.se/duraid-al-khamisi/regnet-luktar-inte-har/recension/bodil-hansson

Helgesson, Stefan. *Efter västerlandet: Texter om kulturell förändring*. Stockholm: Natur och Kultur, 2004.

Helgesson, Stefan and Mads Rosendahl Thompsen. 'Introduction: Why World Literature?' In *Literature and the World*, 1–23, London: Routledge, 2020.

Hogan, Patrick Colm. *Literature and Emotion*. New York: Routledge, 2018.

Holmes, Douglas R. and George E. Marcus 'Cultures of Expertise and the Management of Globalization: Toward the Re-Functioning of Ethnography'. In *Global Assemblages: Technology, Politics, and Ethics as Anthropological Problems*, edited by Aihwa Ong and Stephen J. Collier, 235–52. Oxford: Blackwell, 2005.

Kallifatides, Theodor. *Minnet i exil*. Stockholm: Bonniers, 1969.

Kallifatides, Theodor. *Utlänningar*. Stockholm: Bonniers, 1973.

Kallifatides, Theodor. *Ett nytt land utanför mitt fönster*. Stockholm: Bonnier Pocket, 2017.

Khemiri, Jonas Hassen. *Ett öga rött*. Stockholm: Norstedts, 2003.

Liem, Moa, Thess Steneskog, Ali Zardadi, Yosra Ali, Christie Gutierrez Hadad, Zeinab Muse, Anna Akopyan, Maja Wetterqvist and Naima Oday. *Vi ser, vi känner, vi kämpar*. Stockholm: Bonnier Carlsen, 2018.

Malkki, Liisa H. 'Refugees and Exile: From "Refugee Studies" to the National Order of Things'. *Annual Review of Anthropology* 24 (1995): 495–523.

Meeus, Bruno, Karel Arnaut and Bas van Heur, eds. *Arrival Infrastructures: Migration and Urban Social Mobilities*. New York: Palgrave, 2019.

Naipaul, V. S. *The Enigma of Arrival*. New York: Alfred A. Knopf, 1987.

Narayan, Kirin. 'Placing Lives through Stories: Second-Generation South Asian Americans'. In *Everyday Life in South Asia*, edited by Diane P. Mines and Sarah Lamb, 425–39. Bloomington: Indiana University Press, 2002.

Nilsson, Magnus. 'Swedish "Immigrant Literature" and the Construction of Ethnicity'. *TijdSchrift voor Skandinavistiek* 31, no.1 (2010): 199–218.

Ortner, Sherry B. *Not Hollywood: Independent Film at the Twilight of the American Dream*. Durham, NC: Duke University Press, 2013.

Reed-Danahay, Deborah. *Bourdieu and Social Space: Mobilities, Trajectories, Emplacements*. Oxford: Berghahn, 2019.

Rohi, Pooneh. *Araben*. Stockholm: Ordfront, 2013.

Stahre, Ulrika. 'Splittrad klassresa från Irak till Husby'. *Aftonbladet*, 12 September 2015. www.aftonbladet.se/kultur/bokrecensioner/a/Kva1E7/splittrad-klassresa-fran-irak-till-husby

Stenbeck, Evelina. *Poesi som politik: aktivistisk poetik hos Johannes Anyuru och Athena Farroukhzad*. Lund: Ellerström, 2017.

Wänelöf, Frida. 'Ali flyttar saknaden till pappret', *Huddinge Direkt*. 2017. www.stockholmdirekt.se/kultur/ali-flyttar-saknaden-till-pappret/repqcu!c6kYBk3lYDIFi@oud4Mb1A/

Wiles, Ellen. 'Three Branches of Literary Anthropology: Sources, Styles, Subject Matter'. *Ethnography* 21, no. 2 (2020): 280–95.

Wulff, Helena. 'Introducing the Anthropologist as Writer: Across and Within Genres'. In *The Anthropologist as Writer: Genres and Contexts in the Twenty-First Century*, edited by Helena Wulff. Oxford: Berghahn, 2016.

Wulff, Helena. *Rhythms of Writing: An Anthropology of Irish Literature*. London: Bloomsbury, 2017.

Wulff, Helena. 'Diasporic Divides: Location and Orientations of Rohi's *Araben*'. In *World Literatures: Exploring the Cosmopolitan–Vernacular Exchange*, edited by Stefan Helgesson, Annika Mörte Alling, Yvonne Lindqvist and Helena Wulff, 119–28. Stockholm: Stockholm University Press, 2018.

Wulff, Helena. 'Diversifying from Within: Diaspora Writings in Sweden'. In *The Composition of Anthropology: How Anthropological Texts are Written*, edited by Morten Nielsen and Nigel Rapport, 122–36. London: Routledge, 2018.

Wulff, Helena. 'Writing Truth to Power: Jonas Hassen Khemiri's Work in Stockholm and New York'. *Anthropology & Humanism* 44, no. 1 (2019): 7–19.

Zardadi, Ali. *Ängeln och sparven: Texter av en ensam ungdom på flykt*. Gothenburg: Catoblepas förlag, 2017.

Online Sources

https://sv.wikipedia.org/wiki/Theodor_Kallifatides
www.selmastories.se/forfattarna/intervju/ali-zardadi/
https://ensamkommandesforbund.se/om-oss/
www.scb.se/en/finding-statistics/statistics-by-subject-area/population/
www.scb.se/hitta-statistik/sverige-i-siffror/manniskorna-i-sverige/utrikes-fodda/
www.khemiri.se/en/books/one-eye-red-ett-oga-rott/

Afterword
At home in the world

Deborah Reed-Danahay

This book examines the question of how literature occupies space in the tension between orientation and location. It also concerns questions about the ways in which novelists and other writers, as well as the people about whom they write and readers of what they write, 'claim space'. The entanglements of place, land and power are ever-present in the world, affecting the voices of those who have been less visible in the dominant imaginaries of place on a global scale. Contemporary literary scholars pay attention to the voices of indigenous people, women, the poor and working-class, and migrants. Anthropologists, for their part, study texts produced by the people they study and reflect upon their own writing practices. These trends are leading to new understandings and recognitions of 'place' in textual representations of the world. The chapters in this volume make an important contribution to the so-called spatial turn in the humanities,[1] and tell 'spatial stories'[2] about the works they examine. As an exemplification of new approaches to studies of world literature, this book focuses not only on how texts resonate beyond local, regional and national contexts but also on an exploration of how their authors draw upon vernacular and cosmopolitan orientations.

It is not without some trepidation that I write an Afterword for a book about world literature whose chapters are, with a few exceptions, written by literary scholars. I am an anthropologist, after all, and not trained as a literary scholar and certainly not an expert in the field of world literature. What, I have asked myself, can I contribute to the conversation begun by this insightful set of chapters? My answer has settled upon the ways in which I can highlight the correspondences between the fields of world literature and anthropology. This will lead me to consider how literature and anthropology have both increased their attention to travel and circulation in the contemporary world, without assuming a

---

[1] An introduction and overview regarding the thought of many writers in this vein is offered in Robert T. Tally, Jr., *Spatiality* (London and New York: Routledge, 2013).

[2] Michel de Certeau, *The Practice of Everyday Life*. Trans. Steve Rendell (Berkeley: University of California Press, 1984).

globalization that erases local meanings and interpretations of the people, ideas and things that circulate. In my remarks, I will consider two themes that emerge from the chapters, placed in dialogue with recent trends in my own discipline of anthropology and related fields. I will first consider the troublesome concept of home, by way of which I will address the different orientations and locations that mark the texts analysed in these pages. Then I will turn to a discussion of multi-sited viewpoints in which both vernacular and cosmopolitan orientations come into play.

Home

The subtitle of this Afterword – 'at home in the world' – is a phrase that has been used by many authors with different intentions.[3] Here I put it to work primarily as a provocation. As anthropologist Michael Jackson has written, 'the word "home" is shot through with ambiguity'.[4] This is because of the conflicting impulses of a longing to be emplaced[5] and the desire to cross borders (imaginary, social, geographical). Through its focus on the tensions between the vernacular and the cosmopolitan, this volume prompts further consideration of the place of home in world literature and of what world literature can tell us about the concept of home.

Home is expressed in these chapters through such terms as home, homeland, hometown, home country, homesickness and unhomely. The theme of home as a way of thinking about its absence and the dislocations of not being or feeling at home is one that I have considered in several previous publications[6] and I was therefore drawn to think about ideas of home presented here as they relate

---

[3] I am primarily inspired here by Timothy Brennan's early critical attention to the emphasis on cosmopolitanism in scholarship and in the media. Timothy Brennan, *At Home in the World: Cosmopolitanism Now* (Cambridge, MA: Harvard University Press, 1997). But writers as diverse as a Vietnamese monk based in southern France (Thich Nhat Hanh, *At Home in the World: Stories and Essential Teachings from a Monk's Life* (Berkeley: Parallax Press, 2016)) and an anthropologist of Aboriginal Australia (Michael Jackson, *At Home in the World* (Durham, NC and London: Duke University Press, 1995)) have written books with this title.

[4] Jackson, *At Home in the World*, 3.

[5] Although Jackson uses the terms 'rooted' and 'uprooted' in his book, I prefer emplacement to 'rooted', and so substitute it here.

[6] Deborah Reed-Danahay, 'Leaving Home: Schooling Stories and the Ethnography of Autoethnography in Rural France', in *Auto/Ethnography: Rewriting the Self and the Social*, ed. Deborah Reed-Danahay (Oxford and New York: Berg Publishers, 1997), 123–43; '"This is Your Home Now!" Conceptualizing Location and Dislocation in a Dementia Unit', *Qualitative Research* 1, no. 1 (2001): 47–63; and '"Like a Foreigner in my own Homeland": Writing the Dilemmas of Return in the Vietnamese American Diaspora', *Identities: Global Studies in Culture and Power* 22, no. 5 (2015): 603–618.

to locations and orientations. As noted by Bo G. Ekelund in his Introduction, David Damrosch and David L. Pike have written that one way of approaching world literature is to see what exchanges occur when such works 'travel away from home'.[7] But where do we locate home and what does it mean to travel from home? Home is a multivocal concept that expresses physical locations, orientations and emotional connections. Being and feeling 'at home' are not always the same thing. Texts, authors and characters in stories may all be viewed in terms of how and in what way they may be at home (in the world or at a more local and vernacular level), seek a home, or be relatively homeless. Is location a form of being at home, while dislocation refers to its opposite? And can home be an orientation?

Leaving home can be viewed negatively as a disruptive uprooting or positively as a cosmopolitan desire to experience a wider world. Novelist Jamaica Kincaid, a native of Antigua, referred to these desires in her essay titled 'Homemaking' about a house she purchased in Vermont. In the essay, Kincaid mused on the mobility of American families (like the one in whose house she now lived), who rarely continue to live in the houses where they grew up. She wrote, with what I interpret as an ironic tone, 'Everybody who accomplishes anything leaves home.' I first cited this statement in my analysis[8] of two published ethnographic memoirs, or autoethnographies, written by natives of rural France who had left their villages and expressed ambivalent feelings about having done so. That essay was about leaving home, and concerned writers (internal migrants in France) for whom home had become a nostalgic concept associated with a feeling of loss about the circumstances of their lives in that, as Kincaid expressed it, they had to 'leave home' in order to accomplish things. As I have returned to her essay while writing this Afterword, I find that she continued 'This action, leaving home, has an effect on the people left behind and sometimes, most dramatically, on the new people one meets.'[9] We might interpret this also in terms of texts that circulate and meet new audiences.

There is a valorization of leaving home, which we can observe in the efforts of novelists discussed in this volume to have their work appreciated on a global scale. In anthropology, the value in leaving home to conduct research accompanied several national traditions of anthropology (for example, in the

---

[7] David Damrosch and David L. Pike, 'Preface', *The Longman Anthology of World Literature*, 2nd edition, vol. D: The Seventeenth and Eighteenth Centuries (New York: Longman, 2009), xvi.
[8] Deborah Reed-Danahay, 'Leaving Home'.
[9] Jamaica Kincaid, 'Homemaking: The Life of a House', *The New Yorker* (16 October 1995), 54–64.

United States and the United Kingdom) for a long time, wherein fieldwork 'away' was preferable to fieldwork 'at home'. That is, you had to be a world traveller and go abroad to 'accomplish anything' in anthropology. This trend began to turn in the 1990s, however, when anthropologists began to appreciate fieldwork at home while at the same time renewing interest in 'life history' research – with attention to the life story of the anthropologist and the life stories of our research participants. Ruth Behar, of Cuban ancestry, has written along these lines with reference to her turn towards research in Latin America when she became increasingly conscious that in her earliest scholarship in Spain 'there was no link between this topic and my life'.[10] In the face of pressures from the dominant culture to 'leave home' in not just a physical but an intellectual way, author bell hooks[11] has advocated a focus, especially by academics from ethnic minority and immigrant groups, on ways to incorporate ties to their 'familial and community backgrounds'.[12] hooks was prompted to move in that direction herself when, during her studies at Stanford University, she was taken aback by a comment from her grandmother: 'How can you live so far away from your people?'[13]

Sociologist Jan Willem Duyvendak[14] has remarked on the familiarity that attends the concept of home, and argues that this familiarity is why the concept is rarely interrogated beyond assumptions regarding its connection to belonging. He writes that feeling at home can be 'a rather passive state where things are self-evident because they are so familiar'. Lisa Malkki[15] has offered a cogent critique of the spatial metaphors that underlay the 'naturalness' of Western understandings of territory as the place where one is at home, in ways that assume the naturalness of being rooted in a place and that view forms of spatial mobility as somehow less normal. In her study of refugees from the former Yugoslavia in European cities, Maja Korac[16] examines their emplacements but also points to the darker side of the concept of home for these mobile people. Referencing Mary Douglas's

[10] Ruth Behar, *Translated Woman: Crossing the Border with Esperanza's Story* (Boston: Beacon Press, 1993), 331.
[11] bell hooks, 'Keeping Close to Home: Class and Education', in *Working-Class Women in the Academy: Laborers in the Knowledge Factory*, eds. Michelle M. Tokarczyk and Elizabeth A. Fay (Amherst: The University of Massachusetts Press, 1993), 99–111.
[12] hooks, 'Keeping Close to Home', 111.
[13] hooks, 'Keeping Close to Home', 110.
[14] Jan Willem Duyvendak, *The Politics of Home: Belonging and Nostalgia in Western Europe and the United States* (New York: Palgrave Macmillan, 2011).
[15] Lisa Malkki, 'National Geographic: The Rooting of Peoples and the Territorialization of National Identity Among Scholars and Refugees', *Cultural Anthropology* 7, no. 1 (1992): 24–44.
[16] Maja Korac, *Remaking Home: Reconstructing Life, Place, and Identity in Rome and Amsterdam* (New York and Oxford: Berghahn, 2009).

phrase 'the tyranny of the home', Korac writes: 'alongside intimacy and security … notions of home also entail the oppression, subversion and exclusion of specific groups and/or categories of people, such as the young, the old, women, etc.'[17] If it is viewed as natural for people to remain at home, those who see home as oppressive or dangerous become suspect for not staying home.

This creates ideas of insiders and outsiders that shape how literary texts are received and the role they may play in both national and global contexts. Claims to being 'at home' may be contested, particularly in cases of geographic mobility. This is an issue in the literature of Hawai'i, where the authority to call Hawaiian Islands 'home' is a contentious point not based on birth or residence, but on being the descendant of autochthonous Hawaiians. Sally Anderson Boström describes Lois-Ann Yamanaka's novel *Blu's Hanging* as part of the 'local literature movement', and notes that the author claims a local status on the island of Moloka'i given their sansei identity as a descendant of Japanese migrants, explicitly seeking recognition as a local who is not a 'native Hawaiian'. Another writer, Maxine Hong Kingston, who lived in Hawai'i for almost twenty years but had no claims to ancestry there, did not refer to Hawai'i as her home when writing about it. Instead, as Anderson Boström notes, she describes this as her 'stay' in Hawai'i, and identifies as a visitor not a settler.

Claims to being 'at home' after international migration are similarly ambiguous and frequently contentious. For the migrant writers who moved to Sweden, as portrayed by Helena Wulff, home is associated with memory and emotion: it is what was left behind and what is lost. And yet, the possibility of making a new home through what we can think of as modes of emplacement is also mentioned by one of the writers, who told Wulff in an interview that 'you have to practice to feel at home' in Stockholm. The chapter by Wulff focuses on the arrival stories of those who left home. With a focus on three migrant writers at three historical moments in Swedish immigration history, we can see the initial displacements that become tinged with vernacular orientations to the places they came from and to their new city of Stockholm. At the same time, the broader experience of such migration is a cosmopolitan spatial story. However, it is not one of people who necessarily feel at home anywhere, but of migrants who struggle to 'claim space' in Swedish society not only through their presence there but through their writing.

---

[17] Korac, *Remaking Home*, 195.

Writers discussed in this book are sometimes positioned, either as heroic or provincial, with reference to how much they base their stories in their homelands or hometowns. Writing fiction that draws upon familiar themes and social life in one's hometown can be a double-edged sword in the ways that literature is oriented towards a world stage. In a focus on the gendered aspect of literary locations and dislocations, through the lens of her comparison between the trajectories of novels by a female Nigerian writer, Flora Nwapa, and a much more internationally celebrated male writer, Chinua Achebe, Paula Uimonen illustrates the vernacularization process through which Nwapa's work was for a long time 'located' in Nigeria. Uimonen stresses that Nwapa was admired by some for situating her fiction in her hometown, a place that resonated for other Nigerians. She depicted a social world that was familiar to them. At the same time, Uimonen's ethnographic research shows that local leaders were aware that the characters Nwapa wrote about 'had departed from cultural ideals', which I interpret as exposure to the outside world of what Michael Herzfeld refers to as 'cultural intimacy'.[18]

Like Anderson Boström and Uimonen, Ashleigh Harris juxtaposes different novelists writing in a particular national tradition. She notes that a character in the novel *This Island Now*, a woman of African ancestry living on a fictionalized island in the Caribbean feels that only the islands are 'home' and that one is an 'outsider' everywhere else: 'We're outsiders in continental America, in Europe, in Africa, in Asia. Our ancestors came from these great land masses but they are no longer home to us. And so we're outsiders even among those who are like us but who are not of these islands … We are a new breed, a kind of outpost of the future.'[19] This novel was written by Peter Abrahams, originally from South Africa but writing in exile during the period of apartheid. Harris juxtaposes *This Island Now* with another novel, Sol Plaatje's *Mhudi*, written almost forty years earlier, in the twentieth century and before apartheid. *Mhudi* is set in South Africa during the early nineteenth century. It tells the story of local villagers caught in a period of conflict and violence who are forced to leave their home, and it ends with the main protagonists returning home, coming full circle to more familiar surroundings. *Mhudi* is often hailed as the first English-language novel by a South African, while *This Island Now* has a less secure place in the canon of South African literature. The authority of authors is at stake in the

---

[18] Michael Herzfeld, *Cultural Intimacy: Social Poetics and the Real Life of States, Societies, and Institutions*. 3rd edition (New York: Routledge, 2016).
[19] Ashleigh Harris, Chapter 2.

ways they depict their homeland and in their orientations away from it, but this
is a nuanced business and may change over time as can be seen in the case of
Flora Nwapa. Her credibility as a novelist was enhanced by the fact that she
wrote 'authentically' about local social life; but her gender hindered the wider
circulation of her work.

In the case of Ralph de Boissière's novel *Crown Jewel*, the author was lauded
on the jacket of the German version of his book for 'communicating a true-to-
life image of his homeland and people in a captivating story'.[20] Ekelund shows
that for de Boissière to be a credible proletarian novelist it was necessary that he
'construct a social space marked by a local distribution of symbolic and material
goods'. However, the success of the novel in terms of its broader audiences 'rests on
showing the universal implications of that space'. *Crown Jewel* depicts characters
who move to different locations, with the homeland and site of initial class and
colonial exploitation being the world of creole Trinidad. The vernacular serves
to tell a story of global capitalism that captures the imagination of audiences in
Australia, Eastern Europe and the UK.

Whether or not you can know the world even if you remain always at home
is another question raised in this volume. This is illustrated in the case of the
protagonist in Blasim's short story 'The Market of Stories', as explained by
Tasnim Qutait, who draws upon the concept of 'unhomely' in a consideration
of contemporary Iraqi literature. Previously used by Homi Bhabha,[21] this idea
is about a perception of the disorienting break in the boundary between home
and the world. As he writes, 'the unhomely is the shock of recognition of the
world-in-the-home and the home-in-the-world'.[22] With the phrase 'the aesthetics
of insecurity', Qutait points to the ways in which home becomes not a place of
familiarity and security but one that has changed due to violence and has created
refugees forced to leave. There is disorientation and dislocation, producing a
disruption of a narrative (as well as physical) space that could produce a local
audience for literature and leads storytellers to engage more broadly.

We can view the house in Buffalo inhabited by Muslim-American students
as portrayed in the novel *Taqwacores* as similarly 'unhomely' in Homi Bhabha's
sense. As Adnan Mahmutović notes, the young Muslim punk rockers living there
have created a site in an American location (a house, or 'home') where they are
physically at home while at the same time oriented towards the wider Muslim

[20] Bo G. Ekelund, Chapter 5.
[21] Homi Bhabha, 'The World and the Home', *Social Text* 31/32 (1992): 141–53.
[22] Bhabha, 'The World and the Home', 141.

world. The house is a transnational 'world in the home' but also a 'home in the world'. Mahmutović writes 'Thus we have youngsters located in a house in Buffalo oriented to a house in Mecca. This orientation is both physical/geographic and symbolic, just as their American location is physical and symbolic.'[23] The novel portrays the most literal version of home in this volume – a house in the city of Buffalo. The city plays little part in the narrative, however, so that the location of the novel does not venture into the multicultural city or to any other Muslim sites there (such as mosques). The idea of a global Ummah, as a key element of Islamic tradition and belief, influences the orientations of the students in the house who have not themselves moved far from home geographically to cohabit as university students, but who feel part of a larger social space.

Jobst Welge argues for an understanding of the historical layering (haunting) of space and time in his reading of contemporary Latin American fiction writers. He identifies what I consider a transnational and transhistorical writing strategy on the part of the three authors he discusses, who deliberately seek to find a readership beyond the locations of the texts and to tell stories that also transcend national boundaries. Rather than providing a sense of security and familiarity, the homes depicted in these stories are marked by violence – physical and symbolic. From the violent history of Colombia (Vasquez) to the battles fought by Geronimo (Enrigue) and to the painful experiences of child separation at the Mexican–American border (Luiselli), the vernacular is one of dislocation and disruption. As much as these novelists place their stories in particular locations and in particular historical circumstances, Welge argues, they are purposefully oriented towards a wider readership.

Being at home can be understood both as a physical location and as an emotion and a feeling. Not only in English but also in French (with the term, *chez moi*) there is the idea of physically being there – as in the sentence 'I'll be home tonight if you want to stop by', and to an emotion expressing whether or not one feels that one belongs – as when a migrant may express that they did or did not feel 'at home' in their new location. For the French, this phrase may also connote the idea of ownership and rights, referring to whether or not you are the owner of the house or apartment where you live (rather than a renter). When being at home is associated with rights and positive emotions, therefore, leaving home can be viewed as dislocation and uncertainty rather than a good thing. And even immobile people can stop feeling at home when newcomers arrive in

[23]　Adnan Mahmutović, Chapter 6.

their neighborhoods because of a sense of lost familiarity. As Duyvendak notes 'Whereas cosmopolitans embrace "nomadism" and consider the de-placement of home as a positive development, many others struggle to belong in an increasingly pluriform and mobile society. They deplore the loss of a familiar home.'[24] The theme of emotions connected to home is most salient in the chapters by Wulff (on migrant writers who have travelled far from home) and by Harris (on the loss of a familiar home due to the destruction of war).

Multi-sited viewpoints

The multiple locations and orientations of the texts and authors discussed in this volume articulate the tension between home and the wider world. The contributors locate the texts they analyse with reference to national, ethnic and religious affiliations. There are chapters devoted to African, and more specifically Nigerian, novels (Uimonen), South African novels (Harris), Iraqi fiction (Qutait), Hawaiian literature (Anderson Boström), Muslim-American writing (Mahmutović) and Latin American literature (Welge). Two chapters take a more thematic approach, although they too indicate national locations – as in the chapter on proletarian novels (Ekelund) that references Trinidadian literature, and the chapter on migrant writing set in Sweden (Wulff).

In many ways, these are all multi-sited texts, meaning that they are oriented towards multiple arenas – geographically and socially. In anthropology, the concept of 'multi-sited ethnography' emerged in the mid-twentieth century.[25] George Marcus identified it as a new methodology suited to making connections between local places and the world system. He argued that this type of research entails following the people, following things, following metaphors, following plots and stories, following life histories and following conflicts.

It is not necessary to physically move to have a multi-sited viewpoint, and it can be carried out in one geographic location. The aim is to understand what happens to the subjects of the research in other sites. Marcus refers to this as 'strategically situated ethnography' and argues that good examples of it examine

---

[24] Duyvendak, *The Politics of Home*, 30.

[25] George E. Marcus, 'Ethnography in/of the World System: The Emergence of Multi-Sited Ethnography', *Annual Review of Anthropology* 24 (1995): 95–117. See also Ghassan Hage, 'A Not so Multi-Sited Ethnography of a Not so Imagined Community', *Anthropological Theory* 5, no. 4 (2005): 463–75. Hage offers a critique of several ways in which this concept has been (mis)used since originally mentioned by Marcus.

the implications of what goes on in a particular locale in the context of other related locales.[26] This approach resonates with an earlier statement made by Clifford Geertz: 'anthropologists don't study villages ... they study *in* villages'.[27] Geertz meant that ethnographic research may take place in a local location but it has a more global orientation. I interpret this to mean that Geertz embraced a multi-sited outlook. Although we must not assume that Geertz viewed anthropology as a discipline that only studied villages (a lingering stereotype of my discipline), his point was that any local place in the world is impacted by wider forces and that to narrow one's focus to what lies within the borders of that place would ignore its global connections.

Equally important, the anthropologist aims to provide an ethnography that speaks to broader questions that can be illustrated through what occurs within and around a village (or city, or neighbourhood and so on). I cited this quote from Geertz in my first book,[28] which was based on the ethnographic study of a cluster of rural villages (*commune*) in France, because my intention was to have my book speak to wider implications about state power and social agency that went beyond the particulars of the local people, events and histories that I had collected in my investigations. In some ways, like many of the novelists examined in this volume, I sought to use a vernacular orientation to situate my ethnography in a more cosmopolitan framework. Although my research was not multi-sited in that it was based on one rural region, it had a 'multi-sited' outlook, as do many of the texts analysed in the chapters of this book. A multi-sited outlook characterizes the inquiries offered here as the contributors trace the trajectories of various works and their authors, and try to understand 'what happens' to them in other sites that link the local to the world beyond. For example, Uimonen[29] observes in the context of African literature that when novels circulate beyond the cultural context of the writer, they are also 'relocated into other cultural imaginaries'. Moreover, she notes, Igbo writers, through encounters with readers who are not 'insiders' of the culture, can 'recreate and reconfigure their social worlds'.[30]

Although connections between the local and the global are important to consider in ethnographic and literary studies, to err on the side of too much emphasis on

---

[26] Marcus, 'Ethnography in/of the World System', 106.
[27] Clifford Geertz, *The Interpretation of Cultures* (New York: Basic Books, 1973), 32.
[28] Deborah Reed-Danahay, *Education and Identity in Rural France: The Politics of Schooling* (Cambridge: Cambridge University Press, 1996).
[29] Paula Uimonen, Chapter 1.
[30] Uimonen, Chapter 1.

the global at the expense of the local is another issue that anthropologists have addressed. An example of this is Anna Tsing's[31] critique of globalization theory and her analysis of the 'seductions' of globalization. Marcus[32] identified Tsing as a practitioner of 'strategically situated ethnography'. She defines globalism, whose validity she questions, as 'endorsements of the importance of the global'.[33] Among several other observations that she makes, Tsing points to globalization's 'rhetoric of linkage and circulation as the overcoming of boundaries and restrictions'.[34] She also argues that the metaphor of circulation occludes capitalism's penetration in distant places, noting how circulation is used in the language of corporate expansion but also in the rhetorics of multiculturalism and 'creative hybridity'.[35] Tsing cautions that a focus on the flow, to use a water metaphor, ignores attention to the channel through which it flows. This is very similar to Pierre Bourdieu's criticism of autobiography,[36] whereby he says that to focus on a life without attention to the broader social space in which it is lived is akin to looking at a subway train without understanding the infrastructure of the entire system that surrounds the train and enables it to move. Tsing argues for studying 'the landscape of circulation as well as the flow. How are people, cultures, and things remade as they travel?' The theme of circulation and the social structures in which it occurs is amply illustrated in the chapter by Ekelund, who shows how the author of *Crown Jewel* both creates a localized social space in the story and traces the effects on and products of the colonial and capitalist history of that place in a wider social space.

In addition to the spatial aspects of a multi-sited viewpoint, this volume can be viewed through a temporal lens. Whether or not a story takes place in one location and at roughly the same time period – with the most extreme example being the house in Buffalo inhabited by Muslim punk rockers in the novel *Taqwacores* (Mahmutović) – or across various landscapes and histories, as in the cases of the three Latin American novels discussed by Welge and the novel *Crown Jewel* (Ekelund), the outlook of the writers whose works are analysed is multi-sited historically as well as spatially. Harris traces how the apartheid

[31] Anna Tsing, 'The Global Situation', *Cultural Anthropology* 15, no. 3 (2000): 327–60.
[32] Marcus, 'Ethnography in/of the World System'.
[33] Tsing, 'The Global Situation', 330.
[34] Tsing, 'The Global Situation', 332.
[35] Tsing, 'The Global Situation', 337.
[36] Pierre Bourdieu, 'L'Illusion Biographique', *Actes de la Recherches en Sciences Sociales*, 62/63 (1986): 69–72. See also my extensive discussion of this in chapter 3 of Deborah Reed-Danahay, *Bourdieu and Social Space: Mobilities, Trajectories, Emplacements* (New York: Berghahn Books, 2020).

history of South Africa influenced novels written before and during that system. In her analysis of the literature of Hawai'i, Anderson Boström references the historical interplay of indigeneity and subsequent migrations to the islands as a factor shaping the inclusions and exclusions of this literary field. Uimonen traces an historically-informed literary gendering that affects the trajectories of two Nigerian writers over time. There is also a strong focus on temporality in the analysis of writing about arrival among migrants to Sweden (Wulff), who depict their changing points of view, but also with the focus on different historical moments of migration to Sweden. In her analysis of contemporary Iraqi literature, Qutait mentions an Arabic term that means 'bringing near' in both a temporal and spatial sense. Fiction that addresses war and destruction (Baghdad described as 'unrecognizable' in one of the novels Qutait analyses), may be understood to display the same historical layering and ghosting that Welge identifies in Latin American fiction.

Concluding thoughts

A main contribution of this book is the way in which it decouples the concepts of location and orientation, suggesting that they are not necessarily synonymous. The physical location of a story, therefore, does not dictate the orientations of the writer (towards the local and beyond), and vice versa. This opens up a new way of examining how texts occupy, claim and circulate throughout both social and geographic space. It also leads to new questions about how texts can claim space. These chapters bring spatial issues to the fore and show the possible combinations of orientation and location that can influence how texts circulate and are interpreted in different milieux (at home and abroad). One question raised is that of how the local and the global correspond to the concepts of vernacularism and cosmopolitanism. What is the model of globalization that underlies the view of the world that accompanies world literature? Although it seems straightforward to associate the local with the vernacular, in what ways is the global cosmopolitan? This volume suggests that the interplay between these four concepts deserves more attention.

When reading these chapters in dialogue with each other, new areas emerge that might stimulate further work using the spatial framework of this book. One is that of gender. Although only one chapter (Uimonen) focuses primarily on how gender affected the trajectories of authors and their novels, it would be interesting to consider that question in the other contexts. How does masculinity

affect the authority of a writer and their ability to have their work circulate and
be recognized on a global scale? How does a female writer's topics and national
or historic context affect global recognition of their work? How does a novel by
a female author 'claim space' in a field dominated by men? How do gendered
locations and orientations relate to vernacular and cosmopolitan ones?

Another question is that of how publishers affect the orientations of authors
and their texts, as well as the circulation of those texts. We see in the case of
Latin American texts (Welge) that there were strategic choices made to have
them reach wider audiences. And we see in the case of the novel *Crown Jewel*
(Ekelund) that its publishing and translation history was partly a product of the
appeal of its focus (as a proletarian novel) in different national contexts. How
does the market for world literature shape the vernacular and cosmopolitan
orientations of texts more broadly? And how do internal national conversations
about national literatures affect the wider circulation of texts in relationship
to markets – for example, in Hawai'i (Anderson Boström) and South Africa
(Harris)? When a migrant writer in Sweden writing in Swedish is contributing
to world literature, it is not primarily based on the circulation of their work,
but, as Wulff reveals, on their having brought new insights within another
national context – circulating within rather than beyond. The three migrant
autoethnographers she studies are claiming space within a national context as
outsiders emplacing themselves, which is a different move from that of texts
moving from a national context to claim space at a more diffuse global level. The
theme of human migration is one that intersects with that of world literature, in
that if we follow people or texts we can see how they 'carry things'[37] with them as
they leave home – things with particular and more universal meanings.

Bibliography

Behar, Ruth. *Translated Woman: Crossing the Border with Esperanza's Story.* Boston:
Beacon Press, 1993.
Bhabha, Homi. 'The World and the Home'. *Social Text* 31/32 (1992): 141–53.
Bourdieu, Pierre. 'L'Illusion Biographique'. *Actes de la Recherches en Sciences Sociales*
62/63 (1986): 69–72.
Brennan, Timothy. At *Home in the World: Cosmopolitanism Now.* Cambridge, MA:
Harvard University Press, 1997.

[37] Here I reference Tim O'Brien's book *The Things They Carried* (New York: Houghton Mifflin, 1990).

Certeau, Michel de. *The Practice of Everyday Life*. Trans. Steve Rendell. Berkeley: University of California Press, 1984.

Damrosch, David and David L. Pike. 'Preface'. *The Longman Anthology of World Literature*, 2nd edition. Vol. D. New York: Longman, 2009.

Duyvendak, Jan Willem. *The Politics of Home: Belonging and Nostalgia in Western Europe and the United States*. New York: Palgrave Macmillan, 2011.

Geertz, Clifford. *The Interpretation of Cultures*. New York: Basic Books, 1973.

Hage, Ghassan. 'A Not so Multi-Sited Ethnography of a Not so Imagined Community'. *Anthropological Theory* 5, no. 4 (2005): 463–75.

Herzfeld, Michael. *Cultural Intimacy: Social Poetics and the Real Life of States, Societies, and Institutions*. 3rd edition. New York: Routledge, 2016.

hooks, bell. 'Keeping Close to Home: Class and Education'. In *Working-Class Women in the Academy: Laborers in the Knowledge Factory*, edited by Michelle M. Tokarczyk and Elizabeth A. Fay, 99–111. Amherst: The University of Massachusetts Press, 1993.

Jackson, Michael. *At Home in the World*. Durham, NC and London: Duke University Press, 1995.

Kincaid, Jamaica. 'Homemaking: The Life of a House'. *The New Yorker*, 16 October (1995): 54–64.

Korac, Maja. *Remaking Home: Reconstructing Life, Place, and Identity in Rome and Amsterdam*. New York and Oxford: Berghahn, 2009.

Malkki, Lisa. 'National Geographic: The Rooting of Peoples and the Territorialization of National Identity Among Scholars and Refugees'. *Cultural Anthropology* 7, no. 1, (1992): 24–44.

Marcus, George E. 'Ethnography In/of the World System: The Emergence of Multi-Sited Ethnography'. *Annual Review of Anthropology* 24 (1995): 95–117.

O'Brien, Tim. *The Things They Carried*. New York: Houghton Mifflin, 1990.

Reed-Danahay, Deborah. *Education and Identity in Rural France: The Politics of Schooling*. Cambridge: Cambridge University Press, 1996.

Reed-Danahay, Deborah. 'Leaving Home: Schooling Stories and the Ethnography of Autoethnography in Rural France'. In *Auto/Ethnography: Rewriting the Self and the Social*, ed. Deborah Reed-Danahay, 123–43. Oxford and New York: Berg Publishers, 1997.

Reed-Danahay, Deborah. '"This is Your Home Now!" Conceptualizing Location and Dislocation in a Dementia Unit'. *Qualitative Research* 1, no. 1 (2001): 47–63.

Reed-Danahay, Deborah. '"Like a Foreigner in my own Homeland": Writing the Dilemmas of Return in the Vietnamese American Diaspora'. *Identities: Global Studies in Culture and Power* 22, no. 5 (2015): 603–618.

Reed-Danahay, Deborah. *Bourdieu and Social Space: Mobilities, Trajectories, Emplacements*. New York: Berghahn, 2020.

Tally, Robert T. Jr. *Spatiality*. London and New York: Routledge, 2013.

Tsing, Anna. 'The Global Situation'. *Cultural Anthropology* 15, no. 3 (2000): 327–60.

Index

Abrahams, Peter 14, 59, 72–80, 241
  A Night of their Own 78
  Mine Boy 59
  This Island Now 14, 59, 61–2, 72–80, 241
Abyssinia/Ethiopia 152–4, 163
Achebe, Chinua 17–18, 29–38, 42–4, 50,
  53–4, 241
adab al-ʿālam (world's literature) 85, 106
Adejunmobi, Moradewun xv n18, xvi
Afghanistan 15, 217, 221, 228–9, 231–2
Africa 29–31, 33–4, 43, 45, 50, 77, 221
  (*see also* South Africa)
  African National Congress 63
  Heinemann African Writers Series 31,
    34, 38–9
  literary canon 35–6, 38
  literary vernacularity xv
  literature and writers 29–54, 72, 156,
    158, 245
  novel 32, 38–9, 43, 45
  Pan-Africanism 14, 34, 73–4, 76–9,
    152
  and UNESCO cities of literature 5
  West Africa xvi, 17, 45
  women's literature 36, 43, 46–7
Al-Khamisi, Duraid 23, 221, 224–233
  The Rain Has No Smell Here (*Regnet
    luktar inte här*) 221, 224–7
allegory 18, 94, 97, 99–100, 103
Al-Malaika, Nazik 85–6, 106
ʿammiyya 88, 91
Anderson Boström, Sally 12–13, 111,
  240–41, 247
anglophone xix, 87, 91–2, 116–17, 128,
  200
Anglosphere x, 87–8
anthropology x, xix–xx, 30, 34, 45, 51–2,
  219, 236–9, 244–5
Appadurai, Arjun 86, 170, 183
Apartheid 14, 59–62, 72–4, 77–80, 241,
  246

arrival 15, 23, 217–22, 228, 230–2, 240, 247
audience, readers, readership 96, 100, 113,
  140, 171, 173, 176, 197–9, 238, 243
  Arab 98
  expectations 100–3
  global Muslim 176–7, 179, 181
  international, global, cosmopolitan 14,
    30, 32–4, 37, 54, 71, 73, 88, 92, 94,
    154, 156, 176, 179, 182, 195, 199,
    213, 238, 242
  located 20–1
  mainland (US) 113
  national, local, indigenous 30, 37,
    49, 72, 79, 87, 113, 182, 199,
    232–3, 242
  of peripheries 193
  regional 88, 92
  Russian 157–8
  Second World 158
  Swedish 219
  Western 91, 93, 101, 107
  White South African 78
Auerbach, Erich x
authenticity xiv, 132
authority
  of authors 241, 248
  cosmopolitan authority 128, 149
  cultural and linguistic xiv, xvi, 116,
    127–8, 240
autobiography 144, 157, 217, 220, 231, 246
autochthony 22, 138

Baghdad 8, 85–7, 91–103, 106–7, 221, 224,
  247
Balaz, Joe 119, 120, 126, 131
  'Da Mainland to Me' 119–120
Barber, Karin xix
The Beacon 142–3
Beecroft, Alexander
  ecologies of literature ix, 23, 60–2, 66,
    73, 91, 171, 175, 194

cosmopolitan ecology 88, 128, 176,
194, 213
epichoric ecology xiii, 72
national ecology 80
vernacular ecology xiv, 71, 179
Bhabha, Homi K. xviii, 187, 242
Blasim, Hassan 8–9, 23, 85–9, 91–6,
100–5, 107, 242
The Corpse Exhibition 92–3, 100
'The Market of Stories' 101, 242
Bolaño, Roberto 194, 199–201
borders
border construction and boundary-
work 6, 8, 120–1, 152–3
border-crossing 87, 89, 94, 160, 187–8,
219, 223, 229, 237, 242–3, 246
borderlessness 60, 175
linguistic bordering xv
Mexican–American border 5–7,
201–12, 243
territorial and national borders 2, 170
Bourdieu, Pierre 5n16, 10, 20n57, 232, 246
Buffalo, NY 9, 18, 170, 173, 175, 180,
242–3, 246
Bunyan, John 61
Pilgrim's Progress 61
Busby, Margaret 161–2

Cairo 98
canon
African literary canon 35–6, 38, 45
American literary canon 116
American pacific literary canon 116, 119
counter-canon 32
English literary canon 65
and gender bias 40, 50
literary canon formation 30, 39–40,
48, 116
South African literary canon 59, 61–3,
73, 79, 81, 241
Western literary canon 98
world literary canon 30–2, 36, 39, 72,
94
Caribbean 15, 59, 74, 76–7, 137–40, 146,
241
Casanova, Pascale x, 5n16, 12n36, 15,
19–20, 195
Chamoiseau, Patrick xviii

Chandler, Raymond 3–5
Cheah, Pheng xii, 51, 86
China xxi, 113, 129, 158
circulation of texts x–xi, xx, 13–14, 21, 34,
40, 60, 186, 189, 236–8, 246–8
between Third World and Second
World 141, 145, 161–4
constrained and limited 39, 45–6, 66,
179, 242
global and cosmopolitan 43, 45, 50, 52,
61, 86, 88, 90, 93, 137, 141–2, 154,
163, 170n2, 178, 212, 245
local and national 67, 92, 173
of pirated copies 48
panchoric and regional 69, 88, 99
to and from Sweden xii
citizenship 73, 169–170, 174, 189
Colombia 197–9, 243
Columbus, Christopher 146–7, 158
community and communities
of comprehension xv
ethnic 239
Hawai'ian 120, 122, 128
igbo communities 30
and interface ethnography 219
Islamic 185, 187
Japanese–American 111n4
literary community of Hawai'i 113–14
local community of Flora Nwapa 38,
46, 49
local (epichoric) community 60
Muslim Ummah 175, 180
Taqwacore community 171–5, 177,
180–1, 185–8
Trinidadian 163
comparative literature ix–x, 86
Couzens, Tim 68, 79
creole continuum 22–3, 139–40, 148–9,
153, 163
creolization 139
Cummins, Jeanine 6
American Dirt 6

Damascus 98
Damrosch, David x, 16n46, 19–21, 86,
163, 238
Day, A. Grove and Carl Stroven 116,
118–19, 128

De Boissière, Ralph 22–3, 137–64, 242
    Crown Jewel 22, 137–64, 242, 246, 248
    Life on the Edge: The Autobiography of
        Ralph de Boissière 142–5
decolonization 32, 34, 53, 61, 74, 76n59,
    77–9, 81, 117, 160
decolonize the curriculum 62, 81
Denning, Michael 141, 163
difference 52, 180–2, 187
dislocation 15, 30, 43–5, 72–3, 79, 85, 87,
    89, 95, 96, 103, 107, 218, 221, 231,
    238, 243
dissemination, *see* distribution
distant reading xi–xii, 13, 195
distribution, for the distribution of texts,
        see circulation
    of forms 19, 171, 186
    of gendered orientations 30, 50
    of individuality 140n12
    of places and land and access to them
        2, 15, 17, 24
    of symbolic and material goods 7,
        10–13, 16, 19, 22n61, 142
    of writers and perspectives 15
Du Bois, W. E. B. 66n39, 71
Duyvendak, Jan Willem 239, 244

ecologies of literature, *see* Beecroft,
    Alexander
Egypt 99
Ekelund, Bo G. 1, 22, 137, 238, 242, 246
emotion 13, 44, 87, 93, 217–8, 222, 230–1,
    238, 240, 243–4
Enrigue, Álvaro 21, 23, 204, 207–212
    Ahora me rindo y esto es todo (Now I
        give up and that's all) 207–11
    Muerte súbita (Sudden Death) 207–8
ethnic diversity 232–3
ethnoscapes 170, 183n38, 187
exclusion 60, 111, 217, 231–2, 240

fantasy 93, 97
fieldwork 13, 30, 239
Finland 91, 217
folk tales 63, 67, 70
Foucault, Michel 76
    heterotopia 76, 78
France 93, 238, 245

Frankenstein 8, 85–7, 91–100, 107
Fuentes, Carlos 102, 208
Fujikane, Candace 112n5, 121, 123–5
    Asian Settler Colonialism 112n5,
        117–18, 121, 125
fuṣḥā xiii, 91

Galperina, Evgenyia 155, 158–60
García Lorca, Federico 199, 201
Geertz, Clifford 245
gender 30–1, 35, 39–53, 242
    gender complementarity 30, 31, 49–51,
        53
    literary gendering 30–1, 41–3, 46, 50,
        247
    vernacular gender theory 31, 43, 46–7
genre 32, 42, 89, 91–4, 96, 103, 194, 202,
    231
geoculture 7–9, 11, 13–14, 19, 24, 29–30,
    43, 45, 49, 212
geopolitics xx, 7–9, 95, 116, 119–120, 207
Geronimo [leader of the Chiricahua
        Apache tribe] 204–11, 243
Glissant, Édouard 139, 146
global novel xii, 18, 179, 194n3, 207
globalectics 30–1, 33–5, 50–3
globalization, globalism, the global 51,
    87–8, 99, 107, 121, 139, 164, 172,
    186, 194–5, 237, 242, 247
    archaic globalization 171
    centripetal globalization 170
    economic globalization 219
    global African literature
    global audience(s) 73, 92, 176, 179,
        181–2, 195–6, 199, 213
    global ecology 60–1, 73, 171
    global history 79, 194
    global horror 8, 89, 98–9, 103, 105, 107
    global Latin American novel 194–5, 212
    global novel, globalization of the novel
        18, 179, 193, 207
    global popular culture 90, 174
    global Ummah 184, 189, 243
    global vernacular 175–6, 181, 189
    Tsing, Anna, critique of globalization 246
    unworlding of the world, globalization
        as 86
Gomes, Albert 142–3

Gray, Alasdair 5
    Lanark 5
Gray, Richard 169–70
Greece 15, 217, 221–4, 231

Hamid, Mohsin 169, 170, 174
Hannerz, Ulf 7, 139
Haole 115, 123, 131–3
Harris, Ashleigh 14, 23, 59, 241, 244, 246–8
haunting 21, 196–7, 243
    haunted 198–9, 204–7
Hawaii 111, 124, 240
Hawaiian literature (aka *moʻolelo Hawaiʻi*)
    116–7, 124–5, 128
Hawaiian Sovereignty Movement 114,
    132
Hayot, Eric xi, xii, 4, 13, 51–2
Helgesson, Stefan xi, 21n59, 34n43,
    51n118, 112n6, 180, 189, 218n4,
    219, 221, 230n46
hemispheric 21, 195, 196n10, 198, 200–3,
    208, 211–13
    context 198
    exchange 200
    field 195
    history 203
    scene 196
Herder, Johann Gottfried xv, xv n16
Herrera, Yuri 202
    Señales que precederán al fin del mundo
    (Signs Preceding the End of the
    World) 202
heterogeneous 91, 183, 187, 196, 212
Hofmeyr, Isabel 61n12, 67
home 100–1, 111, 113, 127, 133, 174, 197,
    222, 225, 227, 236–44, 248
    Earth as 16
    homeland, home country 68, 93–4,
    159, 237, 241–2, 249
    homeless 238
    homesickness 133, 230, 232, 237
    hometown 125, 237
    Molokaʻi as home 122, 126
    unhomely 90, 237, 242
    vernacular as 131–3
horror 8–9, 36, 68, 89.90, 92–5, 97–8, 100,
    103–5
    dystopia 94

Horta, Paulo Lemos xviii n26, xix
Hoyos, Hector 195, 212

identity 102, 112, 180, 185, 187, 189
    class 142
    crisis of 170n2, 179
    cultural and linguistic 131
    hybrid 202
    'identity theft' 117
    Latin American 199
    local 117, 121, 128
    Muslim 172–4, 181
    national 194
    sansei 128, 240
Igbo 17, 30–1, 34, 37–8, 42, 44, 46–9,
    53–4, 245
Indigenous Hawaiians (aka Kanaka Maoli)
    122, 125, 226
imagination x, 7, 53, 76, 185, 188, 205,
    207, 242
immigration 203, 217, 240
indigeneity xvii, 133, 247
intertextuality 33, 35, 106
IPAF (International Prize for Arabic
    Fiction) 92–3
Iran 15, 17, 217, 227
Iraq 8–9, 85–6, 92, 94–7, 99–100, 102,
    105–7, 225, 227
    Iraq war, 2003 invasion 87, 92–3, 97, 105

James, C. L. R. 76n59, 142–3, 162
Julien, Eileen 29, 32n22, 45

Kaakinen, Kaisa 196, 207
Kallifatides, Theodor 23, 221–4, 230–3
    Foreigners (Utlänningar) 221–3
Kathmandu, Nepal 11–12, 15
Kenyatta, Jomo 73, 77
Kincaid, Jamaica 11–12, 25, 238, 249
    *Among Flowers: A Walk in the
    Himalayas* 11–12
Kingston, Maxine Hong 13, 111–17, 122,
    129–33, 240
    Hawaiʻi One Summer 13, 111–17, 129–33
Knight, Michael Muhammad 18, 23, 169,
    170–9, 181–9
    Taqwacores 18, 173–6, 179, 181, 183–4,
    187, 189, 242, 246

landscape 17, 116, 125, 128, 132 157, 212, 246
  border 212
  of circulation 246
  desert 202, 212
  of destruction 102
  linguistic 132
  multiply layered and simultaneous, haunted 21, 196-7, 201-7, 210-11
  urban 99
language
  Arabic xiii, xvi, 87-9, 91-2, 103, 175-7, 179, 183, 202
  Bengali xviii
  Creole (*see also* creole continuum) 13, 112, 115n16, 138-141, 148
  English xiv, xvi, xix, 14, 17, 30, 33-4, 36-7, 39, 61-8, 71-4, 80, 88, 92, 115-17, 125, 128-9, 131-3, 139, 147-9, 175-9, 182-3, 202-3, 210, 219, 222, 241, 243
  French xv, xvi, xviii, xix, xxii, 128, 139, 243
  Hawai'i Creole English (HCE) 13, 112, 132
  monolingualism 64, 176
  Pidgin 13, 115, 127-32
  Spanish 139, 199, 203, 210
  translingualism 175-6, 180
Latin America 158, 193-4, 209, 239
  Latin American Boom 19, 20, 200
  Latin American literature 20, 193-4, 196-7, 199-200, 208, 213, 246
  Latin American novel 21, 193-5, 212, 246
  Latin American regionalism 201
leprosy 122-3, 126, 128
literary practice xiii, xvii, xix, xx, xxi, xxii
literature of Hawai'i 12, 111-27, 132-3, 240, 247
Luiselli, Valeria 7, 199-205, 208, 211
  Los ingrávidos (Faces in the Crowd) 199n27
  Lost Children Archive 7, 203, 207
  Tell Me How It Ends: An Essay in Forty Questions 203
Lum, Wing Tek 118, 119, 120, 126
  'East/West Poem' 118, 119
Lu Xun xxii, 4

magic realism 8, 95-6, 102, 107
Mahmutović, Adnan 18, 123, 169, 242-3
Makalela, Leketi 61-2
Mandela, Nelson 77, 79
Marcus, George 244, 245-6
Mecca 180, 243
mediascapes 183, 187
memoir 228, 231
Mendes, Alfred 142-3, 145
metafiction 8, 87, 96
Mexico 5, 130, 200, 202-3, 207-9
  Mexican 102, 199, 201-2, 208-9, 211
  Mexican-American relations 201, 209, 211
  Mexican border 201, 204, 207, 243
Middle East x, 91
migrant 94, 103, 163, 218-19, 222, 224, 227, 231, 240, 243, 248
  encounter 15, 217-18, 231-2
  experiences 217
  literature 218-20, 22, 244
migration x, 6, 104, 133, 200, 211, 217, 219, 221, 223, 230, 232, 240, 247-8
mobility 4, 22-3, 238-40
modernization 193, 202
Moloka'i 122n40
Moretti, Franco ix, x, xi, xii, 15, 19, 21, 89, 195
Mufti, Aamir xvi, 8, 178
Murayama, Milton 127, 131, 132
  All I Asking for Is My Body 123n45
Muslim-American writing 169-72, 189, 244

Naipaul, V. S. 220-2
  The Enigma of Arrival 220
narration 67-8, 127, 131, 194, 208
  auto-fictional narrator 199, 208
  Narrator 68, 101, 103-4, 174, 177, 197-200, 204-5, 208-11, 220-1
Nation x, 18, 38, 60-2, 68, 75, 77, 94, 99, 116, 121, 160, 174-5
New York 4, 5, 19, 42, 143, 170, 199-200, 203-4
New York Times 6, 112, 113
Nigeria 17, 30, 32, 35, 37-8, 47-8, 241
Nkrumah, Kwame 73, 77
Nnaemeka, Obioma 44-5
Nwapa, Flora 17-18, 21, 29-30, 35-9, 41-3, 46, 48-50, 53-4, 241-2

Efuru 21, 30, 35, 37–8, 41–2, 44, 46, 48–50
Nzegwu, Nkiru 42, 44

Oguta 17, 37, 46–50, 54, 57
Okamura, Jonathan 121, 123, 125, 134
  Asian Settler Colonialism 121, 125
'ōlelo Hawai'i (aka Hawaiian language) 117, 132
Orsini, Francesca xii, 10n30
orthography 63, 65, 70, 82, 115
Owen, Gilberto 199–201

pan-African 14, 34, 73–4, 76–9
Paris 4–5, 12, 72
Pilar Blanco, María del 195–6, 201
Plaatje, Sol T. 14, 23, 59, 63–6, 68–72, 73, 79–80, 241
  Mhudi 14, 59, 61–4, 66–73, 79–80, 241
  Native Life in South Africa 63
place
  emplacement 232–3, 239–40
    multi-sited 237, 243, 245–6
plantation 122–3, 126–7, 129, 140, 157
Pollock, Sheldon xiv, xviii, 120
postcolonial xvii 30, 33–4, 39, 42, 50, 74–5, 77, 79, 86, 89–90, 94, 98, 163, 181
post-9/11 170, 173–4, 179
prejudice 44, 217
production 141, 163
  of culture 112, 116, 118, 120–1
  of identity 189
  of literature x, 13, 30, 36, 38, 45, 141, 193, 219
  of location 93
  of space 4
proletarian novel 137, 141–2, 149, 161, 242, 244, 248
proverbs 37, 63–4, 67–72, 80
publishing industry xx, 6
punk 170, 173–4, 177–8, 182, 186–7, 242

Qutait, Tasnim 8, 85, 242, 244, 247

race xv, 32, 36, 40
racism 124, 217, 231–2
  racist 31–4, 54, 123–4, 129, 153
Ramadan, Tariq 174, 185, 187

readers, readership *see* audience
realism 89–90, 94, 97, 100, 103, 107, 145, 157, 159
  magic realism 8, 87, 94–6, 100, 102, 105, 107, 194–5
  socialist realism 145, 157, 159
Realist Writers' Group 142, 144–5, 155
Reed-Danahay, Deborah 232, 236
religion 97, 173, 188
  Allah 177n25, 182
  Bismillah 176–7, 180, 182
  Dar Al–Islam 173–4
  esoteric 101, 188
  fundamentalism 172–3, 185
  Islam 18, 169, 171–8, 180, 182, 184–9
  Muslim 91, 100, 169–89
  Ummah 172, 175–6, 180–1, 184–5, 189, 243
repatriation 71, 79
Robben Island 77–8
Rohi, Pooneh 222, 227
Rulfo, Juan 201, 204
  Pedro Páramo 204

Saadawi, Ahmed 8, 9, 23, 85–7, 89, 91–106
  Frankenstein in Baghdad 85–6, 91, 93, 95–6, 106
scales ix, 9, 12, 16–18, 86
science fiction 91, 94
Sebald, W. G. 197, 207
Second Hawaiian Renaissance 114, 117
Second World 127, 137, 141, 155–8, 160–1, 164, 217
Seddon, Deborah 63–4, 71
Shakespeare, William 64–6, 75, 76
Siskind, Mariano 193–4, 196
solidarity 22, 88, 137–8, 141, 146, 149–160, 163, 200
South Africa 4, 14, 59–63, 67, 72–5, 77–81, 153–4, 163, 241, 244, 247–8
social space 10, 22–3, 142, 146, 151–3, 170, 188–9, 232, 242–3, 246
'spatial stories' 236
Stewart, Charles 139–40
Stockholm 4, 20, 218, 222–5, 227–8, 231, 240
subaltern xvii 92, 172

Sweden x, xii, 4, 15, 188, 217–24, 226–33,
        240, 244, 247

Tageldin, Shaden xvi, 87
Tagore, Rabindranath xviii–xix, 4
Talk Story Conference 114–15, 116, 129,
        131
temporality 16, 62, 205, 247
Third World 101, 137, 161
Thomsen, Mads Rosendahl 19, 219
translation xxi, 100, 105, 193, 199–200
        and cosmopolitan-vernacular dynamic
                xix
        of *Crown Jewel* 141, 155–7, 161–2, 248
        of Iraqi fiction into English 88–93
        of the Latin American Boom 20
        of migrant writers 218–9
        of *Pilgrim's Progress* 61
        by Plaatje, Sol, of Setswana proverbs
                63–71
        by Plaatje, Sol, of Shakespeare 64–5,
                68
        of *Señales que precederán al fin del
                mundo* 202–3
        sociology of xi
        of *Things Fall Apart* 31
        and untranslatability xii, 87, 97
travel xxii, 9, 11, 87, 89, 106, 130, 209, 224,
        236, 238, 246
Trinidad 138, 141–8, 150, 153–4, 156–64,
        220, 242
        Fyzabad 142, 144, 149, 154
        Port-of-Spain 22, 142, 147, 151–2,
                154
typological approach 23, 138, 150–6,
        159–60, 163
        Lukács, Georg, and typology 150
        Tompkins, Jane and typology 150

Uimonen, Paula 17–8, 241, 244–5, 247
uncanny 90, 103, 201
unhomely 90, 237, 242
universality xiii, 51, 179
USA 5–6, 37, 47, 92, 119–20, 126, 144,
        147, 174–5

Vásquez, Juan Gabriel 197–9
        La Forma de las ruinas (The Shape of
                Ruins) 197
Vermeulen, Pieter xi, 178
Vermont 11–2, 238
violence 197–8, 241–3
        Bogotazo 197–8
        class 151
        cultural representations of 103
        drug cartel 6
        history, temporality of 198, 204, 211
        male, against women 44
        military 2
        political violence 230
        post-invasion violence in Iraq, as
                dislocation 8, 87, 89–90, 94–6,
                98–9, 105
        racist 154–4
        vernacular style of 148–9

wa Thiong'o, Ngũgĩ 33, 35
Waititi, Taika 2–3
Wallerstein, Immanuel ix, 7
Warwick Research Collective (WReC) xii, 90
Welge, Jobst 5, 21, 243–7
Western 40, 42, 44–6, 72, 78, 87, 91–4, 96,
        98, 101, 107, 125, 169, 185, 188
Wilson, Rob 119–121
world
        world-creating 196, 206
                worldmaking 41, 43, 47, 50, 52–4
        worlding xii, xx, 1, 5, 52, 85, 104, 105,
                150, 156, 195
world literature ix–xiii, xvi–xxii, 8–9, 12,
        15, 18–20, 23, 29, 31–5, 38–41
Wulff, Helena 15, 240, 244, 247–8

Yamanaka, Lois Ann 13, 23, 112–13, 117,
        120, 122–8, 131–2, 240
        Blu's Hanging 13, 112–3, 122–8, 131, 240
youth culture 184, 189

Zardadi, Ali 221, 228–232
        The Angel and the Sparrow (*Ängeln och
                sparven*) 221

www.ingramcontent.com/pod-product-compliance
Lightning Source LLC
Chambersburg PA
CBHW050409280326
41932CB00013BA/1788